Examining Social Psychology in Virtual Environments

Ruqia Safdar Bajwa
https://orcid.org/0009-0004-8745-6955
Bahauddin Zakariya University, Pakistan

Sarwat Sultan
https://orcid.org/0000-0001-7439-1559
Bahauddin Zakariya University, Pakistan

Asma Yunus
University of Sargodha, Pakistan

IGI Global
Scientific Publishing
Publishing Tomorrow's Research Today

Vice President of Editorial	Melissa Wagner
Director of Acquisitions	Mikaela Felty
Director of Book Development	Jocelynn Hessler
Production Manager	Mike Brehm
Cover Design	Jose Rosado

Published in the United States of America by
IGI Global Scientific Publishing
701 East Chocolate Avenue
Hershey, PA, 17033, USA
Tel: 717-533-8845 | Fax: 717-533-7115
Website: https://www.igi-global.com E-mail: cust@igi-global.com

Library of Congress Cataloging-in-Publication Data

LCCN: 2025038318 (CIP Data Pending)
ISBN13: 9798337358963
Isbn13Softcover: 9798337358970
EISBN13: 9798337358987
British Cataloguing in Publication Data
A Cataloguing in Publication record for this book is available from the British Library.

Table of Contents

Detailed Table of Contents

endure well beyond their intended context. The digital mask offers a powerful lens for understanding identity, anonymity, and behavior online. It is not simply deception but a necessary element of digital life. Masks can liberate or constrain, protect or endanger, depending on the social and technological context. The challenge for individuals and communities is to design technologies, norms, and policies that preserve the protective and creative capacities of digital masks while mitigating their destructive potential. The essential question is not whether we will wear masks in digital life, but under what conditions, for whose benefit, and at whose expense.

Virtual environments operate as dynamic social systems in which technological affordances structure self-processes and social relations. Affordances such as visibility, persistence, editability, and scalability enable communication and actively configure how individuals perceive, perform, and internalise aspects of self. Users co-construct their self-concepts within sociotechnical boundaries through mechanisms such as social feedback, algorithmic curation and audience management. These affordances have been shown to amplify reflexivity and self-awareness, whilst introducing pressures of coherence and performativity across contexts. This chapter utilises sociological and cyberpsychological frameworks to propose that virtual environments have the capacity to reconfigure self-organisation processes by integrating identity negotiation into continuous interaction loops between technological design, social norms, and individual cognition. The self is thus understood as a relational, adaptive construct that is subject to continuous reconfiguration by virtual social systems.

This chapter is aimed to address a very common phenomenon in which many online users voluntarily disclose their personal information, while knowing that such self-disclosure could jeopardize privacy. The concern about privacy invasion and the urge to disclose personal information seem to be at odds, but research suggests that the privacy concern does not really deter or mitigate people's desire to share personal information online. In this chapter, we look into the psychological rewards that encourage or entice people into self-disclosure despite the risks. Considering in some countries self-disclosure could actually lead to legal ramifications or government suppression, the psychological rewards must be significant enough to motivate such behavior. Of course, there can be other types of rewards, such as monetary gains, but this chapter focuses on the psychological aspects.

One of the most visible applications of AI in customer service is the rapid adoption of AI-powered chatbots. This study examines the quality of chatbot services in the banking sector and their influence on customer satisfaction. Using a quantitative design, data were collected from 210 respondents through structured questionnaires. Key variables—functionality, convenience, security, assurance, enjoyment, design, and customization—were analysed statistically to evaluate their impact. Results indicate that chatbot service quality has a significant effect on customer satisfaction, with functionality, customization, security, and convenience as the strongest predictors. Accurate and timely responses were highlighted as critical in enhancing customer experience. Practically, the findings guide banks to enhance chatbot customization, security, and functionality to boost satisfaction and loyalty, thus achieving a competitive edge in digital banking. This research also adds to the limited literature, offering a framework for future AI-based customer service.

Cyber bullying and internet trolling are forms of online aggression that have become increasingly prevalent. Research indicates that individuals engaging in these behaviors often exhibit low self-esteem, low conscientiousness, and low internal moral values (Zezulka & Seigfried-Spellar, 2016).Trolling has been associated with personality traits such as psychopathy, narcissism, and sadism (Aydın et al., n.d.). Studies have found a significant relationship between offline aggression and online trolling behavior, suggesting that aggressive individuals tend to maintain their aggression in online spaces (Strimbu & O'Connell, 2021). However, there are inconsistencies between offline and online self-presentation for highly aggressive individuals. Detecting cyber bullying and aggression on social media platforms like Twitter is possible through machine learning algorithms that analyze text, user, and network-based attributes.

This chapter examines how Malayalam cinema, particularly films like Drishyam (2013), Marco (2022), Pani (2023), and Aavesham (2024), intersects with psychology and criminology through its engagement with realism, moral ambiguity, and cultural specificity. Using theories such as social learning, cognitive scripts, cultivation, and cultural criminology, it explores how cinematic narratives shape identity, moral reasoning, and imitation, especially in the digital era. The rise of OTT platforms and social media has intensified 'cinematic imitation' and real-life 'copycat crimes' in India, rooted in moral disengagement and subcultural identity. Cinema emerges as both a potential trigger for deviant behavior and a tool for ethical reflection. The chapter concludes by advocating for media literacy and interdisciplinary collaboration to reduce harm while preserving artistic freedom.

This study investigates the relationship between design thinking mindset and the psychological well-being of young people in the UAE. In addition, it explores how developing a design thinking mindset can be a psychological prevention to promote sustainable well-being in young people. A quantitative approach was deployed using a cross-sectional study. The participants were young undergraduate students at a federal institute in the United Arab Emirates (UAE). The study's findings suggest that developing a design thinking mindset can act as a psychological prevention to promote the sustainable development of young people's well-being. The study also found a strong positive correlation between design thinking mindsets and psychological well-being. The findings have important implications for educators, policymakers, and practitioners interested in promoting sustainable well-being in young people.

Preface

Digital technologies have become integral to contemporary social life, shaping how individuals think, interact, learn, and construct meaning. Virtual environments, once considered supplementary to offline interaction, now function as primary settings for identity formation, social influence, emotional exchange, and collective behaviour. This transformation raises important questions for social psychology, particularly regarding how established psychological processes are enacted, negotiated, and reconfigured within digitally mediated contexts.

Examining Social Psychology in Virtual Environments brings together a collection of scholarly contributions that address these questions through a social psychological lens. Rather than focusing on technology as an object of analysis in itself, the volume foregrounds the psychological mechanisms that operate within virtual contexts. Its central concern is with how core constructs such as self and identity, social cognition, intimacy, aggression, group processes, psychological safety, and well-being are shaped by the affordances, constraints, and social norms of online and AI-mediated environments.

The chapters included in this volume reflect the diversity and complexity of contemporary virtual experience. They examine issues such as online anonymity and identity performance, self-disclosure and social reward, parasocial relationships, cyberbullying and online aggression, AI-mediated communication, virtual teamwork, digital family dynamics, and student engagement in online classrooms. Several contributions also explore emerging sociotechnical settings, including chatbot interactions, hybrid learning environments, and virtual teams, highlighting how trust, collaboration, and psychological safety are established and maintained in technology-supported systems. Taken together, the chapters demonstrate that virtual environments are neither uniform nor psychologically neutral; they are socially constructed spaces shaped by developmental stage, cultural context, institutional arrangements, and technological design.

A defining strength of this book lies in its theoretical orientation. Contributors engage critically with established social psychological frameworks while extending them to address contemporary digital realities. This approach ensures continuity with foundational theory while recognising the need for conceptual refinement in response to rapid technological change. This book also reflects an interdisciplinary sensitivity, acknowledging that the study of behaviour in virtual environments often intersects with education, organisational psychology, communication studies, and human–computer interaction. Such integration enhances both the analytical depth and practical relevance of the work presented.

This book is intended for researchers, academics, and postgraduate students in social psychology and related disciplines. It may also be of value to educators, practitioners, and designers seeking psychologically informed perspectives on behaviour in online, educational, organisational, and AI-supported settings. By privileging psychological processes over technological novelty, the volume aims to contribute to a more nuanced and responsible understanding of human behaviour in virtual environments.

The editors express their sincere appreciation to the contributing authors for their intellectual rigour and scholarly commitment. Gratitude is also extended to the editorial and development team for their guidance throughout the publication process. It is hoped that this volume will encourage critical reflection, inform future research, and support the continued evolution of social psychology in an increasingly digital world.

ORGANIZATION OF THE BOOK

Chapter 1 sets the intellectual tone for the volume by calling for a fundamental reframing of social psychology in light of digital transformation. Bajwa and Yunus persuasively argue for a shift toward a socio-digital psychology that bridges classical theoretical foundations with contemporary socio-technical realities. By introducing the paradigms of computational authority, networked identity, presence without co-presence, and effortless cognitive regulation, the chapter provides a conceptual scaffold for understanding behavior in increasingly mediated environments. Importantly, the authors balance theoretical innovation with methodological and ethical reflection, highlighting digital trace data, virtual experimentation, and the pressing concerns of privacy, consent, and bias. As editors, we see this chapter as a vital entry point that anchors the volume in both continuity and change within the discipline.

Chapter 2 offers a timely empirical investigation into how individuals across the lifespan engage with artificial intelligence, foregrounding the role of cognitive biases in shaping knowledge acquisition. Barretto and colleagues present a structured examination of age-related differences, revealing distinct bias patterns among younger, middle-aged, and older adults. The findings—ranging from confirmation bias among younger participants to availability bias in older adults—underscore the uneven cognitive landscapes through which AI is interpreted. This chapter contributes not only to cognitive and developmental psychology but also to the broader discourse on digital literacy, reminding readers that engagement with emerging technologies is deeply filtered through pre-existing cognitive tendencies.

Chapter 3 advances a compelling conceptual metaphor by examining the "digital mask" as a lens through which to understand identity, anonymity, and behavior online. Sultan and Kanwal trace the historical and cultural significance of masks and extend this symbolism into virtual environments, where avatars, pseudonyms, and curated identities function as persistent and networked forms of self-presentation. The chapter challenges simplistic notions of deception, instead framing digital masking as both protective and generative. As editors, we value how this contribution foregrounds the ambivalence of anonymity—its capacity to both liberate and harm—while raising critical questions about power, context, and accountability in digital life.

Chapter 4 deepens the exploration of identity by focusing on the reconstruction and performance of the self within virtual environments. Aeniyara and Rudrapati conceptualize digital spaces as dynamic systems where technological affordances—such as visibility, persistence, and scalability—actively shape self-processes. The chapter highlights how individuals continuously negotiate identity through feedback loops involving algorithms, audiences, and social norms. Particularly noteworthy is the framing of the self as a relational and adaptive construct, constantly reconfigured through interaction with socio-technical systems. This perspective aligns closely with the volume's broader emphasis on fluidity and co-construction in digital contexts.

Chapter 5 addresses the paradox of online self-disclosure, where users willingly share personal information despite awareness of privacy risks. Yu's contribution directs attention to the psychological rewards that underpin this behavior, suggesting that intrinsic motivations—such as validation, connection, and self-expression—often outweigh perceived threats. The chapter is especially significant in highlighting that privacy concerns alone are insufficient deterrents, pointing instead to the deeper affective and cognitive drivers of disclosure. As editors, we see this work as an important reminder that digital behaviors cannot be fully understood without accounting for the emotional gratifications embedded within them.

Chapter 6 brings an applied perspective to the volume by examining AI-driven customer service in the banking sector. Khandelwal and colleagues provide a quantitative analysis of chatbot service quality and its relationship to customer satisfaction, identifying functionality, customization, security, and convenience as key determinants. The study offers both theoretical and practical contributions, bridging psychological constructs of satisfaction and trust with technological implementation. We regard this chapter as an important illustration of how socio-digital psychology operates within institutional and commercial domains, where user experience and technological design intersect.

Chapter 7 confronts the darker dimensions of digital interaction by exploring cyberbullying, trolling, and online aggression. Rajput synthesizes existing research to link these behaviors with personality traits such as narcissism, psychopathy, and low moral regulation, while also examining the continuity between offline and online aggression. The chapter further introduces the role of machine learning in detecting harmful behaviors, signaling the growing intersection between psychology and computational tools. As editors, we find this contribution crucial in addressing the ethical and social challenges of digital spaces, emphasizing the need for both psychological insight and technological intervention.

Chapter 8 offers a culturally grounded and interdisciplinary exploration of cinematic influence on behavior, focusing on Malayalam cinema and its psychological and criminological implications. Wani and Rajeev examine how narratives of realism and moral ambiguity can shape cognitive scripts and potentially inspire imitation, particularly in an era amplified by digital distribution platforms. The discussion of "copycat crimes" and moral disengagement situates media consumption within broader socio-cultural and technological contexts. This chapter enriches the volume by extending socio-digital analysis beyond direct interaction to mediated cultural experiences and their real-world consequences.

Chapter 9 concludes the volume on a constructive and forward-looking note by examining the role of a design thinking mindset in promoting psychological well-being among young people. ElSayary's study highlights a strong positive relationship between design thinking and well-being, positioning this mindset as a form of psychological prevention. By linking innovation-oriented thinking with resilience and sustainable development, the chapter offers valuable implications for education and policy. As editors, we view this contribution as an important reminder that the digital age not only presents challenges but also opportunities for cultivating adaptive, creative, and psychologically individuals.

Acknowledgment

The editors would like to express their sincere appreciation to all individuals who contributed to the successful completion of this volume. We are especially grateful to the contributing authors for their valuable scholarly work and dedication. We also extend our thanks to the reviewers for their constructive feedback, which helped improve the quality of the chapters included in this book. Our appreciation is further extended to the editorial and production team at IGI Global Scientific Publishing for their guidance and support throughout the publication process.

We are also thankful to our colleagues, institutions, and families for their encouragement and understanding during the preparation of this work. Above all, we express our deepest gratitude to Allah (SWT) for granting us the strength and wisdom to complete this project, and we send our sincere praise and blessings upon Prophet Muhammad (PBUH), whose teachings continue to inspire the pursuit of knowledge and integrity.

Chapter 1
Reframing Social Psychology for the Virtual Age:
Theoretical Shifts, Digital Realities, and Emerging Paradigms

Ruqia Safdar Bajwa
http://orcid.org/0000-0002-4460-2025
Bahauddin Zakariya University, Pakistan

Asma Yunus
University of Sargodha, Pakistan

ABSTRACT

The chapter proposes a reframing of the discipline toward a socio-digital psychology, integrating classical theory with contemporary socio-technical realities. Four emerging paradigms are identified: computational authority, networked identity, presence without co-presence, and effortless cognitive regulation. Methodological innovations such as digital trace analysis and virtual reality experimentation, alongside ethical considerations concerning consent, privacy, and bias, are also discussed. In doing so, the chapter highlights both the resilience of classical frameworks and the need for interdisciplinary, ethically reflexive approaches to understanding behaviour in the virtual age.

DOI: 10.4018/979-8-3373-5896-3.ch001

1. INTRODUCTION

The digital transformation of human society has unsettled long-standing assumptions within social psychology. Where the mid-twentieth century canon developed its insights in classrooms, laboratories, and community groups, the twenty-first century witnesses the dominance of digitally mediated interaction. Billions of individuals now participate in online platforms, virtual environments, and algorithmically structured spaces that blur boundaries between interpersonal, group, and human–machine communication. For social psychologists, this raises both a challenge and an opportunity: to determine how far classical theories travel into the virtual age and where they require reinterpretation or reframing.

The central claim of this chapter is that human motivations have remained stable but their manifestations have been altered by digital affordances. The drive for cognitive consistency persists, but dissonance reduction now occurs through platform-enabled shortcuts such as muting, blocking, or algorithmic filtering. Group identities remain vital, yet they are magnified by algorithmic curation and destabilised by the fluidity of online roles. Attributional processes continue to structure judgments, though in cue-poor environments they lead to exaggerated dispositional biases and anthropomorphism of machines. Conformity and obedience, once studied in the presence of peers or authorities, now operate through numerical cues, influencers, and computational authority. In each case, classical insights retain explanatory value but demand reframing for environments defined by social media, virtual reality (VR), and artificial intelligence (AI).

This theoretical shift is necessary because classical social psychology was grounded in face-to-face co-presence. Festinger's (1957) cognitive dissonance experiments assumed bounded groups and limited exposure to contradictory information. Asch's (1955) conformity studies relied on the physical presence of confederates delivering incorrect judgments. Tajfel and Turner's (1979) social identity theory presumed group membership was relatively stable and socially demarcated. Heider's (1958) attribution theory assumed that observers had access to behavioural and contextual cues. The digital era unsettles these assumptions. Online spaces collapse contexts (Marwick & Boyd, 2011), render identities performative and ephemeral, and introduce non-human actors as targets of influence or attribution.

In light of these transformations, this chapter pursues three interrelated objectives:

1. To revisit the classical canon of social psychology, highlighting the foundational assumptions and constructs of mid-century theories.
2. To examine how digital realities alter these boundary conditions, particularly in relation to social media, VR, and AI.

3. To propose emerging paradigms that extend classical theory, identifying continuities, shifts, and novel socio-technical processes.

The argument unfolds in seven sections. Following this introduction, Section 2 revisits the classical foundations of social psychology and outlines the trajectory of theoretical shifts leading to the digital turn. Section 3 surveys digital realities and their psychological implications, examining how affordances of social media, VR, and AI reconfigure interaction. Section 4 reinterprets classical theories of dissonance, identity, attribution, and conformity/obedience under these conditions. Section 5 identifies emerging paradigms: computational authority, networked identity, presence without co-presence, and effortless cognitive regulation, that capture novel dynamics of digitally mediated life. Section 6 addresses methodological and ethical implications, emphasising innovations in data collection and the moral stakes of socio-digital research. Section 7 articulates a vision for socio-digital psychology, an integrative framework that bridges classical insight with technological mediation. Finally, Section 8 offers concluding reflections on the endurance and transformation of social psychology in the virtual age.

In taking this approach, the chapter avoids two extremes. On the one hand, it resists the temptation to declare classical theories obsolete in the face of digital change. On the other, it refuses to treat digital contexts as merely new "applications" of timeless principles. Instead, it insists that social psychology must be reframed: continuities in human motivation must be recognised alongside discontinuities produced by technological affordances. Such reframing positions social psychology not only to interpret digital realities but also to shape ethical and policy debates about how digital environments structure collective life.

2. THEORETICAL SHIFTS: FROM CLASSICAL FOUNDATIONS TO DIGITAL REALITIES

2.1 Revisiting the Canon

The mid-twentieth century was the golden era of experimental social psychology, producing theories and paradigms that shaped decades of research. Asch's (1951, 1955) studies on conformity revealed the power of group pressure, demonstrating that individuals often set aside perceptual accuracy in favour of normative acceptance. Festinger's (1957) theory of cognitive dissonance explained the motivational discomfort that arises when attitudes and behaviours conflict, highlighting the drive for psychological consistency. Tajfel and Turner's (1979) social identity theory (SIT) and Turner's self-categorization theory (1987) offered powerful accounts of how group membership structures self-concept and intergroup relations. Heider's (1958) attribution theory established the basic distinction between dispositional and situational explanations, later refined into models of fundamental attribution error (Ross, 1977) and covariation analysis (Kelley, 1967).

These canonical theories share several assumptions. First, they presupposed face-to-face interaction, where co-presence, physical cues, and synchrony shape behaviour. Second, they assumed bounded groups: classroom settings, experimental cohorts, or naturally occurring communities with relatively stable memberships. Third, they operated in contexts where human agents were the only actors, and influence, identity, or attribution was directed solely toward other people. These assumptions reflected the realities of social life in the pre-digital age, where mass communication existed but interpersonal influence was mediated primarily through embodied encounters.

Yet these theories were never static. By the late twentieth century, scholars began questioning their boundary conditions. The emergence of computer-mediated communication (CMC) in the 1980s prompted debates about whether reduced cues would diminish social influence or simply shift its forms (Kiesler, Siegel, & McGuire, 1984). Walther's (1992) hyperpersonal model suggested that lean channels could paradoxically intensify relational closeness through selective self-presentation and idealized perception. Reicher, Spears, and Postmes (1995) developed the Social Identity Model of Deindividuation Effects (SIDE), showing that anonymity in digital contexts did not erode identity but could amplify adherence to salient group norms. These theoretical innovations signaled the start of a digital turn in social psychology.

2.2 The Digital Turn in Social Psychology

The rise of the internet, social networking sites, and mobile communication disrupted the foundational assumptions of the discipline. Social interaction was no longer bound to co-presence; rather, it became mediated, asynchronous, and persistent. Group boundaries became fluid, with individuals participating simultaneously in multiple overlapping online communities. Most radically, digital systems themselves, algorithms, bots, AI-driven agents, emerged as non-human social actors, reshaping the very domain of social psychological inquiry.

The shift to digital realities required new frameworks. Scholars emphasized the role of affordances, technological features that enable or constrain action (Boyd, 2011). Visibility, persistence, and scalability (Treem & Leonardi, 2013) altered how identities, relationships, and influence were enacted online. Algorithmic personalization reshaped exposure to information, amplifying identity salience and selective dissonance regulation (Pariser, 2011). Virtual reality allowed controlled yet immersive replications of classical experiments, demonstrating that conformity and obedience effects persist in simulated environments (Slater et al., 2006; Kyrlitsias & Michael-Grigoriou, 2020).

The digital turn has therefore not displaced classical theories but reframed them. It has demonstrated their continued relevance while exposing their limits under new socio-technical conditions. To understand social behaviour in the twenty-first century, social psychology must account for both continuity in human motivation and transformation in context.

3. DIGITAL REALITIES AND THEIR PSYCHOLOGICAL IMPLICATIONS

The contemporary digital landscape represents more than a change of medium; it constitutes a transformation in the architecture of social interaction. Social psychologists now study behaviours that unfold on social networking sites, immersive virtual environments, and artificial intelligence interfaces, each of which introduces novel affordances and constraints. This section examines three domains—social media, virtual/augmented reality, and AI systems—highlighting their implications for psychological processes of identity, attribution, dissonance, and influence.

3.1 Affordances of Social Media

3.1.1 Algorithmic curation and selective exposure

One of the most significant psychological consequences of social media is algorithmic filtering. Unlike earlier mass media, where exposure to information was broad and undifferentiated, platforms now curate feeds based on prior behaviours. This personalization reinforces selective exposure, facilitating echo chambers and filter bubbles (Pariser, 2011; Cinelli et al., 2021). From a dissonance perspective, this means users can minimize discomfort from contradictory information with minimal cognitive effort (Garrett, 2009). Instead of struggling with competing beliefs, individuals can mute, unfollow, or algorithmically bypass challenges to their worldview.

3.1.2 Metrics as social proof

Social media also transforms conformity and influence. Visible engagement metrics, likes, shares, upvotes—operate as quantitative cues to consensus. Muchnik, Aral, and Taylor (2013) demonstrated that artificially manipulating early upvotes on comments significantly biased subsequent ratings, producing cascades of conformity. This metric-based social proof represents a structural innovation in social environments: the aggregation of group behaviour into a single visible number that influences future actions.

3.1.3 Online identity and performativity

Identity construction online is both fluid and constrained. Users manage self-presentation across multiple platforms, balancing aspirational performances (Duffy, 2017) with the risk of "context collapse" (Marwick & Boyd, 2011). Social identity is co-constructed by platform design (through verification badges, follower counts) and peer interaction. Goffman's (1959) dramaturgical model remains relevant, but the persistence and searchability of digital traces alter role management. Missteps are not ephemeral; they become archived, searchable, and re-circulatable, intensifying identity strain and dissonance.

3.1.4 Digital polarization and affective publics

Social media also fosters polarization and mobilization. Bail et al. (2018) showed that exposure to opposing views on Twitter often increased polarization, not moderation, due to identity-based defensive processing. At the same time, Papacharissi (2015) described the emergence of affective publics: groups mobilized by shared emotions circulating via hashtags and memes. These publics crystallize group identities while also enabling rapid global solidarity.

3.2 Virtual and Augmented Reality

3.2.1 Presence and immersion

Virtual reality (VR) introduces qualitatively new conditions for psychological interaction. Unlike text-based or video-mediated platforms, VR creates a sense of immersion and presence, where users experience avatars and environments as if they were real (Slater & Sanchez-Vives, 2016). Presence intensifies classical phenomena, making VR a valuable testbed for longstanding theories.

3.2.2 Conformity in immersive environments

Replications of Asch's conformity experiments in VR confirm that majority influence persists even when confederates are avatars. Kyrlitsias and Michael-Grigoriou (2020) found significant conformity effects, especially when avatars displayed gaze behaviour directed at participants. The implication is clear: social presence, even without physical co-presence, can evoke conformity.

3.2.3 Obedience to virtual authority

VR also enables ethical replications of Milgram's obedience studies. Slater et al. (2006) found that participants displayed stress responses and compliance when asked to deliver shocks to virtual victims, despite knowing they were simulated. Gonzalez-Franco et al. (2018) similarly demonstrated obedience to virtual authority figures. These findings indicate that the psychological mechanisms of authority and responsibility diffusion remain robust under immersive simulation.

3.2.4 The Proteus effect and identity transformation

Perhaps the most unique contribution of VR is the Proteus effect: users adopt behaviours aligned with their avatars' characteristics (Yee & Bailenson, 2007). Embodying taller avatars led participants to negotiate more aggressively, while attractive avatars increased self-confidence. Beyond behavioural shifts, embodiment has been used to reduce prejudice: White participants embodied in Black avatars displayed reduced implicit racial bias (Peck et al., 2013). VR thus extends social identity theory and self-categorization into domains of embodied transformation.

3.2.5 Augmented reality and shared environments

While VR immerses users in fully digital spaces, augmented reality (AR) overlays digital cues onto physical settings. AR enhances group identity by creating shared reference points, such as Pokémon Go players collaborating in public spaces (Paavilainen et al., 2017). These hybrid realities blur the line between digital and physical identity performance, highlighting the role of technology in shaping group dynamics.

3.3 Artificial Intelligence and Human–Machine Interaction

3.3.1 Anthropomorphism and CASA

Artificial intelligence introduces non-human actors into social life. Early research under the CASA (Computers as Social Actors) paradigm (Reeves & Nass, 1996) showed that humans attribute personality and intent to computers when they display minimal social cues. While CASA effects are less evident for routine desktop interactions today (Heyselaar, 2023), they remain strong for embodied agents, voice assistants, and humanoid robots.

3.3.2 Attribution to machines

Attribution theory is particularly relevant for AI. Edwards and Edwards (2022) found that people commit the correspondence bias more strongly toward robots than humans, attributing internal attitudes even when behaviour is externally programmed. Lauharatanahirun et al. (2024) developed the External–Internal Attribution model, demonstrating that users infer both external (appearance, affordances) and internal (mental states) causes for AI behaviour, shaping trust and compliance.

3.3.3 Algorithmic authority and automation bias

AI also functions as a form of computational authority. Users defer to GPS navigation, recommender systems, and predictive analytics, often at the expense of their own judgment (Lyons et al., 2018). Automation bias (Goddard et al., 2011) and algorithm appreciation (Logg, Minson, & Moore, 2019) demonstrate that people treat algorithms as more competent and reliable than humans in many contexts. This deference echoes Milgram's findings on obedience but extends them to non-human authorities.

3.3.4 Generative AI and dissonance in integrity norms

Generative AI (e.g., ChatGPT, image generators) introduces new tensions. Seran, Kumar, and Lee (2025) found that students experienced **integrity dissonance** when balancing values of originality with pragmatic benefits of AI use. Users reduced dissonance by trivializing originality norms or reframing AI as a neutral tool. These dynamics illustrate how classical dissonance processes adapt to emerging technologies, raising ethical questions for education and work.

3.4 Synthesis

Across social media, VR, and AI, several patterns emerge:

1. **Amplification of classical dynamics**: Conformity, dissonance, attribution, and obedience persist, but are intensified or accelerated by digital affordances.
2. **Emergence of non-human actors**: AI and algorithms are now targets of attribution, trust, and obedience, expanding the scope of social psychology.
3. **Blurring of real and virtual**: VR and AR show that presence without co-presence evokes robust psychological responses, reframing the role of context in classical paradigms.

4. **Structural mediation**: Algorithms and platform designs act not just as environments but as active shapers of social identity, influence, and cognition.

Digital realities thus compel a reframing of classical theory: not abandonment, but reinterpretation in light of socio-technical mediation.

4. REFRAMING CLASSICAL THEORIES

This section systematically revisits classical social psychology theories cognitive dissonance, social identity, attribution, and conformity/obedience and reinterprets them within digitally mediated contexts. Each subsection highlights continuities, boundary shifts, and novel extensions introduced by social media, VR/AR, and AI systems.

4.1 Cognitive Dissonance in the Age of Curation

Festinger's (1957) theory of cognitive dissonance described the motivational discomfort arising from inconsistency between attitudes, beliefs, or behaviours. In digital environments, dissonance persists but is structurally mediated by technology.

4.1.1 Effortless dissonance reduction

Whereas mid-century individuals resolved dissonance through attitude change or rationalization (Festinger & Carlsmith, 1959), today users employ low-cost technological strategies: unfollowing, muting, or algorithmically filtering out dissonant content (Garrett, 2009). This results in echo chambers (Cinelli et al., 2021), which minimize discomfort but also entrench ideological divides.

4.1.2 Multi-platform and fragmented identities

Digital life requires managing multiple overlapping identities. Users may present differently on LinkedIn, Instagram, and Twitter, leading to cross-platform dissonance. Self-discrepancies emerge when online identity clashes with offline behaviour (Toma & Hancock, 2013). Reduction occurs through selective editing, self-affirmation, or reframing of inconsistencies.

4.1.3 Embodiment and immersive dissonance

VR environments generate dissonance through embodied contradiction. The Proteus effect (Yee & Bailenson, 2007) illustrates how avatar traits influence behaviour, producing dissonance if self-concept diverges from embodied representation. Embodying stigmatized avatars can reduce bias (Peck et al., 2013), showing that dissonance may promote positive change under immersive conditions.

4.1.4 Generative AI and integrity dilemmas

Generative AI introduces integrity dissonance, as users reconcile values of originality with pragmatic use of AI outputs (Seran, Kumar, & Lee, 2025). Resolution occurs via trivialization ("AI is just a tool"), justification, or behaviour change. Here, dissonance theory illuminates moral and ethical tensions in human–AI collaboration.

4.2 Social Identity in Networked Societies

Social identity theory (Tajfel & Turner, 1979) and self-categorization theory (Turner et al., 1987) emphasised that self-concept is shaped by group membership. Digital contexts reconfigure this process.

4.2.1 Algorithmic amplification

Social platforms amplify identity salience by curating identity-consistent content. Pariser's (2011) "filter bubble" illustrates algorithmic reinforcement of ingroup norms, while Ribeiro et al. (2020) show how YouTube algorithms channel users into radicalized communities. Hafer et al. (2023) describe this as "networked identity," where human and machine co-construct belonging.

4.2.2 Anonymity and SIDE

The SIDE model (Reicher et al., 1995) reframes anonymity online: rather than eroding individuality, it heightens adherence to salient group norms. Studies confirm that anonymity fosters ingroup solidarity in forums and activist networks (Postmes, Spears, & Lea, 2002).

4.2.3 Fluidity and context collapse

Marwick and Boyd (2011) coined "context collapse" to describe collapsed boundaries across audiences. Users navigate fragmented selves, balancing peer, professional, and family identities. This fluidity complicates SIT, requiring recognition of dynamic, overlapping, algorithmically mediated identities.

4.2.4 Virtual embodiment and identity transformation

VR expands identity work through avatars. The Proteus effect shows that virtual embodiment influences behaviour, while perspective-taking through avatars of marginalized groups reduces prejudice (Peck et al., 2013). Thus, SIT extends into embodied identity performance within immersive spaces.

4.3 Attribution in Low-Cue, High-Tech Environments

Heider's (1958) attribution theory distinguished between dispositional and situational causes of behaviour. In digital contexts, cue scarcity and machine actors reshape attribution dynamics.

4.3.1 Cue scarcity and dispositional bias

CMC reduces nonverbal cues, intensifying the fundamental attribution error (Ross, 1977). Ambiguous online behaviour (delayed responses, terse messages) is often judged dispositional ("they are rude") rather than situational ("they are busy") (Kiesler et al., 1984).

4.3.2 Credibility heuristics

Verification badges, follower counts, and digital markers substitute for interpersonal cues, shaping judgments of credibility (Jiang et al., 2020). Attribution in online environments is increasingly tied to platform-sanctioned heuristics.

4.3.3 Attribution to machines

CASA research (Reeves & Nass, 1996) shows that humans anthropomorphize computers, a tendency that persists in voice assistants and robots (Epley, Waytz, & Cacioppo, 2007). Edwards and Edwards (2022) found that participants applied the correspondence bias more strongly to robots than humans. Lauharatanahirun et al. (2024) propose the EIA model, highlighting how users attribute both external features and internal states to AI, shaping trust.

4.3.4 Algorithmic authority

Users often defer to algorithmic outputs, exhibiting automation bias (Goddard et al., 2011). Logg, Minson, and Moore (2019) demonstrated "algorithm appreciation," where participants preferred algorithmic judgments to human ones. Attribution theory thus extends beyond human behaviour, encompassing trust in computational actors.

4.4 Conformity and Obedience under Algorithmic Authority

Conformity and obedience studies (Asch, 1955; Milgram, 1963) revealed the power of group norms and authority. Digital contexts reshape these dynamics.

4.4.1 Social proof through metrics

Muchnik et al. (2013) found that artificially manipulating early ratings biased subsequent judgments on social media. Engagement metrics aggregate group influence into numerical cues, producing cascades of conformity.

4.4.2 Immersive conformity and obedience

VR replications confirm classical effects: Kyrlitsias and Michael-Grigoriou (2020) found avatar-based conformity, while Slater et al. (2006) showed obedience to virtual authorities. Gonzalez-Franco et al. (2018) demonstrated that immersion heightens compliance, reinforcing Milgram's insights under simulation.

4.4.3 Computational obedience

Users comply with algorithmic guidance, from GPS to recommender systems (Lyons et al., 2018). This "obedience to algorithms" reflects both attributional trust and diffusion of responsibility. Influencers also function as hybrid authorities, blending SIT and obedience mechanisms (Duffy, 2017).

5. EMERGING PARADIGMS IN DIGITAL SOCIAL PSYCHOLOGY

The reinterpretation of classical social psychology in digital contexts reveals not only continuity and boundary shifts but also emergent paradigms. These paradigms extend beyond the reach of mid-century theories, reflecting socio-technical conditions unique to the virtual age. Four are especially salient: computational authority, networked identity, presence without co-presence, and effortless regulation of cognition and affect.

5.1 Computational Authority

5.1.1 From human to algorithmic obedience

Milgram's (1963, 1974) obedience studies highlighted the profound impact of authority figures on individual compliance. In digital contexts, authority is increasingly algorithmic. Recommendation systems, GPS navigation, predictive analytics, and generative AI shape user behaviour, often eliciting deference comparable to human authority (Logg, Minson, & Moore, 2019; Lyons et al., 2018).

5.1.2 Automation bias and diffusion of responsibility

Automation bias (Goddard, Roudsari, & Wyatt, 2011) shows that users over-rely on algorithms even when errors are evident. This phenomenon creates new forms of responsibility diffusion, as accountability is displaced from human decision-makers to opaque computational systems. In organisational settings, algorithmic decisions may be treated as objective, limiting critical scrutiny.

5.1.3 Ethical implications

Computational authority raises normative concerns: when algorithms act as decision-makers, issues of transparency, accountability, and bias become central. Unlike Milgram's experiment, where authority was embodied and visible, algorithmic authority is often hidden, making resistance more difficult.

5.2 Networked Identity and Algorithmic Selves

5.2.1 Human–algorithm co-construction of identity

SIT posits that group membership structures self-concept (Tajfel & Turner, 1979). In digital contexts, algorithms co-construct identity by inferring and amplifying group affiliations. Hafer et al. (2023) describe this as "networked identity," where self-definition is jointly produced by personal choices and algorithmic curation.

5.2.2 Filter bubbles and radicalisation

Pariser's (2011) filter bubble illustrates how personalization reinforces identity salience. Ribeiro et al. (2020) found that YouTube's recommendation system steered users toward increasingly radical content, showing how algorithms function as active agents in shaping identity boundaries.

5.2.3 Identity fluidity and multiplicity

While classical SIT assumed relatively stable group boundaries, digital environments foster identity multiplicity. Users may belong to several algorithmically curated communities simultaneously, each with different norms and saliences. This creates new tensions between fluid self-presentation and algorithmically stabilised categorisation.

5.3 Presence Without Co-presence

5.3.1 Immersive influence

VR demonstrates that psychological presence does not require physical co-presence. Asch's conformity effects have been replicated with avatars (Kyrlitsias & Michael-Grigoriou, 2020), and Milgram's obedience paradigm has been ethically simulated in virtual environments (Slater et al., 2006). The critical factor is not bodily co-location but experienced presence.

5.3.2 Proteus effect and embodied identity

The Proteus effect (Yee & Bailenson, 2007) illustrates how avatar embodiment shapes behaviour. This effect challenges classical theories of identity and dissonance by introducing embodied self-modulation: individuals conform to the traits of their virtual representations, even when inconsistent with offline self-concept.

5.3.3 Implications for social interaction

Presence without co-presence suggests that digital psychology must redefine what counts as "social." Interactions with avatars, bots, or simulated agents can evoke responses traditionally reserved for human-to-human engagement, extending the boundaries of social psychology.

5.4 Effortless Regulation of Cognition and Affect

5.4.1 Technological shortcuts to dissonance reduction

Festinger (1957) argued that dissonance motivates cognitive work to restore consistency. Digital affordances allow effortless regulation: blocking dissenters, curating feeds, or trivializing contradictions with memes. This externalisation reduces motivational struggle but heightens ideological rigidity (Garrett, 2009; Cinelli et al., 2021).

5.4.2 Platform affordances as regulatory scaffolds

Platforms serve as regulatory architectures, scaffolding not only information consumption but also emotional management. For example, muting functions help users avoid distressing content, while algorithmic ranking prioritises emotionally salient posts, shaping affective experiences (Papacharissi, 2015).

5.4.3 Implications for agency and autonomy

Outsourcing cognitive and affective regulation to platforms raises questions about user agency. While dissonance is reduced, critical reflection may decline, and opportunities for growth through discomfort are diminished.

5.5 Synthesis

These paradigms share three features:

1. **Socio-technical hybridity**: Human psychology is now inseparable from algorithmic mediation.
2. **Shifted boundaries**: Presence, identity, and authority are no longer tied exclusively to human actors or physical contexts.
3. **Normative stakes**: Each paradigm introduces ethical and political challenges around transparency, autonomy, and collective well-being.

Together, they suggest the need for a socio-digital psychology that integrates classical insights with the realities of algorithmically structured, immersive, and hybrid environments.

6. METHODOLOGICAL AND ETHICAL CONSIDERATIONS

The reinterpretation of social psychology for the virtual age is not only a theoretical task; it is also a methodological and ethical imperative. Classical theories were developed in tightly controlled laboratory experiments with relatively small participant groups. Today, digital environments generate massive datasets, enable immersive simulations, and involve non-human agents, all of which demand rethinking how research is conducted and evaluated. At the same time, the design and study of digital platforms raise significant ethical challenges concerning consent, manipulation, privacy, and responsibility.

6.1 Methodological Innovations

6.1.1 Digital trace data and big data analytics

Social media and online platforms produce enormous amounts of behavioural data. Unlike self-reports or laboratory tasks, these digital traces (likes, shares, posts, clicks) provide ecologically valid insights into real-world behaviour (Golder & Macy, 2014). Large-scale studies allow researchers to detect patterns in polarization, identity signalling, and social influence across millions of users (Guess, Nagler, & Tucker, 2019). However, such methods raise questions about validity, as observed behaviour may be shaped by opaque algorithms rather than solely psychological processes.

6.1.2 Computational experiments and A/B testing

Platforms routinely conduct randomized controlled trials on users, such as Facebook's emotional contagion study (Kramer, Guillory, & Hancock, 2014). These experiments can provide causal evidence at unprecedented scale but blur the line between research and platform manipulation. While valuable, they challenge the ethical standards traditionally governing psychological experiments.

6.1.3 Virtual reality laboratories

VR offers new methodological opportunities by combining experimental control with ecological immersion. Researchers can replicate classical paradigms (Asch, Milgram) ethically and precisely, while also testing new phenomena like avatar embodiment (Slater & Sanchez-Vives, 2016). VR thus bridges laboratory rigour with ecological validity, but it also raises challenges of generalizability to non-immersive settings.

6.1.4 Human–AI interaction studies

The rise of AI agents requires methodological adaptation. Attributional processes toward robots, trust in algorithms, and AI-mediated decision-making are not easily captured with traditional tools. New paradigms, such as the CASA model (Reeves & Nass, 1996) and the EIA framework (Lauharatanahirun et al., 2024) offer starting points, but more nuanced designs are needed to measure human responses to non-human agents.

6.2 Ethical Challenges

6.2.1 Informed consent and digital manipulation

Classical studies like Milgram's obedience experiments generated controversy for their ethical implications. Today, large-scale digital studies often proceed without explicit consent, raising concerns of manipulation without awareness. Users subjected to algorithmic nudges or experimental interventions may not realise they are participants in research (Kramer et al., 2014).

6.2.2 Privacy and surveillance

The use of digital trace data raises significant privacy concerns. Even anonymized datasets can often be re-identified (Zimmer, 2010). Social psychologists must balance the scientific value of large-scale data with the ethical obligation to protect individuals' rights.

6.2.3 Algorithmic bias and fairness

Platforms themselves embed biases in algorithmic systems. Research on conformity, identity, or attribution in such environments must account for the ways algorithms shape outcomes, potentially reinforcing inequalities (Noble, 2018). Psychologists studying these processes risk becoming complicit in perpetuating bias if such contexts are treated as neutral.

6.2.4 Responsibility and accountability

The extension of obedience and attribution to algorithms raises normative questions: Who is responsible when users follow faulty algorithmic advice? Is accountability located in the user, the designer, or the system itself? These questions mirror classical debates about obedience but in contexts where authority is disembodied and distributed.

6.3 Toward Responsible Socio-Digital Research

The methodological and ethical challenges outlined above point to the need for a responsible research framework in socio-digital psychology. Such a framework should:

- Integrate interdisciplinary methods, combining experimental precision with computational and ethnographic approaches.
- Prioritize transparency and consent, ensuring that participants understand how their data and behaviours are used in research.
- Address algorithmic mediation explicitly, recognising that platform architectures actively shape psychological outcomes.
- Embed reflexivity and ethics at every stage, acknowledging the power of research to influence digital design and governance.

By embedding ethical reflection alongside methodological innovation, social psychology can continue to generate insights into digital realities without compromising its commitment to protecting participants and society.

7. TOWARD A SOCIO-DIGITAL PSYCHOLOGY

The reinterpretation of classical theories in light of digital realities points toward the emergence of what might be called a socio-digital psychology. This is not a rejection of traditional social psychology but its evolution, integrating human motives with socio-technical environments. The challenge is to articulate a framework that respects theoretical continuities while incorporating the unique dynamics of digital mediation.

7.1 Continuities in Human Motivation

At the core, human motivations have remained stable. The drive for cognitive consistency (Festinger, 1957), the need for belonging and identity (Tajfel & Turner, 1979), the tendency to attribute causes (Heider, 1958), and the propensity for conformity and obedience (Asch, 1955; Milgram, 1963) are universal. The persistence of these dynamics in social media, VR, and AI contexts demonstrates their robustness.

Participants conform to avatars as they did to confederates; they attribute agency to robots as to humans; they obey GPS directions as they once obeyed experimenters.

7.2 Shifts in Boundary Conditions

Where socio-digital psychology departs from classical theory is in the boundary conditions:

- **Presence without co-presence**: Conformity and obedience emerge in virtual settings, indicating that physical co-location is not essential.
- **Identity fluidity and multiplicity**: Algorithmic curation enables overlapping, dynamic group memberships, challenging SIT's assumptions of stable ingroups/outgroups.
- **Non-human actors**: Attribution and influence extend beyond human interaction, requiring psychology to treat algorithms and AI as social actors.
- **Effortless regulation**: Platforms provide technological scaffolds that reduce dissonance and manage affect, shifting regulation from internal cognitive processes to external digital affordances.

These shifts highlight the necessity of reframing theory, not because the human psyche has changed, but because the environmental conditions of interaction have transformed.

7.3 Convergence of Theoretical Insights

The socio-digital framework also requires recognising the interconnections between theories:

- Dissonance intersects with identity: algorithmic reinforcement simultaneously reduces discomfort and amplifies group polarization.
- Attribution underpins conformity: heuristic judgments of credibility (badges, follower counts) reinforce social proof.
- Obedience produces dissonance: compliance with algorithmic authority generates ethical tension, prompting rationalisation.
- Identity informs attribution: group membership shapes how AI outputs are trusted or resisted.

This convergence suggests that socio-digital psychology is inherently multitheoretical, requiring synthesis across previously discrete constructs.

7.4 Toward an Integrative Framework

A socio-digital psychology would be characterised by three guiding principles:

1. **Hybrid agency**: Recognising humans, algorithms, and platforms as co-actors in shaping behaviour.
2. **Affordance-sensitive theory**: Building models that explicitly integrate the role of technological affordances (visibility, persistence, algorithmic curation).
3. **Ethical reflexivity**: Embedding normative concerns about transparency, manipulation, and autonomy into theoretical accounts.

Such a framework would bridge classical social psychology with contemporary socio-technical systems, enabling the discipline to remain relevant in a world where human interaction is increasingly mediated by interfaces rather than faces.

7.5 Implications for Future Research

Socio-digital psychology opens several avenues for inquiry:

- **Experimental innovation**: VR and AI provide controlled yet immersive settings to test long-standing theories in new contexts.
- **Computational approaches**: Big data enables population-level analysis of influence, identity, and dissonance.
- **Cross-disciplinary integration**: Collaborations with computer science, communication, and ethics are essential.
- **Applied impact**: Insights can inform platform design, algorithmic transparency, and policies addressing polarization, misinformation, and digital well-being.

8. CONCLUSION

The digital transformation of human interaction represents one of the most profound challenges and opportunities for social psychology since its inception. From the classroom experiments of Asch and Milgram to the immersive simulations of VR and the algorithmic infrastructures of social media, the contexts in which social behaviour unfolds have shifted dramatically. Yet the continuities of human motivation remain evident: individuals still seek cognitive consistency, construct social identities, make attributions, and conform to perceived authority.

What has changed are the conditions under which these processes operate. Cognitive dissonance is now reduced not only through internal rationalisation but also via technological shortcuts like unfollowing or muting. Social identity is reinforced and destabilised simultaneously by algorithmic amplification and fluid online communities. Attribution biases extend to robots and algorithms, with non-human agents treated as intentional actors. Conformity and obedience persist in virtual environments, amplified by metrics, avatars, and computational authority.

The analysis presented in this chapter suggests that classical social psychology must not be abandoned but reframed. Continuity in psychological processes ensures the relevance of foundational theories, while new socio-technical affordances demand theoretical innovation. This reframing yields emergent paradigms: computational authority, where algorithms govern behaviour; networked identity, where selfhood is co-constructed by humans and machines; presence without co-presence, where immersion replaces physical proximity; and effortless regulation, where platforms externalise cognitive and affective labour.

These developments raise pressing methodological and ethical questions. The availability of digital trace data and VR laboratories provides unprecedented opportunities, yet also challenges notions of consent, privacy, and responsibility. Researchers must acknowledge the dual role of platforms as both environments for behaviour and active shapers of social processes. Ethical reflexivity becomes indispensable, ensuring that socio-digital psychology does not merely describe digital influence but also critiques and guides its use.

Looking forward, the task for social psychology is to articulate a socio-digital framework that integrates classical theories with the realities of technological mediation. Such a framework must be interdisciplinary, drawing on computer science, communication, and philosophy, while remaining grounded in the discipline's historical concern with human motivation and behaviour. It must be affordance-sensitive, recognising that the medium is not neutral but structures the message, the interaction, and the identity. And it must be ethically reflexive, confronting the risks of manipulation, surveillance, and algorithmic bias.

Ultimately, the movement from face-to-face to interface underscores both the adaptability and the resilience of social psychology. The discipline's greatest strength lies in its ability to reinterpret enduring questions under new conditions. Just as earlier generations extended theories to mass media and intercultural contexts, today's scholars must extend them to the digital age. By doing so, social psychology not only maintains its explanatory power but also positions itself as a vital lens for understanding and shaping the future of social life.

REFERENCES

Asch, S. E. (1951). Effects of group pressure upon the modification and distortion of judgments. In Guetzkow, H. (Ed.), *Groups, leadership and men* (pp. 177–190). Carnegie Press.

Asch, S. E. (1955). Opinions and social pressure. *Scientific American, 193*(5), 31–35. DOI: 10.1038/scientificamerican1155-31

Bail, C. A., Argyle, L. P., Brown, T. W., Bumpus, J. P., Chen, H., Hunzaker, M. F., Lee, J., Mann, M., Merhout, F., & Volfovsky, A. (2018). Exposure to opposing views on social media can increase political polarization. *Proceedings of the National Academy of Sciences of the United States of America, 115*(37), 9216–9221. DOI: 10.1073/pnas.1804840115 PMID: 30154168

Boyd, D. (2011). Social network sites as networked publics: Affordances, dynamics, and implications. In Papacharissi, Z. (Ed.), *A networked self: Identity, community, and culture on social network sites* (pp. 39–58). Routledge.

Cinelli, M., Morales, G. D. F., Galeazzi, A., Quattrociocchi, W., & Starnini, M. (2021). The echo chamber effect on social media. *Proceedings of the National Academy of Sciences of the United States of America, 118*(9), e2023301118. DOI: 10.1073/pnas.2023301118 PMID: 33622786

Duffy, B. E. (2017). *(Not) Getting paid to do what you love: Gender, social media, and aspirational work.* Yale University Press. DOI: 10.12987/yale/9780300218176.001.0001

Edwards, A., & Edwards, C. (2022). Does the correspondence bias apply to social robots? *Frontiers in Robotics and AI, 8*, 788242. DOI: 10.3389/frobt.2021.788242 PMID: 35059443

Epley, N., Waytz, A., & Cacioppo, J. T. (2007). On seeing human: A three-factor theory of anthropomorphism. *Psychological Review, 114*(4), 864–886. DOI: 10.1037/0033-295X.114.4.864 PMID: 17907867

Festinger, L. (1957). *A theory of cognitive dissonance.* Stanford University Press. DOI: 10.1515/9781503620766

Festinger, L., & Carlsmith, J. M. (1959). Cognitive consequences of forced compliance. *Journal of Abnormal and Social Psychology, 58*(2), 203–210. DOI: 10.1037/h0041593 PMID: 13640824

Garrett, R. K. (2009). Echo chambers online? Politically motivated selective exposure among Internet news users. *Journal of Computer-Mediated Communication, 14*(2), 265–285. DOI: 10.1111/j.1083-6101.2009.01440.x

Goddard, K., Roudsari, A., & Wyatt, J. C. (2011). Automation bias: A systematic review. *Journal of the American Medical Informatics Association : JAMIA, 19*(1), 121–127. DOI: 10.1136/amiajnl-2011-000089 PMID: 21685142

Goffman, E. (1959). *The presentation of self in everyday life*. Anchor Books.

Golder, S. A., & Macy, M. W. (2014). Digital footprints: Opportunities and challenges for online social research. *Annual Review of Sociology, 40*(1), 129–152. DOI: 10.1146/annurev-soc-071913-043145

Gonzalez-Franco, M.. (2018). Obeying virtual authority in immersive VR environments. *Frontiers in Psychology, 9*, 2038.

Guess, A., Nagler, J., & Tucker, J. (2019). Less than you think: Prevalence and predictors of fake news dissemination on Facebook. *Science Advances, 5*(1), eaau4586. DOI: 10.1126/sciadv.aau4586 PMID: 30662946

Hafer, J., Ran, B., & Duimering, P. R. (2023). Social identity dynamics in a networked society. *Frontiers in Psychology, 14*, 1264534. DOI: 10.3389/fpsyg.2023.1264534 PMID: 37637926

Heider, F. (1958). *The psychology of interpersonal relations*. Wiley. DOI: 10.1037/10628-000

Heyselaar, E. (2023). The CASA theory no longer applies to desktop computers. *Scientific Reports, 13*(1), 19559. DOI: 10.1038/s41598-023-46527-9 PMID: 37952037

Jiang, J.. (2020). Badges and credibility: How verification affects trust on Twitter. *Social Media + Society, 6*(3).

Kelley, H. H. (1967). Attribution theory in social psychology. *Nebraska Symposium on Motivation, 15*, 192–238.

Kiesler, S., Siegel, J., & McGuire, T. W. (1984). Social psychological aspects of computer-mediated communication. *The American Psychologist, 39*(10), 1123–1134. DOI: 10.1037/0003-066X.39.10.1123

Kramer, A. D., Guillory, J. E., & Hancock, J. T. (2014). Experimental evidence of massive-scale emotional contagion through social networks. *Proceedings of the National Academy of Sciences of the United States of America, 111*(24), 8788–8790. DOI: 10.1073/pnas.1320040111 PMID: 24889601

Kyrlitsias, C., & Michael-Grigoriou, D. (2020). Social conformity in immersive virtual environments: The Asch paradigm revisited. *Frontiers in Psychology, 11*, 2254. DOI: 10.3389/fpsyg.2020.02254 PMID: 33013589

Lauharatanahirun, N.. (2024). External and internal attributions in human–agent interaction: A neuro-social model. *Human-Machine Communication, 8*(1).

Logg, J. M., Minson, J. A., & Moore, D. A. (2019). Algorithm appreciation: People prefer algorithmic to human judgment. *Organizational Behavior and Human Decision Processes, 151*, 90–103. DOI: 10.1016/j.obhdp.2018.12.005

Lyons, T.. (2018). Obedience to GPS: Human reliance on automated navigation. *Transportation Research Part F: Traffic Psychology and Behaviour, 58*, 479–491.

Marwick, A., & Boyd, D. (2011). I tweet honestly, I tweet passionately: Twitter users, context collapse, and the imagined audience. *New Media & Society, 13*(1), 114–133. DOI: 10.1177/1461444810365313

Milgram, S. (1963). Behavioral study of obedience. *Journal of Abnormal and Social Psychology, 67*(4), 371–378. DOI: 10.1037/h0040525 PMID: 14049516

Milgram, S. (1974). *Obedience to authority*. Harper & Row.

Muchnik, L., Aral, S., & Taylor, S. (2013). Social influence bias: A randomized experiment. *Science, 341*(6146), 647–651. DOI: 10.1126/science.1240466 PMID: 23929980

Noble, S. U. (2018). *Algorithms of oppression: How search engines reinforce racism*. NYU Press. DOI: 10.18574/nyu/9781479833641.001.0001

Paavilainen, J.. (2017). The Pokémon Go experience: A location-based augmented reality mobile game goes mainstream. In *Proceedings of the 2017 CHI Conference on Human Factors in Computing Systems* (pp. 2493–2498). ACM. DOI: 10.1145/3025453.3025871

Papacharissi, Z. (2015). *Affective publics: Sentiment, technology, and politics*. Oxford University Press.

Pariser, E. (2011). *The filter bubble: How the new personalized web is changing what we read and how we think*. Penguin.

Peck, T. C., Seinfeld, S., Aglioti, S. M., & Slater, M. (2013). Putting yourself in the skin of a Black avatar reduces implicit racial bias. *Consciousness and Cognition, 22*(3), 779–787. DOI: 10.1016/j.concog.2013.04.016 PMID: 23727712

Postmes, T., Spears, R., & Lea, M. (2002). Intergroup differentiation in computer-mediated communication: Effects of depersonalization. *Group Dynamics, 6*(1), 3–16. DOI: 10.1037/1089-2699.6.1.3

Reeves, B., & Nass, C. (1996). *The media equation: How people treat computers, television, and new media like real people and places*. Cambridge University Press.

Reicher, S. D., Spears, R., & Postmes, T. (1995). A social identity model of deindividuation phenomena. *European Review of Social Psychology, 6*(1), 161–198. DOI: 10.1080/14792779443000049

Ribeiro, M. H., Ottoni, R., West, R., Almeida, V. A., & Meira, W.Jr. (2020, January). Auditing radicalization pathways on YouTube. In *Proceedings of the 2020 conference on fairness, accountability, and transparency* (pp. 131-141). DOI: 10.1145/3351095.3372879

Ross, L. (1977). The intuitive psychologist and his shortcomings: Distortions in the attribution process. In Berkowitz, L. (Ed.), Vol. 10, pp. 173–220). Advances in experimental social psychology. Academic Press. DOI: 10.1016/S0065-2601(08)60357-3

Seran, S., Kumar, A., & Lee, M. (2025). Generative AI and academic integrity: A dissonance perspective. *Journal of Educational Technology & Society, 28*(1), 45–62.

Slater, M., Antley, A., Davison, A., Swapp, D., Guger, C., Barker, C., & Sanchez-Vives, M. V. (2006). A virtual reprise of the Stanley Milgram obedience experiments. *PLoS One, 1*(1), e39. DOI: 10.1371/journal.pone.0000039 PMID: 17183667

Slater, M., & Sanchez-Vives, M. V. (2016). Enhancing our lives with immersive virtual reality. *Frontiers in Robotics and AI, 3*, 74. DOI: 10.3389/frobt.2016.00074

Tajfel, H., & Turner, J. C. (1979). An integrative theory of intergroup conflict. In Austin, W. G., & Worchel, S. (Eds.), *The social psychology of intergroup relations* (pp. 33–47). Brooks/Cole.

Toma, C. L., & Hancock, J. T. (2013). Self-affirmation underlies Facebook use. *Personality and Social Psychology Bulletin, 39*(3), 321–331. DOI: 10.1177/0146167212474694 PMID: 23359086

Treem, J. W., & Leonardi, P. M. (2013). Social media use in organizations: Exploring the affordances of visibility, persistence, editability, and association. *Communication Yearbook, 36*, 143–189.

Turner, J. C., Hogg, M. A., Oakes, P. J., Reicher, S. D., & Wetherell, M. S. (1987). *Rediscovering the social group: A self-categorization theory*. Blackwell.

Walther, J. B. (1992). Interpersonal effects in computer-mediated interaction: A relational perspective. *Communication Research, 19*(1), 52–90. DOI: 10.1177/009365092019001003

Yee, N., & Bailenson, J. (2007). The Proteus effect: The effect of transformed self-representation on behavior. *Human Communication Research, 33*(3), 271–290. DOI: 10.1111/j.1468-2958.2007.00299.x

Zimmer, M. (2010). "But the data is already public": On the ethics of research in Facebook. *Ethics and Information Technology, 12*(4), 313–325. DOI: 10.1007/s10676-010-9227-5

Chapter 2
Examining Age-Related Differences in Cognitive Biases in Acquiring Knowledge About AI

Adrienne Bethany Barretto
http://orcid.org/0009-0008-7143-1541
Parvatibai Chowgule College of Arts and Science, India

Vanessa Bonita Pereira
http://orcid.org/0009-0003-9392-0577
Parvatibai Chowgule College of Arts and Science, India

Pratiksha Gurudatt Mallya
http://orcid.org/0009-0000-3559-5583
Parvatibai Chowgule College of Arts and Science, India

Shalyn Angel Cardozo
http://orcid.org/0009-0009-1906-5860
Parvatibai Chowgule College of Arts and Science, India

Evira Daniela Pereira
http://orcid.org/0009-0007-8035-2434
Parvatibai Chowgule College of Arts and Science, India

Jeanne Marie Cotta
http://orcid.org/0009-0006-4619-4463
Parvatibai Chowgule College of Arts and Science, India

Saloni Joanna Rodrigues
http://orcid.org/0009-0007-2920-2852
Parvatibai Chowgule College of Arts and Science, India

ABSTRACT

The rise of artificial intelligence (AI) necessitates understanding how cognitive biases shape our perception of this evolving technology. This study examined the relationship between age and susceptibility to biases in acquiring AI-related knowl-

DOI: 10.4018/979-8-3373-5896-3.ch002

edge. It addressed three objectives: to explore the influence of cognitive biases in AI knowledge acquisition, to identify the types of biases involved, and to examine age-related differences. Sixty participants were evenly divided across young, middle, and older adulthood. The findings indicated that younger adults demonstrated higher levels of confirmation bias (80%), middle-aged adults exhibited declinism bias (70%), and older adults displayed availability bias (75%). The least evident biases were distinction bias and authority bias among young adults (30% each), belief bias among middle-aged adults (20%), and belief bias and distinction bias among older adults (30% each). The overall findings provides an understanding of how biases influence AI knowledge acquisition across age groups, laying groundwork for future research.

INTRODUCTION

We humans often pride ourselves on our ability to be objective and rational in our thinking (Holm, 2015). However, at times, we may deny reality because of our tendency to overestimate our own rationality. And one way this happens is through cognitive biases. In our effort to make sense of the world, we often simplify complex information and, in doing so, become vulnerable to these biases. Cognitive biases are unconscious, systematic errors in thinking that occur when people process and interpret information in their surroundings, influencing their decision-making and judgment (Da Silva et al., 2023). These biases can distort an individual's perception of reality, resulting in faulty interpretation of information and decisions that deviate from making rational choices. To better understand why such biases occur and how they challenge our assumptions about human rationality, it's important to examine the theoretical foundations that have long guided our understanding of decision-making. The theory that has dominated all research on making judgments was the "Rational Choice Theory," introduced by Adam Smith (Friedman, 2023). According to this model, the rational man makes his decisions based solely on his assessment of each probable outcome and his ability to maximize utility. He is assumed to evaluate a complete set of information using mathematical logic, which involves calculating the potential utility derived from each option and selecting the one that offers the highest utility within the constraints of their budget (Wong, 2021). On the contrary, evidence suggests that people's assessments of likelihood and risk often deviate from the laws of probability (Gilovich et al., 2002). As a result, this traditional view has been questioned over the past few decades.

This growing skepticism about human rationality paved the way for alternative perspectives on decision-making. In fact, Herbert Simon in 1957 argued against the idea that people make perfectly optimal decisions aimed at maximizing utility

(Raab et al., 2019). He introduced the concept of "bounded rationality," which suggests that while economic rationality is an ideal model, in reality, people's decisions are shaped by their personal limitations and the environment they're in. This means they often make decisions that are just "good enough" or satisfying, rather than perfect, allowing for quicker and more practical choices. Building on Simon's ideas, the heuristics and biases program developed by Amos Tversky and Daniel Kahneman in 1972 focused on identifying the specific limitations or biases that affect human judgment and decision-making (Wilke & Mata, 2017). They proposed that the human mind, much like our perceptual system, is designed to make judgments based on incomplete or imperfect information, which can sometimes lead to errors. These biases were explained as a result of relying on heuristics or simple mental shortcuts. Understanding these foundational theories helps us see why humans often fall short of perfect rationality, paving the way for researchers to identify and categorize the specific cognitive shortcuts, or biases, that frequently influence our everyday judgments and decisions.

For the sake of convenience, the following are some common cognitive biases available to us, which will also frequently appear in this chapter. The most well-known heuristics identified first were the representativeness, availability, and anchoring-and-adjustment heuristics. The anchoring heuristic occurs when people rely too much on the first number they are presented with when making decisions about uncertain quantities, even if that number is random and irrelevant (Teovanović, 2019). People make estimates based on the initial anchor value and gradually adjust from there. However, they often stop adjusting too soon, i.e., as soon as they reach a number that feels reasonable, even though it might not be the best answer. The availability heuristic suggests that people judge how likely or common an event is based on how easily they can remember similar events (Du, 2022). If something is easy to recall, they are more likely to overestimate its chances of happening again. In the representativeness heuristic, people make judgments about probability by asking themselves how closely the target resembles a typical example of the category or group they're thinking about (Teigen, 2004). Essentially, they base their decision on how much the target "looks like" it belongs to that group, rather than considering other relevant factors.

Along with these, there are other biases that also affect how we think and make decisions. The familiarity or mere exposure effect, a term introduced by Zajonc in 1968, refers to the phenomenon where repeated, unreinforced exposure to a stimulus leads to an increased liking for that stimulus (Nickerson, 1998). Authority bias refers to the tendency to favor the opinions of individuals perceived as experts in a specific field (Gültekin, 2024). This bias can lead individuals to unquestioningly follow authority, often resulting in irrational decisions. Further, confirmation bias is the tendency for people to seek out or interpret information in a way that supports their existing beliefs. This bias in decision-making is often unintentional, leading individuals to overlook information that opposes their views. Declinism is the belief, held by many, that their society is deteriorating and that many things of value in the past are being lost or even willfully destroyed in the present (Elchardus, 2017). In distinction bias, people tend to value one option over the other when the two are considered simultaneously (Nalcaci et al., 2019). The differences between the two options become more prominent, and thus one is predicted to contribute more to happiness than the other as opposed to being viewed separately.

Along similar lines, there are a few more biases that further reveal how our beliefs and assumptions can distort logical thinking and perception. Belief bias refers to the tendency for people's beliefs to interfere with logical reasoning. While reasoning, individuals often rely on their existing beliefs instead of following logical principles (Ding et al., 2020). When the conclusion aligns with their beliefs, they are more likely to accept the argument, even if it's flawed, and when the conclusion goes against their beliefs, they are less likely to accept it, even if it's logically sound. Finally, the false consensus effect refers to the tendency for people to view their own behavior and opinions as more common and suitable for the situation while considering other viewpoints or actions as rare or unusual (Choi & Cha, 2019).

COGNITIVE BIASES IN SHAPING PUBLIC ATTITUDES AND OPINIONS

Attitudes and opinions play a significant role in shaping how individuals process information, particularly in the context of cognitive biases. These biases influence how people perceive and interpret information and often stem from deeply held beliefs and prior experiences, leading individuals to selectively focus on information that aligns with their existing views while dismissing contradictory evidence. In recent times, the internet offers a vast repository of information on numerous topics, but the ability to search effectively and evaluate sources critically is crucial. However, our opinions and attitudes are often shaped by what information we encounter online, based on which we come to conclusions (Van Strien et al., 2016).

As a result, this has led researchers to investigate how people process information, particularly when it contradicts their existing beliefs. Three studies have examined how people process information online, particularly when it doesn't align with their existing beliefs. Van Strien et al. (2016) and Knobloch-Westerwick et al. (2014) both share a common finding that individuals with strong attitudes closely scrutinize sources from conflicting websites and stick to arguments supporting their views. Similarly, Meppelink and colleagues (2019), in their research about how people's beliefs about vaccination can influence the information they seek out and how they evaluate that information, also highlighted this bias, showing that people tend to prefer information that supports their existing beliefs even in the case of vaccination.

In a similar view, Van Giesen and colleagues' (2015) study on technology showed that for familiar technologies, people rely on cognition, i.e., their past experiences and knowledge, to shape attitudes, especially those with a high need for analytical thinking. However, with unfamiliar technologies like nanotechnology, emotions (affect) play a larger role, as people without sufficient knowledge often rely on gut feelings. Similarly, authority bias can significantly shape attitudes toward risk. Okushko (2022) found that when an authoritative figure provided input, individuals became more loss-averse, adjusting their risk preferences based on the authoritative opinion.

People's decisions are also influenced by initial reference points. When people are given a low starting point (anchor), they form more positive opinions than when presented with a high anchor. As demonstrated by Shan et al. (2020) in their study on consumer behavior, individuals exposed to a lower anchor value (price) had more favorable attitudes and intentions than those presented with a higher anchor. This shows that people often rely on the information available to them, especially when they are unsure or lack knowledge about a topic. Additionally, this bias affects how individuals perceive and evaluate information, often leading to skewed assessments. Wegener et al. (2010) found that when participants were given extreme anchor values, their later judgments stayed close to these anchors, even when they received more relevant information afterward. This shows how strong initial impressions can influence attitudes and make it hard to think objectively.

Further insights into anchoring bias, particularly in consumer behavior, are provided by Zong & Guo (2022). Their research highlights the variations in anchoring bias concerning price judgments, emphasizing the contextual factors that influence this effect. The study found that both external and internal anchoring effects occur simultaneously when consumers evaluate prices in various scenarios. Based on external anchor values, consumers adjust their price evaluations either upward or downward. Moreover, the study identified several factors that significantly impact the anchoring effect, including gender, Big Five personality traits, expert knowledge and skill, early warning indications, cognitive need, and self-confidence levels. These findings reinforce the complexity of anchoring bias and its implications in influencing the decision-making processes.

Another cognitive bias that affects our attitudes and opinions is the representativeness bias. Wickham (2003) demonstrated this in a study with business students, where their judgments about an entrepreneur's success or failure were influenced by context-related details. This bias, which comes from cognitive shortcuts rather than language or meaning, can lead to poor decision-making, especially in areas like evaluating new ideas.

The false consensus effect (FCE) is yet another bias that strongly influences our opinions and attitudes; however, they do vary in different contexts. Research suggests that the strength of the FCE varies across cultural contexts, with collectivist cultures exhibiting a stronger tendency toward consensus due to their emphasis on conformity and social validation. In contrast, individualistic cultures encourage greater recognition of differing viewpoints, which can result in a reduced FCE. Choi and Cha (2019) conducted a cross-cultural study examining FCE by comparing how Koreans and European Americans estimate others' behaviors based on their own. Their findings indicate that the FCE was more pronounced among Koreans, which the authors attribute to East Asian cultures' heightened sensitivity to information that aligns with broader social consensus, a characteristic rooted in collectivist values. Similarly, Fakhri et al. (2025) explored FCE among Indonesian students, whose cultural context is also shaped by collectivist dynamics. Their study supports the idea that individuals from collectivist societies are more likely to assume that their perspectives are shared by others, reinforcing the notion that cultural background plays a significant role in shaping the FCE.

Attitudes play a significant role in the manifestation of authority bias, where individuals' positive evaluation and agreements are often shaped by the perceived credibility or prestige of an authority figure. A study by Kreimer and Sánchez (2025) aimed to examine the impact of authority figures on beliefs. They investigated whether statements attributed to prestigious individuals were rated more favorably than those attributed to anonymous sources. The results showed that participants rated statements from prestigious figures more favorably, indicating a clear authority bias. This study demonstrates that participants' opinions were shaped not by the content of the statement but by their preconceived attitudes toward the authority of the individual providing the information. Similarly, Tikochinsky & Babad (2022) found that the media bias effect, driven by non-verbal behavior, was moderated by the perceived epistemic authority of the interviewer. When viewers perceived the interviewer as having high authority, the politician was rated more positively if the interviewer exhibited friendly nonverbal behavior. Conversely, if the interviewer was perceived as having low authority, no bias occurred, indicating that the viewers discounted nonverbal cues in favor of other information.

The interplay between these cognitive biases underscores the complexity of opinion formation, especially in the digital age, necessitating critical thinking and source evaluation skills to navigate the vast information landscape and to make decisions effectively.

ROLE OF COGNITIVE BIASES IN DECISION-MAKING

Decision-making is a complex process influenced by various cognitive biases, with confirmation bias affecting how individuals process information. It was seen that managers preferred aligning information with their pre-existing beliefs, avoiding contradictory evidence, which led to biased decisions (Costa et al., 2020; Cai et al., 2022). Due to our limited cognitive and perceptual capacities, we often rely on mental shortcuts to make quick and efficient decisions. Similarly, Cai et al. (2022) researched confirmation bias in analysts' responses to consensus forecasts and found that analysts' responses to consensus forecasts were distorted by their biases, resulting in inaccurate predictions. Both of these study findings indicate that confirmation bias can negatively influence professional decision-making, whether in management or finance.

This bias also plays a significant role in clinical decision-making involving AI. Bashkirova and Krpan (2024) emphasized that psychologists' trust in AI chatbot recommendations when making decisions for mental health diagnoses was influenced by their prior beliefs, specifically, whether the suggestions aligned with their preliminary diagnoses. This indicates that psychologists were more likely to accept and incorporate AI recommendations into their decision-making when they confirmed their preliminary diagnoses.

One well-documented cognitive bias that also affects decision-making is the availability heuristic. Nazlan et al. (2018) explored the effects of the availability heuristic in online consumer reviews, demonstrating how availability cues influence consumers' decision-making that leads to availability bias. Consumers relied on easily accessible information, such as star ratings, written descriptions, and images, when deciding about choosing the restaurants. Negative reviews had a stronger influence on decision-making, aligning with negativity bias, while the presence of both description and ratings led to increased visit intentions. Additionally, visual cues, such as images of menu items, further increased the likelihood of selecting a positively reviewed dish, emphasizing the role of the availability heuristic in shaping decision-making.

Similar to this study, Ly et al. (2023), examined anchoring bias in physician decision-making. They found that physicians were less likely to test for pulmonary embolism in patients with congestive heart failure (CHF) when CHF was mentioned in the triage notes. This demonstrated anchoring bias, where physicians too relied on the initial information when making decisions, making them less likely to consider alternative diagnoses such as pulmonary embolism.

PERCEPTION AND USAGE OF AI ACROSS AGE GROUPS

Artificial intelligence has become an integral part of modern society, influencing various aspects of daily life. However, individuals' perceptions and acceptance of AI vary across different age groups, shaping how they engage with and utilize AI technology. Research indicates that young adults generally perceive AI as a useful tool that can assist with multiple tasks, whereas individuals above 30 tend to view AI's capabilities as more limited (Barbul & Bojescu, 2023). Despite this, both age groups acknowledge AI's usefulness in daily life and evaluate themselves as capable of using AI devices without assistance, suggesting that modern AI has achieved accessible usability. While younger individuals find AI easier to use, both age groups are generally uninfluenced by social opinions regarding AI adoption. Additionally, trust in AI varies by age, with younger adults more likely to believe AI provides accurate information, though both groups consider AI reliable for specific tasks. However, there is a notable objection to AI, as both younger and older adults prefer human interactions over AI-based interactions. This resistance is stronger in individuals over 30, who show a greater inclination to avoid AI in the future.

Preferences for AI also vary by age group; younger adults tend to favor machines that exhibit human-like traits, while middle-aged and older adults are less inclined toward anthropomorphic AI (Pelau et al., 2018). Moreover, younger individuals are generally more aware of how smart devices collect and use personal data, whereas older generations may be less cognizant of these privacy implications. Younger adults are also more optimistic about AI's potential to enhance quality of life compared to older age groups.

Although some studies suggest generational differences in AI perception, others find minimal variance. According to Guo et al. (2024), digital generations currently show no significant differences in their perception of AI's ethical risks, as both "digital natives" and "digital immigrants" are still in the early stages of understanding AI's potential. Factors like cultural assimilation also contribute to this, in which the younger generation transmits knowledge and information to the older generation. Meanwhile, Rahman et al. (2024) found that early adults are more accepting of AI due to its efficiency and availability, whereas middle-aged adults exhibit greater fear related to AI's risks, including job security and bias.

METHODOLOGY

The aim of this chapter is to explore age-related differences in cognitive biases in acquiring knowledge about AI. The objectives of this chapter are to explore the influence of cognitive biases in acquiring knowledge about AI, to determine the types of cognitive biases used in acquiring knowledge about AI, and to identify age-related differences in cognitive biases in acquiring knowledge about AI. To address these objectives meaningfully, it is essential to outline the overall research framework used in the chapter. An exploratory study is a type of research wherein the research problem has not been clearly defined or studied in depth before. Exploratory research usually uses qualitative methods such as interviews, observations, and focus groups for data collection. This type of research method does not aim to provide a final conclusion on a topic but rather leads to more research of the topic.

To ensure appropriate representation for the research objectives, a carefully selected sample was used. Purposive sampling is used in research where the researcher intentionally selects a sample that meets the specific requirements of the study or survey. This involves examining the characteristics of the population and then choosing the sample that aligns with the study's objective. The study employs purposive sampling with 60 participants, male and female, divided into three age groups, to capture diverse perspectives based on the 'Periods of Development' as discussed by Santrock (2012): Young Adults (18-39 years): 20 participants who have grown up with advanced technology and likely have varied familiarity with AI, influencing their cognitive biases. Middle-Aged Adults (40-59 years): 20 participants who have experienced the rapid evolution of technology and may use AI in professional settings, offering insights into practical applications and related biases. Older Adults (60+ years): 20 participants who may have had less exposure to AI or encountered it later in life, providing perspectives on how delayed or limited engagement with technology affects their understanding and biases.

With the sample in place, data collection and analysis followed. An interview schedule, including a sociodemographic form was prepared based on the ten cognitive biases identified. The interview questions were based on information acquired from internet resources. Further, a recording device was used to capture the interview, and an AI-powered transcription tool was employed to transcribe the recorded conversation. The interview schedules were prepared, and data was collected from the three different age groups. This data was then transcribed, and patterns were identified within the text, which were categorized into different cognitive biases. Since this study is qualitative and uses an exploratory research approach, data analysis focuses on examining and interpreting non-numerical data in the form of text. Specifically, thematic analysis is used to identify and analyze patterns and themes within the textual data, enabling a detailed and in-depth exploration of the research findings. This leads to the broader scope of the present study. The primary focus is on how different cognitive biases influence our ability to acquire AI-related information and whether these biases will differ across age groups.

EXPLORING THE AGE-RELATED DIFFERENCES IN COGNITIVE BIASES IN ACQUIRING KNOWLEDGE ABOUT AI

This chapter aimed to explore whether there existed any age-related differences in cognitive biases when acquiring knowledge about AI. The data was collected through interviews and was transcribed, followed by a thematic analysis to identify the recurring themes and patterns that existed within the interview transcriptions. After thorough analysis, the most prevalent cognitive biases across the age groups were identified and are displayed in Table 1 below.

Table 1. Percentages of cognitive biases across all age groups

	Young Adults	Middle-Aged Adults	Older Adults
Representativeness Bias	45%	60%	40%
Familiarity Bias	70%	55%	50%
Availability Heuristic	40%	60%	75%
Confirmation Bias	80%	25%	55%
Declinism Bias	55%	70%	65%
False Consensus Effect	70%	45%	65%
Authority Bias	30%	25%	50%
Anchoring Bias	55%	45%	50%
Distinction Bias	30%	25%	30%
Belief Bias	55%	20%	30%

Representativeness Heuristic

Representativeness Heuristic was measured by describing two AI systems: one humanoid (System A) and one operating on large datasets (System B). Participants' selections were analyzed to determine whether they aligned with their prototype of AI, and the prevalence of this heuristic across different age groups is illustrated in Figure 1 below.

Figure 1. Prevalence of representativeness heuristic across age groups

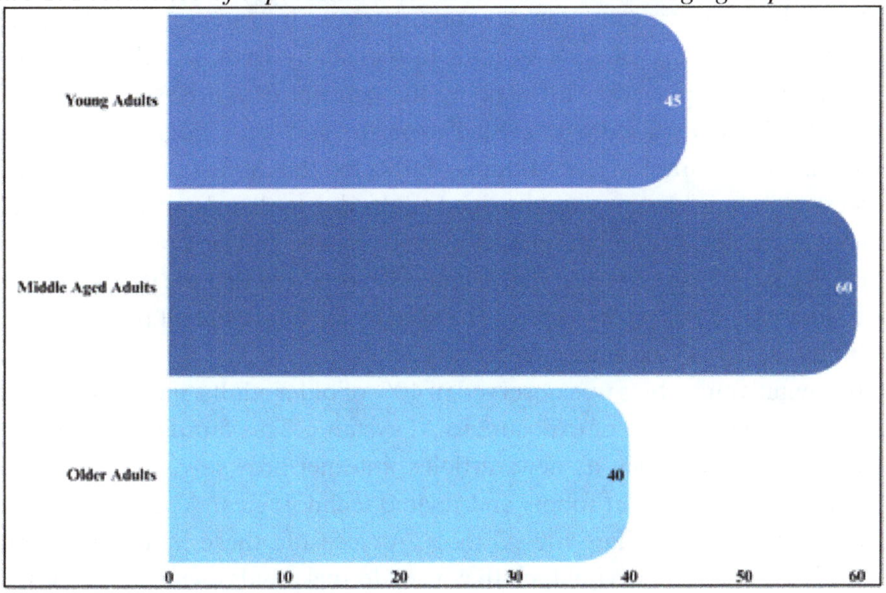

45% of young adults exhibited representative bias in their preferences for AI. Participants had a prototype about AI, which influenced their choices. One key factor was that AI system B aligned with the characteristics of currently available AI, such as tools like ChatGPT. However, none of the participants' responses were based on stereotypes about AI. Instead, they described AI as functioning "behind the scenes" through algorithms for recommendations or automated processes and calculations, rather than envisioning it as humanoid or visible forms. This lack of representativeness bias contrasted with Kahneman and Tversky's (1972) findings, where stereotypes often drove misjudgments. Here, familiarity with real-world AI applications likely reduced such bias.

In the middle-aged sample, 60% of the population demonstrated the presence of the representativeness bias, indicating that more than half of the sample population exhibited this bias while forming opinions about AI. The individual's prototype of AI was, formed by the content they consumed about AI and through their responses on where they got their sources of information about AI from. Since the representativeness heuristic was determined by analyzing those who selected the concept of AI that aligned with their prototype, it was found that the majority of individuals selected System B–the AI system that operates through software applications and large data sets. As the representativeness heuristic was influenced by well-learned schemas and prior knowledge, this aligned with research that showed people defaulted to familiar categories when faced with ambiguous choices (Taylor et al.,

2023). These individuals based it on what they were exposed to the most, either through work or other means, such as coming across information in news articles or through the mere use of such systems in their daily lives, which indicated the role that prototypes played in influencing the concept of AI. Research suggested that trust in robots increased with greater exposure and technological literacy (Oksanen et al., 2020). Similarly, the findings indicated that humanoid robotic AI was not a preferred choice among middle-aged adults due to their limited knowledge of humanoid technology, minimal interaction with robots, and lack of exposure to humanoids in daily life. As a result, individuals also reported that the use of humanoid robotic structures was still projected to be used in the future but, at present, was not something that they came across frequently.

Representativeness bias was observed in 40% of older adults, indicating that they had some prior knowledge or exposure to AI systems. This familiarity likely came from various sources, such as news articles, internet browsing, or conversations with family members about robots and related technologies. A survey found that 12% of people were familiar with AI tools. As a result, these individuals formed mental representations of AI, which they used to make judgments and identify AI in real-life situations. In contrast, the remaining 60% of older adults did not exhibit representativeness bias, suggesting that they lacked sufficient exposure to AI systems. Several factors may have contributed to this lack of exposure. Many of them did not use mobile phones, feared using them, or felt that learning technology at their age was too complex. This finding was supported by research that indicated most older adults who didn't use mobile phones or technology felt it was too complicated or were afraid to try (Yang et al., 2022). Some lived alone, which further reduced their opportunities for social interactions and staying informed about current events, indicating that participating in leisure, social, cultural, and spiritual activities in the community helped seniors stay engaged and informed about current events (WHO, 2010).

Familiarity Bias

Familiarity bias was examined by exposing participants to a news article that opposed their general opinion of AI and assessing whether their beliefs shifted after reading it. Figure 2 below illustrates the prevalence of familiarity bias across different age groups, showing age-related patterns.

Figure 2. Prevalence of familiarity bias across age groups

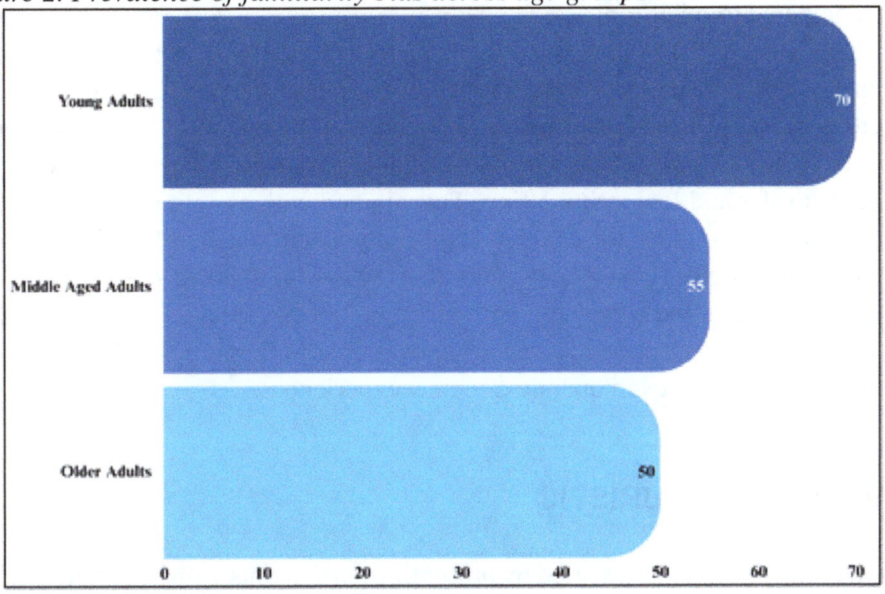

As shown in the figure, 70% of the young adult participants showed familiarity bias. The participants mostly chose the AI that they used in their day-to-day lives, like ChatGPT and Gemini. Learning more about such AI indicated strong familiarity with virtual assistants and computer programs that made them preferred and recognizable AI tools. Positive attitudes were often shaped by frequent use of tools like Siri and Google Assistant. The participants spoke about the usefulness of ChatGPT in writing assignments for college and the use of virtual assistants to do basic tasks while they drove, cooked, or were simply involved in some other work simultaneously, making them able to multitask, as mentioned by a participant. Thus, familiarity created an optimistic view of AI's broader impact. Zajonc (1968) demonstrated how repeated exposure could foster positive attitudes, aligning with this group's bias.

With respect to the middle-aged sample, 55% of the participants were shown to have familiarity bias. Individuals in this age group primarily selected tools such as ChatGPT and Siri or Alexa. When asked for their reasoning, in accordance with the familiarity bias, they mentioned that these tools were the most used by them to aid in various activities such as generation of ideas, creative writing, and drafting work emails. These findings align with Blanchar (2016), who found that participants tended to prefer and select ideologies they had encountered more frequently over those they had seen less often. For those who had negative general opinions about AI, they primarily selected the AI-powered fraud detection system, as it would save vulnerable people from cybercrimes. They claimed that this tool was the 'lesser of evils' compared to other tools on the list.

The equal split (50%) in familiarity bias reflected a divide in how older adults approached decision-making regarding AI tools. Half of the older adults gravitated towards tools or technologies they recognized and understood. Their preference for tools such as ChatGPT or virtual assistants could have been because these options felt safer and less intimidating. This aligned with a preference for comfort and predictability in decision-making, especially when faced with unfamiliar and complex technologies. Conversely, the other 50% who showed openness to less familiar tools suggested a growing curiosity among older adults willing to engage with innovations that seemed relevant or accessible to them, possibly influenced by individual differences in openness to new experiences.

AVAILABILITY HEURISTIC

Availability bias was measured by presenting participants with two short articles tailored to their initial opinions about AI. Those who initially viewed AI positively were shown an article highlighting job displacement due to AI, while those with a negative perception read about AI's advancements in healthcare. This approach aimed to assess whether exposure to new information influenced their initial stance, thereby introducing availability bias. And the prevalence of this bias across three age groups is shown in Figure 3 below.

Figure 3. Prevalence of availability heuristic across age groups

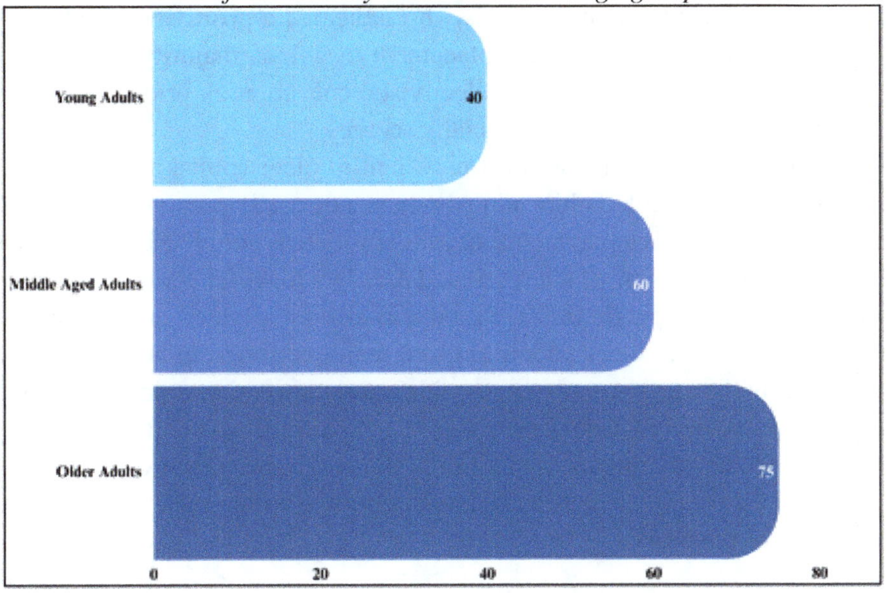

40% of the young adults exhibited the availability heuristic. They expressed concerns about AI-induced unemployment, particularly its impact on vulnerable sectors of the workforce. However, they also mentioned that AI integration could create future opportunities, enhance society by simplifying tasks, and generate new roles, even as it disrupted existing jobs. Some participants explained their reasoning based on personal experiences when the negative article was given, which influenced their agreement with the article. They did so because they believed AI had both positive and negative aspects that had to be considered, which may have influenced their decision. Research by Gupta and Singh (2023) highlighted the role of availability bias in investment decision-making, demonstrating that investors tended to rely on readily available information rather than conducting thorough analysis. Their findings suggested that professional investors were also susceptible to this bias, as they often made decisions based on recent market trends or widely circulated financial news. This aligned with a study which showed that young adults' concerns about AI shifted depending on the available information, further reinforcing how easily accessible data influenced perception and decision-making.

The availability heuristic was the second most common bias found amongst middle-aged individuals. It was found that 60% of the population in the middle-age group, showed availability bias. Individuals with a negative general opinion agreed with the article immediately, as it seemed that the positive article, which was based on advancements in cancer research, showed great sentiment across individuals.

Thus, AI advancements in this particular field had touched the sentiments of individuals. On the other hand, individuals who indicated a positive general opinion expressed a fear over job loss and replacement by AI, as majority of individuals were working. India, known for its collectivistic culture, took pride in work ethic and placed importance on being financially secure.

Availability heuristic was the most prevalent in older adults, affecting 75% of participants; this highlighted older adults' reliance on easily accessible information to form opinions. The high prevalence of availability bias could be linked to the use of health-related examples, which resonated deeply with older adults. Health was a sensitive and crucial topic for this age group, as also highlighted in the research by Zhai et al., 2024, where older people showed major concerns in health and health management. In the current study, many older adults shifted their initially negative views on AI to positive when shown its potential benefits, such as early disease detection or reduced treatment costs. This highlighted how recent examples in areas they prioritized strongly influenced their perceptions, with only a few questioning the reliability of the tools.

CONFIRMATION BIAS

Confirmation bias was measured by asking participants how likely they were to engage with content that contradicted their general opinion of AI and interact with individuals who held opposing views, as shown in Figure 4 below.

Figure 4. Prevalence of confirmation bias across age groups

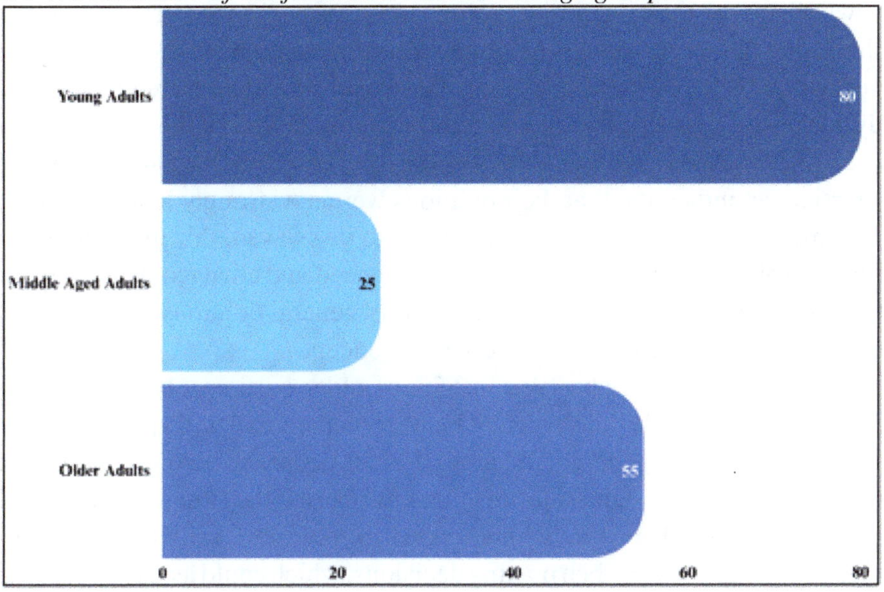

In the young adults, 80% of the participants exhibited confirmation bias. Most had strong pre-existing beliefs about AI. They gave examples of their personal experiences with AI, such as using AI for school and work, where they had hands-on experience with various forms of AI. This further reinforced their existing beliefs of AI as being convenient. Participants who believed AI was largely beneficial disregarded concerns over ethical challenges or biases in AI systems and instead spoke of the long-term benefits, such as increased efficiency and innovation. One particular pattern that was noticed was that the participants repeatedly provided solutions when discussing the potential risks. When engaging with opposing views, participants tended to reiterate their positive perspectives rather than critically evaluate alternative arguments. This aligned with research on confirmation bias and its influence on purchase decision-making, as both findings highlighted how individuals selectively processed information to reinforce their pre-existing beliefs. Just as consumers overlooked negative reviews about the preferred brands, participants in this study disregarded the ethical concerns about AI while emphasizing its benefits (Jin, 2023).

Confirmation bias was reported as being seen in 25% of middle-aged individuals. Those who showed this bias were intent on admitting that they would not specifically go out of their way to read articles. In addition, most individuals believed they would not necessarily ignore the views of others, but these individuals would try to change other people's negative opinions about AI by explaining only the positives.

These people would further dismiss others' concerns or criticism and try to defend their own views, or they would just refuse to be swayed by contrasting opinions. This indicated that professionals exhibited a confirmation bias, favoring AI advice that supported their pre-existing beliefs. Only one individual stated that while AI mostly had positive effects, they would only change their view if they were presented with genuine contradicting evidence. People also chose to continue to engage in conversation, an indication that their opinions were not strongly held. Despite participants mentioning that they would not want to be swayed, this in reality was out of their control, and they could have been influenced and changed their opinions at any time. As a result, most middle-aged persons' general opinions on AI could still have been forming, as it was a relatively new concept.

Confirmation bias was observed in 55% of older participants, indicating that more than half of the older adults relied heavily on their existing views on AI. This was consistent with the general tendency of older people, who often didn't like to change their minds but instead stuck to what information they knew (Waugh, 2023). Research had shown that older adults tended to rely more heavily on their prior knowledge and experience when making decisions, which could lead to confirmation bias (Carpenter & Yoon, 2011). In contrast, the other 45% of participants did not exhibit confirmation bias, possibly because they wanted to know more about AI and were therefore ready to listen to the opposite perspective. This finding was supported by research suggesting that older adults could be motivated to change their attitudes and beliefs when presented with compelling arguments and evidence (APA, 2023).

Declinism Bias

Declinism was assessed by providing statistics on job losses due to AI and evaluating whether participants perceived society as declining because of AI. And the frequency of this bias across different age groups is shown in Figure 5.

Figure 5. Prevalence of declinism bias across age groups

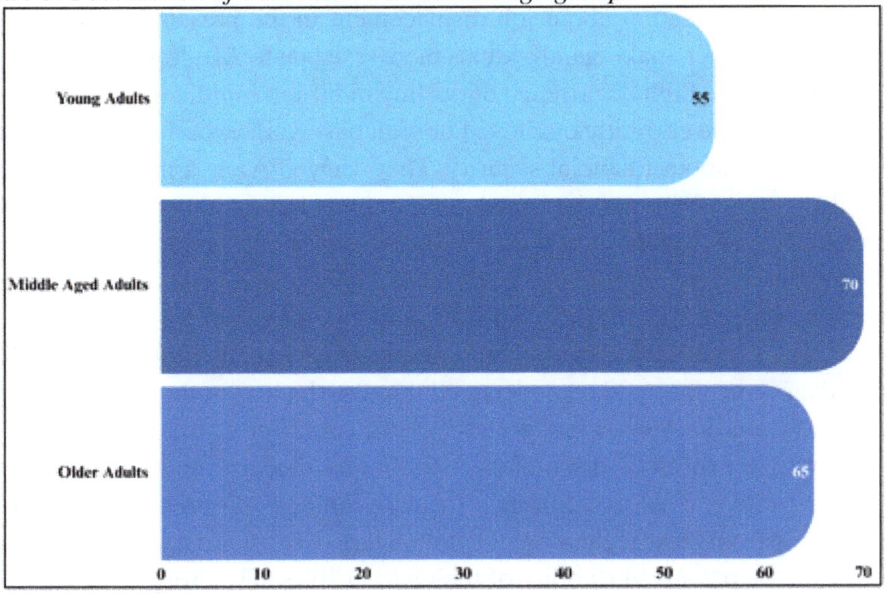

55% of young adults showed declinism bias. Most of the participants agreed that AI advancements were having a negative impact on society compared to its widespread use. All participants expressed apprehension about job loss, particularly for low-income families who might face financial insecurity. This aligned with declinism bias, as participants viewed the future impact of AI in a negative light. These responses aligned with research suggesting that fears of economic disruption contributed to negative perceptions of AI's long-term impact (Frey & Osborne, 2016). However, despite their concerns, the participants noted that these changes would be gradual, providing time for reskilling and workforce adaptation. These participants acknowledged both potential benefits and challenges, emphasizing the importance of reskilling and societal adaptation to AI advancements. They emphasized the importance of education to harness AI's potential and mitigate its negative effects.

Declinism emerged as the most common bias among the middle-aged sample, with 70% of participants exhibiting it. Declinism bias was often driven by rosy retrospection, where individuals recalled the past more positively and perceived the present more negatively. As people grew older, they may have focused more on their past emotional well-being, leading them to remember past events in a more positive light (Adler & Pansky, 2020). Individuals displaying this bias primarily expressed concerns about job loss, similar to those seen in other biases. This was likely due to their extensive work experience. Further, the inclusion of evidence of AI-driven job replacement in the questionnaire may have contributed to the fear, as 'negativity bias,' an aspect of declinism bias, suggested that negative information, like receiving information about job displacement in the present, had a stronger psychological impact, making individuals more resistant to AI adoption (Goldsmith & Dhar, 2013). The high occurrence of declinism bias in middle-aged participants suggested that those currently employed or with past work experience were particularly concerned about financial security. They viewed AI as a potential threat to their ability to meet basic survival needs and, as a result, were more likely to oppose its implementation. Similarly, research indicated that when people perceived AI as highly adaptable, they might have been more likely to worry about AI replacing human jobs, especially if they also saw AI as human-like (Park et al., 2024).

Older adults' widespread declinism bias, particularly concerning rapid technological advancements, could be understood through the lens of the "good old days" phenomenon and the related "rosy view" of the past. For example, 65% of older adults may have expressed discomfort with AI and modern innovations, viewing them as disruptive. This discomfort, especially among those aged 70-82, could have stemmed from these technologies symbolizing overwhelming societal changes compared to the perceived stability of their earlier lives. The "rosy view" research demonstrated how our memories of experiences became more positive over time, minimizing negative feelings encountered when initially facing new technologies. This could have led older adults, especially those less familiar with technology throughout their lives, to perceive current advancements as disruptive compared to their idealized past (Mitchell et al., 1997).

FALSE CONSENSUS EFFECT

The false consensus effect was examined by presenting a statement about AI's popularity and asking participants whether they agreed with the perceived majority opinion. And the age group that agreed with the majority of the opinions is seen in Figure 6 below.

Figure 6. Prevalence of false consensus effect across age groups

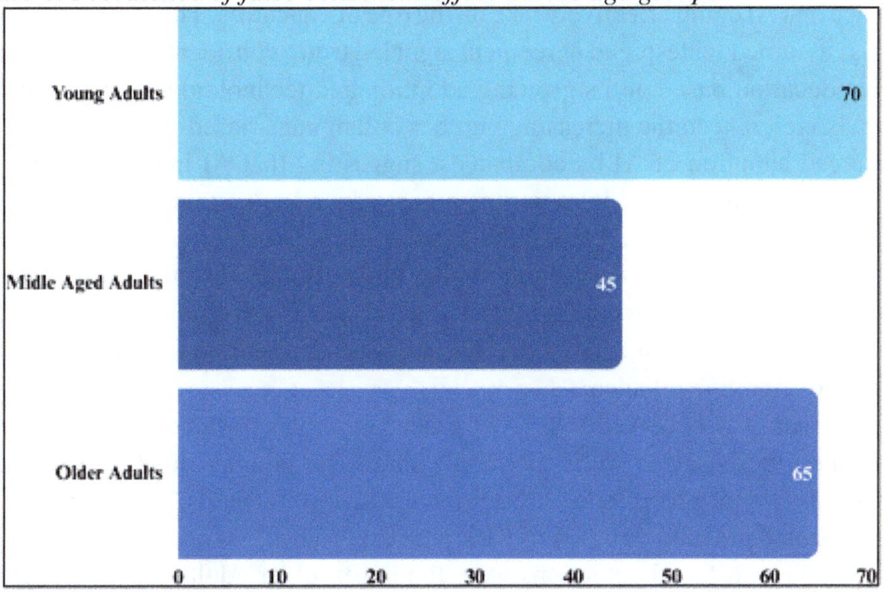

The young adults clearly demonstrated the false consensus effect, with 70% of participants overestimating how widely their views on AI in education were shared by others (Ross et al., 1977). Most respondents agreed that AI would improve education, citing benefits such as personalized learning, automation, and accessibility. Those with direct experience using AI-driven tools expressed even stronger support, reinforcing how personal exposure influenced belief formation. However, when asked whether their peers held similar views, participants consistently overestimated agreement. It was seen that supporters of AI estimated that others shared their opinion, while a few others who raised concerns about reduced human interaction still believed that there would be some, if not many, who agreed with them. This overestimation was driven by selective exposure, as participants likely interacted with like-minded individuals, reinforcing their belief in a general consensus. Additionally, media influence played a role, as the predominant portrayal of AI in education was positive, shaping perceptions of public opinion (Khan, 2023). Those who had personal success with AI tools assumed their experiences were universal, further strengthening their confidence in their stance. The findings confirmed that individuals tended to perceive their views as more widely accepted than they actually were, highlighting how cognitive biases shaped perceptions of social agreement.

The false consensus effect was observed in 45% of middle-aged adults, who tended to believe that if most people agreed with a statement, it must be true. Participants who exhibited this bias expressed confidence in AI's capabilities, often linking their reasoning to anchoring bias, where they perceived technological advancements as evidence that AI could effectively take on the role of educators. Those who exhibited this bias assumed widespread agreement signaled truth, confidently endorsing AI's role in education based on its growing adoption and technological advancements. Many also referenced the increasing number of language-based AI models and the widespread adoption of AI by companies, suggesting that AI integration into the school system was inevitable as part of a dual education system. In contrast, 55% of participants resisted full AI integration due to its lack of human touch, reflecting other studies on parents' views towards AI integration within the school system (Hartley, 2024). Doubts regarding AI's effectiveness in personalized learning and its impact on academic integrity reflected concerns that AI may have reduced originality and cognitive reliance.

This effect was observed in 65% of older participants, showing that many assumed their views on AI were commonly shared by others. This bias was likely influenced by their preference for traditional teaching methods, which they found more personal and effective due to their past experiences. Having grown up in an era where face-to-face interactions were the norm, older adults tended to believe this approach was universally preferred. Their limited exposure to modern teaching methods, like AI-based education tools, further reinforced this belief (Ahmad et al., 2022). Research suggested that older adults often assumed their opinions reflected a general consensus, even when societal views may have been shifting (Vauclair et al., 2016). This pattern was similar to findings on aging and meta-perceptions, where personal beliefs did not always align with broader technological acceptance (Vaportzis et al., 2017).

AUTHORITY BIAS

Authority bias was measured by quoting a statement from a recognized expert speaking positively about AI. Participants were assessed on their willingness to trust recommendations from this authoritative figure (Sundar Pichai). And the extent to which authority bias influences different age groups is depicted in Figure 7 below.

Figure 7. Prevalence of authority bias across age groups

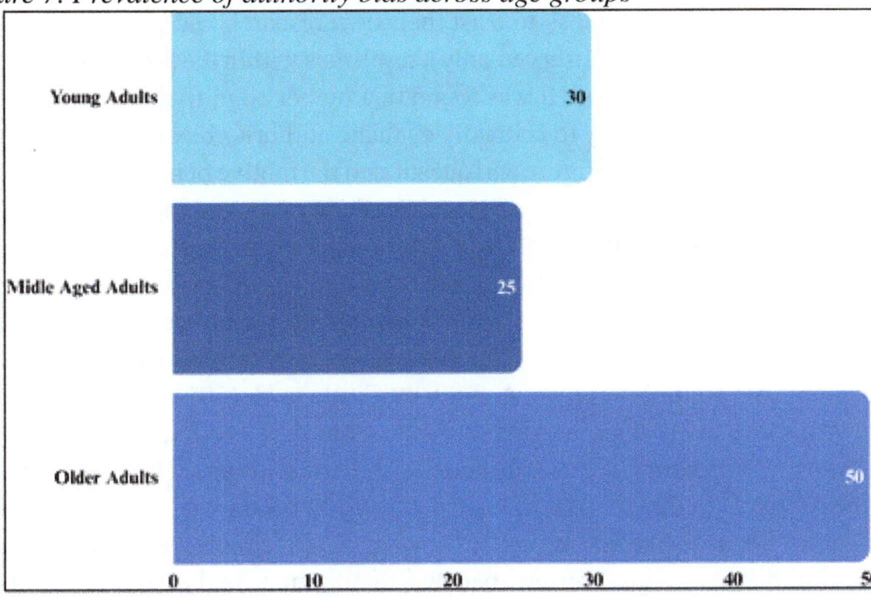

Among the 20 young adult participants, 30% exhibited authority bias, stating that Pichai's role as CEO of Google and his expertise in AI made his endorsement credible. These individuals viewed AI more positively due to his statement, reflecting prior findings that authoritative endorsements could influence attitudes toward technological adoption. Their trust in AI aligned with research suggesting that expert opinion could act as a cognitive shortcut, shaping decision-making without critical evaluation (Milgram, 1963). However, 70% of participants resisted authority bias, stating that their trust in AI was based on personal experience, independent research, or skepticism toward corporate messaging. This aligned with findings that noted that while authority bias existed, it did not universally dictate decision-making, especially among individuals with higher digital literacy and exposure to technological risks (Sabherwal, 2008).

Authority bias was observed in 25% of the middle-aged sample. These individuals had expressed that they would trust the authority figure because it was just a testament to the good that AI had accomplished in technology and other fields. Furthermore, these individuals also stated that not only was he an important figure, but because he was an expert in the field related to AI, they would trust him, as he was not someone who would make statements unless he had concrete evidence. However, some individuals stated that they trusted Pichai only to an extent and agreed with him only because of their own experience with Google or with other types of AI. Contrastingly, most individuals did not fall for this bias because they felt that the figure was trying to promote and advertise their product for their own benefit and hence, would more likely choose to trust their own research and knowledge about AI. This bias may have been observed only a few times within the sample because of the type of sample interviewed. It was found that higher cognitive ability had been associated with greater ability to critically evaluate authority bias; as a result, most individuals had criticized the figure and questioned the motive behind the statement.

The 50% influence of authority figures on older adults could be explained by their tendency to trust credible sources, a habit shaped by generational experiences where teachers, leaders, and traditional media were the primary sources of reliable information. Research supported this, indicating that older adults generally exhibited a higher degree of trust in authority figures, which influenced their acceptance of information from credible sources. A study by Castle et al. (2012) found that older adults were more likely than younger individuals to perceive untrustworthy faces as trustworthy, suggesting a general increase in trust with age. However, when it came to artificial intelligence (AI), this trust did not always translate into acceptance. Older adults often displayed skepticism toward new technologies, with research highlighting that they faced several barriers to adoption, including doubts about the benefits of AI (Smith, 2024).

Anchoring Bias

The anchoring heuristic was assessed by presenting participants with an expert's statement predicting that AI would surpass human capabilities within the next 10 years. Their responses were evaluated to determine whether they were anchored to this statement or maintained differing views, which is seen in Figure 8 below.

Figure 8. Prevalence of anchoring bias across age groups

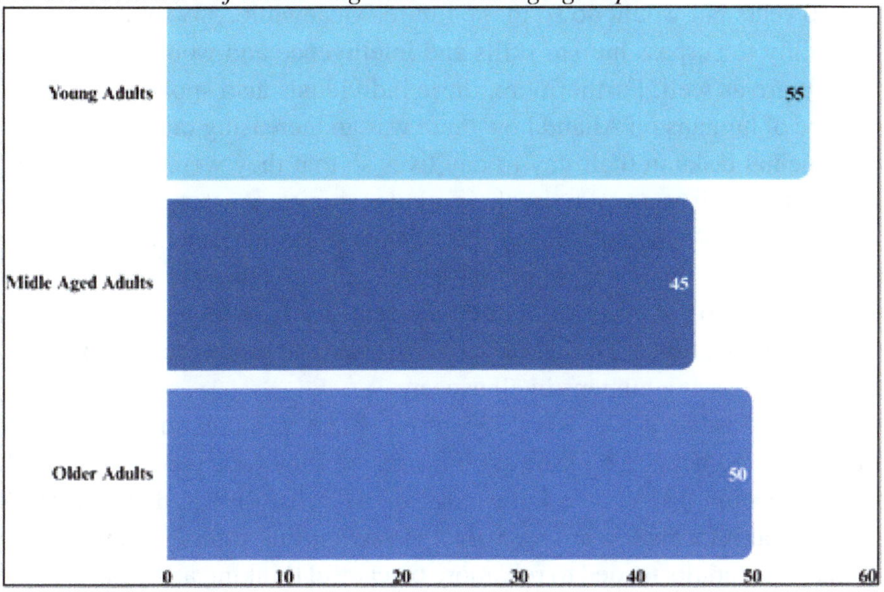

Among the 20 young adult participants, 55% exhibited anchoring bias, basing their views on Musk's 2017 statement. These individuals expressed strong confidence that AI would inevitably surpass human skills, even though current advancements had not yet matched the prediction. This showed the effect of an anchor, which was either numerical or authoritative, that significantly influenced judgments, even when contrary evidence was presented (Tversky & Kahneman, 1974). The presence of this bias suggested that Musk's status as a tech visionary reinforced the belief in AI's dominance, leading participants to interpret AI progress in a way that aligned with the initial anchor. On the other hand, 45% of participants resisted anchoring bias, arguing that AI's advancements had not been as rapid or all-encompassing as predicted. These individuals cited AI's ongoing limitations in creativity, emotional intelligence, and general reasoning as evidence that humans would continue to excel in key areas. This group demonstrated critical thinking, which suggested that effortful reasoning could reduce the impact of anchoring by encouraging individuals to consider alternative perspectives.

It was seen that anchoring bias was observed in 45% of middle-aged individuals, who agreed with the initial statement. These individuals expressed that AI was created by the use of data collected by humans. Thus, they were like sponges ready to absorb and provide information. Interestingly, 44.5% of those who showed anchoring bias seemed to disagree with AI taking over humans in all fields, particularly those that needed and required some "human touch," such as doctors or psychologists.

One individual also indicated that AI was not capable of replacing humans within the next 10 years but would do so in the future. Meanwhile, 55% indicated that AI had the ability to surpass human skills and intelligence and would continue to do so in the future as well. Furthermore, these individuals also spoke about the total dependence of humans on AI and how there was an increasing rate of people using AI to do menial tasks in their day-to-day lives so that they were able to get more free time to themselves and not use their minds as much as intended. Additionally, one individual also talked about the development of a humanoid robot (cat-girl) introduced by Elon Musk who would have the ability to conceive and give birth to children. Relating to this news, the individual mentioned that along with intelligence and skills, AI in the future would also have the ability to procreate just like humans did, thereby surpassing humans in all aspects.

Anchoring bias was observed in 50% of participants, indicating that half of the older adults relied heavily on the first information they received about AI. Many of the older people had limited knowledge of AI, which made them more likely to accept initial information at face value. However, this finding contradicted the notion that older adults tended to rely more on careful thinking and analysis in their decision-making (Koscielniak et al., 2018). In contrast, the other half of the participants did not exhibit anchoring bias. Instead, they tended to stick to their existing knowledge and beliefs, holding onto the notion that the world would remain largely unchanged, with people continuing to work in traditional jobs and societal structures remaining as they had been for decades. However, this finding was supported by research that suggested that as people got older, they tended to be less interested in trying new things and making changes in their lives (Carstensen & Hartel, 2006). They preferred to stick with what they knew and were comfortable with and tended to avoid new experiences and unfamiliar situations. This was a natural part of aging and could actually be a way for older adults to adapt and focus on what was most important to them.

DISTINCTION BIAS

Participants assessed two AI tools: AI X, designed for financial management, and AI Y, aimed at simplifying daily household tasks. Initially, each tool was presented separately to the participants. Afterward, they were shown a side-by-side comparison and asked to rate their preferences. And the results of this particular bias are shown in Figure 9 below.

Figure 9. Prevalence of distinction bias across age groups

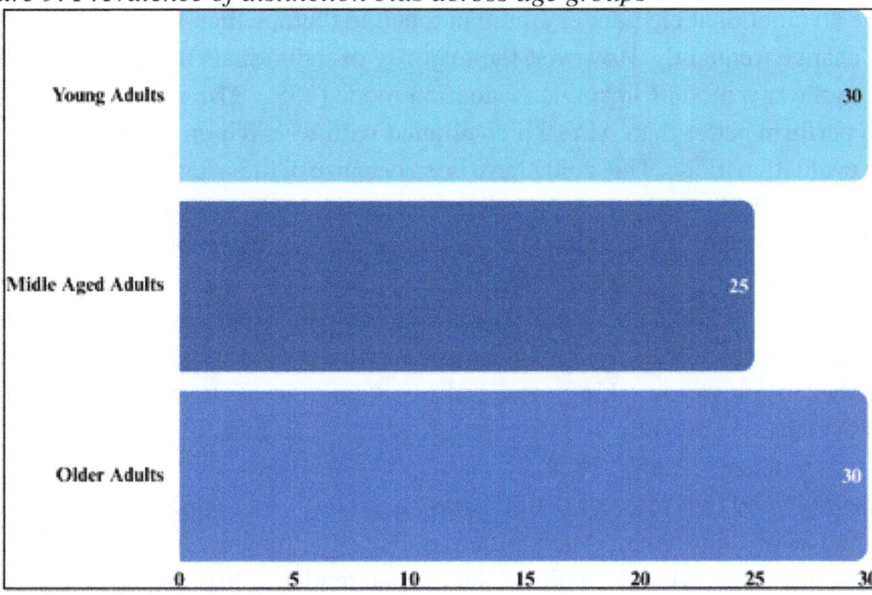

The results revealed that 30% of young adults exhibited distinction bias. These individuals, when presented with the direct comparison, placed undue emphasis on minor differences between the two AI tools, leading to a significant preference for one over the other. For instance, some participants highlighted the real-time fraud alert feature of AI X as a decisive factor, while others focused on the automated reminders of AI Y. This overemphasis on specific features during direct comparison aligned with the concept of distinction bias, where simultaneous evaluation made differences appear more pronounced than they might have in isolation (Hsee and Zhang, 2004). Conversely, 70% of participants did not display distinction bias. Their preferences remained consistent regardless of whether the AI tools were presented separately or together. These participants tended to base their evaluations on the overall utility of the tools in relation to their personal needs, rather than on specific distinguishing features. This finding was consistent with previous research indicating that joint evaluation could make even small differences between options more salient, affecting preferences and choices.

Distinction bias was observed in 25% of people in the middle-aged sample. These individuals expressed that both AIX and AIY were equally important when presented separately; however, when presented in tabular format, they reported that AI1 (the AIX equivalent) would perform better because the data being presented was that which was quantifiable, numerical, and objective, involving more complexity in executing, which was tedious to do without the assistance of AI. Whereas AI 2, which was more simplistic in nature, involved doing those day-to-day activities that needed to have an emotional element or a human touch to them, which was subjective and could change frequently. However, the majority of individuals made a comparison between the two models in single evaluation mode (75%), also reporting that AIX would perform better than AIY, which aligned with research on comparison in the single evaluation mode. This could have been because of the widespread availability of various AI models that served the same purpose as AIX, which appeared to be a key factor in reducing distinction bias (Kyungran et al., 2019). One individual who was a housewife and a working woman chose AIX/1, as usage of AI Y/2 would have led to loss of human activity. This indicated that individuals had the tendency to not allow AI to interfere with matters that were of personal significance to them, maybe because it meant taking more risks or going out of their comfort zone, as AI was known to constrain and restrict self-identity, human autonomy, and social behavior (Valenzuela et al., 2024).

The relatively low score of distinction bias among older adults (30%) could be attributed to several factors. Many older adults (70%) may not have had sufficient exposure to various AI tools, which reduced their tendency to compare and contrast them. This lack of exposure was consistent with research showing that many older adults in India lacked digital literacy, with 86% of senior citizens not knowing how to use digital technology or computers (Édes, 2021). Older adults may have been more focused on the practical applications of AI tools, rather than their unique features. Some may have also been less interested in evaluating the differences between AI tools. Furthermore, older adults may have been more accepting of AI tools as they were, rather than trying to distinguish between them. This suggested that older adults tended to prioritize functionality and practicality when using AI tools. Interestingly, this finding contrasted with research on how people interacted with objects. According to a recent study, people's interactions with objects were heavily influenced by their appearance, size, weight, and material (Potter, 2024). This implied that people generally did consider the unique features of objects when interacting with them. However, the finding suggested that older adults may have been an exception to this rule, as they tended to focus more on the practical applications of AI tools rather than their unique features.

BELIEF BIAS

Belief bias was assessed by first gathering participants' views on alternative medicine and then presenting a scenario where an AI health app recommended alternative treatments without strong supporting evidence. Their responses were analyzed to see if their beliefs were influenced by the AI's recommendation. Figure 10 given below highlights the prevalence of belief bias across different age groups.

Figure 10. Prevalence of belief bias across age groups

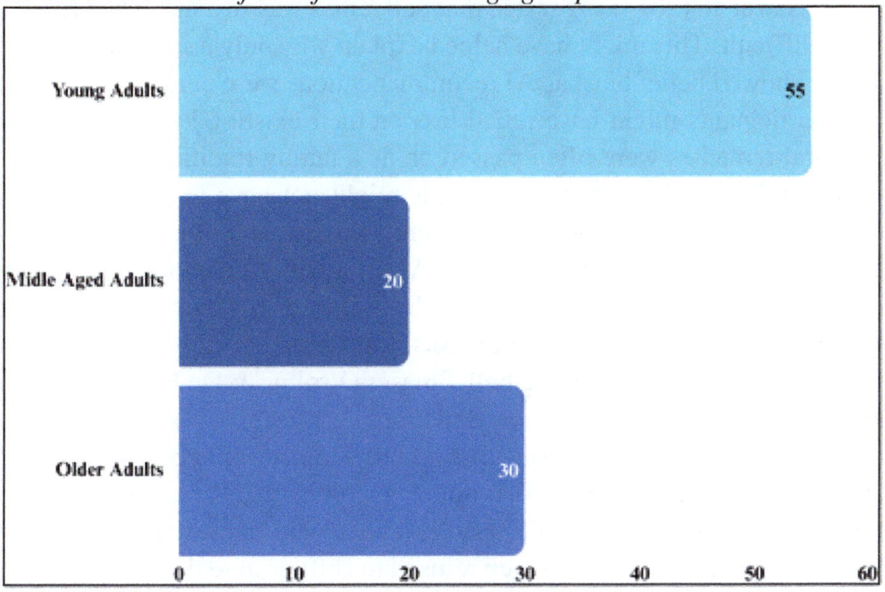

The 55% of young adult participants who exhibited belief bias did so because their preexisting attitudes toward alternative medicine had influenced their trust in AI recommendations, despite the lack of scientific evidence. In this case, participants who already viewed natural remedies positively were more likely to trust the AI health app's recommendations simply because they aligned with their existing beliefs, even if the app lacked empirical validation. Some participants expressed this bias explicitly, making statements such as, "AI was smart, so if it was recommending natural treatments that aligned with my knowledge about those medicines, there must have been some truth to it". Moreover, belief bias led individuals to overlook flaws in supporting information while being more critical of contradictory evidence (Klauer et al., 2000). Some participants dismissed the lack of scientific support, stating, "AI might have been picking up on things researchers hadn't figured out yet." Others reinforced their bias by rejecting opposing views, saying, "There was no problem if there was no scientific backing; it didn't hurt to simply try". The findings highlighted how belief bias could shape decision-making, particularly in health-related AI applications, where individuals might subconsciously favor recommendations that confirmed their preexisting views.

Belief bias was observed only in 20% of the middle-aged sample, indicating that this bias was weak in this age group. Even though all individuals had positive views about alternative medications and natural remedies, they refused to trust recommendations from AI because of the consequences that it might have on their health. Brisson et al. (2014) suggested that belief bias was stronger when reasoning was more difficult. This might have helped explain why only a small percentage of the sample showed belief bias; as AI recommendations were perceived as straightforward, participants might have relied less on their existing beliefs. In addition, since natural remedies were often passed on as a family tradition, because of the personal significance behind it, individuals might not have been keen on going against what was usually followed in the family, highlighting the influence of values and culture in decision-making about AI. In addition, individuals' reluctance to trust AI for health decisions could have been linked to an underlying tendency to confirm fears about potential health risks; this contradicted research, as people were said to have threat-confirming belief biases (Vroling & De Jong, 2010). Thus, participants rejected AI health recommendations despite favoring natural remedies, contradicting research that suggested that AI predictions would be reinforced if the individual had a strong interest in the topic being predicted (Lee, 2024).

Belief bias was observed in 30% of older adults, who answered questions based on their personal opinions, which they refused to shift despite the lack of scientific proof. People tended to evaluate arguments based on their prior beliefs rather than objective logic. This tendency aligned with the findings of a study by (Ding et al., 2020), which also observed that older adults relied heavily on prior knowledge and experience when making decisions. In contrast, the remaining 70% of older adults did not exhibit belief bias, possibly because they did not trust the AI app due to its unfamiliarity, having never seen or experienced anything like this in their time. This finding seemed contradictory to existing research done by Zhang (2023), which suggested that older adults were open to using technology, including unfamiliar ones, for various purposes.

CHALLENGES IN CAPTURING COGNITIVE BIASES ON AI

Our study encountered several limitations that may have influenced the findings in our chapter. One of the key challenges was the confusion among participants regarding the distinction between general technology and AI. This lack of clarity may have impacted their responses and overall understanding of the study's objectives. Future research should aim to mitigate this by providing participants with a clear, standardized definition of AI, along with concrete examples, to ensure a shared understanding before data collection begins.

Another limitation was the variability in AI knowledge among older adult participants. Some individuals had little exposure to AI, which may have affected the accuracy and relevance of their responses. A more effective approach would have been to screen participants based on their AI knowledge through a preliminary survey and select those with a baseline understanding. This would allow for more meaningful insights into the specific biases being investigated.

The phrasing of our interview questions was also one of the limitations, as they may not have optimally captured the biases we aimed to study. For instance, our question designed to assess belief bias did not account for individuals who do not prefer any form of alternative medicine, potentially skewing the results. Future studies should consider incorporating a broader range of response options to accurately capture the spectrum of participants' beliefs.

Additionally, some participants struggled to understand the questions, which may have influenced the consistency and reliability of their responses. This lack of clarity could have introduced unintended biases in the data collection process. Moreover, biases such as distinction bias, which are more evident in real-life settings, were challenging to measure accurately through our survey questions. This suggests a need for developing more nuanced assessment tools or experimental designs that can better capture the prevalence and impact of such biases.

Another problem was the validity of the interview questionnaire, as some questions did not effectively capture the cognitive biases being examined. Certain biases were difficult to measure due to ambiguities in question phrasing, leading to responses that may not accurately reflect participants' true perceptions. Refining the question design by ensuring clarity, using precise language, and incorporating pilot testing to assess comprehension and alignment with the intended biases could have helped avoid this. Providing examples or context within the questionnaire could also enhance participant understanding, leading to more reliable and meaningful insights.

CONCLUSION

In conclusion, this study explored age-related differences in cognitive biases when acquiring knowledge about artificial intelligence (AI), using a qualitative approach with interviews conducted among 60 participants across three age groups. The findings revealed that young adults had a strong understanding of AI and showed high confirmation bias (80%), often seeking information that aligned with their positive perceptions. Middle-aged adults, with moderate knowledge primarily gained through work, exhibited high declinism bias (70%), reflecting cautious attitudes towards AI.

Older adults, who often did not recognize their use of AI tools, demonstrated limited familiarity and showed a high availability bias (75%), relying on familiar examples and experiences. The lowest biases identified were distinction and authority bias in young adults (30%), belief bias in middle-aged adults (20%), and both belief and distinction bias in older adults (30%). These results support existing research and highlight that cognitive biases significantly shape how individuals across age groups perceive and engage with AI. Ultimately, the study offers valuable insights into how age and cognitive bias interact in the context of emerging technologies. Figure 11 and Figure 12 below provide an overview of the most and least prevalent biases across the age groups.

Figure 11. Prevalence of most common biases across age groups

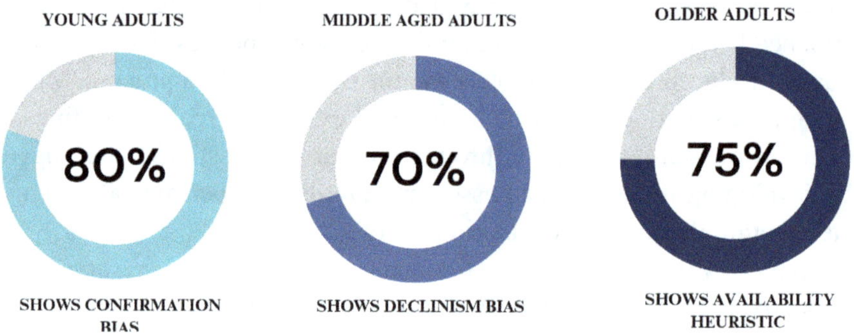

Figure 12. Prevalence of least common biases across age groups

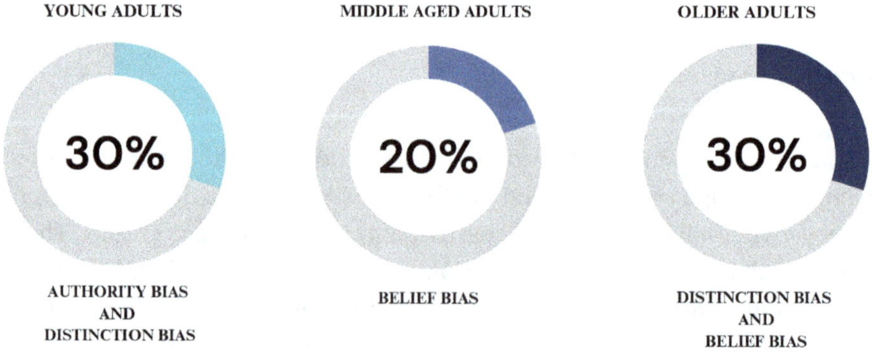

REFERENCES

Adler, O., & Pansky, A. (2020). A "rosy view" of the past: Positive memory biases. In *Elsevier eBooks*.139–171. https://doi.org/DOI: 10.1016/B978-0-12-816660-4.00007-6

Ahmad, N. A., Rauf, M. F. A., & Razak, F. H. (2022). Effectiveness of instructional strategies designed for older adults in learning digital Technologies: A Systematic literature review. *SN Computer Science*, *3*(2), 130. Advance online publication. DOI: 10.1007/s42979-022-01016-0 PMID: 35039803

American Psychological Association. (2023, March). *Ageism is one of the last socially acceptable prejudices. Psychologists are working to change that.* Monitor on Psychology. https://www.apa.org/monitor/2023/03/cover-new-concept-of-

Barbul, M., & Bojescu, I. (2023). Generations' Perception Towards the Interaction with AI. *New Trends in Sustainable Business and Consumption*, 539–546. https://doi.org/DOI: 10.24818/BASIQ/2023/09/041

Bashkirova, A., & Krpan, D. (2024). Confirmation bias in AI-assisted decision-making: AI triage recommendations congruent with expert judgments increase psychologist trust and recommendation acceptance. *Computers in Human Behavior: Artificial Humans.*, *2*(1), 100066. Advance online publication. DOI: 10.1016/j.chbah.2024.100066

Blanchar, J. (2016). Familiarity Bias: Examining a Cognitive-Affective Mechanism Underlying Ideological Support for the Status Quo Underlying Ideological Support for the Status Quo. *Graduate Theses and Dissertations.* Familiarity Bias: Examining a Cognitive-Affective Mechanism Underlying

Brisson, J., De Chantal, P., Forgues, H. L., & Markovits, H. (2014). Belief bias is stronger when reasoning is more difficult. *Thinking & Reasoning*, *20*(3), 385–403. DOI: 10.1080/13546783.2013.875942

Cai, H., Yao, T., & Zhang, X. (2022).Confirmation Bias in Analysts' Response to Consensus Forecasts. *Journal of Behavioural Finances.* https://ssrn.com/abstract=4211686

Carpenter, S. M., & Yoon, C. (2011, October 19). Aging and consumer decision making. *Annals of the New York Academy of Sciences.* https://pmc.ncbi.nlm.nih.gov/articles/PMC3799963/

Carstensen, L. L., & Hartel, C. R. (2006).When I'm 64.*Motivation and behavioral change.* https://www.ncbi.nlm.nih.gov/books/NBK83771/#:~: Choi, I., & Cha, O. (2019). Cross-Cultural examination of the false consensus effect. *Frontiers in Psychology, 10.* https://doi.org/DOI: 10.3389/fpsyg.2019.02747

Castle, E., Eisenberger, N. I., Seeman, T. E., Moons, W. G., Boggero, I. A., Grinblatt, M. S., & Taylor, S. E. (2012). Neural and behavioral bases of age differences in perceptions of trust. *Proceedings of the National Academy of Sciences of the United States of America, 109*(51), 20848–20852. DOI: 10.1073/pnas.1218518109

Costa, D. F., Carvalho, F., Moreira, B. C., & Silva, W. (2020). Confirmation bias in managerial decision-making: an experimental study with managers and accountants. *Journal of Accounting and Organizations.* (PDF) Confirmation bias in managerial decision-making: Da Silva, S., Gupta, R., & Monzani, D. (2023a). Editorial: Highlights in psychology: cognitive bias. *Frontiers in Psychology, 14*, 1242809. Advance online publication. DOI: 10.3389/fpsyg.2023.1242809

Ding, D., Chen, Y., Lai, J., Chen, X., Han, M., & Zhang, X. (2020). Belief bias effect in older adults: Roles of working memory and need for cognition. *Frontiers in Psychology, 10*, 2940. Advance online publication. DOI: 10.3389/fpsyg.2019.02940 PMID: 32038362

Du, R. (2022). Availability Heuristic: An Overview and Applications. *Highlights in Business Economics and Management, 1*, 153–159. DOI: 10.54097/hbem.v1i.2548

Édes, B. (2021, December 22). *Helping India's elderly cross the digital divide as the Country Ages*. Medium. https://bigtrendsguy.medium.com/helping-indias-elderly-

Elchardus, M. (2017). Declinism and Populism. *Clingendael Spectator 3, 71*(1), 1-10. https://spectator.clingendael.org/pub/2017/3/_/pdf/IS-2017-3-elchardus.pdf

Fakhri, N., & Muhajirah, K. Lukman, & Buchori, S. (2025, March 11). *Examining Self-Compassion's Mediating Effects Between Fear of Failure and Academic Self-Handicapping Among University Students*. Journal of Psychological Perspective. https://ukinstitute.org/journals/jopp

Frey, C. B., & Osborne, M. A. (2016). The future of employment: How susceptible are jobs to computerisation? *Technological Forecasting and Social Change, 114*, 254–280. DOI: 10.1016/j.techfore.2016.08.019

Friedman, H. H. (2023). Cognitive Biases that Interfere with Critical Thinking and Scientific Reasoning: A Course Module. SSRN *Electronic Journal*. https://doi.org/ DOI: 10.2139/ssrn.2958800

Gilovich, T., Griffin, D., & Kahneman, D. (2002). *Heuristics and Biases*. Cambridge UniversityPress., http://books.google.ie/books?id=ZGYgAwAAQBAJ&printsec= DOI: 10.1017/CBO9780511808098

Goldsmith, K., & Dhar, R. (2013). Negativity bias and task motivation: Testing the effectiveness of positively versus negatively framed incentives. *Journal of Experimental Psychology. Applied, 19*(4), 358–366. DOI: 10.1037/a0034415 PMID: 24059820

Gültekin, D. G. (2024). Understanding and mitigating authority bias in business and beyond. In *Advances in human resources management and organizational development book series*. 57–72. https://doi.org/ DOI: 10.4018/979-8-3693-1766-2.ch004

Guo, J., Chen, J., & Cheng, S. (2024). Perception of ethical risks of artificial intelligence technology in the context of individual cultural values and intergenerational differences: the case of China. *Research Square (Research Square)*. https://doi.org/ DOI: 10.21203/rs.3.rs-3901913/v1

Gupta, A., & Singh, L. (2023). Checking Influence Of Cognitive Biases On Investment Decision Making And Moderating Role Of Financial Literacy [Journal-article]. *HSBRR, 18–18*(1), 101–113. http://www.gjust.ac.in/department/hsb/hsb_res_journals.html

Hartley, T. (2024, July 16). *AI in Education*. DoodleLearning. https://doodlelearning.com/maths/maths-guides/ai-in-education

Holm, C. (2015). The 25 Cognitive Biases- Uncovering The Myth Of Rational Thinking.

Hsee, C. K., & Zhang, J. (2004). Distinction Bias: Misprediction and Mischoice Due to Joint Evaluation. *Journal of Personality and Social Psychology, 86*(5), 680–695. DOI: 10.1037/0022-3514.86.5.680 PMID: 15161394

Jin, P. (2023). *Research on Confirmation Bias and Its Influences on Purchase Decision-making*. Advances in Economic Management and Political Sciences., DOI: 10.54254/2754-1169/10/20230471

Kahneman, D., & Tversky, A. (1972). Subjective probability: A judgment of representativeness. *Cognitive Psychology, 3*(3), 430–454. DOI: 10.1016/0010-0285(72)90016-3

Khan, R. (2023, November 24). *Media ideology shapes public perception of artificial intelligence.* Open Access Government. https://www.openaccessgovernment.org/media-

Klauer, K. C., Musch, J., & Naumer, B. (2000). On belief bias in syllogistic reasoning. *Psychological Review, 107*(4), 852–884. DOI: 10.1037/0033-295X.107.4.852 PMID: 11089409

Knobloch-Westerwick, S., Johnson, B. K., & Westerwick, A. (2014). Confirmation bias in online searches: Impacts of selective exposure before an election on political attitude strength and shifts. *Journal of Computer-Mediated Communication, 20*(2), 171–187. DOI: 10.1111/jcc4.12105

Koscielniak, M., Rydzewska, K., & Sedek, G. (2018, November 6). *Commentary: The attraction effect in Decision making: Superior performance by older adults.* Frontiers. https://www.frontiersin.org/journals/psychology/articles/10.3389/fpsyg.2018.02321/full

Kreimer, R., & Sánchez, F. (2025). The Impact of Authority Figures in our Beliefs. Experimental Studies on the "Author's Bias." https://www.academia.edu/29898878/The_Impact_of_Authority_Figures_

Kyungran, A. M. A., Kim, T., Ahn, J., & Ahn, J. (2019). A study on the media Consumers' behavior related to Online Communications: Behavioral Economics Perspective. *KSII Transactions on Internet and Information Systems, 13*(5). Advance online publication. DOI: 10.3837/tiis.2019.05.014

Lee, E. (2024). *The Power of Perception in Human-AI Interaction: Investigating Psychological Factors and Cognitive Biases that Shape User Belief and Behavior. arXiv*. Cornell University., DOI: 10.1080/08870440903440707

Ly, D. P., Shekelle, P. G., & Song, Z. (2023). Evidence for anchoring bias during physician decision-making. *JAMA internal medicine.* https://pmc.ncbi.nlm.nih.gov/articles/PMC10294014/#H1-5-IOI230036

Meppelink, C. S., Smit, E. G., Fransen, M. L., & Diviani, N. (2019). "I was Right about Vaccination": Confirmation Bias and Health Literacy in Online Health Information Seeking. *Journal of Health Communication, 24*(2), 129–140. DOI: 10.1080/10810730.2019.1583701 PMID: 30895889

Milgram, S. (1963). Behavioral study of obedience. *Journal of Abnormal and Social Psychology, 67*(4), 371–378. https://www.demenzemedicinagenerale.net/pdf/MilgramOriginalWork.pdf. DOI: 10.1037/h0040525 PMID: 14049516

Mitchell, T. R., Thompson, L., Peterson, E., & Cronk, R. (1997). Temporal adjustments in the evaluation of events: The "Rosy View.". *Journal of Experimental Social Psychology, 33*(4), 421–448. DOI: 10.1006/jesp.1997.1333 PMID: 9247371

Nalcaci, A. A., Girgin, D., Balki, S., Talay, F., Boz, H. A., & Balcisoy, S. (2019). Detection of confirmation and distinction biases in visual analytics systems. *Eurographics Proceedings*, 13–17. https://doi.org/DOI: 10.2312/trvis.20191185

Nazlan, N. H., Tanford, S., & Montgomery, R. (2018). The effect of availability heuristics in online consumer reviews. *Journal of Consumer Behaviour.* https://www.researchgate.net/publication/326376699_

Nickerson, R. S. (1998). Confirmation bias: A ubiquitous phenomenon in many guises. *Review of General Psychology*, *2*(2), 175–220. DOI: 10.1037/1089-2680.2.2.175

Oksanen, A., Savela, N., Latikka, R., & Koivula, A. (2020). Trust toward Robots and Artificial Intelligence: An Experimental Approach to Human–Technology Interactions online. *Frontiers in Psychology*, *11*, 568256. Advance online publication. DOI: 10.3389/fpsyg.2020.568256 PMID: 33343447

Okushko, E. (2022). *Influence of social forces in the form of authority bias and conformity bias on the degree of individuals' risk-aversion* [Master's thesis, Radboud University Nijmegen]. Radboud Repository. https://theses.ubn.ru.nl/server/api/core/bitstreams/

Park, J., Woo, S. E., & Kim, J. (2024). Attitudes towards artificial intelligence at work: Scale development and validation. *Journal of Occupational and Organizational Psychology*, *97*(3), 920–951. DOI: 10.1111/joop.12502

Pelau, C., Nistoreanu, B., & Ene, I. (2018). Differences in the perception on artificial intelligence depending on age. In *ResearchGate* [Online Print]. Proceedings of the 1st International Conference on Economics and Social Science, Bucharest, Romania. https://www.researchgate.net/publication/327721442_

Potter, L. (2024, October 4). *Older people pick up objects in a different way to younger people*. The Conversation. https://theconversation.com/older-people-pick-up-objects-

Raab, M., Bar-Eli, M., Plessner, H., & Araújo, D. (2019). The past, present and future of research on judgment and decision making in sport. *Psychology of Sport and Exercise*, *42*, 25–32. DOI: 10.1016/j.psychsport.2018.10.004

Rahman, M. M., Babiker, A., & Ali, R. (2024). Motivation, concerns, and attitudes towards AI: differences by gender, age, and culture. In *Lecture notes in computer science* (pp. 375–391). https://doi.org/DOI: 10.1007/978-981-96-0573-6_28

Ross, L., Greene, D., & House, P. (1977). The "false consensus effect": An egocentric bias in social perception and attribution processes. *Journal of Experimental Social Psychology*, *13*(3), 279–301. DOI: 10.1016/0022-1031(77)90049-X

Sabherwal, R. (2008). Adoption of information systems innovations by individuals: A study of processes involving contextual, adopter, and influencer actions. *Uark.* https://www.academia.edu/30543160/

Santrock, J. (2012). Life-Span development. McGraw-Hill Higher Education. https://books.google.co.in/books/about/Life_Span_Development.html?

Shan, L., Diao, H., & Wu, L. (2020, August 12). *Influence of the framing effect, anchoring effect, and knowledge on consumers' attitude and purchase intention of organic food.* Frontiers. https://www.frontiersin.org/journals/psychology/articles/10.3389/

Smith, A., (2024). *Older adults and technology use*. Pew Research Center. https://www.pewresearch.org/internet/2014/04/03/older-adults-and-technology-use/

Taylor, M. K., Marsh, E. J., & Samanez-Larkin, G. R. (2023). Heuristic decision-making across adulthood. *Psychology and Aging*. Advance online publication. DOI: 10.1037/pag0000726 PMID: 36757964

Teigen, K. (2004). Judgements by representativeness. In *Cognitive Illusions* (p. 165). Psychology Press., https://www.researchgate.net/publication/256309189_

Teovanović, P. (2019). Individual differences in anchoring effect: Evidence for the role of insufficient adjustment. *Europe's Journal of Psychology*, *15*(1), 8–24. DOI: 10.5964/ejop.v15i1.1691 PMID: 30915170

Tikochinsky, R., & Babad, E. (2022, January 28). Perceived epistemic authority (source credibility) of a TV interviewer moderates the media bias effect caused by his nonverbal behavior - journal of nonverbal behavior. SpringerLink. https://link.springer.com/article/10.1007/s10919-022-00397-3

Tversky, A., & Kahneman, D. (1974). Judgment under Uncertainty: Heuristics and Biases. *In Science.* 4157.1124 –1131. https://www2.psych.ubc.ca/~schaller/Psyc590Readings/TverskyKahneman1974.pdf

Valenzuela, A., Puntoni, S., & Wertenbroch, K. (2024). How artificial intelligence constrains the human experience. *Journal of the Association for Consumer Research*, *9*(3), 241–256. DOI: 10.1086/730709

Van Giesen, R. I., Fischer, A. R. H., Van Dijk, H., & Van Trijp, H. C. M. (2015). Affect and Cognition in Attitude Formation toward Familiar and Unfamiliar Attitude Objects. *PLoS One*, *10*(10), e0141790. DOI: 10.1371/journal.pone.0141790 PMID: 26517876

Van Strien, J. L., Kammerer, Y., Brand-Gruwel, S., & Boshuizen, H. P. (2016). How attitude strength biases information processing and evaluation on the web. *Computers in Human Behavior, 60*, 245–252. DOI: 10.1016/j.chb.2016.02.057

Vaportzis, E., Clausen, M. G., & Gow, A. J. (2017). Older Adults Perceptions of Technology and Barriers to Interacting with Tablet Computers: A Focus Group Study. *Frontiers in Psychology, 8*, 1687. Advance online publication. DOI: 10.3389/fpsyg.2017.01687 PMID: 29071004

Vauclair, C., Lima, M. L., Abrams, D., Swift, H. J., & Bratt, C. (2016). What do older people think that others think of them, and does it matter? The role of meta-perceptions and social norms in the prediction of perceived age discrimination. *Psychology and Aging, 31*(7), 699–710. DOI: 10.1037/pag0000125 PMID: 27831711

Vroling, M. S., & De Jong, P. J. (2010). Threat-confirming belief bias and symptoms of anxiety disorders. *Journal of Behavior Therapy and Experimental Psychiatry, 41*(2), 110–116. DOI: 10.1016/j.jbtep.2009.11.002 PMID: 19942212

Waugh, R. (2023, May 15). *This is why it's so difficult to change old people's Minds*. Yahoo! News. https://uk.news.yahoo.com/this-is-why-its-so-difficult-to-change-old-peoples-

Wegener, D. T., Petty, R. E., Blankenship, K. L., & Detweiler-Bedell, B. (2010). Elaboration and numerical anchoring: Implications of attitude theories for consumer judgment and decision making. *Journal of Consumer Psychology, 20*(1), 5–16. DOI: 10.1016/j.jcps.2009.12.003

Wern Ting Wong, C. (2021, March 4). *Making Rational Decisions*. HU Econ Review. https://www.economicsreview.org/post/making-rational-decisions

Wickham, P. A. (2003). The representativeness heuristic in judgements involving entrepreneurial success and failure. *Management Decision, 41*(2), 156–167. DOI: 10.1108/00251740310457605

Wilke, A., & Mata, R. (2017). Cognitive Bias. In *Elsevier eBooks*. https://doi.org/ DOI: 10.1016/B978-0-12-809324-5.06376-8

World Health Organisation. (2010). *Social Participation*. World Health Organization. https://extranet.who.int/agefriendlyworld/age-friendly-practices/

Yang, C. C., Li, C. L., Yeh, T. F., & Chang, Y. C. (2022, April 28). Assessing older adults' intentions to use a smartphone: Using the meta-unified theory of the acceptance and use of Technology. *International journal of environmental research and public health.* https://pmc.ncbi.nlm.nih.gov/articles/PMC9102817/#:~:text=,
Zajonc, R. B. (1968). Attitudinal effects of mere exposure. *Journal of Personality and Social Psychology, 9*(2, Pt.2), 1–27. https://doi.org/DOI: 10.1037/h0025848

Zhai, S., Zhang, Z., & Chen, J. (2024). Community-dwelling older adults' perspectives on health risks: A qualitative study exploring anxieties, priorities, and expectations in ageing. *BMC Public Health, 24*(1), 1657. Advance online publication. DOI: 10.1186/s12889-024-18878-z PMID: 38907192

Zhang, M. (2023, May 19). Older people's attitudes towards emerging technologies. https://journals.sagepub.com/doi/10.1177/09636625231171677

Zong, Y. & Guo, X.(2022, February 8).An Experimental Study on Anchoring Effect of Consumers' Price Judgment Based on Consumers' Experiencing Scenes.*Frontiers in Psychology*. Frontiers | An Experimental Study on Anchoring Effect of Consumers'

APPENDIX A

Interview Schedule

Q1) In 2017, Elon Musk predicted that AI would outperform humans in almost everything within 10 years. Now, in 2024, while AI has advanced, there are still many areas where humans excel. What do you think about AI's future ability to surpass human skills?

Q2) Imagine Two AI Tools

(Participants are presented with information on two different AI tools separately)

QI

AI X

Imagine AI X, which helps you manage your finances efficiently using artificial intelligence. It provides personalized financial planning, tracks your investments, and offers expert budgeting advice. With AI X, you can make informed decisions about your money and achieve your financial goals. In addition, it analyzes spending habits to suggest cost-cutting opportunities and provides real-time alerts for suspicious transactions, helping you make more informed decisions about your money

AI Y

Imagine AI Y, which simplifies your daily life by managing household chores, organizing shopping lists, and planning family meals. It ensures your home runs smoothly, saving you time and effort. It can also create automated reminders for certain tasks important to you.

i) Is there an AI tool that you would rate better? Why?

Filler Questions:

Q1) Do you believe AI will exceed human intelligence in the next century?

Q2) Would you prefer AI integrated education or traditional teaching methods?

QII The following is information on two AI tools displayed in Table 2 below.

Table 2. Two AI Tools

AI 1	AI 2
Financial planning, investment tracking, budgeting advice, spending habit analysis, fraud alert system.	Household chores, shopping list, meal planning, automated reminders.

ii) Is there an AI tool that you would rate better? Why?

Q3)

AI System A

- Has a humanoid robot appearance with advanced speech capabilities
- Often used for customer service in large tech companies
- Can simulate human emotions and facial expressions

AI System B

- Operates behind the scenes in software applications
- Specializes in analyzing large data sets to predict trends
- Commonly used in finance and healthcare for decision-making processes

Based on these two AI systems, which one do you think best represents what AI is like in real life, and why?

Q4) How do you feel about using alternative medicine, natural remedies? Do you generally have a positive or negative view of these practices?

Now imagine an AI health app that recommends treatments aligning with natural remedies and alternative medications. However, the app's recommendations lack strong scientific proof. How likely are you to trust the recommendation, and why?

Q5) When reading about AI, do you try to stay open to ideas or evidence that might challenge your current understanding of AI ?Can you provide an example about a perspective or evidence that shifted your views on AI?

QI) How do you approach discussions about the positive effects of AI with people who hold opposing views ?

QII) How do you approach discussions about the negative effects of AI when engaging with people who are enthusiastic about its positive impacts?

Q6) You frequently hear on the news or on the internet that most people agree that AI will improve education. Do you accept this information and why?

Q1) You are discussing the advantages and disadvantages of AI with your peers. Do you believe other people hold similar views on the topic that you do? What percentage of people hold similar views ? Elaborate.

Q7) The CEO of Google, Sundar Pichai, has stated that "AI is one of the most profound things humanity is working on". Do you think having a trusted figure like Pichai makes you trust AI recommendations more?

Q8) According to research,14% of workers have experienced job displacement due to AI, and it is expected that AI could replace up to 800 million jobs worldwide by 2030. With this in mind, do you believe AI advancements are having a more negative impact on society compared to the period before its widespread use?

Q9) You're interested in learning more about artificial intelligence (AI). From the following list of AI tools, which one would you choose? And why?"

List of AI tools

Self-driving cars: (Vehicles that can operate without human intervention).

Siri or Alexa: (Virtual assistants that can perform tasks like setting alarms, playing music, and answering questions).

ChatGPT: (A large language model that can generate human-like text in response to a wide range of prompts).

AI-generated art and music: (Creative works created by AI algorithms).

AI-powered fraud detection systems: (Systems that use AI to identify fraudulent activity).

Gemini Ai

Q10) This question is based on the response of their general opinion about AI in the sociodemographic form.

Positive Article for Negative Opinion

"*AI* Revolutionizes Healthcare: Enhancing Diagnostics, Reducing Costs, and Improving Patient Care" AI can detect melanoma (skin cancer) in skin images with over 90% accuracy, allowing for earlier treatment and better care at reduced costs in India- *MIT News 2024*

Negative Article for Positive Opinion

"AI Automation Results in Job Losses: Millions in India Need Reskilling". By 2027, over

16 million workers in India will need reskilling due to AI advancements- *The EconomicsTimes 2024*

QI) How do you currently feel about AI technology? Do you think it's more likely to bring positive changes, like improving healthcare and treatment?

QII) How do you currently feel about AI technology? Do you think it's more likely to bring negative impacts, like job loss and ethical concerns?

Chapter 3
The Digital Mask as Identity, Anonymity, and Behavior in the Online World

Sarwat Sultan
http://orcid.org/0000-0001-7439-1559
Bahauddin Zakariya University, Pakistan

Frasat Kanwal
http://orcid.org/0000-0003-3156-7520
Bahauddin Zakariya University, Pakistan

ABSTRACT

The mask is one of humanity's oldest cultural artifacts, long used in ritual, theater, and carnival to mediate transformation, concealment, and revelation. In the digital age, the mask has migrated into virtual environments, where avatars, pseudonyms, curated profiles, and anonymous forums function as digital masks. Unlike traditional masks, digital ones are persistent, searchable, and networked, leaving traces that endure well beyond their intended context. The digital mask offers a powerful lens for understanding identity, anonymity, and behavior online. It is not simply deception but a necessary element of digital life. Masks can liberate or constrain, protect or endanger, depending on the social and technological context. The challenge for individuals and communities is to design technologies, norms, and policies that preserve the protective and creative capacities of digital masks while mitigating their destructive potential. The essential question is not whether we will wear masks in digital life, but under what conditions, for whose benefit, and at whose expense.

DOI: 10.4018/979-8-3373-5896-3.ch003

INTRODUCTION: WEARING MASKS IN THE DIGITAL AGE

The mask is among the oldest human inventions. Across cultures, masks mediated ritual, performance, and play, serving as devices of transformation, concealment, and revelation. In sacred ceremonies, they allowed dancers to embody gods or spirits. In theatre, they signalled archetypes and emotions, bridging the gap between actor and audience. In carnival, they enabled temporary reversals of hierarchy, freeing peasants to mock nobles and women to parody men (Le Bon, 1895/2002). The mask has always been double-edged: liberating but destabilizing, protective but dangerous.

Today, the mask has migrated to digital space. Avatars, pseudonyms, curetted profiles, encrypted channels, and anonymous forums function as *digital masks*. They shield individuals from exposure, enable exploration of self, and create distance between actor and act (Goffman, 1959). Yet they also provide cover for incivility, deception, and harm (Christopherson, 2007). Unlike traditional masks, digital ones are persistent, searchable, and networked—leaving traces that endure beyond their intended context (Nissenbaum, 2019).

This chapter examines the *digital mask* as both metaphor and analytical lens. It traces its cultural roots, explores its psychological and social functions, and analyzes its ethical and political stakes. Above all, it emphasizes ambivalence: the digital mask is neither inherently liberating nor inherently corrupting, but an amplifier of human motives shaped by platform architectures and cultural norms (Marwick & boyd, 2018).

The Cultural Roots of the Mask

To grasp the novelty of digital masks, we must first recognize their continuity with history.

Ritual Transformation: In ancient societies, masks were portals to the sacred. West African ceremonies and Native American rituals used masks to embody spirits, collapsing the boundary between human and divine. Wearing a mask transformed the self into something larger. Online, pseudonyms and avatars play a similar role, allowing people to step outside embodied identities and experiment with new selves—gendered, ideological, or fantastical (Floridi, 2016).

Theatrical Performance: In Greek theater, masks exaggerated expressions and facilitated role shifts. In Japanese Noh, subtle changes in mask angle conveyed shifting emotions. Digital masks operate comparably: LinkedIn personas, gaming avatars, and pseudonymous handles enable role-playing across contexts. They are not lies but performances, vehicles for expression and storytelling (Goffman, 1959).

Carnival Inversion: Medieval carnival masks temporarily upended order, granting license to mock authority (Le Bon, 1895/2002). Similarly, anonymous online spaces function as digital carnivals—zones of inversion where irreverence, parody, and transgression thrive (Phillips & Milner, 2021). These can foster creativity and critique, but also cruelty and chaos.

Continuity and Difference: What is distinctive today is persistence and scale. Ritual and carnival masks dissolved after the event. Digital masks linger in archives, screenshots, and search engines, sometimes haunting users long after (Zuboff, 2019). They also operate globally, visible far beyond the context in which they were created. The cultural lineage of masking reminds us that the digital mask is not wholly new, but its technological affordances intensify both promise and risk.

Identity, Anonymity, and Pseudonymity

Digital life unfolds along a spectrum of identity presentation: real-name, pseudonymous, and anonymous. Each mode represents a different kind of digital mask, balancing visibility, accountability, and freedom (Goffman, 1959).

Real-Name Identity: Platforms like Facebook and LinkedIn anchor participation in legal identity, promising trust and accountability. When names are tethered to legal selves, deception seems less likely. Yet visibility also constrains freedom. Dissidents in authoritarian states, whistleblowers in corporations, or marginalized users may find real-name spaces unsafe (UN Human Rights Council, 2015). Real-name environments reduce deception but amplify *curated performance*: LinkedIn profiles highlight achievements while minimizing vulnerability, illustrating that authenticity is not guaranteed by exposure (Marwick & boyd, 2018).

Pseudonymity: Handles, gamer tags, and stable aliases offer continuity without full exposure. A Reddit user may cultivate credibility while keeping their legal name hidden. Pseudonyms balance freedom with accountability—missteps can still harm reputation within the community (Brubaker et al., 2016). Yet pseudonyms remain fragile: "doxxing" can pierce the mask, collapsing boundaries carefully maintained across roles (Citron & Norton, 2020).

Anonymity: At the far end lies radical concealment: no stable identifier, as on 4chan or ephemeral chat apps. Here, individuals are reduced to the immediacy of their posts. Anonymity lowers inhibitions, fostering candid disclosure but also aggression (Christopherson, 2007). Classic deindividuation research (Zimbardo, 1969) explains why anonymous groups can produce both heartfelt support and hostility: accountability dissolves, and behavior aligns with prevailing group norms.

Layered Selves: Most people shift across masks daily professional visibility on LinkedIn, playful pseudonymity on Reddit, anonymity in surveys. This layered selfhood is adaptive but precarious. *Context collapse* (Marwick & boyd, 2018)—when identities leak across boundaries—threatens to expose carefully segmented roles. Screenshots, algorithms, and data persistence intensify this fragility, making selective masking both necessary and risky.

The Online Disinhibition Effect

John Suler (2004) coined the *online disinhibition effect* to describe how digital environments loosen ordinary restraints on behavior. Freed from immediate social cues, individuals disclose more, act more impulsively, or express hostility more freely.

Two Faces of Disinhibition

- **Benign disinhibition**: increased openness and emotional disclosure. People share struggles with mental health or trauma in anonymous forums, gaining empathy and support (Brubaker et al., 2016). Vulnerable populations—LGBTQ+ youth, survivors of violence—often rely on this dynamic for solidarity.
- **Toxic disinhibition**: heightened aggression, rudeness, or harassment. Trolls exploit anonymity to provoke, while cyberbullies use it to harm peers (Phillips & Milner, 2021). Extremist recruiters leverage it to normalize radical discourse (Andrejevic, 2019).

Mechanisms of Disinhibition

Suler (2004) identified six factors:

- **Dissociative anonymity** – actions are untraceable.
- **Invisibility** – absence of physical cues.
- **Asynchronicity** – delayed feedback reduces consequences.
- **Solipsistic introjection** – others imagined as characters in one's mind.
- **Dissociative imagination** – online life treated as separate from "real" life.
- **Minimization of authority** – hierarchies less visible in digital space.

Together, these create psychological cover, weakening self-censorship (Christopherson, 2007).

Positive Outcomes: Benign disinhibition supports *digital intimacy*. Studies show that online anonymity encourages self-disclosure that might be stigmatized offline (Snowden, 2019). Shy individuals often gain confidence in online expression, with spillover effects into offline self-esteem (Marwick & boyd, 2018).

Negative Outcomes: Toxic disinhibition contributes to harassment, doxxing, and online radicalization. Research links anonymity to greater likelihood of antisocial behavior (Christopherson, 2007). Bandura's (1999) theory of *moral disengagement* explains how diffusion of responsibility, dehumanization, and moral justification are easier when identities are masked.

Context Matters: Platform cultures mediate outcomes:

- In **health forums**, anonymity fosters care.
- In **gaming spaces**, it often fuels hostility.
- In **political subreddits**, it amplifies both advocacy and vitriol (Phillips & Milner, 2021).

Moderation, algorithms, and community norms shape whether disinhibition becomes supportive or destructive (Citron & Norton, 2020).

Reflection: The online disinhibition effect illustrates the paradox of digital masks. They can empower vulnerability and solidarity or enable cruelty and hate. Disinhibition is not inherently pathological—it is a predictable response to digital affordances. The challenge is to build environments that channel it toward care, creativity, and justice rather than hostility or exploitation (Nissenbaum, 2019).

COLLECTIVE MASKS: GROUP DYNAMICS ONLINE

Masks do not only alter individual behavior; they reshape collective dynamics. When identity is concealed or transformed, groups act differently, sometimes producing extraordinary creativity and solidarity, other times unleashing hostility and chaos.

Deindividuation and Collective Behavior

Classic crowd psychology suggested that anonymity dissolves individuality and intensifies group impulses (Le Bon, 1895/2002). Zimbardo's (1969) deindividuation theory extended this insight, showing that anonymity reduces self-awareness and moral restraint. Online, these processes are amplified. In anonymous forums, individuals often act less as autonomous selves and more as nodes in a collective mask, adopting group norms and emotional tones.

Group Polarization and Echo Chambers: Anonymity interacts with group polarization—the tendency for deliberation to intensify pre-existing views. In digital echo chambers, masked users amplify one another's most extreme expressions, pushing the group further toward radical positions (Phillips & Milner, 2021). This is evident in extremist forums, where anonymity facilitates radicalization, but also in activist spaces, where anonymity protects members and emboldens calls for justice (Snowden, 2019).

Viral Masks and Meme Culture: Memes are themselves collective masks—symbols or phrases repeated until they acquire shared meaning. Viral hashtags like #MeToo illustrate how anonymity allows individuals to contribute personal stories without exposure, while still participating in a powerful collective voice (Citron & Norton, 2020). The anonymity of the many coalesces into a recognizable, collective identity that shapes public discourse.

Platform Architectures: Different platforms enable different collective masks. Reddit's pseudonymous "karma" system builds reputation without exposure; Twitter (now X) combines pseudonymity with virality, producing fast-moving cascades of discourse; 4chan's radical anonymity fosters both creativity and hostility (Phillips & Milner, 2021). Architecture mediates outcome: the same anonymity that enables harassment in one space may enable solidarity in another (Marwick & boyd, 2018).

Ambivalence of the Collective Mask: The collective mask is thus double-edged. It enables communities to pool voices, redistribute power, and resist surveillance, but also facilitates mobs, harassment campaigns, and disinformation. Whether collective masking leads to empowerment or destruction depends less on anonymity itself than on group culture, design choices, and moderation structures (Nissenbaum, 2019).

Ethics, Power, and the Politics of Anonymity

The digital mask is not only psychological or cultural; it is political. Who may wear masks, under what conditions, and with what consequences, is contested by states, corporations, and communities.

Anonymity as a Right: For dissidents, whistleblowers, and marginalized groups, anonymity is essential for safety and expression. The United Nations explicitly recognized anonymity and encryption as enabling rights to privacy and free expression (UN Human Rights Council, 2015). Without masks, voices critical of authoritarian regimes or stigmatized in conservative cultures might never surface.

Anonymity as a Risk: At the same time, anonymity shelters harassment, fraud, and extremism. Law enforcement argues that masking undermines accountability in areas such as child exploitation or terrorism. Research confirms that masked environments can foster antisocial behavior (Christopherson, 2007). Thus, anonymity is framed alternately as liberty or liability, with no easy resolution.

Corporate Gatekeepers: Corporations wield extraordinary influence. Facebook's "real-name" policy, defended as preventing abuse, disproportionately harmed drag performers, LGBTQ+ users, and activists (Marwick & boyd, 2018). Platforms often collect identifying metadata even while permitting pseudonyms, undermining practical anonymity (Zuboff, 2019). These dynamics reveal asymmetries of power: users may mask from peers but not from corporations.

State Surveillance and Regulation: Democratic states struggle to balance freedom with safety, while authoritarian states often suppress anonymity outright. China's real-name registration laws, coupled with facial recognition, illustrate how anonymity can be dismantled to consolidate control (Koltay, 2022). Even in democracies, proposals for mandatory identity verification emerge after crises, raising concerns about surveillance creep (Nissenbaum, 2019).

Inequality of Masks: Masking is unequally distributed. For privileged users, anonymity may be play; for marginalized groups, it is survival. Restrictive identity policies thus tend to harm those most vulnerable (Citron & Norton, 2020). The politics of anonymity reveal how policies that seem neutral often reinforce existing inequalities.

Philosophical Tensions: Debates hinge on authenticity versus freedom. Critics argue masks erode trust and weaken communities; defenders insist they enable dissent, exploration, and survival. Both perspectives hold truth. Hybrid identity systems—stable pseudonyms, context-dependent anonymity—attempt to reconcile these tensions (Floridi, 2016).

CASE STUDIES

- **Whistleblowers** like Edward Snowden relied on anonymity to reveal state surveillance programs; once unmasked, they faced profound consequences (Snowden, 2019).
- **Hacktivist groups** like Anonymous use masks collectively, symbolizing resistance to surveillance but also complicating accountability (Phillips & Milner, 2021).

Reflection: The politics of anonymity remind us that masks are not neutral. They are instruments of freedom, survival, manipulation, or control, depending on who wields them. Preserving their protective functions while mitigating harms requires careful design, ethical foresight, and sensitivity to inequality (Citron & Norton, 2020; Nissenbaum, 2019).

SELECTIVE MASKING AND ADAPTIVE STRATEGIES

Digital masking is rarely absolute. Most individuals practice *selective masking*, adjusting visibility, disclosure, and identity depending on context. This reflects not deception but adaptive navigation of risks, opportunities, and social roles (Goffman, 1959).

Everyday Selectivity: A professional may display real-name achievements on LinkedIn, post hobbies on a semi-private Instagram, and share political opinions under a pseudonymous Reddit account. A gamer might embody a fantastical avatar while using their real name in a Discord group of friends. These choices balance visibility for benefit, concealment for safety, and play for expression (Marwick & boyd, 2018).

Role Segregation and Context Collapse: Goffman's dramaturgical theory highlights how people manage multiple roles—teacher, parent, friend—across contexts. Online, this multiplies. Pseudonyms separate political commentary from professional identity, while anonymous posts isolate intimate disclosures from family. Yet risks of *context collapse* remain high. Screenshots, algorithmic cross-linking, and persistent searchability collapse boundaries, unmasking individuals unintentionally (Phillips & Milner, 2021).

Adaptive Strategies: Marginalized groups especially rely on selective masking:

- **Multiple accounts** maintain separation between personal and activist identities.
- **Disposable pseudonyms** provide cover for one-time disclosures.
- **Technical tools** like VPNs or encrypted messaging enhance concealment.
- **Code-switching** in language or imagery tailors identity to shifting audiences (Nissenbaum, 2019).

For some, such strategies are convenience; for others, survival (Citron & Norton, 2020).

Psychological Benefits: Selective masking supports identity exploration. LGBTQ+ youth, for example, often experiment with identity online before "coming out" offline (Marwick & boyd, 2018). Survivors of trauma disclose in anonymous spaces before confiding in personal networks. Research on self-disclosure shows that anonymity fosters exploration, with potential spillover into authenticity (Christopherson, 2007).

The Burden of Mask Maintenance: Maintaining multiple masks requires vigilance. A single slip—posting under the wrong account, revealing personal details, or being outed—can unravel protective boundaries. The stress of mask maintenance contributes to burnout and inauthenticity (Snowden, 2019).

Community Norms and Moderation: Communities establish norms to govern selective masking. Support forums encourage pseudonymity but prohibit harassment. Many explicitly ban doxxing, recognizing that unmasking violates trust. Moderators act as guardians of the mask, preserving anonymity while enforcing accountability (Phillips & Milner, 2021).

Hybrid Identity Systems: Some platforms design hybrid systems:

- **Stable pseudonyms** build reputational continuity without requiring real names.
- **Verified anonymity** allows platforms to confirm identity privately while protecting public pseudonymity.
- **Contextual anonymity** permits concealment in sensitive spaces but demands identity in others (Floridi, 2016).

These approaches acknowledge that no single model fits all contexts, instead embedding selective masking into platform design.

Reflection: Selective masking illustrates human adaptability. Individuals fluidly manage multiple masks to navigate freedom, safety, and authenticity. Communities develop structures that respect this balance. But these systems are fragile, threatened by surveillance, data persistence, and breaches of trust (Nissenbaum, 2019). The mask here is not deception but a toolkit—an adaptive resource for negotiating identity and power online.

THE FUTURE OF DIGITAL MASKS

The mask is not static. Emerging technologies—artificial intelligence, virtual reality, biometrics—are transforming how masks are created, worn, and regulated. The future will be defined by the tension between *multiplication of masks* and *erosion of masks*.

Generative AI and Synthetic Personas: Generative AI enables synthetic identities: deepfakes, AI-generated profile images, and automated chatbots. Users can fabricate personas indistinguishable from real people, either for play or for deception (Andrejevic, 2019). Entire networks of synthetic identities complicate authenticity and trust. Detection technologies and watermarking are being developed, but an arms race looms (Phillips & Milner, 2021).

Immersive Avatars and the Proteus Effect: Virtual reality (VR) and augmented reality (AR) extend masking into full embodiment. Avatars allow users to adopt new genders, physiques, or fantastical forms. The *Proteus effect* shows that avatar characteristics influence behavior: taller avatars foster confidence, attractive ones sociability (Yee & Bailenson, 2007). Masks in VR thus not only conceal but actively reshape self-perception. As immersive media spreads, identity continuity and relational authenticity will be deeply challenged.

Biometric Surveillance: While AI multiplies masks, biometric surveillance threatens to strip them away. Facial recognition, gait analysis, and digital fingerprinting tether identity to the body, undermining anonymity (Koltay, 2022). China's real-name registration illustrates how masks can be dismantled for state control. Even democracies increasingly debate biometric verification for safety, raising fears of surveillance creep (Zuboff, 2019). The dream of perfect visibility—every mask removed—risks crushing dissent and privacy.

Data Persistence and the Ghost of the Mask: Digital traces persist indefinitely. Unlike ritual masks, which dissolve after performance, digital masks linger. Posts, usernames, and archives may resurface years later. Immutable technologies like blockchain intensify this permanence, reducing the ability to shed outdated identities (Nissenbaum, 2019). The "right to be forgotten" becomes an essential counterbalance.

Algorithmic Mediation of Masks: Algorithms shape how masks are seen. Recommendation systems determine which personas gain visibility and which are buried. This creates identity loops: a performed persona that is algorithmically rewarded may become reinforced, narrowing possibilities for experimentation (Andrejevic, 2019). Conversely, marginalized voices may be suppressed, limiting freedom of expression (Phillips & Milner, 2021).

Hybrid Futures: The most plausible future is hybrid:

- Public anonymity layered with private verification.
- Multiple personas shifting across immersive and traditional platforms.
- Community moderation balancing freedom with accountability.

Masks will not disappear but become institutionalized, embedded in governance structures (Floridi, 2016).

Ethical Horizons: Future debates will revolve around authenticity vs. play, freedom vs. accountability, and privacy vs. surveillance (Nissenbaum, 2019). These are not technical questions alone but ethical ones, requiring negotiation among individuals, corporations, and states.

Reflection: The future of masks is contested. Technologies will simultaneously expand the creativity of masking and intensify pressures to unmask. The human impulse to conceal and reveal selectively will persist, but the conditions under which it is permitted will be reshaped by politics, commerce, and culture (Zuboff, 2019). Whether masks become instruments of freedom or control depends less on technology than on the choices societies make.

CONCLUSION: THE HUMAN WORK OF MASKING

From ancient rituals to networked screens, masks have mediated the tension between self and society. They are not incidental but essential: tools for transformation, concealment, and revelation. The *digital mask* extends this lineage into online life, magnifying both its promise and its risks.

Masks as Mirrors of Human Nature: Even offline, people wear masks—polite smiles at work, parental roles at home, confidant roles among friends. Online, these masks multiply, freed from bodily constraints (Goffman, 1959). Digital masks reveal the elasticity of identity: individuals can try on genders, ideologies, or personas as easily as costumes. This experimentation may lead to discovery or deception, but in either case, it underscores the performative nature of selfhood (Marwick & boyd, 2018).

The Ambivalence of Liberation: Throughout this chapter, ambivalence has been a recurring theme. Masks protect the vulnerable yet shelter the malicious. They invite honesty yet enable cruelty. They foster solidarity yet fuel polarization. This duality reflects what Suler (2004) termed the *online disinhibition effect*: masks loosen constraints, amplifying both prosocial and antisocial impulses. Rather than treat masking as good or bad, it must be seen as a condition that magnifies human motives.

The Architecture of Masks: The consequences of masking depend heavily on context. Platforms, communities, and states act as architects of masks, shaping whether they are protective or harmful (Nissenbaum, 2019). Reputation systems, moderation tools, algorithmic amplification, and identity policies all determine outcomes. A pseudonym on Reddit may empower vulnerable self-disclosure, while anonymity on 4chan may fuel hostility (Phillips & Milner, 2021). The difference lies not in anonymity itself but in the social and technical architectures that surround it.

Power and Inequality: Masking is unevenly distributed. For some, it is play; for others, survival. Real-name policies disproportionately endanger marginalized groups—LGBTQ+ communities, political dissidents, whistleblowers—while doing little to deter determined bad actors (UN Human Rights Council, 2015; Citron & Norton, 2020). Corporations and states wield asymmetrical power: platforms quietly unmask users through data collection (Zuboff, 2019), and governments regulate masks in ways that often reinforce existing inequalities (Koltay, 2022). Ethical responsibility demands that masking protections prioritize the vulnerable rather than merely the convenient.

Future Crossroads: Emerging technologies intensify the stakes. Generative AI multiplies masks, creating synthetic personas at scale (Andrejevic, 2019). Virtual reality expands masks into embodied avatars, where identity itself is reshaped by the Proteus effect (Yee & Bailenson, 2007). Biometric surveillance threatens to strip masks away, tethering identity to the body and undermining privacy (Koltay, 2022). Data persistence ensures that masks, once worn, may return to haunt their wearers indefinitely (Nissenbaum, 2019). Algorithms, meanwhile, mediate which masks are amplified and which are suppressed, shaping identity loops (Phillips & Milner, 2021).

The future of masks will not be a binary of anonymity versus exposure but a hybrid system: layered identities, contextual anonymity, and verified pseudonyms. Whether these arrangements protect freedom or consolidate surveillance depends less on technology than on cultural and political choices (Floridi, 2016).

The Human Work of Masking: Ultimately, masking is a human practice, not merely a technical artifact. It reflects our needs for safety, autonomy, expression, and play, as well as our fears of judgment, stigma, and surveillance. The human work of masking is negotiation: deciding when to reveal and when to conceal, when to risk exposure and when to seek protection. Online, these negotiations are magnified, but they remain fundamentally human.

Bandura's (1999) theory of *moral disengagement* reminds us that masks can enable cruelty when they sever behavior from accountability. But they can also enable honesty and healing when they provide safety for disclosure. The challenge is not to abolish masks but to cultivate wisdom about how to wear them responsibly—individually, collectively, and institutionally.

Toward Responsible Masking: Responsible masking requires balance:

- **Individuals** must reflect on the motives and costs of the masks they wear.
- **Communities** must set norms that preserve protective anonymity while discouraging harm.
- **Platforms** must design architectures that respect privacy while ensuring accountability.
- **States** must regulate in ways that safeguard rights while addressing risks (Citron & Norton, 2020).

Balance is difficult but not impossible. It requires humility—recognizing that masks are here to stay. It requires creativity—finding ways to harness the liberating potentials of masks. And it requires vigilance—ensuring that regulation of masks does not become monopolized by corporations or governments (Zuboff, 2019).

Closing Reflection: The story of the digital mask is the story of visibility in the modern age. As surveillance expands and traces persist, masks are not deceptions but necessities. They carve out spaces for dissent, play, intimacy, and survival. The challenge is not whether we will wear masks—we always will—but under what conditions, for whose benefit, and at whose expense.

The digital mask is a paradox: both danger and defense, illusion and truth. It is also an invitation: to reimagine what it means to be authentic, connected, and free in the online world. Whether it becomes an instrument of liberation or oppression will depend on our collective capacity to balance concealment with accountability, privacy with justice, and freedom with responsibility.

REFERENCES

Andrejevic, M. (2019). *Automated media*. Routledge., DOI: 10.4324/9780429242595

Bandura, A. (1999). Moral disengagement in the perpetration of inhumanities. *Personality and Social Psychology Review*, *3*(3), 193–209. DOI: 10.1207/s15327957pspr0303_3 PMID: 15661671

Brubaker, J. R., Ananny, M., & Crawford, K. (2016). Departing glances: A sociotechnical account of "leaving" Grindr. *New Media & Society*, *18*(3), 373–390. DOI: 10.1177/1461444814542311

Christopherson, K. M. (2007). The positive and negative implications of anonymity in Internet social interactions: "On the Internet, Nobody Knows You're a Dog.". *Computers in Human Behavior*, *23*(6), 3038–3056. DOI: 10.1016/j.chb.2006.09.001

Citron, D. K., & Norton, H. T. (2020). Intermediaries and hate speech: Fostering digital citizenship for our information age. *Boston University Law Review. Boston University. School of Law*, *100*(5), 1605–1636.

Floridi, L. (2016). *The ethics of information*. Oxford University Press.

Goffman, E. (1959). *The presentation of self in everyday life*. Anchor Books.

Koltay, A. (2022). *New media and freedom of expression: Rethinking the constitutional foundations of the public sphere*. Hart Publishing.

Le Bon, G. (2002). *The crowd: A study of the popular mind*. Dover Publications. (Original work published 1895)

Marwick, A. E., & boyd, d. (2018). It's complicated: The social lives of networked teens (Updated edition). Yale University Press.

Nissenbaum, H. (2019). *Privacy in context: Technology, policy, and the integrity of social life*. Stanford University Press.

Phillips, W., & Milner, R. M. (2021). *You are here: A field guide for navigating polarized speech, conspiracy theories, and our polluted media landscape*. MIT Press. DOI: 10.7551/mitpress/12436.001.0001

Snowden, E. (2019). *Permanent record*. Metropolitan Books.

Suler, J. (2004). The online disinhibition effect. *Cyberpsychology & Behavior*, *7*(3), 321–326. DOI: 10.1089/1094931041291295 PMID: 15257832

United Nations Human Rights Council. (2015). *Report of the Special Rapporteur on the promotion and protection of the right to freedom of opinion and expression* (A/HRC/29/32). https://digitallibrary.un.org/record/798709

Yee, N., & Bailenson, J. (2007). The Proteus effect: The effect of transformed self-representation on behavior. *Human Communication Research*, *33*(3), 271–290. DOI: 10.1111/j.1468-2958.2007.00299.x

Zimbardo, P. G. (1969). The human choice: Individuation, reason, and order versus deindividuation, impulse, and chaos. In Arnold, W. J., & Levine, D. (Eds.), *Nebraska symposium on motivation* (Vol. 17, pp. 237–307). University of Nebraska Press.

Zuboff, S. (2019). *The age of surveillance capitalism: The fight for a human future at the new frontier of power*. PublicAffairs.

Chapter 4
Reconstruction and Performance of Self Within Virtual Environments

Aeniyara V. Avanika
http://orcid.org/0009-0000-4422-0062
PES University, India

Megha Rudrapati
PES University, India

ABSTRACT

Virtual environments operate as dynamic social systems in which technological affordances structure self-processes and social relations. Affordances such as visibility, persistence, editability, and scalability enable communication and actively configure how individuals perceive, perform, and internalise aspects of self. Users co-construct their self-concepts within sociotechnical boundaries through mechanisms such as social feedback, algorithmic curation and audience management. These affordances have been shown to amplify reflexivity and self-awareness, whilst introducing pressures of coherence and performativity across contexts. This chapter utilises sociological and cyberpsychological frameworks to propose that virtual environments have the capacity to reconfigure self-organisation processes by integrating identity negotiation into continuous interaction loops between technological design, social norms, and individual cognition. The self is thus understood as a relational, adaptive construct that is subject to continuous reconfiguration by virtual social systems.

DOI: 10.4018/979-8-3373-5896-3.ch004

INTRODUCTION

Virtual environments operate as dynamic social systems in which technological affordances structure self-processes and social relations. The self, as understood through classical social psychological theories, is recognised as a socially constructed and dynamic entity that is emerging from interpersonal interaction and is shaped by cultural contexts and performed according to situational norms (Mead, 1934; Goffman, 1959; Tajfel & Turner, 1986). In offline contexts, identity is shaped through interpersonal interactions, bodily presence and group-based social norms and dynamics. However, as human interactions shift from face-to-face to digitally mediated environments, with affordances such as visibility, persistence, editability, and scalability enable communication and actively configure how individuals perceive, perform, and internalise aspects of self. Users co-construct their self-concepts within sociotechnical boundaries through mechanisms such as social feedback, algorithmic curation and audience management. These affordances have been shown to amplify reflexivity and self-awareness, whilst introducing pressures of coherence and performativity across contexts. This chapter utilises sociological and cyber-psychological frameworks to propose that virtual environments have the capacity to reconfigure self-organisation processes by integrating identity negotiation into continuous interaction loops between technological design, social norms, and individual cognition. The self is thus understood as a relational, adaptive construct that is subject to continuous reconfiguration by virtual social systems.

The present chapter is theoretical in nature and does not rely on primary data collection. Instead, it draws from peer-reviewed psychological literature, digital sociology, and cyberpsychology, synthesising research across disciplines to offer a conceptual framework for understanding identity in technologically mediated contexts. The information has been sourced from various journal databases, including PsycINFO, Google Scholar, and JSTOR, and adheres to the American Psychological Association (APA) 7th edition referencing standards.

CYBERSPACE AS A SOCIAL ENVIRONMENT

Computer-Mediated-Communication (CMC) in recent times, has taken the front stage in human interaction, evolving from simple impersonal e-mails to instant messaging, social media, video conferences, as well as virtual worlds with immersive and embodied interactions, enabling users to interact in environments they aren't physically present in (Schroeder, 2008; Slater & Sanchez-Vives, 2016). The term "cyberspace" is often used while exploring human interactions in the context of virtual environments. Cyberspace is described as a conceptual space where digitally mediated interactions occur. It encompasses the entire realm of networked digital communication, including websites, messaging platforms to MMORPGs and other virtual worlds (Mikhaylova & Mikhaylov, 2024).

Communication mediums can be divided to *lean media* which refers to text messages or emails which offer minimal cues and feedback and *rich media* which comprises modes such as video conferences which provide immediate feedback and more non-verbal cues, such as intonation or facial expressions and social media refers to platforms that enable content creation and sharing among other individuals (Ishii et al., 2019; Bergin, 2016). However, cyberspace is emphasised to be a distinct social environment that shapes human behaviour much more than a neutral medium of communication (Tolnaiová & Gálik, 2020). A foundational difference is the structural properties or "affordances" that set it different from the offline face-to-face interactions.

Affordances, Networked Publics and Virtual Interactions

Offline interactions as well as virtual modes such as voice calls, video conferences and other rich media allow for the communicative process[1] to be immediate and thus *synchronous*. Contrariwise, communication in lean media can be *asynchronous*, wherein participants may not be simultaneously communicating, as in emails or forums. Asynchronity introduces a delay between the message and the feedback, thus changing the dynamic of the interaction. It affords extra time to edit and craft messages, thus enabling a more deliberate self-presentation (Barak & Suler, 2008).

Social Presence Theory (Short et al., 1976) and other early theories argued that communication media differ in their capacity to convey the presence and salience of interaction partners. Lean media, especially text-based interactions, have reduced social cues, i.e., no tone of voice, facial expressions of body language, leading to the user having comparatively weaker sense of others' presence or "low social presence." This absence of non-verbal cues and weakened perceived presence of the sender, can lead to a sense of detachment or de-individuation and increase ambiguity and uncertainty about others' intentions or tone. People, therefore, rely more on their imagination or cognitive biases to fill in the missing information based on their own expectations and personality, which may lead to heightened emotional or exaggerated responses online. Users have now adapted to the reduced cues by developing substitutes such as emojis, acronyms such as "JK" (Just Kidding) and creative use of punctuation to convey tone or emotions like "XD" depicting a smiling face. This is termed as *signalling*, referring to the actions and cues as a deliberate strategy meant to communicate something beyond their face value, to make intentions clearer when communication is inefficient (Pezzulo et al., 2013). For instance, people use "lol" to indicate a friendly attitude, while in actuality, "LOL" is an acronym for "laughing out loud" or typing in all caps to indicate anger, emphasis or urgency. From a socioecological view, it's similar to organisms evolving communication signals suited to a new environment. In the "environment" of cyberspace, humans have developed conventions like emoticons, tone indicators like "/s" to signal sarcasm, or status indicators "typing…" as signals to help interaction flow. These signals form a kind of relational grammar of online interaction that users learn to interpret and thus illustrate ways of conveying mental states, even with constraints. This resulted in the norms of online spaces differing significantly from those of face-to-face interactions. Another contributing factor to the low social presence partial or full anonymity offered by online platforms. Under these conditions of dissociative anonymity, people feel less tied to their offline identity, stripping social filters and lead individuals to disclose more and behave more freely[2].

Boyd (2010) proposed four properties of affordances in online spaces also known as *networked publics:* persistence, replicability, scalability and searchability while Treem & Leonardi (2013) described *organisational affordances*, adding visibility, editability and association to the list. Recent discourse online has highlighted how excessive self-disclosure online due to disinhibition can be an issue as the interactions in cyberspace, unlike in offline contexts, which are ephemeral unless recorded, are automatically logged and archived by the respective platforms and thus tend to leave persistent records. In the context of social media, *persistence* is illustrated as a defining affordance of networked publics as digital content, once posted, by default persists indefinitely unless deliberately deleted (Boyd, 2010). Even then, platforms like Wayback Machine also allow access to currently deleted websites, as the saying goes "the internet never forgets." This persistence can be beneficial: it enables asynchronous discussion (one can catch up on prior messages) and information access across time, but it also blurs the boundary of what's private vs public (Barak & Suler, 2008). Persistence also introduces new social dynamics within this architecture where speech is transient. For instance, mistakes or aggressive outbursts can haunt the user long after the heat of the moment, and context collapse can occur when a message is read by unintended audiences. Thus, this knowledge can influence behaviour as some users may self-censor or cautiously manage what they share.

This persistence of records, also enables replicability—the ease of copying and resharing content—can amplify this behaviour the messages can be screenshot or forwarded, scaling further than the intended audience beyond the original poster's control (Boyd, 2010). A social media post, in theory, can be seen by millions across the globe. This scalability and the presence of algorithm-driven content curation can make some content "go viral" and achieve a reach and visibility disproportionate to the speaker's intent (Harrell, 2025). This potential for high exposure can encourage users to seek attention, viz., chasing likes, performing for virality and fame, but it can also create fear of potential ridicule or anxiety in others (Edwards, 2016).

Cyberspaces can thus be understood as a relational system shaped by these technological architectures and affordances, i.e., what the technology allows or encourages users to do, creating differing norms in social behaviour and dynamics. It is a diverse environment that is subject to constant evolution, thus prompting the necessity to rethink traditional assumptions about social behaviour and to develop updated theories that account for the integration of technology and psycho-social phenomena.

Affordances

Researchers have long debated how to conceptualise affordances in digital contexts, including the distinction between *real* vs. *perceived* affordances. Gibson (2013) originally defined affordances of an environment as actionable properties that it provides to an organism, whether good or ill, and thus are a *relationship* of sorts. In the context of technology, Norman (2004)'s interpretation shifted the emphasis towards perception, i.e., the usefulness of a design lies in the affordances that the users perceive. Norman (2004) suggested that for designed objects (in terms of user interface), an affordance includes both perceived and actual properties of the object, that is, in essence, what a person can believe they can do with it. However, this concept has been criticised due to its current ambiguity, which makes it too broad and thus analytically ineffective (Oliver, 2005). In the context of social interactions, this entails that the interface and features of online platforms mediate user behaviour. For example, if a platform has a "like" button, it becomes easier to provide quick feedback. Contrarily, if the platform only has a comment feature, the dynamic of feedback will differ. Another example would be the new feature on Instagram that allows one to view content their mutuals have liked. This has led to cautious management of liked content and changes in self-presentation, with some individuals going as far as to create anonymous accounts to have freedom as well as judgment on others' liked content. Real and perceived affordances are functional when considering how users use a technology, which makes the structure of the platform shape the norms within it. The character limit on X (formerly Twitter) enforces concise expressions, while the formatting options and lack of such a limit on Tumblr form differing norms, even if the platforms serve similar purposes.

THE SELF AND ITS SOCIAL CONSTRUCTION IN THE VIRTUAL CONTEXT

The American Psychological Association currently defines the self as "the totality of the individual, consisting of all characteristic attributes, conscious and unconscious, mental and physical" (APA Dictionary of Psychology, 2023). However, the "self" has been interpreted and theorised from multiple perspectives that provide insight to the various aspects of the construction and reconfiguration of the self within the cyberspace.

Theories of Self

William James (1890) distinguished between the self as subject "I" and as object "Me". The "I" is illustrated as the inner agent that experiences and acts, and the "me" refers to the aspects that one can reflect upon. The self, according to James, has multiple facets: the "me" can be a material self (body and possessions, a social self (image perceived by others), and a spiritual self (inner self/soul).

The self, can also be an organised set of perceptions and beliefs an individual has about themselves, distinguishing between the real self, who the individual actually is, and the ideal self, who the individual wants to become (Rogers, 1959; Tekke, 2015). Self-Discrepancy Theory (Higgins, 1987) extends this concept of ideal self, introducing three key selves: *the actual self* (attributes an individual believes they currently possess), *the ideal self* (attributes an individual aspires to have) and *the ought self* (attributes an individual feels they should possess).

In contemporary theory, both the differentiation between the "I" and "Me" as well as perceptions are taken into consideration with the self now defined as the reflexive awareness an individual possesses regarding their own identity and self-perception and accordingly, the concept of selfhood is manifested through a sense of self-awareness, or the "I, " and the relatively stable perceptions of the self, or the "me," that individuals discern, construct, and evolve (McAdams et al., 2021).

There is also a need to distinguish the "self" from concepts of "identity" and "personality" as these, at a glance, seem to be superimposing constructs. Identity refers to a specific facet of self, such as social roles and personal commitment among others, thus reflecting a socially contingent concept (Vignoles, 2017). An individual can concurrently have multiple identities, for instance, a gender identity, cultural identity, professional identity and so on. Personality generally refers to the dynamic and relatively stable configuration of characteristics and behaviour that comprises an individual's unique adjustment to life, including major traits, interests, drives, values, self-concept, abilities, and emotional patterns (American Psychological Association, 2018). And thus, the personality constitutes the fundamental components of an individual, i.e., traits and other characteristics, while the self refers to the reflexive perception and understanding that individuals have of themselves, and the identity is the selective role or meaning an individual attaches to themselves within a specific context. However, both personality and identity can be considered to be different aspects that come under the umbrella of "self", with personality reflecting the *intrapersonal* aspect and identity representing the *interpersonal* and *socio-cultural* aspects.

The Self from a Social Context

The aforementioned theories, originating from the West, reflect an "independent" self, thus viewing self as autonomous and bound by internal traits. However, this differed from the self-concepts seen in other cultures, leading to the conceptualisation of an *interdependent self*, that is relational and defined by connections and social roles (Markus & Kitayama, 1991)

Sociologist George Mead (1935) theorised that the self emerges through social interaction, that is, self-awareness is derived by viewing ourselves from others' perspective, which he termed as "role-taking." Mead argued that "I" and "Me" can best be "phases of the self" with the "me" reflecting a social self that is a result of learned behaviour, internalised roles and the "I" being an active self that is unpredictable, spontaneous and only known in retrospect. The notion of a *looking glass self*, substantiates role-taking as the idea that our self-concepts are formed on the basis of how they perceive others' view of them much like a mirror (Cooley, 2025). This became central to the development of *Symbolic Interactionism*, theorising that individuals construct social reality or in this case, self-concept, through social interactions and the sharing of symbols through role-taking and feedback.

Within the social settings, the individual may derive a sense of self from the status and the values of the social group they belong to as well as the emotional significance attached to that group[3], with the salience of personal and social identity shifting with context, i.e., individuals view themselves more as group members when the social identity is salient and vice versa.[4] (Tajfel & Turner, 1986; Turner., et al, 1987).

In the sociological perspective, along with a mirror, the self is also expressed through a theatrical metaphor. Erving Goffman (1959) illustrated a "dramaturgical model" wherein every social interaction reflects a performance in which individuals are actors presenting characters to an audience. The self, rather than an internal identity, is more of an image constructed and projected to others on the "front stage" of life while keeping other aspects in the "backstage". A key aspect to this is *impression management,* the concept of individual regulating and controlling the information they provide to shape others' perception of them. This led to the "self" being viewed as relational and situational, much like identities and roles. The dramaturgical model did not deny the internal consistency of the self but instead focused on how the self is illustrated socially.

Thus, traditional psychological theories understand self as a conscious agent and an object of its awareness that has multiple facets that are adaptive and context-sensitive while also maintaining its *unity* and *overall coherence.* Sociologically, the self as an object also refers to the understanding, we hold of ourselves on the basis of the assumption of how others' perceive us rather than an inherent and intrapersonal construct. This assumption, also makes us consciously project certain aspects of us as "me", while shelving other aspects irrelevant to the context through processes such as impression management.

The contemporary theory, however, rejects the idea of a single unified self and instead describes it as everchanging, context-sensitive, multiple and decentred. The self can be *saturated* with fragments or multiple voices as a result of the diverse relationships and information streams individuals are exposed to in the modern era (Gergen, 1991). Individuals, within these diverse contexts, construct an internal, evolving story that an individual constructs about their life, integration past experiences, present self and future aspirations to a coherent whole termed as the *narrative identity.* It acknowledges the multiple "me" aspects as characters in the story, the continuity of identity with the narrative linking past to the future, and establishes the social context with culturally sensitive scripts as well as themes of personal growth (McAdams, 2011).

Thus, the self is not a singular concept but is instead part trait (personality), part ongoing self-reflection and is selectively expressed (identity) in specific contexts. A core function of narrative identity is to provide *continuity* and *coherence* for the self over time. Personal identity depends on the self's consistency at any moment, and a stable sense of self across time.

The Technoself

In the early 2000s, scholars sought to conceptualise the influence of technology as a part of self-construction and self-experience. This attempt crystallised as an inquiry into how technology affects human identity across the disciplines of psychology, sociology, communication, philosophy and Human-Computer Interaction (HCI), termed as *Technoself Studies* (Luppicini, 2013).

From a worm's eye view, the technoself–meaning identity as co-constituted with technology–depicts the influence of technologies from platforms and algorithms to avatars, shapes self-knowledge, self-presentation, autonomy, memory and social identity. Consequently, two theoretical frameworks have been influential: *postphenomenology* or *mediation theory,* frames technologies as relational systems that mediate perception, action, and self-experience (Ritter, 2021; Mykhailov & Liberati, 2023); and the *onlife condition*, understood within the context of hyperconnected lifeworlds, is a phenomenon that leads to the gradual disintegration of the online/offline distinction, resulting in the perpetual existence of selves in a continuous *infosphere*[5] (Floridi, 2015). Thus, conceptually, the technoself views the self as experienced within the context of technologically configured social environments. It reflects contemporary views on the self as socially constructed, reflexive and contextual.

Social construction of the technoself occurs when individuals engage with peers and audiences via social media, forums, virtual worlds and the like. Individuals create profiles and share content carefully curated to project a desired impression of themselves with the features of different platforms such as profiles, feeds, DMs etc., serving as "frontstages" as per Goffman. The distinctively digital features are editability, persistence, and searchability, that heighten strategic self-presentation, but also induce impression fatigue and vigilance about audience reactions (Marwick & Boyd, 2011). Feedback is received through views, likes, comments etc., that act as mirrors to the looking glass self. For instance, posts that garner appreciation or high relatability may internalise a positive looking-glass self in an individual boosting their self-esteem. These metrics lead the experiences in the cyberspace to undergo *datafication,* i.e., becomes machine processable traces that circulate through platforms, these traces infer the *algorithmic identity* which are the information inferred about an individual from the gathered behavioural data which in turn shape what you see/do on that platform. These platforms and related third-party systems then infer this data and categories such as "parent" or "volleyball enthusiast", for example, are probabilistically assigned and used to modulate opportunities, ads, prices, visibility etc (Cheney-Lippold, 2017). From a socio-psychological perspective, this depicts reflected appraisal and validation with an individual's preferences, interests and opinions may be affirmed with tailored content. This can develop into a normative drift, due to canalisation of preferences and reduction in variety seeking thus restricting value formation and exploration especially in AI-recommendation contexts (Tong et al., 2025).

The technoself studies describe a "quantified self," self-tracking i.e., usage of software to track sleep, habits, mood etc shifts everyday self-knowledge and reflection from introspective narrative judgements to metricised appraisal with "streaks" and "dashboards" thus externalising self-evaluation thereby anchoring identity maintenance and aspects such as self-esteem to numbers rather than meanings (Feng et al., 2020; Lupton, 2016). In parallel, the digital extended self, expanding on James' and Mead's material self, accounts for the migration of possessions to dematerialised assets such as profiles, avatars, in-game items as well as platforms and cloud archives (Belk, 2013; Honarvar & Sepehrinia, 2025). At scale, these dynamics embedded in political-economics regimes or *surveillance capitalism* that appropriate human experience as raw material for prediction and behavioural products, raising questions about the rights to one's data-self (Zuboff, 2019), especially with doubts regarding "ownership" of the self with loss or deplatforming potentially severing identity continuities (Belk, 2013).

Digital media can also act as a prosthetic autobiographical memory with the affordances of cyberspace offering new tools for remembering, editing and sharing one's life story in three ways: providing cues that trigger recall of self-defining stories, allowing users to highlight or give prominence to important narrative threads and by creating opportunities for social uptake of the narratives. Digital profiles also allow individuals to project their preferred narrative publicly (Bortolan, 2024). For example, Instagram allows users to create a "highlight" of posted stories and the "archive" section allows users to view all their posts. Digital photo albums such as Google Photos also enhance autobiographical detail as the pictures and videos are preserved thus allowing users to revisit vivid records of personal events. Features like "memory" or "on this day" in google photos "anchor" memories to specific dates prompting nostalgic recollections. Shared albums also enable reminiscence with other people and thus revoke emotions and contextual detail that strengthen life narrative.

CONSTRUCTION AND PRESENTATION OF THE SELF IN THE CYBERSPACE

The construction of the self or identity in the virtual context is a process of self-presentation where individuals can reveal or hide information about themselves at will. This process is highly flexible with the usual constraints of identity as the audiences do not automatically see traits including physical cues unless the individual deliberately shares the details affording a degree of anonymity or pseudonymity, while also providing high agency and autonomy.

The self-presentation and thus, construction of the self in the cyberspace is best understood through Goffman's Dramaturgy Model (1959). This theory lies at the foundation proposing that individuals perform roles on a front stage for audiences and retreat to a backstage to relax their roles thus comparing social interactions and identity to a theatrical performance. The primary objectives here are impression management and audience segregation. Individuals attempt to regulate how others perceive them in a given situation, as well as ensure that different audiences do not see conflicting versions of themselves. In the digital space, especially in social media, this process complicates with timelines, feeds and profiles being the quasi-public front stages. The backstage becomes thin or invisible unlike in offline spaces, where it works as a "safe zone" of sorts wherein individuals can relax due to absence of an audience (Aspling, 2011; Bullingham & Vasconcelos, 2013). The online audience is broad as well as hard to define due to aspects such as scalability and anonymity, as well as affordances like the interface, algorithms and the norms of the platforms which limit the hidden space one can maintain. Moreover, everything posted online tends to persist and can be shared without knowledge, such as screenshots or even the algorithms delivering the posts to unintended audience, this calls for a much more cautious impression management compressing explicit backstages and merging them to the frontstage. Hogan (2010) argued that social media moves more towards a curated exhibition of artifacts with posts, photos etc., that individuals can asynchronically polish. However, the backstages may survive in private groups, DMs or alternative accounts.

The Audience

To put on an adequate performance, the actor must know the audience. In offline settings, the audiences are identifiable and usually physically present, the feedback is embodied and rich with social cues thus providing immediate feedback. Audience segregation is easier as workplace, family, friends, partners etc., occupy separate physical or social contexts. However, the audience in cyberspace are *partially invisible,* as the user might not know who is viewing the content (Marwick & Boyd, 2011), thus prompting them to construct *imagined audiences* i.e., mental models of who they perceive is viewing the content thus guiding disclosure and style. Imagined audiences are not static but can be of two types: abstract as a vague generalised idea of "followers" or "netizens" or specific as a well-defined group of people the user can visualise (Litt, 2012; Litt & Hargittai, 2016). The imagined audiences also vary across time, platforms or even posts thus evolving depending on contexts and platform affordances. For instance, a user might perceive an audience belonging to a different timezone viewing their posts at night. The self-presentation differs based on the imagined audience as well (De Wolf & Pierson, 2014). For example, let's say an individual is ranting about an event, if their imagined audience involves their colleagues, they might limit oversharing and be cautious with the content (audience limiting behaviour), however if they are imagining their friends, they might use be casual and use slangs (audience reaching behaviour). This further blur the backstage as the audiences is invisible, blended and imagined. Furthermore, the scalablity and persistence, may take the interaction far beyond the intended audience leading to a *context collapse*, i.e., overlap of distinct audience in one context. This can occur in two ways: *context collusion* wherein individuals intentionally collapse or blur the context and *context collision*—when "different social environments unintentionally and unexpectedly come crashing into each other (Davis & Jurgenson, 2014). Both types of collapse have been found to have significant negative impact, even if the individual was partially aware of the potential collapse (Loh & Walsh, 2021). The collapses can lead to misinterpretation of the intentions, and along with persistent records and replicability, the message can reach broader audience through screenshots etc., and pose significant risks. For instance, a personal tweet that leaked to an individual's workplace audience may lead to anxiety due to the overlap of role identities or potential repercussions in the workplace.

Individuals have adapted by learning segmentation of the audience and integration to a coherent self-concept (Yan & Zheng, 2024). For example, an individual might use WhatsApp for family interactions and LinkedIn or X (Formerly Twitter) for professional contexts and Tumblr for their hobbies and interests thus using different platforms for different roles (segmentation) while still maintaining a coherent self by aligning core values across these platforms (integration)

Avatars and Embodiment

In addition to social media posts, virtual environments have enabled creation of avatars, the graphical or textual representations of the self which serve as an embodied interface between the user and the platform (Ducheneaut et al., 2009). Initially, avatars were considered to be tools for symbolic self-presentation however technological advances with VR, AR and metaverse have added an element of immersion where users can experience sensorimotor and emotional identification with a digital body (Yee & Bailenson, 2007; Slater & Sanchez-Vives, 2016). This makes the avatars a psychological extension of the self (Madary & Metzinger, 2016). Recent definitions also frame the avatar as a mediated self-presentation that is controlled by an intelligent user during dynamic interactions (Ratan & Pandita, 2025). This indicates the degree of user control such as full body or limited emotes can moderate the level of identification and behavioural carryover in terms of Proteus Effect. In the current times, full-body avatars are more commonly seen in role-playing games (RPGs) and VTubers, virtual streamers who use live-tracked animation-like avatars. Some RPGs allow slides for physical features and can include body, face, skin, voice, hair, tattoos, scars, gait and such deep customisation tend to increase avatar identification and enable identity encoding (Peng, 2021; Ducheneaut et al., 2009; Boellstorff, 2016). Fantasy-themed RPGs may also include alignment systems such as good/evil or other faction allegiances that enable self-signalling and narrative self-consistency across quests which may prompt avoidance of actions that deviate from their "brand" thus reflecting audience expectation.

VTubers on the other hand, exhibit embodied anonymity wherein they can disclose affect without revealing their offline selves thus lowering risks of self-presentation. At the same time, VTubers also practice dual-layered impression management with maintaining the fictional character's persona as well as meta-authenticity with glimpses of the "actual" self behind the avatars, especially with the performance stage taking place in real-time (Wan & Lu, 2023). This can however lead to heightened emotional labour under platform visibility and parasocial demand.

Avatars also function as prototypes for future or ideal selves with users enhancing appearance or traits aligning with aspirational identities through a process known as *selective idealisation* (Bessière et al., 2007; Markus & Nurius, 1986). And when the avatars align with these aspirational identities, a short-term boost in self-esteem is observed. Long-term usage of avatars can integrate into self-concept, however maintaining multiple avatars across platforms may fragment it, producing cognitive load and strain in authenticity (Zimmermann et al., 2022). Current debates examine where representation ends and embodiment begins, especially when full-body tracking, haptic feedback and first-person perspectives increase physiological coupling (Slater & Sanchez-Vives, 2016). Recent algorithmic systems have also been seen to shape self-presentation through recommendation bias, especially through "trends." In a sense, avatars make Goffman's metaphors literal with selective masking and amplification through idealisation thus making self-presentation both communicative and constitutive of identity.

Impression Management

Self-presentation in digital spaces is highly editable. An individual can delete/edit posts or even log into a different account denoting a fluidity that cannot be found in offline settings. This editability along with proactive construction also demands ongoing maintenance to keep a consistent imagery. In comparison, offline identity maintenance is much less consciously managed on a day-to-day basis and relies more on relatively stable behaviour and reputation. Furthermore, the highly customisable profiles also have been seen to allow individuals to project an ideal self or ought self, more easily than online. Studies have shown that avatars created in-game tend to be closer to the ideal self than their actual self in appearance or abilities (Bullingham & Vasconcelos, 2013). In some cases, the online self can be entirely different from offline reality, as a result of hiding or falsifying characteristics, termed as *identity reconstruction*[6]. For example, individuals are commonly known to embellish, slightly misrepresent themselves by curating information or posting carefully editing their pictures in social media to present a "perfect" life. Motivation for such identity reconstruction include strategic self-presentation, exploration as well as malicious deception (Huang et al., 2021). Identity reconstruction has created tensions between authentic self-expression and idealised self-presentation. The affordances of reward visibility and quantified self-have been pressuring individuals to craft a coherent and marketable identity, regardless of whether an individual is an influencer or not. This came to be known as *personal branding* (Lair et al., 2005). While self-branding has been known to satisfy needs for self-esteem, belonging and competence (Deci & Ryan, 2000) metrics such as likes and followers become externalised cues of competence and social validation (Vogel et al., 2014) while also amplifying contingent self-worth and an esteem dependent on audience approval (Crocker & Park, 2004).

Thus, paradoxically, authenticity, which was originally valued as the antithesis of performance, has become a performative requirement instead (Banet-Weiser, 2012). This can occur through simulated spontaneity i.e. unedited selfies or vulnerability posts that signal sincerity. Influences are also seen to construct narratives around emotional or moral transparency to sustain monetisation (Abidin, 2016). This can lead to authenticity labour, the continuous affective and cognitive effort that is invested to convey genuineness under algorithmic and audience surveillance. This is reinforced when algorithmic engagement metrics reward *staged authenticity* (Maares et al., 2020), thus producing emotional dissonance with a gap experienced between felt and expressed identity.

The debates around authentic and curated self, however, ultimately resemble Rogers' concept of congruence and incongruence between the ideal and actual self. Individuals might compare their real lives to the highly polished lives and experience an *incongruence* however they might also allow expressions of "true" self that some may suppress offline, such as a shy person being able to freely share their opinions online. Thus, authentic self-presentation on social media is positively associated with self-concept clarity (Avci et al., 2024) and healthier functioning (Chan et al., 2025) while heavily idealised or other-comparison-driven presentation predicts identity distress.

In contrast to Goffman's description of episodic impression management, the continuous and infrastructural nature of authenticity labour, have made authenticity in itself, in Gill and Kanai's (2018) words, a "technology of the self." This may manifest in emotional dissonance i.e., the gap between felt and displayed affect and thus impression fatigue (Hollenbaugh, 2021). Studies examining influencers and general social media users have consistently demonstrated a link between perceived pressure to maintain a positive online presence, characterised by likeability, responsiveness, or an "authentic happiness" facade, and symptoms of anxiety, fatigue, and diminished self-concept clarity (Bayer et al., 2015; Reinecke & Trepte, 2014). Impression fatigue arises at the intersection of a self-monitoring overload, ego-depletion cycle (Baumeister et al. 1998) due to continuous use of finite self-control resources, emotional dissonance, context collapse strain and algorithmic hyper-viability. Technological infrastructures, while arguably extending identity's reach, simultaneously increase its maintenance demands. The self's ability to adapt necessitates the ongoing maintenance of identity, which can lead to emotional exhaustion if it is not supported by authentic self-expression, social validation and the ability to periodically disengage.

For impression management within the cyberspace, visibility determines the audience while also facilitating social comparison (Chou & Edge, 2012), editability enables greater message control but also heightens self-monitoring load (Highfield & Leaver, 2016), persistence raises accountability, scalability increases caution and association ties identity to the social networks. Persistence and replicability may influence self-censorship to avoid misinterpretation by unintended or future audiences while visibility and association represent connection management. To illustrate with an example, an individual might consider the audience that views their profile, let's say family and friends (visibility), they engage in identity work by constantly updating their profile (editability), and carefully draft their posts to avoid misinterpretation as they are afraid of their content being shared with screenshots (persistence + replicability) and remove posts that mention their ex-friend to signal broken ties (visibility + association). However, recent discourse has critiqued such status affordance lists as a user's sociocultural context shape how these affordances are enacted upon (Costa, 2018). For instance, visibility might be empowering in individualistic cultures but risky in collectivistic ones. This perspective termed as *affordance-in-practice,* emphasises the dependence of psychological outcomes on a mixture of affordances as well as local norms.

Within the virtual context, the self is thus performed and continuously maintained. Scalability and the quantified feedback have risen the threshold for validation. For example, if 40 others' agreed to an individual's opinion in an offline context, the validation and feedback received would be more impactful than seeing 40 likes the same content as a twitter post. A simple search on Google on the impact of social media describe how it serves negatively increasing pressures toward legibility, coherence, and relentless visibility. Avatars and virtual embodiment allow people to inhabit possible selves; however, metrics and algorithms subtly determine which selves persist. Authenticity thus becomes a form of labour, and the sustained emotional regulation necessary for the maintenance of the ego accumulates as fatigue and dissonance. There has been a rise in individuals disengaging from posting on social media, a phenomenon now termed as "Posting Ennui." From a technoself perspective, identity online can be considered as a social construct that is both user-generated and influenced by external factors, such as audiences and technological infrastructures.

ANONYMITY, PSEUDONOMITY AND IDENTITY FLUIDITY

Anonymity and pseudonymity have long been considered a defining affordance in virtual environments. Visibility and traceability are themselves social regulators, determining how individuals experience accountability, intimacy, and self-control (Bargh et al., 2002; Lapidot-Lefler & Barak, 2012). The absence of a stable, name-anchored identity, in the early internet culture, was considered to be a symbol of liberation from embodied and social constraints, which Suler (2004) termed as the *online disinhibition effect.* The reduction of self-control and social restraint under perceived anonymity and asynchronicity, producing either *benign disinhibition* which can be exhibited as enhanced openness and emotional honesty or *toxic disinhibition* manifesting as aggression, hostility, norm violation.

Unlike common misconceptions, self-disclosure in online spaces cannot be categorised to anonymity, pseudonymity or complete disclosure (usage of real names), it exists in a continuum with different nodes depicting a particular balance of psychological safety, social consequence and affordances of visibility, persistence, editability, and association.

At the extreme end is anonymity, which is operationally defined as the lack of persistent personal identifiers associating an act with an actor (Christopherson, 2007). Anonymous forums like early 4chan or temporary chatrooms, maximise invisibility and untraceability, eliciting higher behavioural variability and moral disengagement (Nitschinsk et al., 2023). These affordances lead to lower valuation anxiety and higher behavioural freedom but minimal reputational constraint, leading to both intimate self-disclosure and antisocial disinhibition (Lapidot-Lefler & Barak, 2012; De Vries et al., 2021).

Pseudonymity falls within the intermediate zone, wherein an alias or handle substitutes for a legal name while persisting across interactions, thereby generating a sense of continuity without identifiability. Van der Nagel and Frith (2015) propose pseudonymity as an affordance that facilitates the establishment of bounded authenticity. In this regard, users are able to construct recognisable reputations and maintain community norms while preserving offline privacy while also facilitating the accumulation of social capital, including karma scores in reddit or follower count without collapsing into real-world accountability. Pseudonymity also enables individuals to express distinct but authentic identity facets across contexts, called the *prismatic self.* An X (Twitter) user may engage politically under one alias, artistically under another, and privately in a support forum under a third, with each segment reflecting a genuine, situated self, this mitigating a context collapse and reintroducing an audience segregation. Most platforms are currently anchored to pseudonymity with audience segregation in texting platforms such as Discord or Telegram or with other platforms like X (Twitter) that allow optional audience limitation through private accounts.

At the other end of the continuum, real-name systems including Facebook and LinkedIn, link digital actions to stable offline identities. They heighten visibility and persistence, increasing impression-management pressures and reactivating the offline audience's normative gaze, thereby reinforcing conformity and self-monitoring. The "real-name Internet," as coined by Zuckerberg, is based on an ideology that prioritises authenticity through transparency, positing that moral and behavioural coherence emerge only when identities are unified. However, empirical evidence indicates that mandated transparency can limit user expression and deter participation, particularly among marginalised users who depend on protective distance for psychological safety (Boyd, 2014). Haimson and Hoffmann (2016) note that real-name enforcement, as a sociotechnical authenticity regime, prioritises singular, stable identity presentations as "truthful", thus leading to authenticity labour. While these regimes may promote civility, they constrain the range of expression and discourage participation from individuals for whom self-expression is a form of protection, such as LGBTQ+ users or activists.

Within a social framework, anonymity can function as an affordance that modifies situational cues to self-awareness, especially in cyberspace with partial cues prompting individuals to rely more on internal states, attributions/assumptions or group signals to guide behaviour. The concept of anonymity has historically been understood through the framework of deindividuation theory which refers to the process by which individuals, when placed in group settings, tend to lose their sense of individual identity and adopt characteristics that are more consistent with the group thus leading to reduced self-evaluation and accountability, allowing behaviours inconsistent with personal norms (Festinger et al., 1952). In digital environments, affordances such as invisibility and scalability, amplify this process.

The deindividuation theory later evolved into the Social Identity Model of Deindividuation Effects (SIDE), which defined deindividuation as a shift from personal to social identity (Reicher et al., 1995; Postmes & Spears, 1998). As per this, anonymity suppresses individuating cues and heightens conformity to perceived in-group norms and the shared identity of the collective. Thus, anonymity is neither inherently antisocial or liberatory in nature, it is dependent on the group standards or norms whether they are prosocial or hostile. Suler's model highlighted the affective mechanism of anonymity wherein the reduced visibility lowers social anxiety and fear of negative evaluation while also promoting social disclosure, thus simultaneously weakening external social control and also strengthening internal or collective cues (Clark-Gordon et al., 2019). This leads to an intensified but highly ambiguous expression. Bandura's (1999) moral disengagement i.e., the cognitive processes through which individuals deactivate self-sanctions that normally prevent unethical behaviour, can also explain these dynamics. Anonymity can facilitate the mechanisms such as diffusion of responsibility and dehumanisation, by obscuring personal authorship and by creating psychological distance from victims and observers (Zhao & Yu, 2021). This elaborates why anonymous collectives online can display solidarity when online communities can act like massive, decentralized support groups, for instance, during the COVID-19 lockdowns, netizens sent grocery funds or supplies to complete strangers across countries, using platforms such as Reddit (r/Assistance) but also display extreme cruelty with mob aggression as displayed by cancel culture and other forms of cyber harassment, as collective anonymity dilutes individual accountability, especially since targets become 'just' screen names or avatars.

Anonymity and pseudonymity can act as a developmental affordance as it enables identity experimentation without real-world repercussions. Within social media, pseudonyms or alternate accounts allow users to enact different gender expressions, political views or effective style. At the same time, without stable identity markers, online communities rely on emergent accountability systems i.e., reputation metrics, moderation algorithms, and communal sanctioning to maintain order. Hine (2020) describes this as *distributed governance*, where social order is produced and enforced through overlapping layers of technological constraint and peer enforcement. When anonymity is paired with persistent pseudonyms or traceable post histories, localised accountability arises (De Vries et al., 2021) such as with Wikipedia edit histories or usage of same usernames on multiple platforms that enable soft identifiability. Completely anonymous boards, however, with no continuity display volatile norm ecologies that fluctuate between humour, hostility, and moral anomie[7] (Phillips, 2015).

Anonymity and Pseudonymity, much like other constructs, are mediated by cultural norms, political structures and collective moral frameworks. Research is heavily focused on a western, individualist contexts. In cultures where moral regulation relies on external evaluation rather than internalised conscience, visibility may enforce the norms. For example, Zeng and Zhu (2021) found that Chinese users experienced online disinhibition differently with anonymity reducing public shame but increasing private guilt, reflecting Confucian relational selfhood. Here, self-presentation online is guided by the need to maintain "face" within dense relational networks. Similarly, Indian and East-Asian studies demonstrate that anonymity enables expression of dissent or taboo emotion without breaching filial or social hierarchies (Khan, 2025). The moral implications of identity masking are influenced by the dynamics of political visibility, beyond the cultural norms. In societies with pervasive surveillance, anonymity serves a defensive function, protecting forms of expression such as dissent, whistleblowing, and minority speech[8].

Anonymity can also be seen through the intentional impermanence of posts, stories, and messages. Unlike classical pseudonymity, which relies on persistence and reputation, ephemeral platforms offer situational anonymity. On these platforms, visibility is brief and context-bound as with Snapchat, BeReal, and Threads' temporary stories. Because the content disappears, users perceive a lower evaluative risk and a greater emotional immediacy. Temporary visibility can encourage "micro-authenticity," defined as the authentic and genuine sharing of personal experiences, often emotional in nature, without the pressure of permanence (Bayer et al., 2015; De Vries et al., 2021).

GROUP DYNAMICS, IDENTITY AND COLLECTIVE SELF

The cyberspace has been observed to contain "digital tribes." A "tribe," in this context, refers to small-to-medium communities or groups formed online around shared interests, ideologies, subcultures, or identities (Grant, 2020). These tribes function as communities with their own norms, symbols, discourse, and boundary work. The tribal metaphor evokes solidarity, binding identity, and inter-tribal rivalry. Digital tribes can be fandom groups, political factions, interest communities such as gaming, crafts, or health groups, or ideological clusters. They often self-organise around expressive symbols, such as emoticons, memes, and badges, and use tight group norms to maintain coherence. Digital tribes are not necessarily rigid; people may belong to multiple overlapping tribes, however, the more isolated a tribe is, the stronger the identity pressure and boundary maintenance tends to be (Maffesoli, 1996; Watson, 2013).

As per Social Identity Theory, an individual's self-concept is partially defined by a social identity that is established by the groups they belong to (Tajfel & Turner, 1986). This particular identity, when salient in a given context, can guide behaviour making individual differences fade and thus behave in more prototypical group norms. The "prototype" here refers to the characteristics attributed to a "typical member" of the group to which members align to with shared symbols, language and other cues making these traits accessible. The predominance of a particular identity is dependent on both comparative fit or the degree to which the group identity aligns with the given context, and normative fit, the extent to which the group identity aligns with established norms, as well as the degree of differentiation between in-group and out-group differences i.e. metacontrast (Turner & Reynolds, 2012). In digital spaces, customised algorithms, social identification and homophily[9] amplify this as they analyse users' habits leading to the creation of filter bubbles and echo chambers. Furthermore, an audience homophily suggests that the content recommended by the audience creates spirals of reinforcement that lead to polarisation over time (Costa Netto & Maçada, 2019; Kaiser & Rauchfleisch, 2020; Stets et al., 2021). While the formation of bubbles is amplified by algorithmic homophily[10], they can emerge from micro-level clustering and feedback dynamics (Kaakinen et al., 2018; Törnberg, 2025). Once these bubbles stabilise, shared norms then emerge rapidly. Members learn the appropriate behaviour through observation, moderator cues, or reward systems such as likes or upvotes. Digital spaces evolve over time, shifting from casual groups to communities characterised by distinct moral vocabularies and behavioural expectations. Fandoms, for instance, functions as a social category in itself with members forming a collective identity rooted in common affect, symbolism and discourse around a shared object of admiration such as an artist or show. The identity salience within fandom is sustained by contextual cues that include shared imagery, linguistics codes, emojis and usernames that signal in-group membership. The group prototype could be an idealised image of a "true fan" which shapes how members express loyalty, enthusiasm and defence of the fandom's values. Members also often orient their discourse toward this imagined prototype, internalising the group norms and thus experiencing depersonalisation. Rather than pathological, this depersonalisation is more of a cognitive shift wherein the self is perceived more as the representative of the collective, embodying its typical traits and stance rather than an autonomous individual. This shift can be magnified when anonymity or reduced individuating cues push people towards group-level categorisation. In online spaces, a number of pseudonyms, profile pictures or information provided in the biography section of an individual tend to reflect the groups they are a part of thus increasing the identification.

Brewer (1991) proposed that individuals tend to have twin motives of inclusion i.e. being part of the group and distinctiveness, being unique within the group. They seek an optimal balance between the group and this dynamic influences how strongly people align with group norms while also trying to stand out. This is known as the *optimal distinctiveness theory*. Going back to the earlier example of fandoms, members would strive to align with the group norms collective activities such as coordinating trends while simultaneously seeking to assert their individuality often using original content such as fanart, edits, commentary threads, fanfiction or witty posts that distinguish them within the in-group without threatening the cohesion of the collective. This represents an ongoing effort to mediate between assimilation and differentiation, which is influenced by the affordances of online platforms. The increased visibility, the utilisation of metrics, and the participatory structure of digital fandoms have the potential to simultaneously enhance opportunities for both conformity and creative self-expression. Anonymity can temporarily lower the cost of distinctiveness by allowing members to experiment with tone, humour, or critique without risking exclusion, while persistent usernames and social media recognition systems such as likes, retweets, reposts also reward alignment with community norms. Furthermore, the optimal distinctiveness point fluctuates as individuals assess how much deviation from the prototype is acceptable before social stigmatisation outweighs the benefits of recognition. As per the SIDE Model, anonymity enables individuals to treat the self and others as prototypes and adhere more to group norms. With minimal personal cues, the brain relies more on categorical processing i.e., group identities rather than feature-based processing of individual uniqueness. Group prototypes become heuristics for deciding what to believe or say. As anonymity suppresses identity signals, decision-making occurs in favour of social identity. Furthermore, this can partially explain Suler's (2004) disinhibition effect by explaining how alignment with group norms may lead to disinhibited behaviour.

Sociological theories also describe a *collective self* that refers to the cognitive, moral, and emotional connection of an individual to a broader collective, category, practice, or institution i.e., the concept of communal unity, characterised by a sense of interconnectedness, shared values, a collective history, common aspirations, symbols, and delineated boundaries (Turkle, 1995). In CMC, collective identity has been conceptualised as a dynamic identity that emerges through ongoing communication patterns across media platforms and hence, according to Barandiaran et al. (2020) be understood as "recurrent, cohesive, coordinated communicative interaction networks". Collective identities can be differentiated between *thick collective identities* that are deep, strongly felt, and stable and include shared narratives, heavy investment, strong boundary maintenance, and clarity about in-group versus out-group members, and *thin collective identities* that are more lightweight, flexible, and prone to fragmentation (Rohlinger & Bunnage, 2018). Digital interactions frequently promote a thin identity due to factors such as high turnover, reduced commitment, and weaker face-to-face grounding. However, digital identity can gradually solidify over time. Networked Publics (Boyd, 2014) explains collective identities are dispersed, mediated, and symbolic formed through shared discourse, memes, hashtags, moderated spaces, and digital symbols. And because digital networks collapse many audiences, context collapse occurs, which complicates identity signals; but within niche communities, more bounded publics can maintain stronger collective identity. Furthermore, collective identity in online spaces is very rarely localised rather it is networked, mediated, negotiated, fragile and often periodic, only activating around certain events, trends or crises.

However, contemporary theories have shifted towards *connective action,* wherein individuals use personal frames, such as their own narratives, emotions, and stories, which are linked via shared symbols or hashtags rather than a unified identity or formal membership that is assumed by collective identity. Action emerges through communication networks rather than formal organisations. A strong collective identity or standard frames aren't required. People coordinate by sharing their own content, linking to others, adopting common hashtags, or editing a meme. Narrative work can be observed through retweets, replies and commentary with repetitive acts such as liking, replying, tagging, or quoting function as ritual affirmations of group membership while also generating emotional energy and commitment (Baym, 2015; Abidin, 2016). Although identity formation under these conditions can be fluid and unstable, online practices still sustain a sense of belonging that motivates collective engagement, particularly within emergent groups where identity bonds are actively negotiated and reinforced (Uysal et al., 2021). However, digitally mediated identities tend to be structurally fragile due to low entry barriers and minimal obligations that allow temporary participation, resulting in fluid membership and weak commitment. Algorithms tend to amplify certain symbols or frames while suppressing others, which can inadvertently distort identity hierarchies within a movement. Finally, digital publics are short-lived and dependent on trending cycles and platform lifespans, so identities can fade quickly unless they are anchored in long-term organisational or offline structures. Information and communication technologies simultaneously amplify identity signalling by easing participation and weaken identity durability through transience and fragmentation (Rohlinger & Bunnage, 2018)

THE INFLUENCE OF ONLINE BEHAVIOURS ON OFFLINE SELF-CONCEPT

The online life or the technoself itself is often compartmentalised as "separate" from offline or actual selves. However, its boundaries extend beyond digital architecture. Online habits of articulation, visibility management, and affective sharing often spill over into one's offline self-concept, altering how individuals perceive their agency, sincerity, and sense of belonging. In digital spaces, individuals have been known to present ideal versions of themselves with editability allowing for careful self-presentations. With partial information and lack of cues, individuals fill in the gaps with assumptions based on their own perceptions, idealising the carefully put together versions of self, thus making virtual relationships feel far more intimate producing the *hyperpersonal effect* (Walther & Whitty, 2020). Users who express vulnerability online perceive higher emotional closeness, though observers rate them as less "authentic," as the vulnerability can feel performative than genuine (Uhl & Knobe, 2025). In social settings, feedback enables adjustment of behaviour both consciously and unconsciously. Feedback in offline contexts can be non-verbal cues making them subtle and bounded by context i.e., you only see it in real time. Virtually, feedback can be asynchronous and quantified, especially in social media contexts with visible metrics such as likes, reposts etc. This transforms social validation into data validating where self-worth and social standing are indicated by numbers and metrics that feed into a datafied self-concept partially constituted by algorithmic feedback loops. (Cheng et al., 2014; Mangiapanello & Hemmes, 2015). Furthermore, the ambient awareness–passive and constant exposure to updates as others' posts show without effort allows an individual to feel subtly informed about everyone's lives (Anderl et al., 2023). This can prompt them to track how they are perceived and further curate self-presentation by adjusting profiles, posts and behaviours to fit what they think the audience expects. Over time, engaging in such adjustment, especially with positive feedback loops, can move it from just behaviour and make them internalise it to their sense of self. Individuals, when the attention is focused on the self, compare their behaviour to internal standards, leading to self-reflection and further down the road, self-monitoring, enabling individuals to regulate self-presentation (Duval & Wicklund, 1973; Fullwood et al., 2016) Identity, thus becomes a project of continuous self-revision guided by mediated feedback and digital media can structure the self-perception by offering constant visual and metric reflection. To illustrate with an example, an individual might see their Instagram story highlights and evaluate their presentation, and then revise it based on satisfaction or personal branding while monitoring engagement insights to gauge authenticity.

Regular digital self-monitoring has been shown to cultivate metacognitive habits that persist beyond the online environment. Individuals become more conscious of their physical appearance in public spaces, a phenomenon often referred to as the "camera mind", and have an internalised audience, i.e., an imagined audience that accompanies the individuals throughout their activities, influencing behaviour even in private moments (Marwick & Boyd, 2011). Thus, the self, which once differentiated between a frontstage and a backstage, now inhibits a permanent semi-public consciousness while creating a *context collapse carryover* with the online reflexivity merging with offline social cognition (Papacharissi, 2014). Oftentimes, we see this expressed with the phrases "the curtains are down, who are you performing for", or "addressing beyond the fourth wall (imagined)."

The relationship between the offline and offline selves is bidirectional. Identity spillover has been a defining property of the technoself (Luppicini, 2013; Michikyan et al., 2014). The technoself and the embodied self-establish a reciprocal feedback loop, wherein online representation influences offline self-concept, and offline experience subsequently alters digital narration. This spillover can occur across cognitive, affective, behavioural and social dimensions as seen with the Proteus effect. The *proteus effect* (Yee & Bailenson, 2007) described a change in self-perception and behaviour based on the characteristics of digital avatars, such as attractive avatars prompting confidence or taller avatars negotiating more assertively. *Self-perception theory* suggests that individuals tend to infer attitudes and traits from observing their own behaviour in its context, and when they behave *through* their avatar, the visual and behavioural cues feed back into self-appraisal through embodied cognition, thus influencing their self-perception. Furthermore, as individuals present themselves online and build their narratives, they learn new visual and behavioural information about the self, which, over time, is internalised through consistent behaviour, which then reconfigures the self-schema. In a neural sense, experiencing an avatar's movement activates sensorimotor regions through neural mirroring, and the body learns through virtual experiences (Adamovich et al., 2009; Maister et al., 2013; Miyamoto et al., 2023). Although originally observed in virtual reality, this can extend towards profile pictures, filters and curated feeds through self-image modification. Although self-enhancing filters can temporarily boost confidence and reduce social anxiety, repeated exposure has been linked to body dissatisfaction (Fardouly & Vartanian, 2016). In essence, profile curation becomes a form of avatar management that reinforces self-beliefs tied to one's portrayed persona. In this sense, online self-presentation becomes a continuous form of avatar management that reinforces the traits and narratives individuals wish to inhabit. Repeated enactment of an avatar's traits updates self-schemas. When congruence between avatar and feedback is established, it enhances self-efficacy and emotional regulation, producing behavioural spillovers offline. Beyond the individual cognitive processes, such interactions give rise to social and normative spillovers. Individuals who experience positive embodiment, validation and social success through a digitally-enhanced self often carry this assurance into real-life interactions. However, inconsistent feedback or identity fragmentation can undermine this sense of coherence and the internalisation of negative or objectifying portrayals can lead to amplified self-surveillance and comparison in embodied contexts. Over time, these digitally rehearsed attributes integrate into autobiographical memory and embody a sense of agency (Michikyan et al., 2014; Wang, 2024), thus transforming cyberspace from a representational platform into a developmental context for the evolving self.

DISCUSSION

The virtual environment and its defining affordances have altered the communicative process and thus the social construction of self. It has created new avenues for self-expression by increasing autonomy and awareness of self-representation through high customisable online personas, with the affordances such as editability and persistence guiding the process. Thus, it enables an exemplary environment for identity exploration and experimentation with different behaviours and interaction styles without the constraints of visible and stable social cues of offline settings as anonymity allows individuals to take on roles and personas they might never risk in real life. The understanding of the self within this context illustrates an amplified performance, flexibility and external influences while raising concerns over authenticity and identity integration. As such, the technoself may be best understood both as the product of and as a means for identity work, that is not an entity external to the self. It is, at its core, a layered, socially constructed self that develops through the interaction of narrative, embodiment, datafication, and social interaction. While the core socio-psychological processes, such as reflected appraisal, social identity, and autobiographical reasoning, remain central, their functioning is filtered through technological affordances that extend, constrain, and reconfigure identity work. This produces a self that is much more malleable, continually reconfigured by metrics, avatars, and algorithmic classifications, yet also much more vulnerable, for coherence must be actively reinforced across platform dependencies. The subjective experience is currently documented through the use of timelines, evaluated via dashboards, embodied in avatars, and inferred by algorithms, all of which are produced in a systemic manner. In the context of social psychology, the challenge lies in ensuring the well-being of individuals' identities, encompassing attributes such as authenticity, coherence, and autonomy. This concern is further intensified due to the predominant role of technology in mediating the conditions that define our sense of self as well as by externalising and quantifying validation. By leveraging its affordances, individuals are better able to explore, create, and express themselves. Consequently, individuals face considerable pressure to establish and maintain a distinct online and offline persona. At the same time, mechanisms such as self-perception, embodied rehearsal, algorithmic feedback, and norm internalisation, digitally enacted identities are progressively absorbed into offline self-schemas, emotions, and conduct. The manner in which individuals engage with technology thus impacts their self-perception and their understanding of the external world.

Limitations and Future Directions

The study provides a conceptual understanding of how the self is influenced by and presented in the virtual environment. Several concepts such as Mirror Culture in VR and their impact on the self were excluded due to insufficient literature discussing mechanisms of the self. Future research should examine the self and related psychological constructs beyond online disinhibition, self-esteem and avatar embodiment as a relational construct rather than isolated constructs. Over-reliance on self-report measures restricts explanatory depth. Much of the literature depends on questionnaires assessing identity, authenticity, or self-esteem, which are vulnerable to social desirability and retrospective bias. Research is disproportionately saturated in Western and Chinese cultures, aspects such as affordances-in-practice can have a variably different impact in other cultures. Finally, ethical and power dimensions are often under-theorized. Algorithmic influence, surveillance, and platform governance are treated as background variables rather than active agents shaping self-concept and autonomy.

Future research must adopt an integrative approach that conceptualises virtual environments as active participants in self-construction given their significant importance in everyday lives. Second, there is a need to examine ways in which narrative coherence is maintained, the role of quantified selves in shaping reflexivity, the potential for challenging algorithmic identities, and the methods of achieving cross-context integration.

REFERENCES

Abidin, C. (2016). "Aren't These Just Young, Rich Women Doing Vain Things Online?": Influencer Selfies as Subversive Frivolity. *Social Media + Society*, *2*(2), 1–17. DOI: 10.1177/2056305116641342

Adamovich, S. V., Fluet, G. G., Tunik, E., & Merians, A. S. (2009). Sensorimotor training in virtual reality: A review. *NeuroRehabilitation*, *25*(1), 29–44. DOI: 10.3233/NRE-2009-0497 PMID: 19713617

American Psychological Association. (2018, April 19). *Personality*. APA Dictionary of Psychology; American Psychological Association. https://dictionary.apa.org/personality

Anderl, C., Levordashka, A., & Utz, S. (2023). Ambient Awareness of Who Knows What: Spontaneous Inferences of Domain Expertise. *Media Psychology*, •••, 1–23. DOI: 10.1080/15213269.2023.2239144

APA Dictionary of Psychology. (2023). *APA Dictionary of Psychology*. Dictionary.apa.org. https://dictionary.apa.org/self

Aspling, F. (2011). *The private and the public in online presentations of the self: A critical development of Goffman's dramaturgical perspective*. https://www.researchgate.net/publication/320346695_The_Private_and_the_Public_in_Online_Presentations_of_the_Self_A_Critical_Development_of_Goffman%27s_Dramaturgical_Perspective

Avci, H., Baams, L., & Kretschmer, T. (2024). A Systematic Review of Social Media Use and Adolescent Identity Development. *Adolescent Research Review*, *10*(2), 219–236. DOI: 10.1007/s40894-024-00251-1 PMID: 40385471

Bandura, A. (1999). Moral Disengagement in the Perpetration of Inhumanities. *Personality and Social Psychology Review*, *3*(3), 193–209. DOI: 10.1207/s15327957pspr0303_3 PMID: 15661671

Banet-Weiser, S. (2012). Authentic: The Politics of Ambivalence in a Brand Culture. In *JSTOR*. NYU Press. https://www.jstor.org/stable/j.ctt9qfmw0

Barak, A., & Suler, J. (2008). *Reflections on the Psychology and Social Science of Cyberspace*. Cambridge University Press., https://www.johnsuler.com/article_pdfs/reflections_psycyber.pdf DOI: 10.1017/CBO9780511813740.002

Barandiaran, X. E., Calleja-López, A., & Cozzo, E. (2020). Defining Collective Identities in Technopolitical Interaction Networks. *Frontiers in Psychology, 11*, 1549. Advance online publication. DOI: 10.3389/fpsyg.2020.01549 PMID: 32848986

Bargh, J. A., McKenna, K. Y. A., & Fitzsimons, G. M. (2002). Can You See the Real Me? Activation and Expression of the "True Self" on the Internet. *The Journal of Social Issues, 58*(1), 33–48. DOI: 10.1111/1540-4560.00247

Baumeister, R. F., Bratslavsky, E., Muraven, M., & Tice, D. M. (1998). Ego depletion: Is the active self a limited resource? *Journal of Personality and Social Psychology, 74*(5), 1252–1265. DOI: 10.1037/0022-3514.74.5.1252 PMID: 9599441

Bayer, J. B., Ellison, N. B., Schoenebeck, S. Y., & Falk, E. B. (2015). Sharing the small moments: Ephemeral social interaction on Snapchat. *Information Communication and Society, 19*(7), 956–977. DOI: 10.1080/1369118X.2015.1084349

Baym, N. K. (2015). Social Media and the Struggle for Society. *Social Media + Society, 1*(1), 205630511558047. DOI: 10.1177/2056305115580477

Belk, R. W. (2013). Extended Self in a Digital World. *The Journal of Consumer Research, 40*(3), 477–500. DOI: 10.1086/671052

Bergin, R. (2016). *Media Richness Theory*. https://www.chds.us/coursefiles/IS4010/lectures/tech_media_richness_long/story_content/external_files/Media%20Richness%20Theory%20Script.pdf

Bessière, K., Seay, A. F., & Kiesler, S. (2007). The Ideal Elf: Identity Exploration in World of Warcraft. *Cyberpsychology & Behavior, 10*(4), 530–535. DOI: 10.1089/cpb.2007.9994 PMID: 17711361

Boellstorff, T. (2016). For Whom the Ontology Turns: Theorizing the Digital Real. *Current Anthropology, 57*(4), 387–407. DOI: 10.1086/687362

Bortolan, A. (2024). Becoming oneself online: Narrative self-constitution and the internet. *Philosophical Studies, 181*(9), 2405–2427. DOI: 10.1007/s11098-024-02169-9

Boyd, D. (2010). *Social Network Sites as Networked Publics: Affordances, Dynamics, and Implications danah boyd*. https://www.danah.org/papers/2010/SNSasNetworkedPublics.pdf

Boyd, D. (2014). It's complicated: the Social Lives of Networked Teens. *Choice Reviews Online, 51*(12), 51–704251–7042. DOI: 10.5860/CHOICE.51-7042

Brewer, M. B. (1991). The social self: On being the same and different at the same time. *Personality and Social Psychology Bulletin, 17*(5), 475–482. DOI: 10.1177/0146167291175001

Bullingham, L., & Vasconcelos, A. C. (2013). The Presentation of Self in the Online world': Goffman and the Study of Online Identities. *Journal of Information Science, 39*(1), 101–112. DOI: 10.1177/0165551512470051

Chan, K. T., Hui, C. L., Cheung, C., Suen, Y. N., Wong, S. M. Y., Wong, C. S., Kam, B. P., & Chen, E. Y. H. (2025). Exploring the Differentiation of Self-Concepts in the Physical and Virtual Worlds Using Euclidean Distance Analysis and Its Relationship With Digitalization and Mental Health Among Young People: Cross-Sectional Study. *JMIR Mental Health, 12*, e60747. DOI: 10.2196/60747 PMID: 39889302

Cheney-Lippold, J. (2017). *We are data: algorithms and the making of our digital selves*. New York University Press. DOI: 10.18574/nyu/9781479888702.001.0001

Cheng, J., Danescu-Niculescu-Mizil, C., & Leskovec, J. (2014). *How Community Feedback Shapes User Behavior*. https://cs.stanford.edu/people/jure/pubs/disqus-icwsm14.pdf

Chou, H.-T. G., & Edge, N. (2012). "They Are Happier and Having Better Lives than I Am": The Impact of Using Facebook on Perceptions of Others' Lives. *Cyberpsychology, Behavior, and Social Networking, 15*(2), 117–121. DOI: 10.1089/cyber.2011.0324 PMID: 22165917

Christopherson, K. M. (2007). The positive and negative implications of anonymity in Internet social interactions: "On the Internet, Nobody Knows You're a Dog.". *Computers in Human Behavior, 23*(6), 3038–3056. DOI: 10.1016/j.chb.2006.09.001

Clark-Gordon, C. V., Bowman, N. D., Goodboy, A. K., & Wright, A. (2019). Anonymity and Online Self-Disclosure: A Meta-Analysis. *Communication Reports, 32*(2), 98–111. DOI: 10.1080/08934215.2019.1607516

Cooley, C. H. (2025). Human nature and the social order by Charles Horton Cooley. In *Project Gutenberg*. Charles Scribner's Sons. (Original work published 1902), https://www.gutenberg.org/ebooks/75145

Costa, E. (2018). Affordances-in-practice: An ethnographic critique of social media logic and context collapse. *New Media & Society, 20*(10), 3641–3656. DOI: 10.1177/1461444818756290 PMID: 30581356

Costa Netto, Y., & Maçada, A. C. G. (2019). THE INFLUENCE OF SOCIAL MEDIA FILTER BUBBLES AND ECHO CHAMBERS ON IT IDENTITY CONSTRUCTION. *Research-In-Progress Papers*. https://aisel.aisnet.org/ecis2019_rip/65/

Crocker, J., & Park, L. E. (2004). The Costly Pursuit of Self-Esteem. *Psychological Bulletin, 130*(3), 392–414. DOI: 10.1037/0033-2909.130.3.392 PMID: 15122925

Davis, J. L., & Jurgenson, N. (2014). Context collapse: Theorizing context collusions and collisions. *Information Communication and Society, 17*(4), 476–485. DOI: 10.1080/1369118X.2014.888458

De Vries, M., & de Jong, R. G. var der Loo, M., de Wolf, P., & Takes, F. W. (2021). The risk of identity disclosure through network structure: anecdotal evidence from a hackathon. In *UNITED NATIONS ECONOMIC COMMISSION FOR EUROPE CONFERENCE OF EUROPEAN STATISTICIANS.* https://www.markvanderloo.eu/files/share/vries2023risk.pdf

De Wolf, R., & Pierson, J. (2014). Who's my audience again? Understanding audience management strategies for designing privacy management technologies. *Telematics and Informatics, 31*(4), 607–616. DOI: 10.1016/j.tele.2013.11.004

Deci, E. L., & Ryan, R. M. (2000). The "What" and "Why" of Goal Pursuits: Human needs and the Self-Determination of Behavior. *Psychological Inquiry, 11*(4), 227–268. DOI: 10.1207/S15327965PLI1104_01

Ducheneaut, N., Wen, M.-H., Yee, N., & Wadley, G. (2009). Body and mind: A study of avatar personalization in three virtual worlds. *Proceedings of the 27th International Conference on Human Factors in Computing Systems - CHI 09*. DOI: 10.1145/1518701.1518877

Duval, S., & Wicklund, R. A. (1973). Effects of objective self-awareness on attribution of causality. *Journal of Experimental Social Psychology, 9*(1), 17–31. DOI: 10.1016/0022-1031(73)90059-0

Edwards, F. (2016). An Investigation of Attention-Seeking Behavior through Social Media Post Framing. *Athens Journal of Mass Media and Communications, 3*(1), 25–44. DOI: 10.30958/ajmmc.3.1.2

Fardouly, J., & Vartanian, L. R. (2016). Social Media and Body Image Concerns: Current Research and Future Directions. *Current Opinion in Psychology, 9*, 1–5. DOI: 10.1016/j.copsyc.2015.09.005

Feng, S., Mäntymäki, M., Dhir, A., & Salmela, H. (2020). How Self-tracking and the Quantified Self Promote Health and Well-being: A Systematic Literature Review (Preprint). *Journal of Medical Internet Research, 23*(9). Advance online publication. DOI: 10.2196/25171

Festinger, L., Pepitone, A., & Newcomb, T. (1952). Some consequences of de-individuation in a group. *Journal of Abnormal and Social Psychology*, *47*(2), 382–389. DOI: 10.1037/h0057906 PMID: 14937978

Floridi, L. (2015). *The Onlife Manifesto* (Floridi, L., Ed.). Springer International Publishing., DOI: 10.1007/978-3-319-04093-6

Fullwood, C., James, B. M., & Chen-Wilson, C.-H. (2016). Self-Concept Clarity and Online Self-Presentation in Adolescents. *Cyberpsychology, Behavior, and Social Networking*, *19*(12), 716–720. DOI: 10.1089/cyber.2015.0623 PMID: 27830930

Gergen, K. J. (1991). *The saturated self: Dilemmas of identity in contemporary life*. Basic Books.

Gibson, J. J. (2013). *The Ecological Approach To Visual Perception*. Psychology Press. (Original work published 1979) DOI: 10.4324/9780203767764

Gill, R., & Kanai, A. (2018). Mediating Neoliberal Capitalism: Affect, Subjectivity and Inequality. *Journal of Communication*, *68*(2), 318–326. DOI: 10.1093/joc/jqy002

Goffman, E. (1959). The Presentation of Self in Everyday Life. *American Sociological Review*, *21*(5), 631. Advance online publication. DOI: 10.2307/2089106

Grant, A. (2020). DIGITAL TRIBALISM AND THE INTERNET OF THINGS: CHALLENGES AND OPPORTUNITIES. *Issues in Information Systems*. Advance online publication. DOI: 10.48009/2_iis_2020_213-220

Haimson, O. L., & Hoffmann, A. L. (2016). Constructing and enforcing "authentic" identity online: Facebook, real names, and non-normative identities. *First Monday*, *21*(6). Advance online publication. DOI: 10.5210/fm.v21i6.6791

Harrell, N. (2025). The Mechanisms of Virality in Online Public Discourse. In *Purdue University*. https://s3-eu-west-1.amazonaws.com/pstorage-purdue-258596361474/53964152/Harrell_final_thesis_4.pdf?X-Amz-Algorithm=AWS4-HMAC-SHA256&X-Amz-Credential=AKIAI5YTMH46SYYEBHKA/20250914/eu-west-1/s3/aws4_request&X-Amz-Date=20250914T140558Z&X-Amz-Expires=10&X-Amz-SignedHeaders=host&X-Amz-Signature=b14993f2d675e568e57392c6d8367eaaaa5177ec59b760733321233183e3b99c

Higgins, E. T. (1987). Self-discrepancy: A theory relating self and affect. *Psychological Review*, *94*(3), 319–340. DOI: 10.1037/0033-295X.94.3.319 PMID: 3615707

Highfield, T., & Leaver, T. (2016). Instagrammatics and digital methods: Studying visual social media, from selfies and GIFs to memes and emoji. *Communication Research and Practice*, *2*(1), 47–62. DOI: 10.1080/22041451.2016.1155332

Hine, C. (2020). *Ethnography for the Internet*. Routledge., DOI: 10.4324/9781003085348

Hogan, B. (2010). The Presentation of Self in the Age of Social Media: Distinguishing Performances and Exhibitions Online. *Bulletin of Science, Technology & Society, 30*(6), 377–386. DOI: 10.1177/0270467610385893

Hollenbaugh, E. E. (2021). Self-Presentation in Social Media: Review and Research Opportunities. *Review of Communication Research, 9*(2255-4165), 80–98. DOI: 10.12840/ISSN.2255-4165.027

Honarvar, R., & Sepehrinia, M. (2025). Refashioning Belk's Theory of Digital Extended Self for a Datafied Society: A Review and Research Agenda. *SAGE Open, 15*(3), 21582440251357241. Advance online publication. DOI: 10.1177/21582440251357241

Huang, J., Kumar, S., & Hu, C. (2021). A Literature Review of Online Identity Reconstruction. *Frontiers in Psychology, 12*(1), 696552. Advance online publication. DOI: 10.3389/fpsyg.2021.696552 PMID: 34497560

Ishii, K., Lyons, M. M., & Carr, S. A. (2019). Revisiting media richness theory for today and future. *Human Behavior and Emerging Technologies, 1*(2), 124–131. DOI: 10.1002/hbe2.138

James, W. (1890). The Principles of Psychology. By WILLIAM JAMES 2 vols. (American Science Series, Advance Course.) New York, Holt. 8Dagger. *Science, ns-16*(401), 207–208. DOI: 10.1126/science.ns-16.401.207-a

Kaakinen, M., Sirola, A., Savolainen, I., & Oksanen, A. (2018). Shared identity and shared information in social media: Development and validation of the identity bubble reinforcement scale. *Media Psychology, 23*(1), 1–27. DOI: 10.1080/15213269.2018.1544910

Kaiser, J., & Rauchfleisch, A. (2020). Birds of a Feather Get Recommended Together: Algorithmic Homophily in YouTube's Channel Recommendations in the United States and Germany. *Social Media + Society, 6*(4), 205630512096991. DOI: 10.1177/2056305120969914

Khan, A. (2025, July 10). *How India's Emerging Surveillance Regime Threatens the Right to Anonymity Online*. Yale Law School. https://law.yale.edu/isp/initiatives/wikimedia-initiative-intermediaries-and-information/wiii-blog/how-indias-emerging-surveillance-regime-threatens-right-anonymity-online

Lair, D. J., Sullivan, K., & Cheney, G. (2005). Marketization and the Recasting of the Professional Self. *Management Communication Quarterly, 18*(3), 307–343. DOI: 10.1177/0893318904270744

Lapidot-Lefler, N., & Barak, A. (2012). Effects of anonymity, invisibility, and lack of eye-contact on toxic online disinhibition. *Computers in Human Behavior*, *28*(2), 434–443. DOI: 10.1016/j.chb.2011.10.014

Litt, E. (2012). Knock, Knock. Who's There? the Imagined Audience. *Journal of Broadcasting & Electronic Media*, *56*(3), 330–345. DOI: 10.1080/08838151.2012.705195

Litt, E., & Hargittai, E. (2016). The Imagined Audience on Social Network Sites. *Social Media + Society*, *2*(1), 1–12. DOI: 10.1177/2056305116633482

Loh, J., & Walsh, M. J. (2021). Social media context collapse: The consequential differences between context collusion versus context collision. *Social Media + Society*, *7*(3), 1–15. DOI: 10.1177/20563051211041646

Luppicini, R. (2013). *HANDBOOK OF RESEARCH ON TECHNOSELF: identity in a technological society* (Vol. 1). Information Science Refer. DOI: 10.4018/978-1-4666-2211-1

Lupton, D. (2016). The diverse domains of quantified selves: Self-tracking modes and dataveillance. *Economy and Society*, *45*(1), 101–122. DOI: 10.1080/03085147.2016.1143726

Maares, P., Banjac, S., & Hanusch, F. (2020). The labour of visual authenticity on social media: Exploring producers' and audiences' perceptions on Instagram. *Poetics*, *84*, 101502. DOI: 10.1016/j.poetic.2020.101502

Madary, M., & Metzinger, T. K. (2016). Real Virtuality: A Code of Ethical Conduct. Recommendations for Good Scientific Practice and the Consumers of VR-Technology. *Frontiers in Robotics and AI*, *3*. Advance online publication. DOI: 10.3389/frobt.2016.00003

Maffesoli, M. (1996). The Time of the Tribes: The Decline of Individualism in Mass Society. *Sage (Atlanta, Ga.)*. Advance online publication. DOI: 10.4135/9781446222133

Maister, L., Sebanz, N., Knoblich, G., & Tsakiris, M. (2013). Experiencing ownership over a dark-skinned body reduces implicit racial bias. *Cognition*, *128*(2), 170–178. DOI: 10.1016/j.cognition.2013.04.002 PMID: 23680793

Mangiapanello, K. A., & Hemmes, N. S. (2015). An Analysis of Feedback from a Behavior Analytic Perspective. *The Behavior Analyst*, *38*(1), 51–75. DOI: 10.1007/s40614-014-0026-x PMID: 27606167

Markus, H., & Nurius, P. (1986). Possible selves. *The American Psychologist*, *41*(9), 954–969. DOI: 10.1037/0003-066X.41.9.954

Markus, H. R., & Kitayama, S. (1991). *Culture and the Self: Implications for Cognition, Emotion, and Motivation*. ResearchGate., DOI: 10.1037/0033-295X.98.2.224

Marwick, A. E., & Boyd, D. (2011). I Tweet honestly, I Tweet passionately: Twitter users, Context collapse, and the Imagined Audience. *New Media & Society*, *13*(1), 114–133. DOI: 10.1177/1461444810365313

McAdams, D. P. (2011). Narrative Identity. *Handbook of Identity Theory and Research, 1*, 99–115. DOI: 10.1007/978-1-4419-7988-9_5

McAdams, D. P., Trzesniewski, K., Lilgendahl, J., Benet-Martinez, V., & Robins, R. W. (2021). Self and Identity in Personality Psychology. *Personality Science*, *2*(1), e6035. Advance online publication. DOI: 10.5964/ps.6035

McPherson, M., Smith-Lovin, L., & Cook, J. M. (2001). Birds of a feather: Homophily in social networks. *Annual Review of Sociology*, *27*(1), 415–444. DOI: 10.1146/annurev.soc.27.1.415

Mead, G. H. (1935). Mind, Self and Society. From the Standpoint of a Social Behaviorist. *The Journal of Philosophy*, *32*(6), 162. DOI: 10.2307/2016046

Michikyan, M., Subrahmanyam, K., & Dennis, J. (2014). Can you tell who I am? Neuroticism, extraversion, and online self-presentation among young adults. *Computers in Human Behavior*, *33*(1), 179–183. DOI: 10.1016/j.chb.2014.01.010

Mikhaylova, A. A., & Mikhaylov, A. S. (2024). Cyberspace: A systematic review of 30 years of social and economic research. *Journal of Infrastructure. Policy and Development*, *8*(8), 6178. DOI: 10.24294/jipd.v8i8.6178

Miyamoto, Y., Uchitomi, H., & Miyake, Y. (2023). Effects of avatar shape and motion on mirror neuron system activity. *Frontiers in Human Neuroscience*, *17*, 1173185. Advance online publication. DOI: 10.3389/fnhum.2023.1173185 PMID: 37859767

Mykhailov, D., & Liberati, N. (2023). Back to the technologies themselves: Phenomenological turn within postphenomenology. *Phenomenology and the Cognitive Sciences*. Advance online publication. DOI: 10.1007/s11097-023-09905-2

Nitschinsk, L., Tobin, S. J., Varley, D., & Vanman, E. J. (2023). Why Do People Sometimes Wear an Anonymous Mask? Motivations for Seeking Anonymity Online. *Personality and Social Psychology Bulletin*, *0*(0). Advance online publication. DOI: 10.1177/01461672231210465 PMID: 37997811

Norman, D. (2004, January 1). *Affordances and Design*. ResearchGate. https://www.researchgate.net/publication/265618710_Affordances_and_Design

Oliver, M. (2005). The Problem with Affordance. *E-Learning and Digital Media*, *2*(4), 402–413. DOI: 10.2304/elea.2005.2.4.402

Papacharissi, Z. (2014). *Affective publics: Sentiment, technology, and politics. Affective Publics: Sentiment*. Technology, and Politics., DOI: 10.1093/acprof:oso/9780199999736.001.0001

Peng, T. (2021). *THE ROLE OF CUSTOMIZATION ON AVATAR IDENTIFICATION AND PERFORMANCE IN A KART RACING GAME*. https://repository.library.northeastern.edu/files/neu%3Abz617n18m/fulltext.pdf

Pezzulo, G., Donnarumma, F., & Dindo, H. (2013). Human Sensorimotor Communication: A Theory of Signaling in Online Social Interactions. *PLoS One*, *8*(11), e79876. DOI: 10.1371/journal.pone.0079876 PMID: 24278201

Phillips, W. (2015). This Is Why We Can't Have Nice Things: Mapping the Relationship between Online Trolling and Mainstream Culture. In *JSTOR*. The MIT Press., https://www.jstor.org/stable/j.ctt17kk8k7

Postmes, T., & Spears, R. (1998). Deindividuation and antinormative behavior: A meta-analysis. *Psychological Bulletin*, *123*(3), 238–259. DOI: 10.1037/0033-2909.123.3.238

Ratan, R., & Pandita, S. (2025). 12 Avatar, That an Intelligent User Controls during Dynamic Interactions. *The Oxford Handbook of Media Psychology*, 241.

Reicher, S. D., Spears, R., & Postmes, T. (1995). A Social Identity Model of Deindividuation Phenomena. *European Review of Social Psychology*, *6*(1), 161–198. DOI: 10.1080/14792779443000049

Reinecke, L., & Trepte, S. (2014). Authenticity and well-being on social network sites: A two-wave longitudinal study on the effects of online authenticity and the positivity bias in SNS communication. *Computers in Human Behavior*, *30*(30), 95–102. DOI: 10.1016/j.chb.2013.07.030

Ritter, M. (2021). Postphenomenological Method and Technological Things Themselves. *Human Studies*, *44*(4), 581–593. DOI: 10.1007/s10746-021-09603-5

Rogers, C. R. (1959). A Theory of Therapy, Personality, and Interpersonal Relationships: As Developed in the Client-Centered Framework. In Koch, S. (Ed.), *Psychology: A Study of a Science. Formulations of the Person and the Social Context* (Vol. 3, pp. 184–256). McGraw Hill.

Rohlinger, D. A., & Bunnage, L. A. (2018). COLLECTIVE IDENTITY IN THE DIGITAL AGE: THIN AND THICK IDENTITIES IN MOVEON.ORG AND THE TEA PARTY MOVEMENT*. *Mobilization: An International Quarterly (San Diego, Calif.)*, *23*(2), 135–157. DOI: 10.17813/1086-671X-23-2-135

Schroeder, R. (2008). Defining Virtual Worlds and Virtual Environments. *Journal of Virtual Worlds Research*, *1*(1). Advance online publication. DOI: 10.4101/jvwr.v1i1.294

Short, J., Williams, E., & Christie, B. (1976). The social psychology of Telecommunications. *Contemporary Sociology*, *7*(1), 32. DOI: 10.2307/2065899

Slater, M., & Sanchez-Vives, M. V. (2016). Enhancing Our Lives with Immersive Virtual Reality. *Frontiers in Robotics and AI*, *3*(74). Advance online publication. DOI: 10.3389/frobt.2016.00074

Stets, J. E., Aldecoa, J., Bloom, Q., & Winegar, J. (2021). Using Identity Theory to Understand Homophily in Groups. *Frontiers in Sociology and Social Research*, 285–302. DOI: 10.1007/978-3-030-76966-6_14

Suler, J. (2004). The online disinhibition effect. *Cyberpsychology & Behavior*, *7*(3), 321–326. DOI: 10.1089/1094931041291295 PMID: 15257832

Tajfel, H., & Turner, J. C. (1986). *Social identity and intergroup relations*. Cambridge University Press.

Tekke, M. (2015, December). *Rediscovering Rogers's self theory and personality*. ResearchGate. https://www.researchgate.net/publication/286456614_Rediscovering_Rogers%27s_Self_Theory_and_Personality

Tolnaiová, S. G., & Gálik, S. (2020). Cyberspace as a New Living World and Its Axiological Contexts. In www.intechopen.com. IntechOpen. https://www.intechopen.com/chapters/71568

Tong, Z., Liu, H., Feng, J., Wang, W., Wu, H., & Xu, J. (2025). Trapped by AI Recommendation: How Identity Concerns Reduce Variety-Seeking Behavior. *MDE. Managerial and Decision Economics*, *46*(5), 3200–3211. Advance online publication. DOI: 10.1002/mde.4524

Törnberg, P. (2025). *Online Homogeneity Can Emerge Without Filtering Algorithms or Homophily Preferences*. ArXiv.org. https://arxiv.org/abs/2508.10466

Turkle, S. (1995). *Life on the Screen: Identity in the Age of the Internet*. Simon & Schuster Paperbacks, Dr.

Turner, J. C., Hogg, M. A., Oakes, P. J., Reicher, S. D., & Wetherell, M. S. (1987). *Rediscovering the social group: A self-categorization theory*. Basil Blackwell.

Turner, J. C., & Reynolds, K. J. (2012). Self-Categorization Theory. *Handbook of Theories of Social Psychology, 2*, 399–417. DOI: 10.4135/9781446249222.n46

Uhl, M., & Knobe, J. (2025). The Inauthentic Online Self: Perceptions of Naturalness Drive Judgments of Authenticity. *Philosophy & Technology, 38*(2), 1–25. DOI: 10.1007/s13347-025-00871-y

Uysal, M. S., Akfırat, S. A., & Cakal, H. (2021). The social identity perspective of social media leadership in collective action participation. *Journal of Community & Applied Social Psychology*, *32*(6), 1001–1015. Advance online publication. DOI: 10.1002/casp.2502

Van der Nagel, E., & Frith, J. (2015). Anonymity, pseudonymity, and the agency of online identity: Examining the social practices of r/Gonewild. *First Monday, 20*(3). Advance online publication. DOI: 10.5210/fm.v20i3.5615

Vignoles, V. (2017, May). *Identity: Personal and Social*. ResearchGate. https://www.researchgate.net/publication/316790231_Identity_Personal_AND_Social

Vogel, E. A., Rose, J. P., Roberts, L. R., & Eckles, K. (2014). Social comparison, social media, and self-esteem. *Psychology of Popular Media Culture, 3*(4), 206–222. DOI: 10.1037/ppm0000047

Walther, J. B., & Whitty, M. T. (2020). Language, Psychology, and New New Media: The Hyperpersonal Model of Mediated Communication at Twenty-Five Years. *Journal of Language and Social Psychology*, *40*(1), 120–135. DOI: 10.1177/0261927X20967703

Wan, Q., & Lu, Z. (2023, July 20). *Investigating VTubing as a Reconstruction of Streamer Self-Presentation: Identity, Performance, and Gender*. ArXiv.org. https://doi.org//arXiv.2307.11025DOI: 10.48550

Wang, Q. (2024). The online extension of autobiographical memory: A psycho-cultural perspective. In Wang, Q., & Hoskins, A. (Eds.), *The remaking of memory in the age of the internet and social media* (pp. 15–31). Oxford University Press.

Watson, I. (2013). Digital Natives or Digital Tribes? *Universal Journal of Educational Research, 1*(2), 104–112. DOI: 10.13189/ujer.2013.010210

Wood, J. T. (2009). *Communication in our lives* (4th ed.).

Yan, M., & Zheng, S. (2024). Segmentation or integration? The managerial approach to work-family balance in the age of virtual team work. *Xinli Kexue Jinzhan, 32*(5), 754. DOI: 10.3724/SP.J.1042.2024.00754

Yee, N., & Bailenson, J. (2007). The Proteus Effect: The Effect of Transformed Self-Representation on Behavior. *Human Communication Research, 33*(3), 271–290. DOI: 10.1111/j.1468-2958.2007.00299.x

Zeng, R., & Zhu, D. (2021). Fear of Evaluation and Online Self-Disclosure on WeChat: Moderating Effects of Protective Face Orientation. *Frontiers in Psychology, 12*, 530722. Advance online publication. DOI: 10.3389/fpsyg.2021.530722 PMID: 34512427

Zhao, L., & Yu, J. (2021). A Meta-Analytic Review of Moral Disengagement and Cyberbullying. *Frontiers in Psychology, 12*, 681299. Advance online publication. DOI: 10.3389/fpsyg.2021.681299 PMID: 34916984

Zimmermann, D., Wehler, A., & Kaspar, K. (2022). Self-representation through avatars in digital environments. *Current Psychology (New Brunswick, N.J.), 42*(25), 21775–21789. Advance online publication. DOI: 10.1007/s12144-022-03232-6

Zuboff, S. (2019). Surveillance Capitalism and the Challenge of Collective Action. *New Labor Forum, 28*(1), 10–29. DOI: 10.1177/1095796018819461

KEY TERMS AND DEFINITIONS

Affordances: Properties of the user interface or a platform that allow an individual to perform certain actions.

Anonymity: Completely hiding one's identity.

Asynchronous Communication: Communication where the sender and the receiver are not simultaneously communicating. E.g., a message from a sender might be seen by the receiver at different times.

Audiences and Context Collapse: The audience is who views any content you post on the web. Context collapse occurs when those content reaches and interacts with an unintended audience.

Avatar: A virtual representation of a person used for online interaction, ranging from profile pictures to in-game characters.

Collective Self: The identity one derives from the groups they belong to.

Cyberspace: A space wherein all types of digital communication occur, ranging from texts and websites to games.

Datafication: The conversion of experiences to data that is machine-processable and circulates on the internet. E.g., shopping for cameras on Amazon will be converted to data and circulated, which is then processed by another machine entity like Instagram, wherein you see it as ads.

Dramaturgy: Self-presentation and perception explained through a theatrical performance. The front stage is where one performs (e.g., a student in a classroom), the backstage is where one relaxes and drops the role (e.g., home), and the performance is impression management.

Hyperpersonal Effect: Due to reduced cues online, individuals project their assumptions onto their interaction partner, which makes the relationship seem more genuine and closer compared to those offline.

Identity Construction: Creating a digital self-image.

Identity Reconstruction: Crafting a digital self by deliberately choosing what parts to portray.

Impression Management: The conscious or unconscious process of controlling how others perceive you.

Networked Publics: Spaces formed and structured by digital technology, such as social media.

Proteus Effect: When characteristics of online personas or avatars influence behaviour offline.

Pseudonymity: Hiding your identity while using a consistent pseudonym.

Signalling: Cues and behaviours made to convey intentions when communication is inefficient.

Staged Authenticity: Curating a "genuine" image to seem relatable to an audience that seeks authenticity.

Technoself: The experience of the self in digital environments.

ENDNOTES

1 Interactive Model of Communication: a two-way process where the participants take turns to convey a message and provide feedback, forming a continuous loop (Wood, 2009)

2 Online Disinhibition Effect (Suler, 2004). This will be further discussed in section 4.

3 Social Identity Theory (Tajfel & Turner, 1986)

4 Self-categorisation Theory (Turner et al., 1987)

5 The infosphere is the total environment of information, encompassing all data, communication, and knowledge, both online and offline, where informational entities (like humans, AI, and data) interact. It's a metaphysical space or a "global shell" of information, representing our information-saturated reality, raising ethical questions about data, privacy, and identity (Floridi, 2015).

6 Different from identity construction, which is the development of a self-definition (Huang et al., 2021).

7 a societal state where shared moral standards break down, leading to confusion, instability, and a loss of purpose, as people become uncertain about what's right or wrong (Emile Durkheim, through Gonzales, 2024).

8 Research in political psychology, particularly concerning authoritarian regimes, has shown an association between anonymity and increased civic engagement, attributed to reduced fear of reprisal (Haimson & Hoffmann, 2016; Khan, 2025). In a networked authoritarianism, states may instead employ "real-name Internet" policies to consolidate social control, reframing authenticity as loyalty, thereby portraying pseudonymity as deception.

9 Individuals, in general, tend to associate and bond with similar others, by beliefs, attitudes, identity, demographics, this is known as *homophily* (McPherson et al., 2001). This association validates their shared meanings, which strengthen and reinforce their shared identity. As a result, they form stronger bonds and increase their social distance from those who are perceived as different, or the out-group

Chapter 5
The Psychological Rewards of Online Self-Disclosure

Szde Yu
http://orcid.org/0009-0007-2771-6075
Wichita State University, USA

ABSTRACT

This chapter is aimed to address a very common phenomenon in which many online users voluntarily disclose their personal information, while knowing that such self-disclosure could jeopardize privacy. The concern about privacy invasion and the urge to disclose personal information seem to be at odds, but research suggests that the privacy concern does not really deter or mitigate people's desire to share personal information online. In this chapter, we look into the psychological rewards that encourage or entice people into self-disclosure despite the risks. Considering in some countries self-disclosure could actually lead to legal ramifications or government suppression, the psychological rewards must be significant enough to motivate such behavior. Of course, there can be other types of rewards, such as monetary gains, but this chapter focuses on the psychological aspects.

INTRODUCTION

In today's hyperconnected digital world, online self-disclosure has become a defining feature of modern communication. From status updates and personal stories on social media platforms to in-depth discussions in forums and comment sections, people are increasingly choosing virtual spaces to reveal their inner thoughts, emotions, and life experiences (Yau & Reich, 2019). While concerns about oversharing,

DOI: 10.4018/979-8-3373-5896-3.ch005

privacy breaches, and the potential negative consequences of digital vulnerability often dominate public discourse, there is another side to this phenomenon that deserves closer attention: the psychological rewards that come with sharing online.

Research in psychology and communication studies suggests that self-disclosure whether in person or online plays a crucial role in building and maintaining relationships, fostering emotional resilience, and promoting a sense of identity and belonging (Blackwell, Birnholtz, & Abbott, 2014; Walther, 1996). In digital environments, these benefits can be amplified by the unique features of online interaction, such as perceived anonymity, asynchronous communication, and the ability to connect with niche communities across geographical boundaries (Amichai-Hamburger & Ben-Artzi, 2003).

For many individuals, the internet offers a safe and accessible space to express themselves authentically without fear of immediate judgment or real-world repercussions. This can be especially empowering for those who struggle with face-to-face communication or belong to marginalized groups seeking understanding and solidarity (Subrahmanyam & Greenfield, 2008). Moreover, receiving likes, comments, and supportive messages in response to shared content can reinforce feelings of validation, acceptance, and social connectedness (Utz & Beukeboom, 2011).

Studies have also shown that emotional disclosure online can lead to improved mood and well-being, particularly when it results in positive feedback and reciprocal interactions (Chen & Liang, 2020). However, it's important to note that not all forms of self-disclosure yield positive outcomes as context, audience, and motivation play critical roles in determining whether the experience is beneficial or detrimental (Fox, Moreland, & Joiner, 2015).

This article delves into the psychological motivations behind online self-disclosure and examines the emotional and mental health benefits it can provide.

THE FORMS OF SELF-DISCLOSURE

Written Disclosure

Written self-disclosure refers to the act of revealing personal thoughts, emotions, experiences, or information about oneself through written communication. Written self-disclosure can take place in various formats, such as diary entries, journaling, letters, blog posts, status updates on social media, forum comments, and messages in online support groups (Subrahmanyam & Greenfield, 2008; Yau & Reich, 2019).

One of the key advantages of written self-disclosure is that it allows individuals time to reflect, edit, and control how much they reveal. This level of control can reduce anxiety and increase the likelihood of disclosure, especially among those who are shy or experience social anxiety (Blackwell, Birnholtz, & Abbott, 2014). Additionally, writing allows for asynchronous communication, meaning people can disclose at their own pace and receive responses later, which can be particularly beneficial in digital environments like online communities or therapy platforms (Amichai-Hamburger & Ben-Artzi, 2003).

Research has shown that written self-disclosure can lead to emotional relief and improved mental health. For example, expressive writing—writing about traumatic or stressful events—has been linked to reduced symptoms of depression and anxiety, as well as improved immune function (Pennebaker & Seagal, 1999). In digital spaces, sharing personal stories on platforms such as Facebook, Reddit, or personal blogs can also provide therapeutic benefits by fostering social support and validation from others (Utz & Beukeboom, 2011; Chen & Liang, 2020).

However, not all forms of written self-disclosure are equally beneficial. Disclosing to strangers without reciprocity or receiving negative feedback can lead to increased distress or vulnerability (Fox, Moreland, & Joiner, 2015). Therefore, the context, audience, and motivation behind the disclosure significantly influence its psychological outcomes.

In summary, written self-disclosure serves as both a tool for self-expression and a mechanism for emotional regulation. Whether through personal journals, digital storytelling, or online interaction, the written form enables individuals to process emotions, seek connection, and construct a coherent narrative of their identity.

Visual Disclosure

Visual self-disclosure refers to the act of revealing personal information, emotions, identity, or experiences through visual content such as photographs, videos, selfies, infographics, and digital art shared on social media platforms. In the digital age, platforms like Instagram, TikTok, Snapchat, and YouTube have transformed how individuals express themselves, allowing for a shift from primarily text-based communication to visually rich forms of self-presentation and storytelling (Chua & Chang, 2016; Manago, Taylor, & Greenfield, 2012).

Unlike written self-disclosure, visual self-disclosure offers a more immediate and emotionally resonant way to communicate one's inner world. A single image or short video can convey complex emotions, body language, environment, and identity markers that words alone may not capture effectively (Zywica & Danowski, 2008). This form of disclosure often plays a key role in impression management, relationship building, and emotional expression, especially among younger users who prioritize authenticity and visual connection (Utz & Muscanell, 2021).

Studies show that visual self-disclosure can enhance feelings of social connectedness and validation when met with positive feedback such as likes, comments, or shares (Chen & Liang, 2020). For example, posting a selfie or a personal photo can serve as an invitation for others to respond with empathy, support, or affirmation, thus reinforcing the discloser's sense of belonging and self-worth (Baker & Moore, 2008). Moreover, platforms like TikTok have become spaces for marginalized groups to share lived experiences through video diaries, contributing to mental health awareness and community building (Fox, Moreland, & Joiner, 2015).

However, visual self-disclosure also carries potential risks. Overexposure or pressure to maintain a curated online image can lead to anxiety, lowered self-esteem, or even identity fragmentation (Tandoc, Ferrucci, & Duffy, 2015). Additionally, the permanence and reach of visual content mean that disclosures can be misinterpreted, archived indefinitely, or used without consent, which poses unique privacy challenges compared to textual self-disclosure.

In sum, visual self-disclosure represents a powerful and evolving mode of communication that blends emotion, identity, and technology. Whether through a carefully edited Instagram post or a candid TikTok story, individuals continue to use visual media to connect, heal, and assert their presence in the digital world.

Audio Disclosure

Audio self-disclosure refers to the act of revealing personal thoughts, emotions, and experiences through spoken words shared via audio formats. This form of self-expression has gained popularity with the rise of digital platforms such as podcasts, voice messages, voice-based social apps (e.g., Clubhouse, Discord), and live-streamed audio conversations. Unlike written or visual self-disclosure, audio allows individuals to convey tone, emotion, and nuance without relying on physical appearance or text-based interpretation (Lambton-Black et al., 2021; Zhao, 2020).

One of the key psychological benefits of audio self-disclosure is its ability to foster intimacy and emotional connection. Hearing someone's voice can create a sense of closeness and authenticity that text alone may not achieve (Bull, 2016). For example, sharing a vulnerable story in a podcast episode or during an audio discussion can encourage reciprocal disclosures from listeners or participants, thereby building a sense of community and mutual understanding (Fox & Moreland, 2018).

Additionally, audio self-disclosure can serve therapeutic purposes. Voice journaling, for instance, has been used in mental health practices to help individuals process emotions and reflect on their experiences (Pennebaker & Smyth, 2016). Similarly, anonymous voice-sharing platforms allow users to express difficult emotions without fear of being visually identified, offering a safer space for those hesitant to disclose in face-to-face or video settings (Naslund et al., 2020).

However, like other forms of self-disclosure, audio sharing comes with potential risks. Once recorded and shared, audio content can be saved, replayed, and potentially misused, raising concerns about privacy and consent (Marwick & boyd, 2014). Moreover, the permanence of audio recordings can lead to anxiety over how one's voice or message might be perceived over time.

Despite these challenges, audio self-disclosure remains a powerful mode of communication. It enables individuals to share their inner lives in a way that feels both personal and expressive, bridging the gap between private reflection and public connection.

Behavioral/Implicit Disclosure

Behavioral or implicit self-disclosure refers to the unintentional or indirect ways individuals reveal personal information about themselves through their actions, particularly in digital environments. Unlike explicit forms of self-disclosure, such as writing a post, sharing a photo, or recording a voice message behavioral disclosure occurs through patterns of online behavior, including search queries, browsing history, app usage, geolocation data, and even typing speed or mouse movements (Zuboff, 2019; Lutz & Ranzini, 2020).

These forms of disclosure are often automatic and occur without conscious intent, yet they can reveal a wealth of personal information, including interests, emotional states, political views, and even psychological traits (Matz et al., 2017). For example, frequent visits to mental health websites may signal emotional distress, while late-night social media activity might reflect insomnia or mood fluctuations (De Choudhury, Gamon, & Counts, 2013).

From a psychological perspective, behavioral self-disclosure plays a subtle but powerful role in shaping digital identities and social impressions. Algorithms on platforms like Facebook, Instagram, and YouTube interpret these behavioral signals to tailor content, advertisements, and recommendations, effectively constructing a profile of the user based on their digital footprint (Andreassen et al., 2017). This can lead to a sense of personalization and relevance, enhancing user engagement and perceived connection to the platform (Naslund et al., 2020).

However, unlike intentional self-disclosure, behavioral disclosure often occurs without users' full awareness or consent, raising significant concerns about privacy, autonomy, and surveillance (Stoycheff, 2016). Because this form of self-disclosure is not always controllable, individuals may unknowingly reveal sensitive aspects of their identity or mental health, which can be exploited by third parties for commercial or political purposes (Couldry & Mejias, 2019).

Despite these risks, behavioral self-disclosure also has potential benefits, particularly in the field of mental health. Researchers have used digital behavior patterns, such as smartphone usage and social media activity to detect early signs of depression, anxiety, and other psychological conditions (Insel, 2017). These insights open new avenues for passive, real-time monitoring and intervention, especially in remote or underserved populations.

In conclusion, behavioral or implicit self-disclosure is an increasingly influential aspect of digital life. While it enables personalization and offers new tools for psychological insight, it also challenges traditional notions of privacy and consent. As technology continues to evolve, understanding the implications of these subtle forms of self-revelation becomes essential for both users and researchers.

Anonymous/Pseudonymous Disclosure

Anonymous and pseudonymous self-disclosure refers to the act of sharing personal thoughts, emotions, or experiences online without revealing one's real identity or using a fabricated or alternate identity (pseudonym). This form of self-expression is common in digital spaces such as discussion forums (e.g., Reddit), anonymous confession platforms (e.g., Whisper, Yik Yak), multiplayer gaming communities, and comment sections across social media and news websites (Blank, 2017; Zhao, 2020).

Psychologically, anonymity can lower barriers to self-disclosure by reducing fear of judgment, social repercussions, or damage to one's offline reputation (Joinson, 2001). This sense of safety enables individuals, especially those from stigmatized or marginalized groups to share deeply personal stories, mental health struggles, or taboo topics that they might otherwise withhold in identifiable settings (Baker & Moore, 2008). For example, users on subreddits like r/Depression or r/Anxiety often report feeling more comfortable disclosing emotional distress when their identities are concealed (Naslund et al., 2016).

Pseudonymity, where individuals use consistent but non-identifying usernames, offers an additional layer of control over self-presentation. It allows for sustained relationships and community building while still preserving privacy (Marwick & boyd, 2014). In this way, pseudonymous identities can become meaningful extensions of the self, enabling exploration of different aspects of personality, sexuality, or life experiences in a socially safe environment (Döring & Mohseni, 2019).

Research has shown that anonymous and pseudonymous disclosures can have therapeutic effects, including reduced psychological distress and increased feelings of support and validation (Chen & Liang, 2020). These forms of self-disclosure also foster inclusivity and diversity of voices in online discourse, especially among individuals who may feel silenced or judged in face-to-face interactions.

However, anonymity can also lead to negative behaviors such as trolling, cyberbullying, or misinformation, due to the perceived lack of accountability (Suler, 2004). Moreover, the absence of real-world consequences may encourage excessive self-disclosure that can be emotionally destabilizing or exploited by others (Fox, Moreland, & Joiner, 2015).

Despite these risks, anonymous and pseudonymous self-disclosure remains a vital part of the digital landscape. It provides a unique space for vulnerable populations to express themselves freely, seek help, and connect with others who share similar experiences, which offers both psychological relief and a sense of belonging.

THE PURPOSES OF SELF-DISCLOSURE

Emotional Regulation

Self-disclosure, whether verbal or written, explicit or implicit, public or private, plays a central role in how individuals construct identity, form relationships, and manage psychological well-being. Across various digital platforms and communication modes, people engage in self-disclosure to fulfill a range of emotional, social, and cognitive needs. From revealing deeply personal experiences to subtly signaling preferences through online behavior, self-disclosure is a multifaceted process that reflects both individual motivations and broader sociocultural dynamics (Walther, 1996; Utz & Beukeboom, 2011).

One of the primary purposes of self-disclosure is emotional regulation and psychological relief. Expressing one's thoughts and feelings whether through writing a journal entry, posting a photo on Instagram, recording a voice message, or anonymously sharing on a forum can help individuals process emotions, reduce internal conflict, and achieve a sense of catharsis (Pennebaker & Smyth, 2016; Chen & Liang, 2020). This is especially true when disclosures are met with empathy, validation, or support, reinforcing the therapeutic potential of self-expression in both clinical and informal settings (Baker & Moore, 2008; Naslund et al., 2016).

Emotional regulation refers to the processes individuals use to influence their own emotional experiences, expressions, and responses (Gross, 1998). Online self-disclosure can be a powerful tool for managing emotions due to its accessibility, perceived anonymity, and the potential for social support.

How Online Self-Disclosure Facilitates Emotional Regulation

1. Catharsis and Affective Release

Sharing personal experiences online can provide a cathartic effect, allowing individuals to release pent-up emotions in a safe space. Writing or speaking about emotional events has been shown to reduce distress and improve well-being (Pennebaker & Beall, 1986). This process may be enhanced online because users can choose when, how much, and with whom to share.

2. Self-Awareness and Reflection

Online self-disclosure often involves articulating internal states, which can lead to greater self-awareness and emotional clarity. Expressing emotions in writing or verbal form helps individuals make sense of their experiences, contributing to better emotional regulation (Rude et al., 2004).

3. Social Support and Validation

Receiving feedback from others after disclosing online can validate one's feelings, normalize emotional experiences, and offer coping strategies. Social support is a key component in emotion regulation, especially during times of stress or crisis (Bar-Kalifa et al., 2019).

4. Controlled Disclosure

Compared to face-to-face interactions, online environments allow users to control the depth and timing of disclosure. This perceived control can reduce anxiety around sharing vulnerable information and facilitate healthier emotional expression (Subrahmanyam & Greenfield, 2008).

5. Reduced Inhibitions

The relative anonymity and physical distance provided by online platforms can lower inhibitions, making it easier for individuals to express emotions they might suppress in offline settings (Joinson, 2001). This reduced self-monitoring can promote more honest and emotionally revealing communication.

Relationship Building and Maintenance

Another key function of self-disclosure is relationship building and maintenance. Sharing personal information fosters trust, intimacy, and connection, even in online environments where physical presence is absent (Blackwell, Birnholtz, & Abbott, 2014). Whether it's through exchanging selfies, participating in voice chats, or engaging in pseudonymous conversations, individuals use self-disclosure to initiate and strengthen bonds with others, often creating virtual communities based on shared experiences or values (Döring & Mohseni, 2019; Manago, Taylor, & Greenfield, 2012).

Online self-disclosure plays a crucial role in forming and maintaining interpersonal relationships. In digital environments, where face-to-face interaction is limited or absent, sharing personal information becomes a primary means of establishing trust, intimacy, and connection (Walther, 1996). Through gradual and reciprocal exchanges of increasingly personal content, individuals build relational bonds that can mirror or even surpass those formed offline.

Key Mechanisms Linking Online Self-Disclosure to Relationship Development

1. Reciprocity and Social Exchange One of the foundational principles of relationship formation is reciprocity, which means when one person discloses something personal, the other often responds in kind (Altman & Taylor, 1973). Online environments facilitate this process by allowing users to control the depth and timing of their disclosures, enabling gradual relationship development at a comfortable pace.

2. Development of Trust and Intimacy Self-disclosure fosters perceived closeness and trust between individuals. Research shows that people who disclose more about themselves online are seen as more likable and trustworthy (Walther, 1996). As relationships progress, deeper levels of disclosure contribute to emotional intimacy, even in text-based interactions.

3. Maintenance of Existing Relationships Social media and messaging platforms allow individuals to maintain contact with friends and family across time and space. Regular updates, personal stories, and shared experiences help sustain feelings of connectedness, especially when physical interaction is not possible (Baker & Moore, 2018).

4. Identity Expression and Affiliation Online self-disclosure enables individuals to express their identities and values, which can attract like-minded others and strengthen group belonging. This is particularly important for marginalized communities or individuals seeking peer support (Blackwell et al., 2015).

5. Supportive Communication Sharing personal struggles or successes online often elicits supportive responses, reinforcing relational bonds. These interactions provide emotional validation and reinforce commitment, key components of healthy and enduring relationships (Fox & Moreland, 2015).

Online self-disclosure is a powerful mechanism for both initiating and sustaining relationships. By facilitating reciprocity, fostering trust and intimacy, enabling ongoing communication, and promoting identity expression, digital self-disclosure supports meaningful social connections. As technology continues to shape how we interact, understanding these dynamics becomes essential for navigating modern relationships.

IDENTITY CONSTRUCTION AND EXPLORATION

Self-disclosure also supports identity construction and exploration. In digital spaces, users can experiment with different aspects of their personality, beliefs, or appearance, particularly through visual and pseudonymous disclosure, without fear of immediate judgment (Marwick & boyd, 2014; Chua & Chang, 2016). This is especially valuable for marginalized or vulnerable populations who may find greater freedom and acceptance online than in offline contexts (Subrahmanyam & Greenfield, 2008; Fox, Moreland, & Joiner, 2015). Thus, online self-disclosure plays a significant role in how individuals construct, express, and explore their identities. These platforms serve as dynamic environments for both identity performance and self-discovery, especially during developmental stages like adolescence and emerging adulthood.

Key Mechanisms Linking Online Self-Disclosure to Identity Development

1. Self-Presentation and Impression Management

Social media and online communities allow individuals to curate their self-presentation through text, images, and multimedia content. By selectively disclosing personal information, users shape how others perceive them, reinforcing or redefining aspects of their identity (Goffman, 1959; Zhao, Grasmuck, & Martin, 2008).

2. Identity Experimentation

The relative anonymity and flexibility of online environments provide opportunities for users to try out different versions of themselves without the immediate consequences of face-to-face interactions. This can be particularly valuable for individuals exploring marginalized or stigmatized identities (Subrahmanyam & Greenfield, 2008).

3. Feedback and Affirmation

Reactions from others to one's disclosures help validate or challenge emerging identities. Positive reinforcement from peers can strengthen self-concept, while critical responses may prompt further reflection and identity refinement (Murray & Coulson, 2010).

4. Community Affiliation and Belonging

Sharing experiences related to identity (e.g., cultural background, sexual orientation, political views) helps individuals connect with like-minded communities. These affiliations contribute to a sense of belonging and reinforce personal identity narratives (Blackwell, Birnholtz, & Abbott, 2015).

5. Narrative Self-Construction

Regular self-disclosure on platforms such as blogs, vlogs, or social media allows users to craft a coherent narrative about themselves over time. This ongoing storytelling process supports the integration of past experiences, current feelings, and future aspirations into a unified sense of self (Bamberg & Andrews, 2004).

Online self-disclosure serves as a powerful tool for identity construction and exploration. Through curated self-presentation, experimentation, peer feedback, community affiliation, and narrative development, individuals use digital platforms to actively shape and understand who they are. As technology continues to evolve, so too do the ways in which people engage in identity work online, making this an essential area of psychological inquiry.

Practical and Functional

Moreover, self-disclosure serves practical and functional purposes, such as seeking advice, gaining social validation, or accessing resources. Behavioral self-disclosure, though often unintentional, plays a growing role in shaping personalized experiences online, influencing everything from targeted advertising to mental health monitoring (Zuboff, 2019; Insel, 2017). While these insights can enhance user experience, they also raise ethical concerns about consent, surveillance, and data privacy (Couldry & Mejias, 2019; Stoycheff, 2016).

Among these, self-promotion and professional networking stand out as increasingly important motivations for disclosing personal information online. In a world where digital presence can significantly influence career opportunities, reputation, and social capital, individuals strategically use self-disclosure to shape perceptions, build networks, and advance their professional goals (Zhao, Grasmuck, & Martin, 2008).

Strategic Self-Promotion Through Online Self-Disclosure

Self-promotion refers to the deliberate effort to present oneself in a favorable light in order to gain social or professional advantages (Leary & Kowalski, 1990). In digital contexts, this often involves disclosing achievements, skills, affiliations, and experiences that align with one's desired image.

1. Curated Personal Branding: Platforms like LinkedIn, Twitter/X, and even Instagram allow users to construct a consistent narrative about who they are professionally and personally. By selectively sharing accomplishments, articles, speaking engagements, or endorsements, individuals craft a personal brand that reflects expertise, credibility, and visibility (Mazman & Usluel, 2010).
2. Visibility and Recognition: Many professionals use platforms such as blogs, podcasts, or YouTube to share knowledge and insights. These forms of self-disclosure not only showcase competence but also increase digital visibility, which can lead to invitations for collaborations, media appearances, or job offers.
3. Highlighting Soft Skills and Cultural Fit: Beyond technical abilities, employers and collaborators often seek individuals who fit well within organizational cultures. Disclosing personal values, teamwork experiences, or leadership moments allows individuals to demonstrate soft skills like communication, adaptability, and emotional intelligence (Hargittai & Hinnant, 2008).
4. Portfolio Building: Freelancers, artists, designers, and other creatives often use platforms like Behance, GitHub, or personal websites to disclose work samples. This type of self-disclosure functions both as a portfolio and as evidence of ongoing engagement in their field.
5. Networking for Visibility: Posting regularly about industry trends, commenting on others' content, or participating in discussions increases the likelihood of being noticed by potential mentors, clients, or recruiters. These behaviors serve as digital impression management strategies that enhance one's perceived value in professional circles (Walther, 1996).

Professional Networking and Career Development

1. Online self-disclosure plays a pivotal role in forming and maintaining professional connections. The ability to manage impressions, articulate qualifications, and engage meaningfully with others has made platforms like LinkedIn essential tools for career advancement.
2. Building a Digital Résumé: Unlike traditional résumés, online profiles allow for richer, multimedia-enhanced representations of one's experience. Individuals disclose employment history, certifications, recommendations, and project highlights often with embedded links and visual elements to create a dynamic professional identity (Boyd, 2014).
3. Connecting with Industry Peers: Social media platforms enable users to follow thought leaders, join niche groups, and participate in virtual events. By disclosing interests, asking questions, and sharing insights, users can establish themselves within professional communities and initiate meaningful connections.

4. Job Searching and Recruitment: Employers frequently review candidates' online presence before making hiring decisions. Therefore, individuals may proactively disclose relevant credentials, volunteer work, or side projects to enhance employability and differentiate themselves from other applicants (Hargittai & Shafer, 2006).
5. Collaboration Opportunities: Disclosing research findings, publications, or creative works online can attract interest from peers seeking collaborators. Academics, entrepreneurs, and innovators often use platforms like ResearchGate, Medium, or GitHub to share progress and invite feedback or partnerships.
6. Maintaining Professional Relationships: Regular updates, comments, and messages help sustain long-distance professional relationships. These disclosures keep individuals "top of mind" and maintain rapport over time, even when face-to-face interaction is limited (Ellison, Steinfield, & Lampe, 2007).

Ethical and Psychological Considerations

While self-promotion and professional networking through online self-disclosure offer tangible benefits, they also raise ethical and psychological concerns:

1. Authenticity vs. Performance: Overly curated personas can blur the line between authenticity and performance. Users must balance the desire to impress with the need to remain genuine, as audiences often respond negatively to perceived inauthenticity (Marwick & boyd, 2011).
2. Privacy Trade-offs: Sharing professional details online often requires revealing personal information, potentially compromising privacy. Users must weigh the benefits of visibility against risks such as data misuse or unwanted exposure.
3. Social Comparison: Constant exposure to others' professional successes can foster feelings of inadequacy or competition. This phenomenon, known as upward social comparison, may reduce self-esteem among frequent users (Chou & Edge, 2012).

Online self-disclosure extends beyond emotional expression and relationship-building to serve critical functional roles in professional development. Through self-promotion and strategic networking, individuals use digital platforms to manage reputations, access opportunities, and build careers. As the boundaries between personal and professional identities continue to blur in digital spaces, understanding how and why people disclose information online becomes essential for both users and organizations.

Other Practical and Functional Purposes

1. Accessing Services and Building Digital Trust

Many online services, such as banking, healthcare portals, and educational platforms require some level of self-disclosure to verify identity and provide personalized experiences. Users often disclose personal information to access tailored content or secure services (Dinev & Hart, 2006).

2. Reputation Management

Individuals strategically disclose or withhold information online to shape how they are perceived by others. This includes managing impressions on dating apps, job candidate profiles, or community forums, where reputation can influence real-life outcomes (Zhao et al., 2008).

3. Community Participation and Civic Engagement

People engage in self-disclosure to participate in discussions about social issues, politics, or advocacy efforts. Sharing personal perspectives can foster collective action and enhance civic engagement, especially among younger populations (Bennett, 2008).

4. Seeking Advice and Problem-Solving

Online forums, Q&A sites (e.g., Reddit, Stack Exchange), and social media groups allow users to disclose personal challenges in order to receive advice, feedback, or solutions from knowledgeable peers (Nadkarni & Hofmann, 2012).

5. Marketing and Consumer Behavior

Consumers often disclose preferences, demographics, and behaviors through likes, shares, and reviews. Companies use this data for targeted advertising, product development, and customer relationship management, turning self-disclosure into a transactional tool (Turow, Hennessy, & Draper, 2015).

Beyond its psychological and social implications, online self-disclosure has significant practical value. It enables individuals to navigate professional landscapes, access essential services, manage their digital reputations, contribute to civic discourse, solve problems collaboratively, and participate in consumer culture. Understanding these functional dimensions is crucial for both users and organizations seeking to leverage digital platforms effectively.

Advocacy/Activism

In recent years, online self-disclosure has become a powerful vehicle for advocacy and activism, allowing individuals to share personal stories that raise awareness, mobilize support, and drive social change. By disclosing experiences related to discrimination, mental health, gender identity, political injustice, or other socio-political issues, users can transform their personal narratives into public discourse that challenges dominant ideologies and promotes collective action (Bennett & Segerberg, 2013).

How Online Self-Disclosure Supports Advocacy and Activism

1. Personal Stories as Political Tools One of the most significant ways people engage in activism online is through personal narrative disclosure—sharing lived experiences of marginalization, trauma, or resilience. These disclosures humanize abstract issues, making them more relatable and compelling to broader audiences. For example, the #MeToo movement gained momentum through survivors sharing their stories of sexual harassment and assault on social media platforms (Gill & Orgad, 2018).

2. Amplifying Marginalized Voices Online spaces provide a platform for historically underrepresented groups, such as LGBTQ+ individuals, racial minorities, and people with disabilities to disclose their realities and challenge systemic inequities. This form of digital testimony empowers marginalized voices and contributes to counter-narratives that resist dominant cultural discourses (Jackson et al., 2020).

3. Fostering Solidarity and Collective Identity When individuals publicly disclose shared struggles, they contribute to the formation of collective identities around specific causes. This sense of solidarity can galvanize communities and encourage coordinated action, such as participating in protests, signing petitions, or supporting policy changes (Tufekci, 2017).

4. Accessing and Mobilizing Networks Social media platforms enable rapid dissemination of advocacy messages. Personal disclosures about injustices or personal hardships often go viral, reaching wide audiences and prompting engagement from influencers, journalists, and policymakers. The networked nature of digital platforms allows individual acts of self-disclosure to scale into large-scale social movements (Earl & Kimport, 2011).

5. Emotional Engagement and Empathy Building Emotional storytelling is a key component of effective advocacy. Disclosing vulnerability or pain can evoke empathy

and motivate others to act. Research shows that emotionally charged content is more likely to be shared, increasing its visibility and impact (Pew Research Center, 2018).

6. Creating Safe Spaces for Disclosure Online communities often serve as supportive environments where individuals feel safe to disclose sensitive experiences related to activism. Hashtags like #BlackLivesMatter, #EndSARS, or #MyDepressionStory create virtual spaces where people can express themselves without fear of immediate judgment or retaliation (Bonilla & Rosa, 2015).

Online self-disclosure plays a vital role in modern advocacy and activism, transforming personal experiences into tools for social change. By sharing stories of injustice, individuals not only raise awareness but also build communities, inspire empathy, and mobilize action. As digital platforms continue to evolve, so too does the capacity for self-disclosure to influence public opinion and shape societal progress.

Performaing/Entertaining

In addition to fulfilling emotional, relational, professional, and activist functions, online self-disclosure also serves as a form of performance and entertainment. Many individuals use digital platforms not only to share information about themselves but also to craft engaging personas, entertain audiences, and participate in creative expression. This phenomenon is particularly evident on platforms like TikTok, Instagram, YouTube, Twitch, and Twitter/X, where users often blend personal disclosure with humor, storytelling, and aesthetic presentation to attract followers and build communities (Marwick, 2013).

How Online Self-Disclosure Functions as Performance and Entertainment

1. Digital Persona Construction Users curate and disclose aspects of their lives to construct a consistent and appealing digital persona, that is, a stylized version of themselves that aligns with the content they produce. This persona may include exaggerated traits, specific aesthetics, or recurring character roles that enhance entertainment value (Zhao, Grasmuck, & Martin, 2008). For example, influencers often disclose personal routines, opinions, or challenges while maintaining a charismatic and relatable image.

2. Audience Engagement Through Disclosure To maintain attention and grow their audience, content creators strategically disclose personal stories, emotions, and experiences that resonate emotionally or humorously with viewers. These disclosures are often crafted for maximum engagement, using humor, surprise, or vulnerability to keep audiences entertained and coming back for more (Burgess & Green, 2018).

3. Parasocial Relationships Regular self-disclosure helps creators foster parasocial relationships, such as one-sided emotional connections in which audiences feel personally connected to someone they follow online. By disclosing daily life events, struggles, or behind-the-scenes moments, creators simulate intimacy and familiarity, making viewers feel like they "know" them (Cohen, 2004).

4. Creative Storytelling and Aesthetic Expression Many users treat social media as a stage for creative performance, using multimedia tools to edit, script, and present their self-disclosure in visually and narratively compelling ways. Platforms like TikTok encourage users to combine music, filters, and choreography with personal narratives, transforming even mundane disclosures into entertaining performances (Abidin, 2016).

5. Viral Content and Meme Culture In meme culture and viral trends, self-disclosure often takes the form of humorous or ironic self-representation. Users post photos, videos, or captions that exaggerate personal flaws, quirks, or experiences for comedic effect. This type of disclosure blurs the line between authenticity and performance, as it is both self-expressive and intentionally entertaining (Davison, 2012).

6. Gamification of Identity On platforms such as Twitch or YouTube, performers often incorporate real-time interaction with their audience, turning self-disclosure into an interactive experience. Viewers may influence what the creator shares next, creating a gamified relationship where disclosure becomes part of a live, evolving show (Lewis et al., 2014).

Psychological and Social Motivations

1. Need for Recognition and Validation: The desire to be seen, liked, and followed motivates many to perform and entertain through self-disclosure. Likes, comments, and shares function as immediate feedback, reinforcing the behavior and encouraging continued performance (Chou & Edge, 2012).

2. Self-Expression and Identity Exploration: For some, performing online offers a space to explore different versions of the self in a playful, low-risk environment. This can be especially important for youth or marginalized groups seeking creative outlets (Subrahmanyam & Greenfield, 2008).

3. Monetization and Career Aspirations: Many creators view their online presence as a career path. In this context, self-disclosure becomes a strategic tool for building brand identity and attracting sponsorships or ad revenue (Abidin, 2018).

Risks and Ethical Considerations

1. Burnout and Emotional Labor: Constantly producing content and managing a public persona can lead to exhaustion and mental health strain.
2. Authenticity vs. Performance: Audiences may perceive over-curated content as inauthentic, potentially damaging trust and engagement.
3. Exploitation of Personal Life: Some creators disclose sensitive experiences primarily for views, risking emotional harm or exploitation.

Online self-disclosure has evolved beyond mere communication to become a form of digital performance and entertainment. Whether through curated personas, parasocial relationships, or creative storytelling, users engage in self-disclosure not only to connect or express themselves but also to captivate and amuse others. As digital platforms continue to blur the lines between private and public life, understanding the motivations and implications of this performative aspect of self-disclosure becomes increasingly important.

EXTERNAL FACTORS

Although self-disclosure seems to be an voluntary act, like many human behaviors that are inevitably subject to external influences and environmental limitations, online self-disclosure can be affected by many factors beyond the user's control.

AUDIENCE

While individuals often engage in online self-disclosure with specific intentions, such as emotional expression, relationship building, identity exploration, or entertainment, the audience to which they disclose remains an external and uncontrollable factor. Unlike face-to-face interactions, where speakers can gauge audience reactions and adjust disclosures accordingly, digital environments complicate this dynamic due to the asynchronous, public, and often unpredictable nature of online audiences (Walther, 1996).

Why the Audience Is Considered an External Factor

1. Unpredictable Composition

One of the most significant challenges of online self-disclosure is that users cannot always know who will view their content. A post intended for close friends may be seen by coworkers, family members, or strangers, leading to unintended consequences (boyd, 2014). This unpredictability makes it difficult for users to tailor disclosures effectively.

2. Context Collapse

Scholars use the term context collapse to describe the phenomenon in which multiple social contexts merge into one, making it hard for users to manage different relationships simultaneously (Marwick & boyd, 2014). For example, a humorous or personal story shared on social media might reach both professional contacts and intimate friends, creating confusion about how to interpret or respond to the message.

3. Lack of Immediate Feedback

In offline settings, individuals receive immediate nonverbal cues, such as facial expressions, body language, tone of voice that help them regulate how much and what they disclose. In contrast, digital platforms often delay or obscure audience feedback, leaving users uncertain about how their disclosures are being received (Walther, 1996).

4. Audience Interpretation and Misinterpretation

Once content is posted online, users lose control over how it is interpreted. Even carefully crafted disclosures can be misunderstood, taken out of context, or used against the discloser. Memes, screenshots, or quotes can circulate independently of the original intent, further distancing the user from the narrative (Papacharissi, 2011).

5. Viral Spread and Loss of Control

Content shared online can go viral, reaching millions of people beyond the original intended audience. While viral fame can be beneficial for influencers or activists, it also exposes users to scrutiny, criticism, and even harassment from unexpected quarters (Abidin, 2018).

Psychological and Behavioral Implications

1. Self-Censorship: Due to concerns about audience interpretation, many users practice self-censorship, choosing not to disclose certain thoughts or experiences online (De Choudhury et al., 2016).

2. Strategic Disclosure: Some users attempt to mitigate risks by adjusting their privacy settings, using pseudonyms, or crafting ambiguous posts. However, these strategies are not foolproof and do not eliminate the influence of external audiences entirely (Lampe, Ellison, & Steinfield, 2007).
3. Emotional Impact: Negative audience reactions, such as trolling, cyberbullying, or shamin can have serious emotional consequences, including anxiety, depression, and decreased self-esteem (Tokunaga, 2010).
4. Reputation Management: Given the visibility of online disclosures, users must constantly monitor and manage how they are perceived by diverse audiences, especially when balancing personal and professional identities (Zhao, Grasmuck, & Martin, 2008).

The audience plays a critical role in shaping the experience and consequences of online self-disclosure, yet it remains largely outside the direct control of the individual. Because of the unpredictable composition, potential for misinterpretation, and lack of real-time feedback, users must navigate a complex and often risky landscape when deciding what to share. Understanding the dynamics of audience influence is essential for both researchers studying self-disclosure and users seeking to manage their digital presence responsibly.

CONTROL

In the context of online self-disclosure, control refers to the extent to which individuals can regulate what they reveal about themselves, who accesses this information, and how it is used or interpreted. While users may attempt to exert control through privacy settings, selective sharing, or strategic language, digital environments inherently limit full control, making it an external and partially uncontrollable factor in the self-disclosure process (Joinson, 2008).

Why Control Is Considered an External Factor

1. Limited Control Over Information Spread

Once something is posted online, users cannot fully control its distribution or permanence. Even with privacy settings enabled, content can be shared, screenshotted, or archived without consent, leading to unintended visibility and long-term exposure (Trepte & Reinecke, 2013).

2. Platform Algorithms and Visibility

Social media platforms use algorithms to determine what content appears in users' feeds, often prioritizing engagement over user intent. As a result, a post intended for a small audience might reach many more people due to algorithmic amplification, or conversely, be hidden from those the user intended to see it (Gillespie, 2010).

3. Third-Party Access and Data Mining

Users often have little insight into how their disclosed data is collected, stored, or used by third parties such as advertisers, governments, or researchers. Platforms may monetize personal data or experience breaches, further diminishing user control over self-disclosed information (boyd & Crawford, 2012).

4. Interpretation Beyond User Intent

Just as users cannot control who sees their content, they also cannot dictate how others interpret it. Disclosures may be misunderstood, misquoted, or taken out of context—especially when shared beyond the original audience (Marwick & boyd, 2014). This loss of narrative control can lead to reputational damage or emotional distress.

5. Regret and Post-Disclosure Emotions

Due to the irreversible nature of online disclosures, users may later regret what they shared. However, even if posts are deleted, they may persist in cached versions, archives, or in the memories of those who viewed them (Blank, 2017).

Psychological and Behavioral Implications

1. Privacy Concerns and Risk Perception: Awareness of limited control leads many users to engage in privacy protective behaviors, such as limiting what they disclose, using pseudonyms, or avoiding certain platforms altogether (Dienlin & Metzger, 2016).
2. Strategic Self-Censorship: Some users choose not to disclose at all or only selectively due to fears of misuse, judgment, or surveillance. This self-censorship can impact emotional expression and social connection (De Choudhury et al., 2016).
3. Trust in Platform Governance: Users' willingness to disclose depends on their perceived trustworthiness of platform policies. When platforms fail to protect user data or enforce community guidelines effectively, trust erodes, and disclosure decreases (Larose & Rifon, 2007).

4. Digital Literacy and Agency: Those who understand digital systems better, such as how algorithms work, how data is tracked, or how screenshots spread are more likely to make informed disclosure decisions, though they still face external constraints (Livingstone, 2008).

Control is a critical yet externally constrained element in the process of online self-disclosure. While users may intend to manage what they share and with whom, the realities of digital environments, such as algorithmic visibility, data extraction, and unpredictable dissemination limit their ability to fully control outcomes. Recognizing these external constraints is essential for understanding both the risks and motivations behind online self-disclosure behavior.

ANONYMITY

Anonymity plays a significant role in shaping how individuals engage in online self-disclosure. Unlike face-to-face interactions, where identity is typically known and visible, digital environments often allow or even encourage users to disclose personal information without revealing who they are. This external condition of anonymity can significantly affect the depth, honesty, and emotional tone of self-disclosure (Joinson, 2001). However, because anonymity is not always fully within a user's control (e.g., due to platform design or data tracking), it functions as an external factor that influences but is not entirely determined by individual choice.

Why Anonymity Is Considered an External Factor

1. Platform Design Determines Identity Options

Whether or not users can remain anonymous depends largely on the design and policies of the platform. For example, platforms like Reddit and Whisper offer pseudonymous or fully anonymous posting options, whereas others like Facebook require real-name registration. Thus, anonymity is not solely under the user's control as it is shaped by the digital environment (Marwick & boyd, 2014).

2. Reduced Accountability and Inhibition

Anonymity reduces perceived accountability for one's actions, which can lead to both increased openness and risky or antisocial behaviors. This phenomenon, known as the online disinhibition effect, allows users to express thoughts and emotions they might suppress in identifiable contexts (Suler, 2004).

3. Unpredictable Exposure Risk

While some users believe they are anonymous online, metadata, IP tracking, or de-anonymization techniques can reveal their identities without consent. As such, true anonymity is often uncertain, making it an externally mediated condition rather than a guaranteed state (Zimmer, 2010).

4. Audience Uncertainty

When disclosing anonymously, users often lack information about who will view their content or how it will be used. This uncertainty about audience further distances them from full control over the consequences of their disclosures (Lapidot-Lefler & Barak, 2012).

5. Temporal Nature of Anonymity

Content posted anonymously may become associated with a real identity over time, especially if users later link accounts or if their identity is revealed through social connections. Therefore, anonymity may be temporary rather than absolute, reinforcing its status as an external and shifting condition (Tufekci, 2014).

Psychological and Behavioral Impacts of Anonymity

1. Increased Emotional Disclosure: Research consistently shows that people tend to disclose more vulnerable, emotional, or taboo topics when they believe they are anonymous (Baker & Moore, 2018). This makes anonymous platforms valuable for mental health support and crisis intervention.
2. Support for Marginalized Voices: Anonymity enables individuals from stigmatized or vulnerable groups, such as LGBTQ+ youth, survivors of abuse, or political dissidents to speak freely without fear of retaliation (Harper et al., 2019).
3. Risk of Misuse and Trolling: On the flip side, anonymity can facilitate toxic communication, harassment, and misinformation, as users feel less bound by social norms or consequences (Postmes, Spears, & Lea, 1998).
4. Emotional Relief and Catharsis: Disclosing anonymously can provide a sense of relief, particularly when individuals feel unable to share sensitive experiences in identifiable settings (Rains, 2017).
5. Trust in the System: Users' willingness to disclose under anonymity often depends on their trust in the platform to maintain confidentiality. Breaches of

trust, such as leaks or identity exposure can discourage future self-disclosure (Dienlin & Metzger, 2016).

Anonymity is a powerful external factor that shapes the nature and extent of online self-disclosure. It can enable greater openness and emotional expression, especially among those who fear judgment or harm. However, because anonymity is influenced by platform policies, technological capabilities, and unpredictable exposure risks, it remains partially beyond the user's direct control. Understanding this dynamic is essential for researchers, designers, and users alike, particularly when considering how anonymity affects well-being, community building, and digital safety.

RISKS

Another key external factor that is often beyond the user's control is risk. There are several potential risks associated with self-disclosure.

Psychological Risks

1. Mental Health Consequences

Excessive or inappropriate self-disclosure online has been linked to various mental health issues, including depression, anxiety, and low self-esteem. Research suggests that individuals who frequently post personal content may experience heightened social comparison, particularly when they perceive others' lives as more fulfilling or successful (Chou & Edge, 2012). These comparisons can lead to feelings of inadequacy and decreased well-being.

Moreover, oversharing intimate details without receiving the expected emotional support can result in disappointment, loneliness, and even rejection from peers (Fox & Moreland, 2015).

2. Loss of Privacy Awareness

Frequent self-disclosure can desensitize individuals to the long-term consequences of revealing personal information. Over time, people may develop a diminished sense of privacy, leading to habitual disclosure of sensitive data without fully considering the implications (Bartsch & Dienlin, 2016).

Social Risks

1. Damaged Relationships

Online self-disclosure can strain interpersonal relationships, especially when shared content is misinterpreted or considered inappropriate. For instance, posting private conversations, grievances about friends or partners, or controversial opinions can lead to conflicts, misunderstandings, or social ostracism (McDaniel & Coyne, 2016).

Additionally, the permanence of online content means that past disclosures can resurface and affect current relationships, sometimes years after the original post.

2. Reputational Harm

Personal disclosures, especially those involving risky behavior, controversial views, or unprofessional conduct, can negatively impact an individual's reputation among colleagues, employers, or educational institutions. Employers often review applicants' social media profiles, and inappropriate content can lead to hiring discrimination (Hargittai & Litt, 2019).

Security and Identity Risks

1. Identity Theft and Fraud

Sharing personal details such as birth dates, addresses, phone numbers, or family members' names can provide cybercriminals with enough information to commit identity theft or fraud. Phishing attacks and targeted scams often exploit publicly available personal data to manipulate victims (Dinev & Hart, 2006).

2. Cyberstalking and Harassment

Oversharing can make individuals vulnerable to cyberstalking, harassment, or real-world threats. Personal location check-ins, daily routines, and relationship statuses can be exploited by malicious actors to track or target individuals (Spitzberg & Hoobler, 2002).

3. Data Exploitation by Third Parties

Even when users attempt to control their privacy settings, personal information shared online can be harvested by third parties through data mining, cookies, or breaches. This data can be used for targeted advertising, political manipulation, or sold on the black market (Zuboff, 2019).

Legal and Ethical Considerations

Self-disclosure can have legal ramifications, particularly when it involves defamation, hate speech, or the unauthorized sharing of others' private information. In some jurisdictions, individuals have faced lawsuits or criminal charges for content posted online (Solove, 2007).

Ethically, users must consider the impact of their disclosures on others, especially when sharing content that includes friends, family, or colleagues without consent.

While online self-disclosure offers opportunities for connection and expression, it also presents substantial risks across psychological, social, and security domains. Users must remain vigilant about what they share, how they share it, and with whom. Educating individuals, particularly younger users about responsible digital behavior, privacy settings, and the potential consequences of oversharing is essential. As technology continues to evolve, so too must our understanding of its impacts on personal safety and well-being.

PSYCHOLOGICAL REWARDS

Despite the risks, online self-disclosure is still a prevalent phenomenon. This phenomenon known as the privacy paradox describes the contradiction between individuals' concerns about online privacy and their willingness to disclose personal information on digital platforms (Barkhuus & Tashiro, 2013; Dienlin & Metzger, 2016). Research suggests that despite being aware of potential risks such as data misuse or identity theft, users often prioritize social benefits, self-expression, and connection over privacy protection (Goswami & Saxena, 2020; Kokilaj, 2020). This behavior is particularly prevalent among younger generations, who engage in strategic self-disclosure to manage their online identities, even when they recognize the associated dangers (Lanier & Chitrapornprasert, 2019; Taddicken, 2014). The persistence of this paradox highlights the complex decision-making processes involved in online self-disclosure, where perceived utility and social norms frequently outweigh privacy concerns (Bolton et al., 2018; Xu et al., 2012).

Conceivably, there must be sugnificant psychological rewards stemming from online self-disclosure to mitigate or offset the fear of risk.

EMOTIONAL CATHARSIS & STRESS REDUCTION

One of the most significant psychological rewards of online self-disclosure is its role in emotional release. Writing or talking about deeply felt emotions, even in a virtual space, can help individuals process and manage their feelings more effectively. This phenomenon aligns with the concept of catharsis, where expressing repressed emotions leads to a sense of relief and mental clarity (Pennebaker & Seagal, 1999). Social media platforms, blogs, and online forums often serve as outlets for such expression, allowing users to articulate complex emotions that they may not feel comfortable sharing in face-to-face interactions.

Moreover, studies have found that online self-disclosure can reduce psychological stress by activating social support networks. When individuals share personal struggles online, they often receive empathy, validation, and advice from others in similar situations (Barak et al., 2008). This feedback loop can enhance feelings of connectedness and belonging, which are essential for emotional well-being. In particular, anonymous online communities provide a safe environment for discussing stigmatized issues such as mental health, trauma, or addiction, thereby lowering barriers to emotional expression (Baker & Moore, 2008).

Neurological evidence also supports the idea that self-disclosure activates brain regions associated with reward and pleasure. Research using functional MRI scans has shown that sharing personal information triggers dopamine release, reinforcing the behavior and making it psychologically rewarding (Tamir & Mitchell, 2012). This neurochemical response may explain why people continue to engage in self-disclosure online despite potential risks to privacy.

Additionally, expressive writing, a structured form of self-disclosure, has been linked to improved mood and reduced symptoms of depression and anxiety (Smyth, 1998). Although traditionally conducted offline, many individuals now use digital tools and platforms to journal their thoughts, suggesting that the therapeutic benefits of expressive writing extend into the online realm.

In sum, while online self-disclosure carries certain risks, it also offers important psychological rewards, especially in the form of emotional catharsis and stress relief. By providing a platform for emotional expression and social support, digital environments can play a constructive role in mental health management when used mindfully and responsibly.

SOCIAL VALIDATION & BELONGING

Online self-disclosure serves not only as a means of self-expression but also as a powerful mechanism for seeking social validation and fostering a sense of belonging.

These psychological rewards play a crucial role in motivating individuals to continue engaging in self-disclosure behaviors, even when they are aware of potential risks such as privacy breaches or social judgment.

One of the most immediate benefits of online self-disclosure is the feedback it generates from others. Likes, comments, shares, and direct messages often function as forms of social validation, reinforcing users' self-worth and identity (Chua & Chang, 2016). This external affirmation can be particularly rewarding for individuals who struggle with low self-esteem or who seek reassurance in their offline lives. The positive reinforcement provided by digital interactions activates reward-related neural pathways, encouraging repeated engagement in self-disclosure (Burke et al., 2010).

Moreover, online self-disclosure facilitates a sense of belonging by connecting individuals with like-minded peers. Social media platforms, forums, and interest-based communities allow users to share personal stories and experiences with others who may have similar backgrounds or emotional struggles (Bessi et al., 2016). This shared experience fosters social bonds and reduces feelings of isolation, which is especially important in today's increasingly digital and sometimes socially fragmented world.

For adolescents and young adults, the need for peer approval and group inclusion is especially strong. Research indicates that this demographic frequently uses self-disclosure as a tool to build and maintain social identities online (Steinfield et al., 2008). By sharing aspects of their lives, individuals signal alignment with certain values, lifestyles, or ideologies, thereby gaining acceptance within specific online communities.

In summary, while online self-disclosure carries potential risks, it also offers significant psychological benefits, particularly through the mechanisms of social validation and belonging. These rewards help explain why people continue to disclose personal information despite concerns about privacy, underscoring the complex interplay between social needs and digital behavior.

IDENTITY EXPLORATION & CLARIFICATION

Online self-disclosure offers individuals a unique space for identity clarification and exploration, particularly during formative life stages such as adolescence and young adulthood. These psychological rewards contribute significantly to the appeal of digital self-expression, allowing users to refine their self-concept, experiment with different personas, and receive feedback from others in a relatively low-risk environment.

One of the key psychological benefits of online self-disclosure is its role in identity clarification. By articulating their beliefs, values, and experiences through posts, comments, or multimedia content, individuals gain greater insight into who they are and how they perceive themselves (Subrahmanyam & Greenfield, 2008). The act of self-disclosure encourages introspection and reflection, helping users organize and make sense of their internal experiences. This process is especially valuable during developmental periods when identity formation is central to psychological growth.

In addition to clarifying existing aspects of identity, online environments also support identity exploration. Digital spaces allow individuals to present alternative versions of themselves, try out new social roles, and engage with diverse communities that may not be accessible offline (Turkle, 1995). For example, marginalized youth or individuals questioning their gender, sexuality, or cultural identity often use online platforms to explore these dimensions safely and anonymously. Such experimentation can foster greater self-acceptance and resilience by validating emerging identities through peer interaction and support.

Furthermore, the interactive nature of online platforms enhances this process by enabling users to receive real-time responses to their disclosures. Feedback from others helps individuals assess how their self-presentations are perceived, which can further inform their evolving self-concept (Papacharissi, 2011). In this way, online self-disclosure functions not only as an individual act of self-reflection but also as a dynamic, socially mediated process of identity development.

In conclusion, beyond its emotional and social benefits, online self-disclosure plays a crucial role in facilitating identity clarification and exploration. By offering a flexible and responsive environment for self-expression, digital platforms empower users to better understand and shape their identities, contributing to healthy psychological development and self-awareness.

ENHANCED SOCIAL CONNECTION & INTIMACY

Online self-disclosure plays a critical role in fostering social connection and intimacy, particularly in an era where digital communication increasingly supplements or replaces face-to-face interaction. While concerns about privacy and oversharing are well documented, research consistently shows that strategic self-disclosure online can deepen interpersonal relationships, build trust, and enhance emotional closeness.

One of the primary ways online self-disclosure contributes to enhanced social connection is by facilitating ongoing communication across time and space (Ellison et al., 2007). Social media platforms, instant messaging apps, and video calls allow individuals to maintain contact with friends and family regardless of physical distance. By sharing updates, photos, and personal reflections, users create a continuous sense of presence and involvement in each other's lives, which strengthens relational bonds and fosters a feeling of connectedness.

Moreover, self-disclosure in digital environments can promote emotional intimacy, even among individuals who have never met in person. Research suggests that computer-mediated communication can support "hyperpersonal" interactions, where individuals disclose more personal information than they might in offline settings, often leading to stronger emotional ties (Walther, 1996). This phenomenon is particularly evident in long-distance relationships, online support groups, and close friendships maintained primarily through digital means.

In romantic relationships, online self-disclosure also plays a significant role in building intimacy and maintaining relational satisfaction. Couples who engage in frequent and meaningful communication via digital platforms report higher levels of emotional closeness and trust (Fox & Moreland, 2015). The ability to share thoughts and feelings instantly allows partners to remain emotionally attuned, even when physically apart.

In conclusion, while online self-disclosure carries potential risks, it also offers powerful psychological rewards, especially in terms of enhancing social connection and intimacy. By enabling deeper communication and sustained emotional engagement, digital self-disclosure supports meaningful relationships in both virtual and real-world contexts.

SENSE OF CONTROL

One of the primary ways online self-disclosure enhances a sense of control is through self-presentation management. Unlike face-to-face interactions, digital platforms allow individuals to carefully select, edit, and time their disclosures (Walther, 1996). This ability to craft and refine one's self-image gives users a heightened sense of agency over how they are perceived by others, which can be especially empowering for those who feel less confident in unstructured social settings. The option to delete, revise, or withhold content before posting allows individuals to maintain a desired identity and avoid unwanted misinterpretations.

Additionally, online self-disclosure can offer a sense of control over emotional expression. Digital environments provide a space where individuals can disclose at their own pace and on their own terms, often without the immediate pressure of real-time interaction (Lampe et al., 2014). This flexibility can be particularly valuable for individuals dealing with sensitive or traumatic experiences, as it allows them to share when they feel emotionally ready and in a context where they can manage the level of detail and audience response.

Moreover, the selective nature of disclosure online contributes to a greater sense of autonomy. Users can control who sees their content through privacy settings, friend lists, and group memberships, enabling them to disclose personal information only to trusted individuals or communities (Chua & Chang, 2016). This perceived control over audience and context enhances users' confidence in managing their digital identities and social relationships.

Thus, beyond its emotional and relational benefits, online self-disclosure provides individuals with a psychologically rewarding sense of control, allowing them to manage self-presentation, regulate emotional expression, and shape their social environments in a way that aligns with their personal needs and goals.

ALTRUISM

Online self-disclosure can also serve as a vehicle for altruistic behavior, offering individuals a sense of purpose and fulfillment through helping others. This psychological benefit is particularly evident in contexts where users share personal struggles, offer advice, or advocate for social causes, contributing to broader communal well-being while fulfilling their own emotional and social needs.

One of the key ways online self-disclosure fosters altruism is by enabling peer-to-peer support within digital communities. Platforms such as mental health forums, parenting groups, and chronic illness networks allow individuals to disclose personal challenges and coping strategies, often with the intent of helping others who are experiencing similar difficulties (Barak et al., 2008). This form of prosocial self-disclosure not only benefits recipients by providing emotional validation and practical guidance but also enhances the discloser's sense of empathy, competence, and social responsibility.

Moreover, online self-disclosure plays a central role in digital activism and advocacy, where individuals share personal stories related to social justice, discrimination, or personal trauma to raise awareness and inspire change (Fox et al., 2015). These disclosures can humanize complex issues and mobilize collective action, reflecting an altruistic motivation to contribute to societal progress. The anonymity and reach of online platforms often empower individuals to speak out in ways they might not feel comfortable doing offline.

Research also suggests that engaging in altruistic self-disclosure online activates reward-related brain regions, reinforcing prosocial behavior and contributing to greater psychological well-being for the discloser (Pavey et al., 2011). This dual benefit where both the individual and the community gain from the act of disclosure highlights the unique psychological value of altruistic motivations in digital communication.

In conclusion, beyond its personal and relational rewards, online self-disclosure can be driven by and result in altruistic outcomes, allowing individuals to support others, advocate for important causes, and derive a sense of meaning and fulfillment from their digital interactions.

REDUCED STIGMA & NORMALIZATION

Online self-disclosure can play a powerful role in reducing stigma and promoting the normalization of topics that are often considered taboo or socially uncomfortable. By enabling individuals to openly discuss issues such as mental health, chronic illness, sexuality, trauma, and other stigmatized experiences, online environments foster greater understanding, empathy, and social acceptance.

One of the most impactful ways online self-disclosure contributes to reduced stigma is by humanizing experiences that are often misunderstood or marginalized (Berry et al., 2017). When individuals share their personal stories, they provide visibility to conditions or circumstances that others may not fully understand. This transparency can challenge stereotypes, dispel myths, and encourage more compassionate attitudes within broader communities. For example, public disclosures about mental health struggles on platforms like Instagram, Twitter, or YouTube have been shown to increase awareness and reduce negative perceptions associated with psychological disorders (Naslund et al., 2016).

Moreover, the collective nature of online disclosure fosters normalization, particularly when multiple users share similar experiences. As more people speak openly about previously hidden topics, these experiences become integrated into everyday discourse, shifting cultural narratives and reducing feelings of isolation for those who identify with them (Christensen, 2009). This normalization effect is especially significant for individuals from stigmatized or minority groups, who may find validation and solidarity through shared disclosures in online spaces.

Additionally, online self-disclosure allows individuals to reclaim agency over their narratives. Rather than having their experiences defined by societal labels or media portrayals, users can assert their own voices and perspectives, contributing to a more nuanced and inclusive public understanding of diverse life experiences (Gillies et al., 2021).

Thereby, online self-disclosure serves as a powerful tool for reducing stigma and promoting normalization by empowering individuals and communities to reshape public perceptions and foster greater social inclusion.

COGNITIVE PROCESSING & PROBLEM SOLVING

One particularly compelling psychological reward is the cognitive processing and problem-solving enhancement that can result from articulating one's thoughts and emotions in an online environment.

Cognitive Processing Through Expression

One of the primary ways in which online self-disclosure contributes to psychological well-being is through its role in cognitive processing. When individuals write or speak about their experiences, they are often forced to organize their thoughts in a coherent manner. This process of externalizing internal states helps clarify complex emotions and events, allowing for more effective meaning-making (Pennebaker & Seagal, 1999). Writing or speaking about a problem forces individuals to structure their narrative, identify key themes, and begin to make sense of otherwise chaotic or overwhelming situations.

Online platforms, such as blogs, social media, or mental health forums provide accessible spaces where users can engage in this kind of reflective writing. Research suggests that expressive writing, even in informal digital formats, can lead to improved mood and reduced stress levels (Smyth, 1998). These benefits are thought to stem from the cognitive restructuring that occurs when individuals translate subjective experiences into language.

Problem-Solving Enhancement Through Feedback

Beyond individual reflection, online self-disclosure often invites feedback from others, which can significantly enhance problem-solving capabilities. Social media networks, support groups, and online communities provide opportunities for individuals to receive diverse perspectives, advice, and validation. This collaborative aspect of online disclosure can lead to novel insights and alternative strategies for dealing with personal challenges (Naslund et al., 2016).

For example, someone struggling with anxiety might post about their difficulties on a mental health forum and receive coping strategies from others who have faced similar issues. This exchange not only provides emotional support but also introduces practical solutions that the individual may not have considered independently. The availability of multiple viewpoints encourages critical thinking and expands the user's repertoire of coping mechanisms.

While online self-disclosure carries potential risks, it also offers significant psychological rewards in the domains of cognitive processing and problem-solving. By encouraging structured reflection, inviting collaborative feedback, promoting emotional regulation, and enhancing self-awareness, digital self-expression can be a powerful tool for personal growth and mental clarity. As online communication continues to evolve, understanding and harnessing these benefits can help individuals use digital platforms more intentionally and constructively.

CONCLUSION

This chapter provides a comprehensive view on voluntary sharing of personal thoughts, emotions, or experiences on digital platorms, also known as onilne self-disclosure. Different forms of self-disclosure provide different functionalities and serve different purposes. However, it is important to note that human behavior can serve more than one purpose or can be motivated by more than one desire. Therefore online self-disclosure can serve multiple purposes for the same person as well. Despite the different purposes and methods, the underlying mindset is similar in that people who actively engage in online self-disclosure must be gaining or at least seeking some rewards. While much research has focused on the risks associated with sharing personal experiences online (e.g., privacy concerns, vulnerability to cyberbullying), less attention has been paid to the psychological rewards that individuals may derive from such disclosures. Such rewards must be significant enough to help users disregard or tolerate those potential risks as also discussed previously in this chapter. There can be many types of rewards, but the scope of this chapter focuses on the psychological rewards.

Online self-disclosure is a way of life now for many people rather than something that should be banned or discouraged. Life is never without risks and flaws. While the downside needs to be concerned about, the bright side also deserves to be looked at. By addressing the psychological rewards, we can gain a better understanding on cyber behavior and cyber psychology, both of which are of paramount importance in studying today's social issues and human behavior since so much social interaction and transaction is happening via digital avenues nowadays. It helps rationalize what seems to be risk-taking decisions and therefore develop proper measures to reduce risk instead of simply telling people not to do it. It also helps raise awareness about potential psychological manipulation often seen in online propaganda, scam, and various cybercrimes. Furthermore, it has the potential to develop digital resources that can assist in the treatment of mental illness or psychotherapy.

REFERENCES

Abidin, C. (2016). Visibility labour: Engaging with influencers' fashion brands and #OOTD advertorial campaigns on Instagram. *Media International Australia, Incorporating Culture & Policy*, *161*(1), 86–100. DOI: 10.1177/1329878X16665177

Abidin, C. (2018). "Aren't these just young, rich women doing vain things?" Influencer vetting and branding on a micro-celebrity farm. *Social Media + Society*, *4*(2), 1–11. DOI: 10.1177/2056305118768687

Altman, I., & Taylor, D. A. (1973). *Social penetration: The development of interpersonal intimacy*. Holt, Rinehart & Winston.

Amichai-Hamburger, Y., & Ben-Artzi, E. (2003). Loneliness and sociability in cyberspace: A four-wave theory on the development of the Internet. *Computers in Human Behavior*, *19*(1), 7–28. DOI: 10.1016/S0747-5632(02)00076-1

Andreassen, C. S., Pallesen, S., & Griffiths, M. D. (2017). The relationship between addictive use of social media, narcissism, and self-esteem: Findings from a large national survey. *Addictive Behaviors*, *64*, 287–293. DOI: 10.1016/j.addbeh.2016.03.006 PMID: 27072491

Baker, E. K., & Moore, S. M. (2008). Internet support groups for depression: A review of the literature. *Archives of Psychiatric Nursing*, *22*(1), 20–28. DOI: 10.1016/j.apnu.2007.04.005 PMID: 18207053

Baker, K., & Moore, P. J. (2018). Social networking site use and perceived social capital: The role of perceived authenticity and self-disclosure. *Computers in Human Behavior*, *87*, 227–234. DOI: 10.1016/j.chb.2018.05.039

Baker, K. M., & Moore, S. M. (2008). Online support groups for illness: A review of empirical data. *Patient Education and Counseling*, *70*(3), 297–303. DOI: 10.1016/j.pec.2007.10.004

Bamberg, M., & Andrews, M. (2004). *Considering counter-identities: Introduction*. In M. Bamberg & M. Andrews (Eds.), *Considering counter-identities* (pp. 1–15). Narrative Inquiry Book Series.

Bar-Kalifa, S., Rafaeli, E., & Hall, J. A. (2019). The role of emotional support and reciprocal self-disclosure in affective outcomes: An observational study of online peer support. *Journal of Consulting and Clinical Psychology*, *87*(6), 536–549. DOI: 10.1037/ccp0000405

Barak, A., Hen, L., Boniel-Nissim, M., & Shapira, N. (2008). A comprehensive review and a meta-analysis of the effectiveness of internet-based psychotherapeutic interventions. *Journal of Technology in Human Services, 26*(2–4), 109–160. DOI: 10.1080/15228830802094429

Barkhuus, L., & Tashiro, C. (2013). Privacy vs. self-expression: Young adults' use of social media. In *Proceedings of the SIGCHI Conference on Human Factors in Computing Systems* (pp. 757–766). DOI: 10.1145/2470654.2466118

Bartsch, A., & Dienlin, T. (2016). Can't help myself: An experience sampling study on the role of self-control in young adults' problematic use of social network sites. *Computers in Human Behavior, 61*, 295–305. DOI: 10.1016/j.chb.2016.03.055

Bennett, W. L. (2008). Changing citizenship in the digital age. In Bennett, W. L. (Ed.), *Playing citizen: Youth, participatory politics, and the biographical frame* (pp. 1–29). University of Michigan Press.

Bennett, W. L., & Segerberg, A. (2013). *The logic of connective action: Digital media and the personalization of contentious politics*. Cambridge University Press. DOI: 10.1017/CBO9781139198752

Berry, N., Lobban, F., & Emsley, R. (2017). Social media use in psychosis: Benefits, risks and opportunities for research. *Current Opinion in Psychology, 18*, 45–50. DOI: 10.1016/j.copsyc.2017.07.023

Bessi, A., Petroni, F., Barrat, A., Cattuto, C., Castillo, C., Menczer, F., & Scala, A. (2016). User baseline popularity and attention half-life in social media. *EPJ Data Science, 5*(1), 39. DOI: 10.1140/epjds/s13688-016-0099-y

Blackwell, C., Birnholtz, J., & Abbott, A. (2014). Seeing myself through you: Emotional disclosure and relational closeness in online social networks. *Computers in Human Behavior, 36*, 161–170. DOI: 10.1016/j.chb.2014.03.052

Blackwell, C., Birnholtz, J., & Abbott, A. (2015). Seeing and being seen: Co-situation and impression formation using Grindr, a location-aware gay dating app. *New Media & Society, 17*(7), 1117–1136. DOI: 10.1177/1461444814521595

Blank, G. (2017). The Internet and the mass repersonalization of society. *Information Communication and Society, 20*(1), 1–19. DOI: 10.1080/1369118X.2016.1148186

Blank, G. (2017). The myth of internet anonymity: Why everything you do online can be traced. *First Monday, 22*(6). Advance online publication. DOI: 10.5210/fm.v22i6.7462

Bolton, R. N., Parasuraman, A., Hoefnagels, A., Migchels, N., Poulis, E., Blankaert, I., & Silvestre, B. S. (2018). Understanding Generation Z through innovation adoption lens: Implications for existing scale items. *Journal of Business Research, 93*, 343–354. DOI: 10.1016/j.jbusres.2017.12.023

Bonilla, Y., & Rosa, J. (2015). # Ferguson: Digital protest, hashtag ethnography, and the racial politics of social media in the United States. *American Ethnologist, 42*(1), 4–17. DOI: 10.1111/amet.12112

boyd, d., & Crawford, K. (2012). Critical questions for big data: Provocations for a cultural, technological, and scholarly phenomenon. *Information, Communication & Society, 15*(5), 662–679. DOI: 10.1080/1369118X.2012.678878

boyd, D. (2014). *It's complicated: The social lives of networked teens*. Yale University Press.

Bull, S. (2016). *Sound: An auditory anthropology*. Routledge.

Burgess, J., & Green, J. (2018). *YouTube: Digital media and society series* (2nd ed.). Polity Press.

Burke, M., Marraccini, M. E., & McGannon, K. R. (2010). The measurement of social network site usage and its relationship to social capital and well-being. *Proceedings of the SIGCHI Conference on Human Factors in Computing Systems*, 1191–1200. DOI: 10.1145/1753326.1753502

Chen, W., & Liang, Y. (2020). The emotional benefits of online self-disclosure: A meta-analysis. *Journal of Communication, 70*(4), 513–537. DOI: 10.1093/joc/jqaa019

Chou, H. G., & Edge, N. (2012). "They are happier and having better lives than I am": The impact of using Facebook on perceptions of others' lives. *Cyberpsychology, Behavior, and Social Networking, 15*(2), 117–121. DOI: 10.1089/cyber.2011.0324 PMID: 22165917

Christensen, K. S. (2009). The paradox of participation: Online personal narratives as performances of breast cancer. *Health Communication, 24*(3), 254–265. DOI: 10.1080/10410230902806948

Chua, T. H. H., & Chang, L. (2016). Follow me and like my beautiful, happy, successful life: The impact of following celebrity Instagram accounts on adolescent girls' body image satisfaction. *Body Image, 19*, 115–124. DOI: 10.1016/j.bodyim.2016.09.010

Cohen, J. (2004). Parasocial break-up: Responses to the ending of favorite TV programs. *Journal of Broadcasting & Electronic Media, 48*(4), 582–596. DOI: 10.1207/s15506878jobem4804_5

Couldry, N., & Mejias, U. A. (2019). *The costs of connection: How data is colonizing human life and appropriating it for capitalism.* Stanford University Press.

Davison, P. (2012). The language of internet memes. In Mandiberg, M. (Ed.), *The social media reader* (pp. 120–134). NYU Press. DOI: 10.18574/nyu/9780814764077.003.0013

De Choudhury, M., Gamon, M., & Counts, S. (2013). Predicting depression via social media activity. *Proceedings of the International AAAI Conference on Web and Social Media, 7*(1), 128–137.

Dienlin, T., & Metzger, M. J. (2016). An extended privacy calculus model for SNSs: Incorporating trust and social capital in privacy concerns. *Journal of Computer-Mediated Communication, 21*(5), 354–371. DOI: 10.1111/jcc4.12163

Dinev, T., & Hart, P. (2006). An extended privacy calculus model for e-commerce transactions. *Information Systems Research, 17*(1), 61–83. DOI: 10.1287/isre.1060.0080

Döring, N., & Mohseni, M. R. (2019). Digital intimacy: Conceptualizing intimate communication in computer-mediated contexts. *New Media & Society, 21*(3), 629–649. DOI: 10.1177/1461444818803962

Earl, J., & Kimport, K. (2011). *Digitally enabled social change: Activism in the Internet age.* MIT Press. DOI: 10.7551/mitpress/9780262015103.001.0001

Ellison, N. B., Steinfield, C., & Lampe, C. (2007). The benefits of Facebook "friends:" Social capital and college students' use of online social network sites. *Journal of Computer-Mediated Communication, 12*(4), 1143–1168. DOI: 10.1111/j.1083-6101.2007.00367.x

Fox, J., & Moreland, J. J. (2018). The role of social networking sites in romantic relationships: Effects on emotional intimacy and jealousy. *Cyberpsychology, Behavior, and Social Networking, 21*(5), 305–311. DOI: 10.1089/cyber.2017.0650

Fox, J., Moreland, J. J., & Joiner, T. E. (2015). The dark side of Facebook: The impact of rumination and self-disclosure on depressive symptoms. *Social Media + Society, 1*(1), 1–9. DOI: 10.1177/2056305115581158

Fox, J., Moreland, J. J., & Warber, K. M. (2015). Social networking site use and the gratification of perceived social capital and emotional support: The influence of communicative behaviors. *Communication Research Reports, 32*(3), 276–285. DOI: 10.1080/08824096.2015.1051633

Gill, R., & Orgad, S. (2018). The "me too" movement, digital media, and culture. *European Journal of Cultural Studies, 21*(4), 363–369. DOI: 10.1177/1367549418782894

Gillespie, T. (2010). The politics of "platforms.". *New Media & Society, 12*(3), 347–364. DOI: 10.1177/1461444809342738

Gillies, J., Strong, T., & Patel, V. (2021). Mental health-related discourses on social media: A systematic review. *International Journal of Environmental Research and Public Health, 18*(1), 346. DOI: 10.3390/ijerph18010346 PMID: 33466436

Goffman, E. (1959). *The presentation of self in everyday life*. Doubleday.

Goswami, D., & Saxena, K. (2020). Privacy paradox in social media usage: A systematic literature review. *Telematics and Informatics, 46*, 101312. DOI: 10.1016/j.tele.2019.101312

Gross, J. J. (1998). The emerging field of emotion regulation: An integrative review. *Review of General Psychology, 2*(3), 271–299. DOI: 10.1037/1089-2680.2.3.271

Hargittai, E., & Hinnant, A. (2008). Digital inequality: Differences in young adults' use of the Internet. *Communication Research, 35*(5), 602–621. DOI: 10.1177/0093650208321782

Hargittai, E., & Litt, E. (2019). The tweet in court: How do employers interpret Facebook and Twitter activity when evaluating job candidates? *New Media & Society, 21*(3), 603–623. DOI: 10.1177/1461444818797082

Hargittai, E., & Shafer, S. (2006). Differences in actual and perceived online skills: The role of gender. *New Media & Society, 8*(3), 437–451. DOI: 10.1177/1461444806061956

Harper, G. W., Carver, L. J., & Hamilton, W. E. (2019). "I'm not scared anymore": Exploring the impact of an online storytelling forum on LGBTQ+ youth's psychosocial development. *New Media & Society, 21*(2), 336–353. DOI: 10.1177/1461444818787369

Insel, T. (2017). Digital phenotyping: Technology for a new science of behavior. *Journal of the American Medical Association, 318*(13), 1215–1216. DOI: 10.1001/jama.2017.11295 PMID: 28973224

Jackson, S. J., Bailey, M., & Foucault Welles, B. (2020). *HashtagActivism: Networks of race and gender justice*. MIT Press. DOI: 10.7551/mitpress/10858.001.0001

Joinson, A. N. (2001). Self-disclosure in computer-mediated communication: The role of self-awareness and visual anonymity. *European Journal of Social Psychology, 31*(2), 177–192. DOI: 10.1002/ejsp.36

Joinson, A. N. (2008). Looking at, looking up or keeping up with people? Motives and use of Facebook. *Proceedings of the SIGCHI Conference on Human Factors in Computing Systems*, 1027–1036. DOI: 10.1145/1357054.1357213

Kokilaj, S. (2020). Is there a trade-off between privacy concerns and online self-disclosure? A meta-analytic review. *Social Science Computer Review, 38*(2), 181–198. DOI: 10.1177/0894439318823326

Lambton-Black, G., Whittaker, A., & Woods, R. (2021). Listening in lockdown: Podcasts and well-being during the coronavirus pandemic. *Media and Communication, 9*(2), 135–144. DOI: 10.17645/mac.v9i2.3811

Lampe, C., Ellison, N., & Steinfield, C. (2007). A familiar face(book): Profile elements as signals in an online social network. *Proceedings of the SIGCHI Conference on Human Factors in Computing Systems*, 435–444. DOI: 10.1145/1240624.1240695

Lampe, C., Wohn, D. Y., Ellison, N., Vitak, J., & Gray, R. (2014). Under the covers: Self-disclosure in a social networking site for families. *Proceedings of the 17th ACM Conference on Computer Supported Cooperative Work & Social Computing*, 865–875. DOI: 10.1145/2531602.2531674

Lanier, J., & Chitrapornprasert, W. (2019). Self-presentation and privacy management among college students on social networking sites. *Computers in Human Behavior, 90*, 214–221. DOI: 10.1016/j.chb.2018.08.041

Lapidot-Lefler, N., & Barak, A. (2012). Effects of anonymity, invisibility, and lack of eye-contact on toxic online communications. *Computers in Human Behavior, 28*(2), 434–443. DOI: 10.1016/j.chb.2011.10.014

Larose, R., & Rifon, N. J. (2007). Value orientations, perceived risks, and Internet privacy concerns. *Journal of Applied Security Research, 2*(2), 71–87. DOI: 10.1300/J374v02n02_06

Leary, M. R., & Kowalski, R. M. (1990). Impression management: A literature review and two-component model. *Psychological Bulletin, 107*(1), 34–47. DOI: 10.1037/0033-2909.107.1.34

Lewis, K., Kaufman, J., & Christakis, N. (2014). The taste for privacy: An analysis of college student privacy settings in an online social network. *Journal of Computer-Mediated Communication, 14*(4), 1005–1024. DOI: 10.1111/j.1083-6101.2009.01474.x

Livingstone, S. (2008). Taking risky opportunities in youthful content creation: Teenagers' use of social networking sites for intimacy, privacy and self-expression. *New Media & Society, 10*(3), 393–411. DOI: 10.1177/1461444808089415

Lutz, C., & Ranzini, G. (2020). The emotional experience of privacy: A qualitative study on how people feel about behavioral targeting. *Information Communication and Society, 23*(5), 685–701. DOI: 10.1080/1369118X.2018.1540634

Manago, A. M., Taylor, T., & Greenfield, P. M. (2012). Me and my 400 friends: The anatomy of college students' Facebook networks, their communication patterns, and well-being. *Developmental Psychology, 48*(2), 369–380. DOI: 10.1037/a0026338 PMID: 22288367

Marwick, A., & boyd, . (2014). Networked privacy: How teenagers negotiate context in social media. *New Media & Society, 16*(7), 1051–1067. DOI: 10.1177/1461444814543995

Marwick, A. E. (2013). *Status update: Celebrity, publicity, and branding in the social media age*. Yale University Press.

Marwick, A. E., & boyd, . (2011). I tweet honestly, I tweet passionately: Twitter users, context collapse, and the imagined audience. *New Media & Society, 13*(1), 114–133. DOI: 10.1177/1461444810365313

Matz, S. C., Kosinski, M., Nave, G., & Stillwell, D. J. (2017). Psychological targeting as an effective approach to digital mass persuasion. *Proceedings of the National Academy of Sciences of the United States of America, 114*(48), 12714–12719. DOI: 10.1073/pnas.1710966114 PMID: 29133409

Mazman, S. G., & Usluel, Y. K. (2010). Modeling educational usage of Facebook. *Computers & Education, 55*(2), 444–453. DOI: 10.1016/j.compedu.2010.02.008

McDaniel, B. T., & Coyne, S. M. (2016). "Technoference": The interference of technology in couple relationships and implications for women's relational satisfaction. *Psychology of Popular Media Culture, 5*(1), 85–98. DOI: 10.1037/ppm0000065

Murray, C., & Coulson, N. S. (2010). An investigation of identity construction and Facebook use among university students. *British Journal of Guidance & Counselling, 38*(1), 55–65. DOI: 10.1080/03069880903373039

Nadkarni, A., & Hofmann, S. G. (2012). Why do people use Facebook? *Personality and Individual Differences, 52*(3), 243–249. DOI: 10.1016/j.paid.2011.11.007 PMID: 22544987

Naslund, J. A., Aschbrenner, K. A., Marsch, L. A., & Bartels, S. J. (2016). The future of mental health care: Peer-to-peer support and social media. *Epidemiology and Psychiatric Sciences, 25*(2), 113–122. DOI: 10.1017/S2045796015001067 PMID: 26744309

Naslund, J. A., Aschbrenner, K. A., Marsch, L. A., & Bartels, S. J. (2020). Digital technology to deliver cognitive behavioral therapy for depression: Applications in low- and middle-income countries. *Global Mental Health (Cambridge, England), 7*, e22. DOI: 10.1017/S204579602000020X

Papacharissi, Z. (2011). *A networked self: Identity, community, and culture on social network sites*. Routledge.

Pavey, L., Greitemeyer, T., & Sparks, P. (2011). Can giving a little help vibrate with happiness? The psychological benefits of altruistic behavior. *Social Psychology*, *42*(2), 99–104. DOI: 10.1027/1864-9335/a000051

Pennebaker, J. W., & Beall, S. K. (1986). Confronting a traumatic event: Toward an understanding of inhibition and disease. *Journal of Abnormal Psychology*, *95*(3), 274–281. DOI: 10.1037/0021-843X.95.3.274 PMID: 3745650

Pennebaker, J. W., & Seagal, J. D. (1999). Forming a story: The health benefits of narrative. *Journal of Clinical Psychology*, *55*(10), 1243–1254. DOI: 10.1002/(SICI)1097-4679(199910)55:10<1243::AID-JCLP6>3.0.CO;2-N PMID: 11045774

Pennebaker, J. W., & Smyth, J. M. (2016). *Opening up by writing it down: How expressive writing improves health and eases emotional pain* (3rd ed.). Guilford Press.

Pew Research Center. (2018). *Social media and political engagement*. https://www.pewresearch.org/internet/2018/09/27/social-media-and-political-engagement/

Postmes, T., Spears, R., & Lea, M. (1998). Breaching or building social boundaries? SIDE-effects of computer-mediated communication. *Communication Research*, *25*(6), 689–715. DOI: 10.1177/009365098025006006

Rains, S. A. (2017). Communicating about health online. In Rubin, R. N., Sharoff, B. F., Housel, E. M., & Merwin, Y. I. (Eds.), *Health communication in the 21st century* (pp. 127–146). Wiley.

Rude, S. S., Gortner, E. M., & Pennebaker, J. W. (2004). Language use of depressed and depression-vulnerable college students. *Cognitive Therapy and Research*, *28*(3), 321–338. DOI: 10.1023/B:COTR.0000032361.44816.9d

Smyth, J. M. (1998). Written emotional expression: Effect sizes, outcome types, and moderating variables. *Journal of Consulting and Clinical Psychology*, *66*(1), 174–184. DOI: 10.1037/0022-006X.66.1.174 PMID: 9489272

Solove, D. J. (2007). "I've got nothing to hide" and other misunderstandings of privacy. *The San Diego Law Review*, *44*, 797–833.

Spitzberg, B. H., & Hoobler, G. (2002). Cyberstalking and the technologies of interpersonal terrorism. *New Media & Society*, *4*(1), 71–92. DOI: 10.1177/14614440222226271

Steinfield, C., Ellison, N. B., & Lampe, C. (2008). Social capital, self-esteem, and use of online social network sites: A longitudinal analysis. *Journal of Applied Developmental Psychology*, *29*(6), 434–445. DOI: 10.1016/j.appdev.2008.07.002

Stoycheff, E. (2016). Under surveillance: How the "watched" self silences political expression online. *New Media & Society*, *18*(5), 807–824. DOI: 10.1177/1461444814559371

Subrahmanyam, K., & Greenfield, P. (2008). Online communication and adolescent relationships. *The Future of Children*, *18*(1), 119–146. DOI: 10.1353/foc.0.0006 PMID: 21338008

Suler, J. (2004). The online disinhibition effect. *Cyberpsychology & Behavior*, *7*(3), 321–326. DOI: 10.1089/1094931041291295 PMID: 15257832

Taddicken, M. (2014). The "privacy paradox" in the context of social network sites – A longitudinal analysis of user attitudes and behavior. *Computers in Human Behavior*, *35*, 341–353. DOI: 10.1016/j.chb.2014.03.011

Tamir, D. I., & Mitchell, J. P. (2012). Disclosing information about the self is intrinsically rewarding. *Proceedings of the National Academy of Sciences of the United States of America*, *109*(50), 21277–21280. DOI: 10.1073/pnas.1202129109 PMID: 22566617

Tandoc, E. C., Ferrucci, P., & Duffy, M. (2015). Frat boys vs. humblebrags: Self-presentation on social media. *Atlantic Journal of Communication*, *23*(1), 3–15. DOI: 10.1080/15456870.2014.943456

Tokunaga, R. S. (2010). Following you home from school: A critical review and synthesis of research on cyberbullying victimization. *Computers in Human Behavior*, *26*(1), 1–15. DOI: 10.1016/j.chb.2009.11.014

Trepte, S., & Reinecke, L. (2013). The role of identity construction and self-determination in online self-disclosure. In Trepte, S., & Reinecke, L. (Eds.), *The psychology of social networks* (pp. 137–154). Springer.

Tufekci, Z. (2014). Big questions for social media big data: Representativeness, validity and other methodological pitfalls. *Proceedings of the Eighth International AAAI Conference on Weblogs and Social Media*, 506–515. DOI: 10.1609/icwsm.v8i1.14517

Tufekci, Z. (2017). *Twitter and tear gas: The power and fragility of networked protest*. Yale University Press.

Turkle, S. (1995). *Life on the screen: Identity in the age of the internet*. Simon & Schuster.

Turow, J., Hennessy, M., & Draper, N. (2015). The trade-off fallacy: How marketers are misrepresenting American consumers and opening them up to exploitation. SSRN *Electronic Journal*. DOI: 10.2139/ssrn.2820060

Utz, S., & Beukeboom, C. J. (2011). The role of emotion in online word-of-mouth: An analysis of attribution and expression. *International Journal of Electronic Commerce, 15*(4), 5–24. DOI: 10.2753/JEC1086-4415150401

Walther, J. B. (1996). Computer-mediated communication: Impersonal, interpersonal, and hyperpersonal interaction. *Communication Research, 23*(1), 3–43. DOI: 10.1177/009365096023001001

Xu, H., Teo, H. H., Tan, B. C., & Agarwal, R. (2012). The personalization privacy paradox: An empirical evaluation of informational privacy concerns and post-adoption behaviors in location-based services. *Information Systems Research, 23*(4), 1348–1369. DOI: 10.1287/isre.1110.0412

Yau, J. C., & Reich, S. M. (2019). Digital Strangers: Who do adolescents self-disclose to online? *New Media & Society, 21*(6), 1328–1346.

Zhao, S. (2020). From text to voice: Emerging vocal communication in mobile instant messaging. *New Media & Society, 22*(10), 1774–1792. DOI: 10.1177/1461444819883732

Zhao, S., Grasmuck, S., & Martin, J. (2008). Identity construction on Facebook: Digital empowerment in anchored relationships. *Computers in Human Behavior, 24*(5), 1816–1836. DOI: 10.1016/j.chb.2008.02.012

Zimmer, M. (2010). "But the data is already public": On the ethics of research in Facebook. *Ethics and Information Technology, 12*(4), 313–325. DOI: 10.1007/s10676-010-9227-5

Zuboff, S. (2019). *The age of surveillance capitalism: The fight for a human future at the new frontier of power*. PublicAffairs.

Zywica, J., & Danowski, J. (2008). The faces of Facebookers: Investigating social enhancement and social compensation hypotheses. *Proceedings of the American Society for Information Science and Technology, 45*(1), 1–13. DOI: 10.1002/meet.2008.145045025

KEY TERMS AND DEFINITIONS

Emotional Regulation: The ability to manage and respond to emotional experiences in a way that maintains psychological balance, adaptability, and appropriate behavior.

Identity Construction: The process through which individuals develop and shape their sense of self, including personal values, beliefs, roles, and social identities, often influenced by experiences, relationships, and cultural contexts.

Online Self-Disclosure: The voluntary sharing of personal, emotional, or private information about oneself with others through digital platforms such as social media, blogs, forums, or messaging apps.

Psychological Rewards: The internal or emotional benefits that individuals experience as a result of certain behaviors or events.

Risk of Self-Disclosure: The potential for negative outcomes, such as privacy breaches, emotional harm, misinterpretation, or social judgment, resulting from sharing personal information online.

Self-Promotion: The act of actively presenting oneself in a favorable light to enhance one's image, reputation, or social standing, often by highlighting achievements, skills, or positive traits.

Social Validation: The process of seeking and receiving approval, acceptance, or affirmation from others to confirm one's thoughts, feelings, or behaviors as correct or appropriate.

Chapter 6
Chatbot Service Quality in Banking:
Analysis of Customer Satisfaction

Aditi R. Khandelwal
IIS (Deemed to be) University, India

Ratisha Yadav
http://orcid.org/0000-0002-6193-1007
IIS (Deemed to be) University, India

Mahima Agnani
http://orcid.org/0009-0003-2964-4651
IIS (Deemed to be) University, India

Senthil Kumar A.V.
http://orcid.org/0000-0002-8587-7017
Nehru Institute of Information Technology and Management, India

ABSTRACT

One of the most visible applications of AI in customer service is the rapid adoption of AI-powered chatbots. This study examines the quality of chatbot services in the banking sector and their influence on customer satisfaction. Using a quantitative design, data were collected from 210 respondents through structured questionnaires. Key variables—functionality, convenience, security, assurance, enjoyment, design, and customization—were analysed statistically to evaluate their impact. Results indicate that chatbot service quality has a significant effect on customer satisfaction, with functionality, customization, security, and convenience as the strongest predictors. Accurate and timely responses were highlighted as critical in enhancing customer experience. Practically, the findings guide banks to enhance

DOI: 10.4018/979-8-3373-5896-3.ch006

chatbot customization, security, and functionality to boost satisfaction and loyalty, thus achieving a competitive edge in digital banking. This research also adds to the limited literature, offering a framework for future AI-based customer service.

INTRODUCTION

In today's modern digital age, the rapid pace of technological innovation has brought about a profound transformation in the way businesses function and deliver services, especially within the service-oriented industries. With continuous advancements in digital tools, automation, and artificial intelligence, organizations are rethinking their traditional business models and adopting smarter approaches to remain competitive in a dynamic environment. Among the most groundbreaking developments in recent years is the increasing incorporation of artificial intelligence (AI) into multiple facets of customer service. AI has enabled businesses to elevate the quality of customer interactions, simplify complex processes, and streamline overall service delivery to ensure faster and more effective results.

One of the most visible and impactful applications of AI within customer service is the rapid rise of AI-powered chatbots. These intelligent virtual assistants have moved beyond being optional add-ons and are now considered essential components of modern customer support frameworks. Unlike conventional systems that often require significant human intervention, AI chatbots are capable of autonomously managing a wide range of tasks—ranging from responding to basic customer queries and resolving frequently asked questions to providing instant assistance and guiding users through routine transactions. Their ability to respond within seconds not only saves valuable time for both customers and service providers but also increases the overall efficiency of service operations.

This global shift toward AI-driven customer support is especially prominent in the banking and financial services sector, where customer demands for speed, security, and convenience are at their peak. Banks and financial institutions are increasingly deploying chatbots to deliver 24/7 support, enabling customers to access assistance at any time of the day without waiting in long queues or depending solely on human representatives. These chatbots are designed to provide real-time answers to customer inquiries, simplify day-to-day banking activities such as balance checks, fund transfers, and bill payments, as well as effectively address repetitive queries that often consume large amounts of staff time. According to research such as Eren (2021), the adoption of AI chatbots in banking not only enhances customer satisfaction but also reduces the operational workload on employees, minimizes costs associated with human resources, and significantly improves the overall efficiency of banking operations. Ultimately, the integration of AI in this sector reflects a larger trend where technology is not just supporting but actively reshaping how financial institutions connect with and serve their customers.

This introduction explores the rising adoption of chatbot services in the banking industry, emphasizing their role in improving customer experience and operational efficiency. Additionally, it examines the broader implications of AI integration in banking, highlighting its potential to reshape traditional banking models and redefine customer engagement (Ruan, 2022). Drawing on various studies and industry reports, this discussion aims to contextualize current research on AI-powered chatbot services in the financial sector.

The banking industry, traditionally recognized for its strong focus on security, reliability, and customer trust, has increasingly turned to advanced technologies to remain competitive and meet the evolving expectations of its clientele. Over the past decade, the rapid growth of digital banking and the rising complexity of financial services have made it essential for banks to adopt innovative solutions that not only improve efficiency but also enhance the quality of customer interactions. Among these innovations, artificial intelligence (AI) has emerged as a transformative force, helping banks streamline internal processes, optimize resource management, and deliver faster, more personalized services to customers.

One of the most prominent applications of AI within the financial sector is the use of AI-driven chatbots. These intelligent software tools, designed to simulate human-like conversations, have become vital in addressing customer needs for convenience, speed, and accuracy. Unlike traditional customer service models that rely heavily on human staff and operate within limited hours, chatbots provide banks with the ability to extend round-the-clock support, ensuring that customers can access assistance at any time, regardless of location or time zone. By handling common inquiries, assisting with routine transactions, and guiding customers through processes such as fund transfers or account updates, chatbots significantly reduce waiting times and improve the overall customer journey.

Moreover, the adoption of chatbots allows financial institutions to achieve multiple operational benefits simultaneously. Not only do they help enhance user engagement by offering instant and consistent responses, but they also contribute to cost reduction by minimizing the need for large customer service teams. Although the technology is still evolving and continues to face challenges such as improving natural language understanding and managing complex queries, it has already demonstrated remarkable potential in creating a more seamless banking experience. Ultimately, by combining efficiency with personalization, AI-powered chatbots are proving to be a powerful tool for banks striving to maintain customer loyalty, strengthen relationships, and adapt to the growing demands of the digital era.

According to a study by Cheng (2022), chatbots are capable of offering personalized and engaging customer service experiences, especially in industries where customer interaction is crucial. In the banking sector, their ability to handle large volumes of transactions and queries without human intervention has made them an invaluable tool for improving operational efficiency and reducing service delivery times. These benefits are particularly significant in the context of digital banking, where customers increasingly expect immediate responses to their queries and seamless service across all channels.

Furthermore, the introduction of AI-powered chatbots has played a crucial role in significantly enhancing customer satisfaction within the banking sector. Unlike traditional service channels that often restrict assistance to business hours, chatbots are capable of offering 24/7 availability, ensuring that customers can access support at any time of the day or night. This constant accessibility not only reduces long wait times but also provides immediate resolutions to a wide variety of common banking needs, including routine services such as checking account balances, transferring funds, applying for loans, and resolving frequently asked questions (Eren, 2021). As a result, customers experience a more seamless, convenient, and reliable interaction with their banks, which strengthens overall trust and satisfaction.

In addition to improving customer experience, chatbots deliver substantial operational advantages for financial institutions. By automating a large portion of customer queries and day-to-day banking tasks, banks are able to minimize their reliance on large customer service teams, thereby significantly reducing staffing and training costs. This shift allows human representatives to focus more on complex, high-value cases that require empathy and detailed attention, further boosting efficiency. Beyond these fundamental benefits, the more advanced versions of AI-driven chatbots utilize data analytics and machine learning to perform sophisticated tasks, such as offering personalized financial advice tailored to individual spending habits, detecting unusual activity to provide fraud alerts, and delivering proactive banking solutions like reminders for upcoming payments or customized investment suggestions. Collectively, these features elevate the overall user experience by blending efficiency with personalization, positioning chatbots as not just cost-saving tools but also as strategic assets for building stronger customer relationships in an increasingly competitive digital banking environment.

Chatbots bring with them a wide range of important advantages for the banking industry, fundamentally transforming both customer service and internal operational efficiency. Perhaps the most significant benefit lies in their ability to provide round-the-clock assistance, which ensures that customers are no longer limited by the restrictions of traditional business hours. With this continuous availability, clients can conveniently access services and carry out essential banking activities at any time of day, whether early in the morning, late at night, or even during weekends and holidays. This flexibility is particularly critical for handling time-sensitive financial matters, where delays could have serious consequences. For instance, customers can instantly check their account balances, monitor recent transaction histories, initiate fund transfers, or receive guidance on urgent loan-related queries without waiting for human intervention (Klein, 2023).

In addition to improving accessibility and convenience, chatbots also play a crucial role in maintaining financial security and preventing risks. Their ability to provide real-time notifications and immediate fraud alerts allows users to respond quickly to unusual activities, thereby reducing the likelihood of monetary losses and identity theft. By leveraging AI and machine learning, chatbots can detect irregular spending patterns or suspicious login attempts and immediately notify the customer, prompting faster corrective action. This proactive feature not only minimizes potential financial mishaps but also reassures customers that their bank is actively safeguarding their assets. As a result, chatbots do more than just answer queries; they serve as vital tools for building trust, enhancing customer confidence, and strengthening the overall reliability of digital banking services.

Another major advantage of implementing chatbots in the banking sector is their ability to manage large volumes of customer queries simultaneously, something that traditional human-staffed support systems often struggle to achieve. During peak hours, when customer inquiries tend to surge, human agents can easily become overwhelmed, resulting in long wait times, inconsistent service quality, and potential frustration for clients. In contrast, chatbots are designed to handle multiple requests at the same time without any decline in speed or accuracy, thereby ensuring that each customer receives timely and reliable assistance. This capacity to scale support operations on demand makes them particularly valuable in today's fast-paced digital environment, where efficiency and instant responses are highly valued.

By providing consistent response times and accurate information, chatbots create a seamless interaction experience for users. Research, including the study conducted by Eren (2021), highlights that customers often report higher levels of satisfaction when interacting with chatbots for routine tasks, precisely because of the speed, efficiency, and accessibility they provide. Common banking needs such as balance inquiries, transaction updates, password resets, or loan-related questions can be resolved almost instantly, which helps reduce frustration and enhances customer loyalty. Beyond these basic functions, modern AI-powered chatbots are capable of continuous learning through machine learning algorithms. Every interaction helps the chatbot refine its language processing abilities and improve its contextual understanding, enabling it to provide more personalized and context-aware responses over time. This means that as customers continue to engage with the chatbot, the system becomes smarter, more intuitive, and better equipped to anticipate individual needs ultimately creating a more tailored and satisfying banking experience.

One of the most remarkable and valuable advantages of integrating chatbots into the banking sector is their capacity to deliver deeply personalized services, which is steadily reshaping and modernizing the way financial institutions communicate and engage with their customers. Unlike traditional customer support systems that often provide generic responses, chatbots use advanced technologies such as machine learning algorithms and natural language processing to go beyond surface-level interactions. They can carefully examine a wide range of customer information, including personal account details, transaction histories, spending behaviours, and even recurring financial patterns. Based on this comprehensive analysis, the chatbot is able to generate responses and recommendations that are closely aligned with each customer's unique lifestyle, preferences, and financial goals.

This level of personalization results in a much richer and more meaningful customer experience. For example, rather than simply answering queries, the chatbot can suggest banking products or investment options that are most relevant to the individual, provide proactive financial advice at the right time, and even offer customized solutions such as tailored budgeting strategies, reminders for bill payments, or smart investment suggestions. By making interactions more relevant and supportive, chatbots not only improve convenience for customers but also build stronger trust and loyalty toward the financial institution, ultimately transforming the overall customer–banking relationship.

Beyond convenience, personalization also fosters customer trust and loyalty, as individuals feel valued when their unique concerns and preferences are acknowledged. According to Li (2021), chatbot reliability and assurance were key factors in promoting customer satisfaction in the travel industry, a finding that is equally applicable to banking. When chatbots provide accurate, context-aware assistance, they contribute to a more engaging and seamless banking experience, ultimately strengthening customer relationships and brand reputation.

Furthermore, chatbots are valuable tools for reducing operational costs. By automating routine tasks, banks can allocate human resources to more complex customer service issues, thereby increasing efficiency. This cost-saving aspect of chatbot implementation is especially appealing to banks, which are continually seeking ways to optimize their resources in an increasingly competitive marketplace. According to (Nadarzynski, 2019), the use of AI-driven chatbots in customer service can significantly reduce the burden on human staff, allowing them to focus on higher-value tasks while maintaining high levels of customer satisfaction.

Customer satisfaction is a critical metric for assessing the effectiveness of chatbot services in banking, as it directly influences customer loyalty and long-term engagement. Service quality, defined by factors such as accuracy, responsiveness, reliability, and personalization, plays a key role in shaping customer perceptions of chatbot interactions. A well-designed chatbot must not only provide quick responses but also ensure that the information delivered is precise and relevant to the customer's needs (Petersson, 2023).

Moreover, responsiveness is crucial, as customers expect instant support, particularly in urgent situations such as fraudulent transactions or failed payments. Reliability, on the other hand, ensures that chatbots function seamlessly across various banking platforms, minimizing errors and maintaining consistent service. Research has consistently shown that high-quality service, whether delivered by human agents or AI-powered chatbots, leads to increased customer satisfaction, trust, and retention (Carvalho, 2023). By continuously improving chatbot capabilities through advanced AI and customer feedback, banks can enhance digital service experiences and strengthen customer relationships.

A study by Ashfaq (2020) highlighted the importance of service quality in determining customer satisfaction with chatbot interactions. The research found that chatbot performance—particularly in terms of information accuracy, ease of use, and response time—was a major factor influencing how customers perceived and engaged with chatbot services in the banking sector. When chatbots deliver precise and relevant information efficiently, they enhance the overall customer experience by reducing frustration and improving service accessibility.

Similarly, Hsu (2023) demonstrated that customers who interacted with AI chatbots in e-commerce were more likely to be satisfied when the chatbot provided timely, accurate, and contextually relevant responses. These findings suggest that high-performing chatbots, regardless of the industry, contribute significantly to customer satisfaction by streamlining interactions and ensuring smooth digital service experiences. In banking, where trust and reliability are paramount, maintaining high service quality in chatbot interactions can lead to stronger customer relationships, increased loyalty, and improved operational efficiency.

In the banking sector, the concept of service quality extends beyond the chatbot's ability to provide accurate information. It also encompasses the security and privacy of customer data, as well as the chatbot's ability to handle complex financial transactions. (Lei, 2021) compared customer perceptions of chatbots and human agents in the hospitality industry and found that while chatbots were effective for handling simple tasks, customers preferred human agents for more complex issues. This finding underscores the importance of balancing AI automation with human oversight in the banking industry, particularly when it comes to sensitive or high-stakes interactions.

However, it is important to note that not all customers perceive chatbot services in the same way. A study by (Ruan, 2022) found that customer satisfaction with chatbots varied depending on the nature of the task and the type of product or service being offered. For example, customers were more likely to be satisfied with chatbot interactions when dealing with functional products, such as account inquiries or transaction histories, compared to experiential products, where human interaction was valued more highly. This suggests that banks should consider the specific needs and preferences of their customer base when designing and implementing chatbot services.

LITERATURE REVIEW

Chatbots and AI

Chatbots, functioning as AI-driven conversational interfaces, are specifically developed to communicate with users in a manner that closely resembles human conversation, thereby making digital interactions more natural, intuitive, and user-friendly. Unlike rigid, menu-based systems that require customers to follow preset options, chatbots utilize sophisticated technologies to engage in free-flowing conversations, allowing users to express their concerns or queries in everyday language. This conversational approach not only reduces the complexity of digital communication but also significantly enhances overall efficiency, as customers are able to obtain accurate information and guidance almost instantly without navigating through complicated processes.

At the core of chatbot functionality lie natural language processing (NLP) techniques combined with machine learning algorithms. NLP equips chatbots with the ability to understand and interpret human language, breaking down user inputs into meaningful components such as intent, context, and sentiment. Meanwhile, machine learning algorithms allow these systems to continuously adapt by recognizing patterns in user interactions and improving the accuracy of their responses over time. By leveraging these technologies, chatbots can do more than just provide generic answers—they can analyze queries in real time, interpret the underlying intent behind customer requests, and deliver contextually relevant solutions. Through repeated interactions and continuous learning, chatbots evolve into more intelligent systems, capable of offering increasingly refined, accurate, and personalized responses. This technological sophistication ensures that chatbots not only streamline communication but also strengthen customer engagement and satisfaction in the long run.

As Hsu et al. (2023) suggest, chatbots play a crucial role in automating repetitive tasks, such as answering frequently asked questions, handling transaction requests, and assisting with account management. By doing so, they significantly reduce human effort, allowing banking professionals to focus on more complex customer inquiries that require personalized attention. Additionally, chatbots enhance service consistency by providing standardized responses, minimizing human errors, and ensuring that customers receive reliable support across multiple digital platforms, ultimately improving overall customer satisfaction.

The development and evolution of chatbots can generally be divided into two broad categories: rule-based systems and AI-based systems. Rule-based chatbots represent the earlier and more traditional form of this technology. These systems operate strictly within predefined boundaries, relying on structured sets of commands, scripted dialogues, and decision trees to generate responses to user queries (Yen, 2020). Essentially, they are programmed to recognize specific keywords or phrases and then provide corresponding outputs, which makes them particularly effective in addressing straightforward, repetitive, and predictable questions such as FAQs, basic account inquiries, or step-by-step instructions for simple tasks. Their strength lies in their reliability and consistency, as they follow pre-programmed logic without deviation.

However, despite these advantages, rule-based chatbots face significant limitations when the conversation moves beyond routine scenarios. Because they cannot process the subtleties of natural language or handle unexpected input, these systems often fail when confronted with complex, ambiguous, or multi-layered customer requests. For instance, if a customer phrases a query in an unfamiliar way or asks for assistance that requires contextual understanding, a rule-based chatbot is likely to provide irrelevant or incomplete answers, leading to customer frustration. This lack of adaptability restricts their usefulness in dynamic environments such as modern banking, where customer expectations are increasingly diverse and demand greater personalization. As a result, while rule-based chatbots serve as a foundation for digital interaction, they are gradually being replaced or supplemented by more advanced AI-driven chatbots, which are designed to overcome these limitations through learning and contextual awareness.

In contrast, AI-based chatbots leverage deep learning, natural language processing (NLP), and machine learning algorithms to adapt to user inputs and continuously improve over time. These intelligent systems can understand context, recognize intent, and generate more nuanced and personalized responses. AI-based chatbots, such as OpenAI's ChatGPT and Google's Dialogflow, have significantly advanced conversational capabilities, making interactions more dynamic and human-like (Chung et al., 2020). Their ability to learn from past interactions enables them to refine their responses, offer predictive assistance, and provide more accurate and context-aware support, ultimately enhancing the customer experience in industries such as banking, e-commerce, and customer service.

Customer Satisfaction

This study examines how luxury fashion brands can sustain high levels of customer satisfaction and deliver brand-aligned value through AI-driven e-services, particularly chatbots (Chung et al., 2020). In the luxury sector, customer satisfaction is deeply tied to a chatbot's ability to replicate the personalized, high-touch service traditionally provided in-store. Unlike mass-market brands, luxury brands thrive on exclusivity, prestige, and exceptional service, making it crucial for chatbots to not only provide accurate and efficient responses but also uphold the brand's distinct identity and values.

An essential determinant of customer satisfaction in the use of chatbots lies in their ability to foster trust and deliver high-quality communication that aligns with the values of exclusivity, consistency, and reliability—qualities particularly emphasized in premium and luxury service industries. Customers interacting with digital interfaces often seek the same level of credibility and reassurance they would expect from direct human interactions. Therefore, a chatbot must not only provide accurate information but also create a sense of security and reliability, ensuring that the customer perceives the interaction as professional, transparent, and dependable. This is especially important in sectors where brand reputation heavily depends on customer trust and perceived value.

Evidence from industries such as banking and e-commerce highlights how specific trust-enhancing features significantly improve customer experiences. For example, the integration of secure transaction capabilities reassures users that their sensitive financial or personal information is well protected. Similarly, the ability of chatbots to deliver precise, data-driven recommendations and demonstrate contextual awareness—by recognizing user preferences, purchase history, or financial behaviour—creates a personalized service experience that mirrors human-like attentiveness (Eren, 2021; Cheng & Jiang, 2022). These elements help strengthen user confidence and loyalty, as customers feel the chatbot is not only efficient but also attuned to their individual needs.

Beyond functional trust and efficiency, researchers also point to the role of entertainment-driven and anthropomorphic design features in boosting engagement. By incorporating conversational tones, humor, or even human-like traits such as empathy and warmth, chatbots can make interactions feel more immersive, engaging, and relatable. Studies in food e-commerce, for instance, demonstrate that customers respond positively when chatbots adopt an approachable persona, thereby making the digital shopping journey more enjoyable and less mechanical (Klein & Martinez, 2023). When effectively combined, these two dimensions functional reliability and human-like engagement—position chatbots as powerful tools for elevating the customer experience, blending efficiency with emotional connection.

Furthermore, customization and efficient problem-solving are crucial in the luxury retail industry, where consumers expect highly personalized recommendations, proactive engagement, and seamless issue resolution. Unlike mainstream shoppers, luxury customers prioritize exclusivity, attention to detail, and premium service experiences, which AI-driven chatbots must replicate to maintain brand prestige. Advanced chatbot solutions, powered by machine learning and natural language processing (NLP), can analyze customer preferences, purchase history, and browsing behaviour to provide tailored product recommendations, style advice, and concierge-level support. This hyper-personalized approach ensures that each customer interaction feels bespoke and aligned with the brand's premium positioning.

Efficient problem-solving is another critical factor in luxury chatbot success. High-net-worth consumers expect swift and accurate resolutions to their inquiries, whether related to product availability, order modifications, or post-purchase services such as returns, repairs, and exclusive privileges. AI chatbots equipped with predictive analytics and sentiment analysis can preemptively detect potential dissatisfaction or service issues, allowing brands to proactively address concerns and enhance the overall customer experience. Additionally, integrating seamless human handover options ensures that complex requests are escalated to human luxury advisors, preserving the brand's commitment to superior service.

Findings from the hospitality and tourism industries provide compelling evidence of the growing significance of value co-creation through digital technologies. In these sectors, customers are no longer passive recipients of services; instead, they actively participate in shaping and customizing their own experiences, which in turn leads to enhanced perceptions of value and stronger satisfaction levels (Carvalho & Alves, 2023). For instance, travelers increasingly engage with digital platforms to design personalized itineraries, provide real-time feedback, and interact with service providers through AI-enabled systems. This active involvement not only empowers customers but also creates a sense of ownership and emotional investment in the service process, thereby deepening loyalty and overall satisfaction.

The same principle is directly applicable to the luxury retail sector, where exclusivity, personalization, and engagement are critical to customer perception. Clients in this market segment value immersive and interactive digital experiences that go beyond simple transactions, elevating the shopping journey into something unique and memorable. Tools such as AI-powered personal shoppers, virtual stylists, and concierge-style chatbot services allow luxury brands to replicate the attentiveness of in-store interactions in digital spaces. These technologies enable customers to receive tailored recommendations, personalized styling guidance, and exclusive offers in real time, all while maintaining the convenience of digital access. By blending efficiency with exclusivity, such interactive services reinforce the luxury brand's image and enhance customer satisfaction, while also fostering a co-creative environment where clients feel their preferences and individuality are central to the experience.

Ultimately, the success of AI-driven chatbots in luxury retail depends on their ability to blend advanced technology with brand heritage, ensuring that interactions remain personalized, engaging, and aligned with luxury standards (Chung et al., 2020). By refining AI capabilities such as emotion recognition, predictive personalization, and seamless omnichannel integration luxury brands can enhance customer satisfaction, foster long-term loyalty, and drive digital transformation without compromising exclusivity.

Factors Influencing Customer Satisfaction with Chatbots

The success of chatbot services in Banking depends largely on key factors such as functionality, ease of use, personalization, and trust. As digital banking continues to expand, chatbots play a vital role in enhancing accessibility and efficiency in financial services. However, their adoption and effectiveness vary across different customer demographics. A study conducted by Das and Dutta (2021) explored customer perceptions of chatbot services in both urban and rural areas, highlighting a stark contrast in acceptance levels. Their findings indicated that urban customers, being more familiar with digital platforms, are more likely to trust and adopt chatbots as a convenient alternative to traditional banking channels. Conversely, rural customers exhibited skepticism, often favoring human interaction over AI-powered tools due to concerns about accuracy, security, and lack of digital literacy.

Another critical factor influencing chatbot success is their ability to handle complex queries. Research by Gupta et al. (2022) revealed that while Banking chatbots perform well in facilitating basic transactions, such as balance inquiries and bill payments, they often struggle with addressing more intricate issues like loan applications, investment advice, or fraud dispute resolutions. This shortcoming can lead to customer frustration, reducing overall satisfaction and trust in AI-driven banking services. To overcome these limitations, banks must invest in more advanced AI algorithms, natural language processing (NLP), and machine learning capabilities. By improving chatbot intelligence, enabling multilingual support, and integrating human assistance when needed, Banks can enhance customer confidence and ensure a seamless, efficient banking experience across diverse populations.

Chatbot Service Quality

Chatbot service quality is defined by key dimensions such as reliability, understandability, assurance, responsiveness, and service recovery, all of which are crucial for ensuring user satisfaction and fostering continued engagement with the service (Hsu & Lin, 2023). These factors determine how effectively chatbots can replicate human-like interactions while delivering accurate and timely responses. High-quality chatbot interactions significantly enhance user experiences, particularly in industries where quick and effective problem resolution is essential, such as travel and banking (Li et al., 2021; Eren, 2021).

A user-centered design that caters to specific needs and preferences plays a vital role in improving chatbot acceptance. For example, healthcare chatbots that prioritize patient-centered interactions, offering empathetic and precise communication, tend to be more readily embraced by users (Nadarzynski et al., 2019). Similarly, banking chatbots must instill a sense of trust and security by ensuring accurate financial guidance and fraud detection support. However, factors such as technology anxiety and skepticism can moderate users' satisfaction with chatbot service quality. These concerns are particularly prevalent in sectors like healthcare and among demographics in emerging markets, where security, data privacy, and AI expertise are significant considerations (Mogaji et al., 2021; Ruan & Mezei, 2022).

Each industry presents unique challenges that shape user expectations. In travel and hospitality, chatbots must maintain consistency in customer engagement across multiple touchpoints, ensuring seamless itinerary management and personalized recommendations. In contrast, banking chatbots must prioritize user assurance by handling sensitive transactions with high accuracy and security (Cheng & Jiang, 2022; Petersson et al., 2023). Ultimately, ensuring superior chatbot service quality—characterized by reliability, responsiveness, effective issue resolution, and adaptability to industry-specific concerns is vital for enhancing chatbot effectiveness, strengthening user trust, and fostering long-term customer loyalty.

Banking Sector

The Banking sector has undergone significant transformation due to the rapid adoption of technology, fundamentally reshaping customer service and financial operations. With the rise of digital banking, artificial intelligence (AI)-powered chatbots have become an integral part of enhancing service delivery and operational efficiency (Das & Agarwal, 2022). These intelligent virtual assistants are designed to provide seamless interactions by offering quick resolutions to customer queries, handling routine transactions, and assisting with financial advice, ultimately improving the overall user experience (Singh & Gupta, 2023).

As banks continue to invest in AI-driven solutions, chatbots are playing a crucial role in reducing service wait times, automating repetitive tasks, and ensuring 24/7 customer support (Kvale, 2020). However, while these technologies bring numerous advantages, their adoption also presents challenges such as trust issues, limitations in handling complex queries, and digital literacy gaps, particularly in rural areas. This literature review explores key studies that analyze the adoption, effectiveness, challenges, and future potential of chatbot services in the Banking context. By examining existing research, this review aims to provide insights into how chatbots are shaping the Banking experience, the factors influencing customer acceptance, and the innovations needed to enhance their capabilities in the evolving financial landscape.

Benefits of Chatbots in the Banking Sector

Chatbots provide several key benefits to the banking industry. First and foremost, they enable banks to offer round-the-clock service, ensuring that customers can access support and perform basic banking tasks outside of regular business hours. This feature is especially valuable for resolving time-sensitive issues such as account balances, transaction histories, or fraud alerts. In addition, chatbots can handle high volumes of queries simultaneously, reducing wait times and improving the overall customer experience. Studies, such as one conducted by Eren (2021), suggest that customers appreciate the convenience and speed of chatbot interactions, particularly when dealing with routine inquiries.

Another highly significant advantage of adopting chatbots in the banking industry is their capacity to deliver personalized services, which represent a key driver of customer satisfaction in today's competitive digital environment. Unlike generic customer service systems that provide standardized responses, AI-powered chatbots can make use of machine learning algorithms and advanced data analytics to study customer profiles, transaction histories, and behavioural patterns. By processing this information, chatbots are able to generate tailored responses that directly address individual customer preferences, financial needs, and lifestyle habits. For example, a chatbot may recommend suitable savings plans for a customer who frequently transfers funds into fixed deposits, or provide customized loan options to a client whose financial behaviour indicates upcoming large expenditures.

This emphasis on personalization offers several important benefits. First, it significantly enhances the overall customer experience, as clients feel that the service is relevant, attentive, and responsive to their unique circumstances. Second, it helps foster trust and long-term loyalty, since customers are more likely to value and repeatedly engage with a bank that demonstrates an understanding of their personal needs rather than treating them as just another account number. Evidence from other industries reinforces this point. For instance, a study by Li et al. (2021) in the travel sector revealed that chatbot features such as reliability and assurance were critical in driving customer satisfaction. These findings are highly transferable to the banking context, where trust, accuracy, and personalized guidance form the foundation of customer–institution relationships. Thus, personalization through chatbots not only improves day-to-day interactions but also strengthens long-term customer commitment to the bank.

Furthermore, chatbots are valuable tools for reducing operational costs. By automating routine tasks, banks can allocate human resources to more complex customer service issues, thereby increasing efficiency. This cost-saving aspect of chatbot implementation is especially appealing to banks, which are continually seeking ways to optimize their resources in an increasingly competitive marketplace. According to Nadarzynski et al. (2019), the use of AI-driven chatbots in customer service can significantly reduce the burden on human staff, allowing them to focus on higher-value tasks while maintaining high levels of customer satisfaction.

Challenges of Chatbot Implementation in Banking

Despite their many advantages, chatbot implementation in the banking sector is not without its challenges. One of the primary concerns is the issue of trust. Many customers, particularly in emerging markets, remain skeptical of AI-driven services, fearing that chatbots may not be able to provide the same level of accuracy, security, and reliability as human agents. This skepticism can hinder the widespread adoption of chatbot services, as customers may prefer to engage with human representatives for sensitive or complex issues.

Mogaji et al. (2021) explored the interaction between customers and banking chatbots in Nigeria, an emerging market, and found that trust and perceived expertise were significant factors influencing customer engagement. In many cases, customers were reluctant to fully rely on chatbots due to concerns about the accuracy and security of the information provided. As chatbots continue to evolve, addressing these concerns through improved security measures and more advanced AI capabilities will be essential for fostering customer trust and encouraging greater adoption.

Another challenge is the technical limitations of chatbots, particularly in understanding and processing natural language. While advancements in natural language processing (NLP) have improved the ability of chatbots to engage in more meaningful and accurate conversations, there are still limitations in their ability to handle complex or ambiguous queries. Petersson et al. (2023) noted that while banking chatbots in Norway were generally effective at handling basic tasks, users expressed frustration when the chatbot failed to understand more complex requests, leading to a decline in user satisfaction.

Additionally, the design and customization of chatbot interfaces can also impact their effectiveness. Customers expect user-friendly and visually appealing interfaces that allow them to easily navigate through banking services. Poorly designed chatbots can lead to frustration and reduced engagement. Carvalho et al. (2023) emphasized the importance of user-centric design in AI applications, noting that personalized and customizable interfaces are crucial for maintaining high levels of customer satisfaction.

Chatbot Service Quality and Customer Satisfaction

Customer satisfaction is a critical metric for assessing the effectiveness of chatbot services in banking, as it directly influences customer trust, engagement, and long-term retention. Service quality, defined by key factors such as accuracy, responsiveness, reliability, and personalization, plays a fundamental role in shaping customer perceptions of chatbot interactions. Accuracy ensures that chatbots provide precise and relevant information, minimizing errors that could lead to frustration or distrust. Responsiveness is equally crucial, as customers expect instant support, especially for time-sensitive issues like failed transactions or fraud alerts (Lo Presti, 2021).

Reliability, which refers to the chatbot's ability to function seamlessly across digital platforms without glitches, further enhances user confidence in AI-driven banking services. Additionally, personalization improves the customer experience by tailoring responses based on user history and preferences, making interactions feel more intuitive and human-like. Research has consistently shown that high-quality service, whether delivered by human agents or AI-powered chatbots, leads to increased customer satisfaction, greater brand loyalty, and improved customer retention rates. As banking institutions continue to integrate AI chatbots into their customer service models, maintaining superior service quality will be essential in fostering trust, enhancing user experiences, and ensuring the long-term success of AI-driven banking solutions.

A study by Ashfaq et al. (2020) highlighted the crucial role of service quality in determining customer satisfaction with chatbot interactions. The research emphasized that chatbot performance particularly in terms of information accuracy, ease of use, and response time directly impacts how customers perceive and engage with AI-driven services. When chatbots provide precise, up-to-date information, users are more likely to trust their reliability and continue using them for future inquiries. Additionally, ease of use plays a significant role in adoption, as intuitive chatbot interfaces improve accessibility for users across different demographics. Response time is another key factor, as customers expect instant resolutions, especially in industries where quick service is essential, such as banking and retail.

Similarly, Hsu et al. (2023) demonstrated that customers who interacted with AI chatbots in e-commerce exhibited higher satisfaction levels when the chatbot delivered timely, accurate, and relevant responses. This finding underscores the importance of chatbot efficiency in fostering positive user experiences across various industries. As AI technology advances, ensuring that chatbots are well-optimized to handle diverse customer needs with speed and accuracy will be essential in driving customer satisfaction, loyalty, and overall engagement with digital services.

In the banking sector, the concept of service quality extends beyond just a chatbot's ability to deliver accurate information; it also includes security, privacy, personalization, and the capability to handle complex financial transactions. Given the highly sensitive nature of banking interactions, customers expect chatbots to not only provide swift and precise responses but also to ensure data confidentiality, fraud prevention, and seamless transaction processing. Any failure in these areas can lead to diminished trust and reluctance to use AI-driven services.

Research by Lei et al. (2021) compared customer perceptions of chatbots and human agents in the hospitality industry, revealing that while chatbots efficiently managed simple tasks, customers preferred human agents for complex concerns requiring deeper understanding. This insight is highly relevant to banking, where tasks like loan processing, investment advice, and dispute resolution often necessitate human intervention.

These findings highlight the need for a hybrid approach in banking, where chatbots handle routine inquiries while human representatives step in for more intricate or emotionally sensitive issues. Banks must focus on enhancing chatbot intelligence through machine learning and NLP advancements while maintaining accessible human support for high-stakes transactions. By striking this balance, financial institutions can maximize efficiency, improve customer experience, and build trust in AI-driven banking solutions.

Figure 1. Conceptual framework

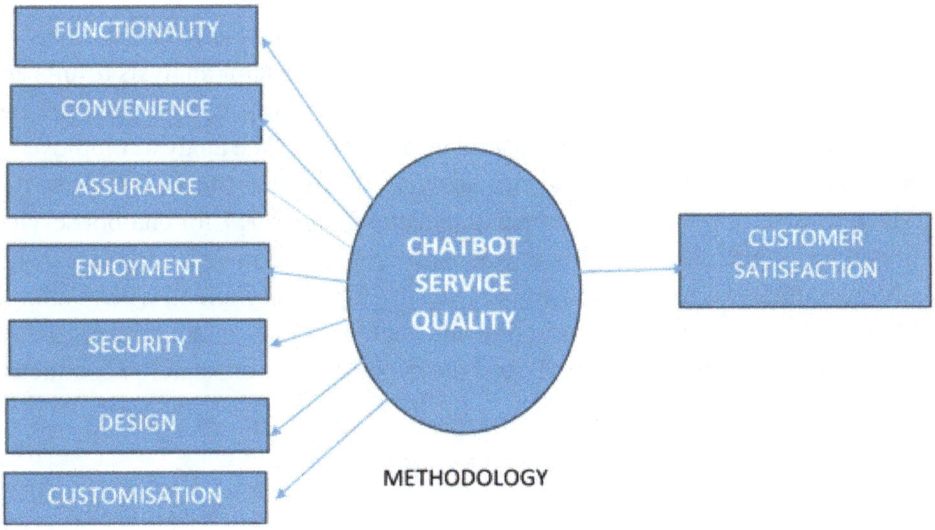

METHODOLOGY

METHODOLOGY

This study adopts a quantitative research approach to examine the impact of chatbot services on customer satisfaction and perceived value in the banking sector. A survey-based methodology is employed to collect relevant data, providing insights into how chatbot service quality influences customer perceptions and overall experience. The primary data collection tool is a structured questionnaire, designed to assess key aspects such as chatbot functionality, convenience, security, enjoyment, design, customization, and assurance. These factors serve as independent variables, while customer satisfaction acts as the dependent variable in the study.

To ensure a comprehensive analysis, statistical software tools are utilized to evaluate and test hypotheses regarding the relationship between these variables. This approach allows for an in-depth understanding of the factors driving customer satisfaction with chatbot interactions. The study focuses on the banking sector in Jaipur, with data collected over a period of two months. By analyzing user responses, the research aims to provide valuable insights into how AI-driven chatbot services can be optimized to enhance customer experiences and foster long-term trust in digital banking.

DATA ANALYSIS PROCEDURE

For data analysis, IBM SPSS version 22 was utilized. Factor analysis results are displayed in Table 1 to evaluate the alignment of dimensions used to measure the impact of chatbot service quality on customer satisfaction. The analysis employed a varimax rotation method with Kaiser normalization. The Kaiser-Meyer-Olkin (KMO) test yielded value of 0.848 for customer satisfaction, and 0.917 for chatbot service quality, indicating that the instrument was well-suited for dimensional loading. Internal consistency was measured using Cronbach's alpha coefficient, with results of 0.842 and 0.912 for customer satisfaction and chatbot service quality, respectively, all indicating acceptable reliability. To test the hypotheses, the researcher conducted Regression and ANOVA analyses.

Table 1. Reliability and VALIDITY test

Variables	Measures	Factor Loading
Customer satisfaction Cronbach Alpha Value= 0.842 Kaiser-Meyer Olkim (KMO)= 0.848	Happy with Service Provided	.671
	Task More Efficiently	.771
	Adds Significant Value	.782
	Meets Expectations	.805
	Satisfied with Performance	.806
Chatbot Service Quality Cronbach alpha value=0.912 Kaiser-Meyer Olkim(KMO)=0.917	Easy to Use	.741
	Trust Chatbot Information	.634
	Responds Queries Promptly	.732
	Security System	.701
	Enjoy Using Chatbot	.767
	Interface Visually Appealing	.712
	Customised Specific Needs	.717
	Effectively Resolves Issues	.714
	Consistent Service	.776
	Tailored Responses	.763
	Fun to Use	.769

Table 2. Respondents characteristics

Demographics	Characteristics	Frequency	Percentage
Occupation	Self-Employed	44	21.0
	Employed	65	31.0
	Student	97	46.2
	Any other	4	1.9
Qualification	Secondary	6	2.9
	Senior Secondary	43	20.5
	Graduate	100	47.6
	Any other	7	3.3
	Post Graduate	54	25.7
Used Chabot Services	Yes	202	96.2
	No	8	3.8
Digital Banking Platform	Yes	208	99.0
	No	2	1.0

Data Analysis and Results

The data indicates a predominantly tech-savvy and well-educated demographic, reflecting a strong inclination toward digital banking solutions. A significant majority of respondents are students (46.2%), highlighting a young, adaptable user base that is highly engaged with digital technology. This is followed by employed individuals (31.0%) and self-employed professionals (21.0%), suggesting that chatbot adoption is widespread across different career paths. The high percentage of graduates and postgraduates (73.3%) further reinforces the notion that the respondents are well-informed, comfortable with technological advancements, and open to integrating AI-driven solutions into their financial activities.

The overwhelming adoption rates 96.2% having used chatbot services and 99.0% utilizing digital banking platforms illustrate a deeply embedded digital banking culture, with minimal resistance to technology. This suggests that chatbots have seamlessly integrated into everyday banking experiences, proving their value in streamlining operations. However, the small minority yet to adopt these technologies presents an opportunity for banks to expand outreach programs, enhance digital literacy, and build trust among hesitant users.

1. To understand the concept of chatbot service quality in banking.

The objective "To understand the concept of chatbot service quality in banking" involves a comprehensive exploration of how AI-driven chatbots enhance customer interactions and streamline banking operations. This begins with defining 'chatbot service quality', which includes identifying critical characteristics such as response accuracy, response time, user experience, and contextual understanding. These factors determine how effectively chatbots address customer queries, resolve issues, and provide personalized assistance.

Beyond basic functionality, chatbot service quality is also evaluated through key dimensions such as reliability, empathy, security, and adaptability. Reliability ensures that chatbots consistently deliver correct information without errors, while empathy though challenging in AI interactions refers to the chatbot's ability to provide reassuring and human-like responses. Security remains paramount, as customers need to trust that their data is protected. Additionally, adaptability measures how well chatbots learn from interactions and refine responses over time.

By understanding these elements, banks can optimize chatbot performance, ensuring seamless, efficient, and customer-centric digital experiences. Understanding customer expectations is crucial; customers seek fast responses, 24/7 availability, and accurate information, and benchmarking these expectations against actual chatbot performance highlights areas for improvement. Evaluating performance metrics, including customer satisfaction scores and resolution rates, enables banks to measure effectiveness and implement feedback mechanisms for continuous enhancement. Analyzing the customer interaction experience through mapping the user journey helps identify pain points and moments of satisfaction, while assessing personalization capabilities ensures chatbots meet individual customer needs.

Additionally, recognizing the role of chatbots in digital transformation highlights their potential to streamline operations, reduce service bottlenecks, and enhance customer engagement, ultimately fostering long-term loyalty. By automating routine inquiries, chatbots allow human agents to focus on complex, high-value tasks, improving overall service efficiency. Their ability to provide instant responses, personalized recommendations, and seamless multi-channel support makes them an essential tool for banks looking to modernize customer interactions.

However, challenges persist, such as limitations in natural language processing (NLP), integration with legacy banking systems, and concerns regarding customer trust and data security. While AI-powered chatbots have improved significantly, misunderstandings and inadequate responses to nuanced queries still pose obstacles. Additionally, factors like customer skepticism, privacy concerns, and resistance to AI-driven interactions influence adoption rates. Addressing these issues through continuous AI advancements, improved chatbot training, and transparency in data handling is essential for maximizing chatbot effectiveness.

By focusing on these aspects, this objective aims to offer a comprehensive understanding of chatbot service quality in banking, helping financial institutions refine their chatbot strategies. By aligning technological advancements with evolving customer expectations, banks can enhance customer satisfaction, boost operational efficiency, and strengthen their competitive edge in the digital banking landscape.

2.To study the impact of chatbot service quality on consumer satisfaction & value.

Ha1: Chatbot service quality of banks significantly influences customer satisfaction & value.

Table 3. Model summary

Model Summary				
Model	**R**	**R Square**	**Adjusted R Square**	**Std. Error of the Estimate**
1	.892[a]	.795	.794	.28604

a. Predictors: (Constant), Chatbot Service Quality

Source: Primary Data Processing in SPSS.

The model summary offers significant details about the model's overall efficacy. Based on the model's predictors of customer value & satisfaction towards the coefficient of determination (R-squared) value, which is 0.795, shows that 79.5% of the variance in barriers to completion can be explained. This shows that even while the model has some explanatory power, a significant amount of the variance is still unexplained.

Table 4. ANOVA

ANOVA[a]						
Model		**Sum of Squares**	**Df**	**Mean Square**	**F**	**Sig.**
1	Regression	65.977	1	65.977	806.396	.000[b]
	Residual	17.018	208	.082		
	Total	82.995	209			

a. Dependent Variable: Customer Satisfaction
b. Predictors: (Constant), Chatbot Service Quality
Source: Primary Data Processing in SPSS.

The F-statistic ($F = 806.396, p < 0.05$) in the ANOVA table, which evaluates the regression model's overall significance, is significant. It is evident from this that the regression model, which takes into consideration the customer value & satisfaction towards as predictors, is a major predictor of the barriers associated with completing.

Table 5. Coefficients

Coefficients[a]						
Model		**Unstandardized Coefficients**		**Standardized Coefficients**	**t**	**Sig.**
		B	**Std. Error**	**Beta**		
1	(Constant)	.455	.106		4.303	.000
	Chatbot Service Quality	.879	.031	.892	28.397	.000

a. Dependent Variable: Customer Satisfaction
Source: Primary Data Processing in SPSS.

The regression analysis shows that the intercept for barriers to completion is .879. The coefficient (0.000) is not significant ($p = 0.263$), indicating it does not strongly influence barriers. However, the coefficient (0.455) is significant ($p < 0.001$), suggesting a positive impact on reducing barriers, with a standardized coefficient (Beta) of 0.892, showing a moderate effect.

FINDINGS

The findings of the study reveal that an overwhelming 96% of respondents have used chatbot services in banking, indicating not only a high level of awareness but also widespread adoption of AI-driven customer support tools. This strikingly high adoption rate reflects the growing comfort of digital banking users with automation and AI-powered interactions. It suggests that customers are no longer hesitant about engaging with non-human interfaces, but instead are beginning to view chatbots as an integral part of their day-to-day banking experience. The widespread use also highlights a shift in consumer expectations, where immediacy, efficiency, and digital convenience are becoming non-negotiable elements of service quality in financial institutions.

Customers in the study generally perceive chatbots in a positive light, particularly emphasizing their functionality, convenience, and security. The ability to perform essential banking tasks instantly whether checking balances, transferring funds, or blocking a lost debit card has positioned chatbots as reliable digital assistants. Efficiency and time-saving stand out as the most valued aspects, as customers prefer resolving queries instantly rather than spending time visiting physical branches or waiting in long queues to connect with customer service representatives. For many respondents, chatbots have redefined customer service in banking by making interactions quicker, more efficient, and available anytime, anywhere.

The study further establishes a strong and statistically significant positive correlation between chatbot service quality and customer satisfaction. Three primary factors functionality, convenience, and assurance emerge as key contributors to satisfaction. Customers particularly appreciate the round-the-clock availability of chatbot services, which eliminates the constraints of traditional banking hours and significantly enhances the overall experience. The capacity of chatbots to provide instant responses reduces customer frustration associated with long waiting times, thereby fostering higher satisfaction. Beyond speed, personalization plays a critical role. Chatbots have the ability to tailor suggestions and recommendations based on customers' past transactions, spending behaviour, and stated preferences, thus creating a more individualized and engaging interaction. This ability to provide quick and relevant solutions not only increases utility but also strengthens the perceived value of AI-enabled banking services.

In terms of service quality, dimensions such as responsiveness, reliability, assurance, and security are particularly crucial in shaping the overall effectiveness of chatbot interactions. Responsiveness ensures that users feel heard and supported in real time, while reliability reinforces trust through consistent, error-free service delivery. Assurance and security, on the other hand, are fundamental to customer trust in a sector as sensitive as banking, where customers must feel confident when sharing personal or financial information. A seamless, glitch-free experience combined with robust security protocols reassures users that their data is safe and protected. Beyond functional aspects, emotional factors also influence satisfaction. Elements such as enjoyment, ease of use, and trust shape the emotional dimension of service quality. Customers who perceive chatbot interactions as intuitive, engaging, and user-friendly are not only more likely to use them consistently but also more inclined to build long-term trust in AI-driven financial services.

Despite these strengths, the study underscores that customer satisfaction levels are not uniform across all types of banking interactions. The level of satisfaction often depends on the complexity of the tasks being handled. While chatbots are efficient at addressing routine and straightforward tasks such as FAQs, balance checks, or fund transfers, customers may encounter dissatisfaction when attempting to resolve more complex issues. Tasks involving loan applications, investment guidance, or dispute settlements often exceed the current capabilities of most chatbots. In these situations, customers may feel frustrated if the chatbot is unable to provide adequate assistance or if escalation to a human agent is delayed.

To overcome this limitation, a hybrid model of customer service where chatbots handle initial, routine queries and seamlessly escalate complex problems to human representatives emerges as a practical solution. This blended approach allows banks to retain the efficiency and cost-effectiveness of automation while ensuring that customers receive personalized and empathetic support for more complicated concerns. Furthermore, continuous improvements in chatbot capabilities through advanced artificial intelligence, natural language processing, and machine learning algorithms hold the potential to bridge these gaps. By enhancing their ability to manage complex queries, predict customer needs, and deliver more human-like interactions, chatbots can move beyond being simple transactional tools to becoming strategic assets that foster higher customer satisfaction, deeper trust, and long-term loyalty.

LIMITATIONS

While the sample size provides valuable insights into chatbot service quality, certain limitations should be noted. The study focuses primarily on customers already using digital banking services, which may exclude perspectives from individuals who prefer traditional banking methods. For instance, elderly populations or those less comfortable with technology may still rely on face-to-face interactions and remain hesitant to adopt AI-powered banking solutions. Without accounting for these groups, the findings may not reflect the full spectrum of customer experiences and satisfaction with chatbots in banking.

Another limitation is the study's exclusive focus on banking chatbots, which restricts the generalizability of its findings to other industries. In banking, chatbot design often emphasizes security, accuracy, and efficiency. By contrast, customers in sectors like e-commerce, healthcare, or hospitality may value personalization, engagement, or convenience more highly. Extending research beyond the banking sector could provide a broader understanding of how chatbot service quality is perceived across industries.

The study also does not address other AI-driven tools that are reshaping financial services, such as robo-advisors or voice-activated banking assistants. Robo-advisors are already transforming investment and wealth management by offering automated, data-driven recommendations, while voice-enabled assistants integrated into smart devices are making banking more accessible. Future research that incorporates these emerging technologies could present a more complete view of how AI is redefining customer service in finance and beyond.

SUGGESTION

Future research should aim to cover a broader demographic scope by including diverse regions across Country, encompassing both urban and rural populations. . A larger and more representative sample size could capture variations in digital literacy, banking habits, and trust levels in AI-driven services across different population segments. Additionally, incorporating customers who are less familiar with digital banking such as elderly individuals or those with limited internet access would offer valuable insights into the barriers to chatbot adoption and potential areas for improvement.

A comparative analysis between chatbots and human agents would also offer deeper insights into the strengths and weaknesses of AI-driven services, particularly in handling complex or emotionally sensitive banking interactions. While chatbots excel in providing quick responses and handling repetitive tasks, they may lack the empathy and nuanced problem-solving abilities of human representatives. Studying customer preferences for AI versus human support in different banking scenarios such as resolving fraud disputes, loan approvals, or financial planning could help banks refine their customer service strategies. Furthermore, understanding how chatbot interactions impact customer emotions, frustration levels, and overall satisfaction compared to human-led services would be crucial for improving chatbot design and effectiveness.

Beyond service efficiency, further studies could explore the influence of chatbots on customer trust and long-term loyalty. Trust is a key determinant of customer retention, especially in the financial sector, where data security, privacy, and reliability are top concerns. Investigating how AI-driven interactions build (or undermine) trust over time, and how they affect customer loyalty, could provide banks with strategic insights into enhancing customer relationships. This research would be particularly relevant in private banking and wealth management, where personalized service and trust are fundamental to customer satisfaction.

Moreover, future studies could examine the impact of emerging technologies, such as AI-powered voice assistants, sentiment-aware chatbots, and hybrid AI-human customer support models. Voice-activated banking assistants, integrated into smart devices, are becoming more prevalent and may offer a more seamless and intuitive way for customers to interact with their banks. Similarly, hybrid models that combine AI chatbots with human intervention at critical touchpoints could improve service efficiency while maintaining the personal touch required for sensitive financial matters. Exploring these advancements would contribute to a deeper understanding of how customer service in banking is evolving and offer new perspectives on optimizing service delivery for enhanced customer satisfaction.

CONCLUSION

The study concludes that chatbots play a crucial role in enhancing customer satisfaction and adding significant value to banking services by offering fast, reliable, and personalized assistance. Their ability to provide instant responses, handle multiple queries simultaneously, and operate 24/7 has improved customer convenience and streamlined banking operations. By reducing wait times and automating routine tasks such as account inquiries, fund transfers, and transaction tracking, chatbots contribute to greater operational efficiency, benefiting both banks and their customers. Additionally, chatbots enhance service accessibility, allowing users to engage with their banks at any time and from any location, which is especially valuable in today's fast-paced digital banking environment.

Despite these advantages, the study emphasizes that for chatbots to meet rising customer expectations, particularly in handling complex banking tasks, continuous improvements in AI capabilities are essential. Advancements in natural language processing (NLP) and machine learning can enhance chatbot accuracy, allowing them to better interpret user intent, manage sophisticated queries, and provide context-aware responses. Additionally, improvements in user interface (UI) design and conversational flow can create a more seamless and intuitive interaction experience, making chatbot services more engaging and user-friendly. Personalization is another key area for development by leveraging customer data and behavioural insights, chatbots can deliver more tailored recommendations, proactive support, and customized banking solutions that align with individual financial needs.

Furthermore, the study highlights the growing importance of chatbot services in the digital transformation of banking, paving the way for further innovation and customer-centric developments. As AI-driven banking solutions evolve, future advancements may include integration with voice assistants, enhanced sentiment analysis for empathetic responses, and hybrid AI-human support models to ensure a more personalized and effective banking experience. Banks that invest in refining chatbot technology will not only enhance customer satisfaction but also strengthen brand loyalty and maintain a competitive edge in the rapidly evolving financial sector.

REFERENCES

Ashfaq, M. Y. (2020). I, Chatbot: Modeling the determinants of users' satisfaction and continuance intention of AI-powered service agents. *Telematics and Informatics*.

Carvalho, P., & Alves, H. (2023). Customer value co-creation in the hospitality and tourism industry: A systematic literature review. *International Journal of Contemporary Hospitality Management, 35*(1), 250–273. DOI: 10.1108/IJCHM-12-2021-1528

Cheng, Y., & Jiang, H. (2022). Customer–brand relationship in the era of artificial intelligence: Understanding the role of chatbot marketing efforts. *Journal of Product and Brand Management, 31*(2), 252–264. DOI: 10.1108/JPBM-05-2020-2907

Chung, M., Ko, E., Joung, H., & Kim, S. J. (2020). Chatbot e-service and customer satisfaction regarding luxury brands. *Journal of Business Research, 117*, 587–595. DOI: 10.1016/j.jbusres.2018.10.004

Das, A., & Agarwal, P. (2022). Enhancing customer experience through AI-powered chatbots in Banking. *Journal of Banking and Technology Innovations, 15*(4), 112–129.

Das, P., & Dutta, S. (2021). Customer perception of chatbots in urban and rural banking in India. *Indian Journal of Business Studies*, 34-48.

Eren, B. A. (2021). Determinants of customer satisfaction in chatbot use: Evidence from a banking application in Turkey. *International Journal of Bank Marketing, 39*(2), 294–311. DOI: 10.1108/IJBM-02-2020-0056

Gupta, R., Sharma, V., & Mehta, K. (2022). Assessing the effectiveness of chatbots in Banking: Opportunities and challenges. *International Journal of Financial Services, 8*(3), 78–93.

Hsu, C. L., & Lin, J. C.-C. (2023). Understanding the user satisfaction and loyalty of customer service chatbots. *Journal of Retailing and Consumer Services, 71*, 103211. DOI: 10.1016/j.jretconser.2022.103211

Klein, K., & Martinez, L. F. (2023). The impact of anthropomorphism on customer satisfaction in chatbot commerce: An experimental study in the food sector. *Electronic Commerce Research, 23*(4), 2789–2825. DOI: 10.1007/s10660-022-09562-8

Kvale, K. F. (2020). Understanding the user experience of customer service chatbots: what can we learn from customer satisfaction surveys? *In International Workshop on Chatbot Research and Design.*

Lei, S. I., Shen, H., & Ye, S. (2021). A comparison between chatbot and human service: Customer perception and reuse intention. *International Journal of Contemporary Hospitality Management, 33*(11), 3977–3995. DOI: 10.1108/IJCHM-12-2020-1399

Li, L. L., Lee, K. Y., Emokpae, E., & Yang, S.-B. (2021). What makes you continuously use chatbot services? Evidence from chinese online travel agencies. *Electronic Markets, 31*(3), 575–599. DOI: 10.1007/s12525-020-00454-z PMID: 35603227

Lo Presti, L. M. (2021). The role of the chatbot on customer purchase intention: towards digital relational sales. *Italian Journal of Marketing*.

Mogaji, E. B., Balakrishnan, J., Nwoba, A. C., & Nguyen, N. P. (2021). Emerging-market consumers' interactions with banking chatbots. *Telematics and Informatics, 65*, 101711. DOI: 10.1016/j.tele.2021.101711

Nadarzynski, T. M., Miles, O., Cowie, A., & Ridge, D. (2019). Acceptability of artificial intelligence (AI)-led chatbot services in healthcare: A mixed-methods study. *Digital Health, 5*, 2055207619871808. DOI: 10.1177/2055207619871808 PMID: 31467682

Petersson, A. H. (2023). Investigating the factors of customer experiences using real-life text-based banking chatbot: A qualitative study in Norway. *Petersson, A. H., Pawar, S., & Fagerstrøm, A.*

Ruan, Y., & Mezei, J. (2022). When do AI chatbots lead to higher customer satisfaction than human frontline employees in online shopping assistance? Considering product attribute type. *Journal of Retailing and Consumer Services, 68*, 103059. DOI: 10.1016/j.jretconser.2022.103059

Singh, M., & Gupta, N. (2023). The future of chatbots in Banking: Trends and opportunities. *AI and Financial Services Journal, 7*(1), 45–60.

Yen, C.-H., Teng, H.-Y., & Tzeng, J.-C. (2020). Innovativeness and customer value co-creation behaviours: Mediating role of customer engagement. *International Journal of Hospitality Management, 88*, 102514. DOI: 10.1016/j.ijhm.2020.102514

Chapter 7

Cyber Bullying, Trolling, and Online Aggression

Rubi Rajput
http://orcid.org/0000-0002-1912-667X
Swami Vivekanand Subharti University, Meerut, India

ABSTRACT

Cyber bullying and internet trolling are forms of online aggression that have become increasingly prevalent. Research indicates that individuals engaging in these behaviors often exhibit low self-esteem, low conscientiousness, and low internal moral values (Zezulka & Seigfried-Spellar, 2016).Trolling has been associated with personality traits such as psychopathy, narcissism, and sadism (Aydın et al., n.d.). Studies have found a significant relationship between offline aggression and online trolling behavior, suggesting that aggressive individuals tend to maintain their aggression in online spaces (Strimbu & O'Connell, 2021). However, there are inconsistencies between offline and online self-presentation for highly aggressive individuals. Detecting cyber bullying and aggression on social media platforms like Twitter is possible through machine learning algorithms that analyze text, user, and network-based attributes.

1. INTRODUCTION

Digital communication technologies, such as social media platforms, messaging apps, online gaming environments, and emerging immersive environments like the metaverse, have become central to communication, learning, and relationship-building between young and old. Along with these opportunities, these spaces have given rise to new forms of hate and harassment, collectively known as cyber bullying. This term encompasses cyber bullying, trolling, verbal abuse, privacy violations, and

DOI: 10.4018/979-8-3373-5896-3.ch007

coordinated harassment campaigns, each varying in ideology, intensity, and social impact. Schools, families, policymakers, and platform designers are increasingly recognizing that cyber bullying is not an isolated problem but a social engineering phenomenon shaped by human consciousness, platform power, and digital culture. Despite extensive research in psychology, communication studies, education, and human-computer interaction, the field remains fragmented. Definitions vary across studies, measurement instruments are inconsistent, and prevalence estimates vary widely depending on sampling methods, age groups, and instruments used. As the reviewers of this manuscript rightly point out, many reports provide estimates without clarifying the methodology, making it difficult to compare findings or draw conclusions based on evidence. This lack of consistency limits theory building and undermines the development of effective prevention and intervention strategies. To address these challenges, this chapter uses a survey research approach. Survey research is appropriate for this topic because it allows for a systematic mapping of definitions, theoretical models, measurement instruments, prevalence, level content, and interventions across different research traditions. The survey is not intended to produce broad general statistics; rather, it is intended to clarify how online bullying is conceptualized and measured, the types of intervention models that are consistently reported, and the extent to which knowledge gaps remain.

Figure 1. Cyber Bully at Global Level

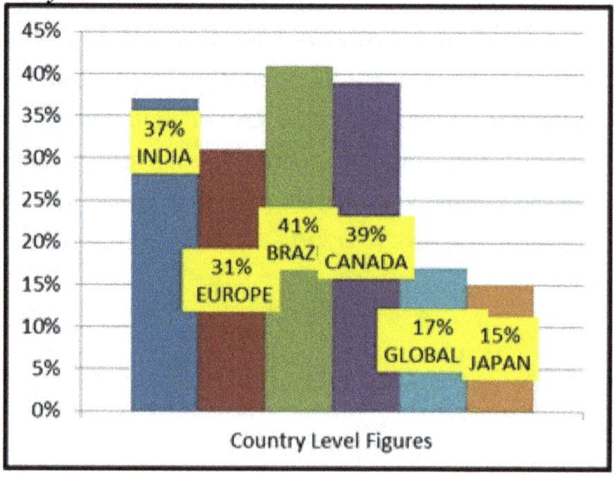

1.1 Psychology of Virtual Bullying

Virtual bullying, often referred to as cyber bullying, is not simply face-to-face aggression. Rather, it stems from a unique set of psychological processes that shape the structure of online aggression. Several mechanisms interact to enhance hostility, and create autonomy, resulting in a context in which people can behave as they would in physical environments. Internal autonomy is a fundamental characteristic, which can be weakened in digital contexts. In offline environments, direct social feedback-expressions, from facial expressions to physical reactions-encourage empathy and instill norms. However, online communication removes or delays these signals. Rather than relying on emotional cues, text-based interactions, avatars of emotional signals, provide some information about the emotional state of another person. This lack of physical feedback reduces anticipatory guilt and weakens self-monitoring, creating conditions in which aggressive impulses can be expressed with fewer psychological constraints. Digital environments often combine discursive insecurity, invisibility, asynchrony, reduced authority, and solipsistic imagery. Together, these factors create a sense of psychological disconnect between one's actions and their consequences. Importantly, this does not arise from name alone; even semi-identified users can engage in aggressive behavior when communication is asynchronous or when community norms reward impulsive behavior. Thus, toxic disinhibiting-manifested as hostile, provocative antisocial acts-can emerges in spaces that foster rather than tolerate aggressive expression. Group identity processes also fuel online aggression. Social media, forums, and gaming communities are designed to connect through groups that reinforce shared values, stories, and emotional climates. A strong intra-group identity can foster empathy for outsiders and more disconnected approaches such as humanizing the distribution of roles. In these environments, hostile acts can be reframed as humor, "defense of the group," or rational retaliation. Trolling behavior often exploits this dynamic: users seek reactions not only from viewers but also from followers, and gain entertainment status through disruption. Group-based trolling can quickly escalate into coordinated harassment when members give their consent, indirectly or explicitly through giving likes, sharing supportive comments, and so on.

1.2 Short-Circuiting of the Internal "Policeman"

Classical theories of moral action-particularly Bandura's work on moral self-regulation-suggest that individuals adjust to social norms through mechanisms such as guilt, shame, empathy, and inhibitory self-evaluations. These processes work together as an "internal policeman," guiding behavior and discouraging actions that violate personal or social norms. In physical, face-to-face settings, this internal system is constantly activated by direct feedback: the presence of others, nonverbal cues, social evaluation, and the tangible visibility of harm. In virtual environments, however, several factors can weaken or "short-circuit" these regulatory processes. **First**, reduced social presence reduces emotional resonance. Without facial expressions, tone, or physical cues, individuals receive fewer signals that their actions may be harmful. This weakens predictive guilt-the mechanism that typically prompts people to think about how their behavior will affect another person. When emotional cues are absent, empathy becomes less spontaneous and it is easier to act out an attack. **Second**, psychological distance and detachment allow individuals to feel separate from their online persona. Even if users are not completely anonymous, the feeling of operating through a digital identity can create a mental barrier between the self and the action. This detachment reduces self-justification, making harmful actions feel less personal and less morally meaningful. **Third**, asynchrony-a feature of many online platforms-gives individuals time to formulate responses without seeing immediate consequences. Because victims' reactions are not always visible or immediate, moral feedback is delayed or absent. In turn, the psychological cost of an attack is reduced, and the internal "policeman" is less likely to intervene. **Fourth**, audience effects and the diffusion of responsibility in group contexts can further undermine autonomy. When harmful behavior is normalized, condoned, or encouraged by an online community, individuals experience less personal responsibility. They may see their actions as part of collective moral choices rather than individual choices, making moral disengagement strategies (e.g., harm reduction, victim blaming, moral justification) more readily available. At last, algorithmic and platform capabilities can change autonomy. Interfaces that encourage rapid posting, reward provocative content, or regulate ambiguous responses may inadvertently encourage people to express unfriendly emotions and reduce opportunities for reflective thinking-another important component of self-regulation. These factors suggest that the weakening of internal moral constraints in digital spaces is not simply a matter of anonymity or inadequacy. It reflects a complex interplay between psychological processes, technological opportunities, and social dynamics. Understanding how and why this "short circuit" occurs is essential for developing interventions that aim to strengthen digital self-regulation, increase reflective awareness, and promote responsible online behavior.

1.3 Moral Disengagement

People may cognitively restructure their acts so that they are not perceived as hurting others (e.g. "It's just banter," "They deserved it," "Everybody does it"), displace responsibility ("I was just following what the group said"), dehumanize the target, or minimize the consequences (Bandura's mechanisms). Research shows that online disinhibition correlates positively with moral disengagement, which in turn predicts more frequent cyber aggression (e.g. in cyber-dating abuse).

1.4 Anonymity

When individuals feel they can hide behind an anonymous or pseudonymous identity, the sense of direct personal responsibility is diluted; this weakens the anticipatory guilt or social sanction fears.

1.5 A Synchronicity and Lack of Real-Time Feedback

In many online interactions, a bully can issue a comment, insult, or post and then disconnect before seeing the full emotional response. This "fire and forget" mode reduces the emotional feedback loop that might otherwise restrain aggression.

1.6 Cognitive Dissonance Avoidance

The online environment may allow perpetrators to mentally "bracket off" their online persona from their offline self, reducing dissonance and making it easier to act harmfully online without feeling it reflects on their "real" self.

2. DEFINITIONS

2.1. Online Aggression

The digital ecosystem has created new spaces for interaction, learning, and entertainment, but it has also produced novel modes of hostility that differ in form, function, and impact from traditional face-to-face aggression. Online aggression is an umbrella term that encompasses a range of behaviors aimed at inflicting harm, distress, or disruption through digital means. While these behaviors overlap, scholars differentiate between cyber bullying, trolling, flaming, and organized harassment as distinct but interconnected categories (Kowalski et al., 2014; Zezulka et al., 2016). Clear conceptualization is essential because each form is associated with different motivations, psychological traits, and social consequences. These behaviors have garnered significant scholarly attention due to their profound impact on young people's mental health, academic performance, and social well-being.

2.2. Cyber Bullying

Cyber bullying is perhaps the most widely studied form of online aggression. It refers to the deliberate, repeated use of electronic communication technologies to intimidate, harass, or threaten an individual who may find it difficult to defend themselves (Kowalski et al., 2014). Unlike traditional bullying, cyber bullying transcends temporal and spatial boundaries: harmful content can be disseminated widely, persist for extended periods, and reach audiences far beyond the immediate peer group. Victims of cyber bullying frequently report anxiety, depression, suicidal ideation, social withdrawal, and academic decline (Wachs et al., 2022). The persistent and pervasive nature of cyber bullying often intensifies its psychological impact compared to face-to-face bullying. Furthermore, anonymity afforded by digital platforms reduces perpetrators' accountability; encouraging behaviors that may not manifest offline (Suler, 2004). *Example behaviors include (i)* Sending threatening or abusive messages (ii) Sharing humiliating photos or videos without consent (iii) Excluding peers from online groups or chats (iv) Spreading rumors or misinformation on social media. Cyber bullying is particularly concerning in educational settings, where students are both high users of digital technologies and highly vulnerable to peer influence. Global statistics suggest that between 30–60% of adolescents report experiencing cyber bullying at least once in their lives (Cyber bullying Research Center, 2025).

2.3. Trolling

Trolling is another prominent manifestation of online aggression, but it differs from cyber bullying in scope. Trolling refers to the deliberate posting of provocative, offensive, disruptive messages with the primary goal of eliciting emotional reactions, derailing conversations, and creating conflict (Strimbu et al., 2021). While some trolling may be framed as humor and mischief, research increasingly links trolling behavior to personality traits such as psychopathy, narcissism, and sadism (Aydın et al., 2021). Unlike cyber bullying, trolling is not always directed at a specific individual; instead, it often targets groups, online communities, or public discussions. Trolling can range from mild antagonism (sarcasm, deliberate misinformation) to severe hostility (hate speech, personal attacks). Its ambiguity makes it challenging to regulate, since some perpetrators claim that their behavior is "just a joke." Nevertheless, trolling can escalate into harassment, exacerbate polarization, and contribute to toxic online cultures.

2.4. Flaming

Flaming represents one of the earliest forms of online aggression identified in digital communication studies. It involves hostile, insulting, and inflammatory exchanges between users, typically in the form of heated arguments or verbal abuse (Chatzakou et al., 2017). Unlike cyber bullying and trolling, flaming is often reciprocal and occurs in real time, such as in comment sections, forums, multiplayer gaming chat rooms. Key features of flaming include: (i) Use of offensive and vulgar language (ii) Escalating cycles of retaliation (iii) Occurrence in public digital spaces, witnessed by others. While flaming may appear less targeted than cyber bullying, it still has negative consequences. Research shows that exposure to frequent online hostility contributes to emotional exhaustion, desensitization, and normalization of aggression (Cortis & Handschuh, 2015). Flaming can quickly evolve into organized harassment when multiple users collectively attack an individual.

2.5. Organized Harassment

*S*ometimes called dog piling; occurs when a group of individuals coordinates to target and overwhelm a specific person or group with abusive messages, threats, with harmful content. This form of aggression is often amplified by algorithmic systems that boost controversial and emotionally charged content, making harassment campaigns highly visible and damaging (Chatzakou et al., 2017; Sadiq et al., 2021). Examples: (i) Coordinated attacks using hash tags (e.g., during political and social controversies) (ii) Mass reporting of an individual's social media account to force suspension (iii) Collective spamming of derogatory comments on a victim's posts. Organized harassment often has devastating consequences, including reputational damage, psychological trauma, and withdrawal from digital spaces. In some cases, targets may even face offline threats, demonstrating the blurred boundaries between virtual aggression and real-world harm. Table 1 comparative Characteristics While all four types cyber bullying, trolling, flaming, and organized harassment fall under the umbrella of online aggression, they differ in intent, target, and structure:

Table 1. Forms of online aggression – definitions, contexts, and impacts

Form of Aggression	Intent	Target	Typical Context	Psychological Impact
Cyber bullying	To harm, intimidate, or dominate	Specific individual (often weaker peer)	Social media, messaging apps, school settings	Anxiety, depression, academic decline
Trolling	To provoke, disrupt, or amuse	Individuals, groups, or public forums	Comment sections, gaming platforms	Anger, frustration, toxic online culture
Flaming	To attack or retaliate during conflict	One or more individuals	Forums, chat rooms, multiplayer games	Emotional exhaustion, hostility normalization
Organized Harassment	To overwhelm and silence	Specific individual or group	Social media campaigns, hash tag activism	Trauma, reputational damage, withdrawal

3. THEORETICAL PERSPECTIVES

3.1. Online Aggression

Understanding online aggression requires more than just documenting behaviors; it also demands an exploration of the psychological, social, and technological mechanisms that facilitate such conduct. Scholars have developed several theoretical models to explain why individuals act aggressively in digital spaces. Four particularly influential frameworks are de-individuation theory, the online disinhibition effect, social identity theory, and moral disengagement theory. Together, these perspectives illustrate how anonymity, group dynamics, and cognitive processes interact to foster online hostility.

3.1.1 De-individuation Theory

De-individuation theory originates from social psychology, where it was first proposed to explain crowd behavior. It suggests that when individuals lose their sense of personal identity and accountability within a group, they are more likely to engage in antisocial and aggressive behavior (Festinger et al., 1952; Zimbardo, 1969). In digital environments, De-individuation occurs through: (i) Anonymity (users conceal personal identity) (ii) Large group size (mass interactions dilute personal responsibility) (iii) Physical invisibility. This state of reduced self-awareness diminishes self-regulation and amplifies impulsivity, leading individuals to act in ways they would normally avoid offline. For example, in an online forum, users may participate in flaming because they feel shielded by the collective identity of the group. Empirical studies confirm that de-individuation increases aggressive and norm-violating behavior in online settings, particularly where moderation is weak (Postmes et al., 2001). Empirical research increasingly associates toxic online disinhibition with cyber bullying. For example, among adolescents, toxic disinhibition amplifies the effect of trait anger on cyber bullying behaviors Disinhibition is a key psychological lens to understand why people behave more harshly online.

3.1.2 Effect of online Disinhibition (ODE)

The effect of online disinhibition is a double-edged sword, leading to both positive (benign) and negative (toxic) outcomes. While it can foster increased self-disclosure and help for others, it also fuels negative behaviors like toxic drama, rudeness, cyber bullying, and hatred due to factors such as anonymity, invisibility, and delayed communication. Suler (2004) concept of the online disinhibition effect (ODE) is one of the most widely cited explanations for toxic digital behavior. The theory posits that individuals feel less restrained in online interactions, leading to a spectrum of behaviors ranging from benign disinhibition (self-disclosure, seeking support) to toxic disinhibition (verbal aggression, threats, harassment). Suler identifies six psychological factors driving ODE: (i) Dissociative anonymity – Users feel unidentifiable, reducing accountability.(ii) Invisibility; Others cannot see facial expressions or physical reactions. (iii) A synchronicity; Delays in communication allow users to detach emotionally.(iv) Solipsistic introjection; People assign imagined characteristics to others online.(v) Dissociative imagination; The online world feels like a separate reality.(vi) Minimization of authority; Absence of visible power structures encourages norm violations. For instance, a teenager might engage in cyber bullying by sending hateful direct messages because the asynchronous, anonymous nature of the medium shields them from immediate consequences.

3.1.3 Social Identity Theory

While de-individuation and ODE emphasize anonymity and loss of self, social identity theory (SIT) provides a complementary perspective. Tajfel et al., 1979 argue that individuals derive part of their identity from group memberships. In online spaces, where communities form around shared interests, ideologies, or demographics, group identity becomes a powerful driver of behavior. Key implications for online aggression: (i) In-group favoritism: Users defend their group and attack outsiders. (ii) Out-group derogation: Hostility intensifies when differences are highlighted (e.g., political trolling, hate speech). (iii) Conformity pressures: Members mirror aggressive behavior to maintain group status. For example, political trolling campaigns often emerge within online subcultures that reinforce group-based hostility. Social media algorithms further exacerbate this by creating echo chambers, amplifying group identities, and polarizing discourse. Thus, SIT helps explain why organized harassment frequently takes the form of collective aggression targeted at out-groups, rather than isolated individual misbehavior.

3.1.4 Moral Disengagement Theory

Bandura's (1999) moral disengagement theory focuses on the cognitive processes that allow individuals to commit harmful acts without experiencing guilt or self-condemnation. Online aggressors often employ moral disengagement strategies to justify their actions:

Moral justification: Framing aggression as serving a higher purpose ("I'm exposing the truth").

Euphemistic labeling: Using softened language to disguise harm ("It's just banter").
Advantageous comparison: Minimizing behavior by comparing it to worse acts ("At least I didn't threaten violence").
Displacement of responsibility: Blaming platform norms or peer pressure ("Everyone does it online").
Diffusion of responsibility: Sharing blame across a group during harassment campaigns.
Dehumanization: Viewing victims as less than human or unworthy of empathy.

3.2. Integrating the Theories

Each theory highlights a different facet of online aggression:

- **De-individuation** → explains how anonymity erodes accountability.
- **ODE** → explains why digital communication lowers inhibitions.
- **SIT** → explains how group dynamics intensify hostility.
- **Moral disengagement** → explains how aggressors neutralize guilt.

4. PSYCHOLOGICAL AND SOCIAL IMPACTS OF ONLINE AGGRESSION

4.1 Online Aggression

including cyber bullying, trolling, flaming, and organized harassment has far-reaching consequences for individuals' psychological well-being, social relationships, and academic or professional functioning. Unlike traditional face-to-face aggression, online hostility is amplified by the features of digital platforms: content can spread quickly, persist indefinitely, and reach wide audiences, leaving victims with little control over their exposure. This creates conditions where the emotional damage often surpasses that of offline bullying (Kowalski et al., 2014;).

4.2 Psychological Trauma

is one of the most frequently documented effects. Victims of online aggression often report heightened levels of stress, anxiety, and depression, as well as feelings of helplessness and shame (Modecki et al., 2014). In extreme cases, prolonged exposure to cyber bullying and harassment has been linked to self-harm and suicidal ideation, particularly among adolescents and young adults who are highly active on digital platforms (Hinduja & Patchin, 2019). Research indicates that the anonymity and permanence of online abuse intensify its emotional impact, as individuals relive their victimization each time the content resurfaces or is shared by others (Slonje et al., 2013). The consequences of online aggression extend beyond individual mental health, affecting social relationships and community belonging. Victims frequently experience social alienation, withdrawing from online and offline interactions due to fear of further harassment (Barlett & Chamberlin, 2017). Such withdrawal can create a cycle of isolation, where reduced social support exacerbates psychological distress. Moreover, the stigma associated with being targeted can erode self-esteem and damage peer relationships, especially in educational contexts where reputation is closely tied to social inclusion (Wachs et al., 2017). In educational and professional settings, the negative outcomes are particularly concerning. Studies reveal that students who experience cyber bullying often demonstrate lower academic achievement, reduced concentration, and decreased motivation to engage in classroom activities (Schneider et al., 2012). Similarly, in workplace environments, online harassment—sometimes referred to as cyber incivility—has been associated with decreased job satisfaction, burnout, and turnover intentions (Farley et al., 2016). These findings illustrate that the consequences of online aggression are not confined to private emotional suffering but extend into measurable declines in productivity and performance. An additional dimension is the intergenerational impact of online aggression, where victims' families, peers, and educators are also affected. Parents of bullied adolescents report feelings of helplessness and frustration, while teachers and school administrators face the challenge of addressing cyber incidents that often occur outside formal school hours but directly affect students' learning and classroom climate (Smith et al., 2018). The ripple effect of online aggression underscores its broader societal cost, not just as an individual psychological burden but also as a structural challenge for educational institutions and communities. The normalization of aggressive online culture poses risks for broader social cohesion. When trolling, flaming, and cyber bullying are tolerated as "entertainment" and "right to free expression," they contribute to toxic online environments where hostility becomes the norm. This normalization discourages constructive dialogue, reduces trust in digital communities, and perpetuates cycles of aggression (Cheng et al., 2017). Over time, such environments risk desensitizing individuals to harmful behaviors, lowering empathy, and reinforcing divisive social identities. Taken together, these findings demonstrate that online aggression cannot be dismissed as trivial digital behavior. Its consequences are profound, encompassing psychological trauma, social alienation, academic and workplace disruptions, and broader societal harm.

4.3 Effect on Bystanders and Victims

4.3.1 Emotional and Psychological Damage

Victims of cyber bullying can suffer:

Anxiety, depression, and low self-esteem: Numerous studies link cyber bullying victimization with higher symptoms of depression, internalizing problems, and lowered well-being.
Post-traumatic stress reaction: Persistent ongoing harassment can provoke symptoms akin to PTSD (intrusive thoughts, hyper vigilance, and avoidance).
Somatic symptoms: Sleep disturbances, headaches, abdominal pain, and psychosomatic complaints are commonly reported in youth under cyber bullying stress.
Academic decline, attention problems, and social withdrawal: Victims may withdraw from social or educational engagement for fear of further harassment.
Risk of self-harm or suicidal ideation: In extreme cases, sustained cyber bullying has been linked to suicidal attempts.

4.3.2 Bystanders and Witnesses May Also Experience

Emotional distress and guilt: Witnessing harm without intervening can lead to helplessness, guilt, or moral conflict.
Vicarious trauma: Repeated exposure to harassment may tax one's emotional boundaries, leading to anxiety or stress.
Desensitization: Over time, seeing frequent bullying may numb individuals to its effects, reducing sensitivity and responsiveness.

4.3.3 Self-Censorship and Reputation Damage

When people observe aggressive online norms, they often self-censor:

Fear of backlash: Potential critics or counter speakers may stay silent to avoid becoming targets.
Reduced expression: People may avoid controversial opinions, to not attract aggression.
Reputation management: Individuals may avoid posting, participating, or engaging deeply to reduce exposure to harassment or misinterpretation.

Who is online Victim ? Victims whose reputation is attacked online (e.g. via rumors, defamation, boxing) suffer damage to their social standing, which can ripple into real-world consequences (educational, professional, relational).

4.3.4 Moral Disengagement of Bystanders

Bystanders often rationalize non-intervention through mechanisms of moral disengagement:

Diffusion of responsibility: "Someone else will step in."
Minimizing harm: "It's just joking."
Victim-blaming: "They asked for it."
Dehumanization of victims: "They're overreacting."

4.4 Summative Effects and Long-Term Trauma

Over time, the cumulative impact can be profound:

Chronic anxiety or depression: Sustained harassment may produce enduring mental health challenges.
Identity disturbance: Victims may internalize negative messages, altering self-concept or reducing confidence.
Social avoidance or isolation: To avoid future harm, victims may withdraw from online or offline social life.
Erosion of trust: Trust in social platforms, peers, and institutions may degrade.
Normalization of hostility: In communities where bullying is frequent, cruelty can become normalized, making recovery harder.
Spillover into offline life: Online aggression can fuel real-world harassment or stress, affecting relationships, schooling, or work.

5. PLATFORM AND CONTEXTUAL INFLUENCES ON ONLINE AGGRESSION

The technological environment in which digital interactions occur plays a decisive role in shaping the prevalence and intensity of online aggression. Unlike offline spaces, online platforms create unique conditions-such as anonymity, algorithmic amplification, and asynchronous communication-that influence how individuals behave and how aggression manifests. The design of digital platforms is therefore not neutral; instead, it actively structures the opportunities and constraints that govern user conduct (Cheng et al., 2017; Keipi et al., 2017). A central factor is anonymity, which reduces accountability and increases the likelihood of aggressive behavior. When individuals are free from the risk of being personally identified, they are more inclined to use hostile language or engage in harassment that they would avoid in face-to-face contexts. Research has consistently shown that anonymous users on forums and social media are more likely to engage in flaming, trolling, and hate speech compared to users whose real identities are visible (Lapidot-Lefler et al., 2012). This finding connects with de-individuation theory and the online disinhibition effect, which highlight how anonymity and invisibility lower self-regulation and foster hostility. Another important factor is algorithmic amplification. Social media platforms rely on algorithms designed to maximize user engagement, often by prioritizing content that generates strong emotional responses. Unfortunately, provocative and aggressive posts tend to attract more attention, clicks, and shares, which mean that hostility is disproportionately amplified by platform design. Studies of Twitter, for example, show that hostile and toxic content spreads more widely and quickly than neutral or positive content (Chatzakou et al., 2017). This amplification not only increases the visibility of aggression but also normalizes it, as users are repeatedly exposed to hostile communication in their feeds. The asynchronous nature of online communication also shapes aggressive behavior. Unlike face-to-face interactions, digital exchanges often occur with time delays, allowing aggressors to craft and escalate hostile messages without immediate social cues or feedback from victims. This lack of instant reaction reduces empathy and increases the likelihood of extreme responses (Suler, 2004). Victims, too, may experience greater distress due to the unpredictability of when and how hostile content will appear. Audience interrelations in online spaces further influence aggression. Social media platforms are inherently public, and hostile behavior can be performed not only against a victim but also for the entertainment or validation of an audience. The presence of bystanders can either exacerbate or mitigate aggression: some users may join in collective harassment campaigns, while others may intervene in defense of the victim. Research suggests that when aggression is rewarded with likes, shares, or approval from peers, individuals are more likely to continue or escalate hostile behavior (Wright, 2017). The affordances of specific platforms such as comment sections, direct messaging or group chat functions provide varying opportunities for aggression. Gaming platforms with competitive features often foster trash talk and flaming, while anonymous apps like Ask.fm or Yik Yak historically facilitated cyber bullying due to their lack of identity checks. Virtual classrooms and professional forums, while designed for constructive engagement, are not immune; misuses of chat tools, discussion boards, and collaborative spaces can also result in exclusion, ridicule, or harassment (Barlett & Chamberlin, 2017). Taken together, these factors show that online aggression is not only a matter of individual psychology but also of structural and contextual design.

6. PREVENTION AND INTERVENTION

Preventing and mitigating online aggression requires a comprehensive, multi-layered approach that integrates education, technology, governance, and cultural change. Cyber aggression-including cyber bullying, trolling, flaming, and doxing—emerges from a complex interplay of individual psychological factors, social dynamics, and platform design features (Kowalski et al., 2014). Consequently, effective strategies must address personal competencies, digital architecture, community norms, and regulatory frameworks simultaneously, rather than relying solely on punitive measures.

6.1 Educational Intervention

Education represents the foundational layer of prevention, aiming to develop both cognitive and socio-emotional competencies that reduce the likelihood of hostile online behavior. Emotional literacy programs, for instance, equip adolescents with the ability to recognize, label, and regulate emotions such as anger, shame, and envy, which have been empirically linked to aggressive online conduct. Scenario-based simulations and role-play exercises provide experiential learning opportunities, allowing students to practice conflict resolution and constructive responses when provoked, thereby strengthening self-regulation and social problem-solving skills. Media literacy is another critical component, particularly as algorithmic curation, echo chambers, and the affordances of anonymity influence online behavior. Instruction that emphasizes critical evaluation of digital content, the mechanisms of information amplification, and the ethical responsibilities of bystanders has been shown to reduce both victimization and inadvertent participation in cyber aggression (Livingstone et al., 2017). Complementary interventions focused on perspective-taking and empathy—through narrative exercises, immersive simulations, or peer testimony—have consistently demonstrated reductions in aggressive tendencies by enhancing the ability to understand and consider others' emotional experiences (Wachs et al., 2019). Moral reasoning and ethical deliberation further strengthen online conduct. Structured dialogues that challenge students to articulate community norms, assess the social cost of silence, and evaluate the consequences of online aggression cultivate internalized standards of behavior and foster pro-social decision-making (Narvaez & Lapsley, 2009). Skill-based training in counter-speech and micro-interventions enables adolescents to actively disrupt aggression in real time, whether by providing supportive replies, redirecting conversations, or gently challenging hostile remarks. Peer-led initiatives and mentorship programs, such as digital peer mentors, reinforce these skills by modeling positive online behavior and establishing socially endorsed norms of conduct.

6.2 Platform Design and Technological Safeguards

Digital platforms constitute a critical structural determinant of online behavior, influencing both the frequency and severity of aggression. Thoughtful platform design can introduce "friction layers" to mitigate impulsive or reactive aggression. Examples include confirmation prompts such as "Are you sure you want to post this?" temporary cool down timers, throttling mechanisms that limit rapid reposting or mass commenting, and normative nudges that display reminders of community standards or visualize the potential impact of a message on recipients (Cheng et al., 2017). Automated moderation systems powered by machine learning enhance the detection and mitigation of abusive content. Advanced algorithms can identify harassment patterns, sentiment anomalies, and repeated aggressive behavior with high precision, enabling rapid intervention before escalation occurs (Sadiq et al., 2021). AI-driven "tone checkers" and sentiment analyzers provide users with real-time feedback, prompting reconsideration or rephrasing of potentially harmful messages, thereby encouraging self-regulation while maintaining user agency. Anonymity management represents another pivotal factor. While anonymous interaction can encourage open communication, it also facilitates disinhibition and antisocial behavior (Lapidot-Lefler et al., 2012). Platforms can balance anonymity with accountability by implementing optional identity verification, visible reputation scores, or limiting full anonymity in high-risk contexts. Simultaneously, robust user controls—such as granular blocking, muting, keyword filters, and streamlined reporting mechanisms—empower individuals to protect themselves and manage exposure to aggression with minimal friction. The integration of these technological measures with educational and social interventions is essential. Platforms alone cannot eliminate online hostility; likewise, individual or school-based interventions are insufficient without supportive digital environments. A synergistic approach, combining preventive education, user empowerment, and platform accountability, aligns with ecological models of behavior that emphasize multi-level influence on aggression, from intrapersonal to societal scales. Addressing online aggression requires an evidence-based, multi-faceted strategy. Educational programs enhance socio-emotional competence and ethical reasoning, technological interventions create friction and accountability in digital environments, and community norms reinforce pro social behavior. By integrating these dimensions, stakeholders can reduce the prevalence and impact of online aggression, fostering digital spaces that support respectful, constructive, and psychologically safe interactions.

6.3 Parental & Community Interventions

Parental and community engagement represents a crucial ecological layer in the prevention and mitigation of online aggression. Research consistently demonstrates that adolescents whose parents actively monitor, guide, and discuss online behavior are less likely to engage in cyber aggression or become victims (Wright, 2017). Importantly, the nature of parental involvement matters: strategies emphasizing open communication, collaborative rule-setting, and co-use of digital platforms are significantly more effective than restrictive, punitive controls alone. These approaches foster trust, promote self-regulation, and encourage adolescents to internalize norms of responsible online conduct rather than merely complying out of fear of punishment. Parental mediation can take multiple forms. Active mediation involves parents discussing online experiences, explaining potential risks, and encouraging reflective thinking about digital interactions. Restrictive mediation, such as setting screen-time limits or blocking websites, can reduce exposure to harmful content but is less effective in cultivating intrinsic ethical reasoning or resilience. Co-use mediation, in which parents engage alongside adolescents in online activities, helps model positive behavior, exposes youth to appropriate norms, and strengthens parent-child relationships, creating a protective buffer against aggression. Community-based interventions further amplify the protective effect of parental involvement by establishing broader social support networks. Peer networks, youth organizations, and local institutions can provide safe spaces for adolescents to discuss negative online experiences and seek guidance without fear of judgment. Participation in structured peer support programs has been linked to increased empathy, perspective-taking, and a reduced likelihood of retaliation or internalization of aggressive behaviors (Heiman & Olenik-Shemesh, 2020). In addition, community organizations can facilitate restorative justice practices, where perpetrators of online aggression are encouraged to recognize the impact of their behavior and take corrective action, fostering accountability while promoting rehabilitation rather than stigmatization. The integration of parents and community actors is also critical for reinforcing cultural norms around acceptable online conduct. Social learning theory posits that behavior is influenced not only by individual cognition but also by observation of and interaction with role models in the environment (Bandura, 1999). When parents, educators, and community leaders consistently demonstrate respectful online behavior and intervene constructively in instances of aggression, they provide adolescents with models for pro social conduct. Campaigns and initiatives led by community organizations that highlight the real-world consequences of cyber aggression, while celebrating positive digital engagement, have been shown to shift collective norms and reduce tolerance for online hostility (Cheng et al., 2017). Moreover, parental and community involvement synergizes with educational and technological strategies. For example, when parents reinforce lessons from school-based digital citizenship programs or support the responsible use of platform tools, adolescents are more likely to internalize pro social norms. Likewise, community programs that train volunteers or mentors in recognizing early signs of cyber aggression can complement AI-driven moderation, ensuring that interventions are responsive and contextualized to local needs. Finally, fostering resilience through parental and community support is vital. Adolescents who experience online hostility may develop stress, anxiety, or social withdrawal; supportive adults and peer networks provide both emotional validation and practical coping strategies. Encouraging cognitive reframing, guided problem-solving, and access to professional mental health resources reduces long-term psychological harm and promotes adaptive coping (Schenk et al., 2012). Importantly, resilience-building should not be construed as shifting responsibility onto victims; rather, it functions as a complementary protective mechanism within a comprehensive, multi-layered strategy that includes education, technology, and systemic safeguards. In summary, parental and community involvement strengthens the multi-dimensional framework required to prevent and mitigate online aggression.

6.4 Governance and Policy

Effective governance supports healthy norms and accountability. Platforms should maintain streamlined reporting workflows with clear feedback to reporters. Tiered escalation—beginning with user moderators and extending to trained staff—ensures swift action. Community or peer moderators, supported by reputation-based systems, can mediate disputes and guide norms in real time. Transparent appeals processes and public transparency reports build trust by showing how often content is flagged, removed, or reinstated. Because harassment often crosses platform boundaries, cross-platform cooperation is vital. Shared standards, interoperable reporting tools, and privacy-safe threat-intelligence sharing can prevent aggressors from simply moving to a new venue. Legal frameworks should clearly define harassment and outline proportional penalties, while partnerships with independent oversight bodies can audit fairness and protect free expression.

6.5 Norms and Counter-Speech

Sustainable mitigation of online aggression requires not only individual skills and technological safeguards but also a fundamental shift in social norms surrounding digital interaction. Social norms—shared beliefs about acceptable behavior—play a critical role in regulating conduct in online communities. When norms tolerate hostility or trivialize harassment, aggressive behavior becomes socially reinforced, perpetuating cycles of cyber bullying, trolling, and flaming. Conversely, clearly communicated, widely endorsed norms of civility can reduce aggression by shaping both perceived expectations and behavioral intentions. Prominent, plain-language codes of conduct serve as explicit signals of community expectations, reducing ambiguity regarding acceptable behavior and providing a reference point for enforcement. Empirical studies indicate that platforms and institutions that maintain visible community guidelines see lower rates of reported harassment, particularly when these guidelines are coupled with consistent enforcement (Gorwa et al., 2020). The principle of social proof can be leveraged to encourage compliance: messaging that emphasizes positive behavioral trends e.g., "Most users respond politely" capitalizes on individuals' tendency to conform to perceived majority behavior. This normative framing reinforces pro social conduct by making civility the expected, visible standard. Counter-speech campaigns constitute a proactive mechanism for norm reinforcement. These initiatives involve public, deliberate responses to harmful content, often mobilizing peers to challenge aggression, defend victims, and provide alternative narratives. Examples include has hash tag campaign, viral video content, influencer-led endorsements, and organized bystander interventions. Research demonstrates that counter-speech can reduce the visibility of toxic content, empower victims, and foster a culture of accountability. Platforms can amplify these effects through interface design highlighting top civil comments, showcasing exemplary interactions, or providing recognition for constructive engagement—to prime users toward respectful participation. Narrative-based interventions further enhance norm internalization. Sharing personal stories of victims, detailing the emotional consequences of online aggression, or celebrating bystander heroes humanizes the issue and strengthens empathetic responses among the audience. Social-cognitive theories suggest that observing models of pro social behavior particularly relatable peers encourages imitation and adoption of similar behaviors (Bandura, 1999). In educational and organizational contexts, embedding anti-cyber bullying norms into honor codes, disciplinary policies, or institutional campaigns reinforces the expectation that respectful conduct is both valued and required. Longitudinal studies in school environments indicate that such norm-based interventions, when combined with restorative practices and peer-led initiatives, significantly reduce incidents of harassment and repeat offenses (Tokunaga, 2010). Campaigns should be culturally sensitive, avoid inadvertently amplifying aggression, and ensure that marginalized voices are represented. Evidence suggests that when counter-speech is perceived as authentic and community-driven rather than top-down enforcement, it is more effective at shaping attitudes and behaviors. Addressing online aggression necessitates not only individual-level interventions and platform-level safeguards but also systemic cultural change. Establishing clear norms of civility, leveraging social proof, and implementing counter-speech campaigns foster an environment in which respectful behavior is visible, valued, and rewarded. When integrated with educational programs, parental and community involvement, and technological safeguards, these norm-based strategies create a digital ecosystem that reduces the prevalence of online hostility and encourages constructive, empathetic, and socially responsible engagement.

6.6 Limitations of Interventions and Research Gap

Future efforts could integrate mental-health resources directly into platforms, offering immediate links to counseling or crisis hotlines when harassment is detected. Gamified reward systems might give badges or courtesy scores for constructive participation. Collaborative "digital neighborhood watch" groups could blend volunteer moderators with AI monitoring to spot coordinated harassment early. Finally, resilience-building programs that teach stress management and cognitive reframing help individuals withstand inevitable exposure to online conflict without normalizing it.

6.7 Comprehensive Strategies for Preventing and Mitigating Online Aggression

Efforts to address online aggression must move beyond punitive approaches and toward comprehensive strategies that integrate prevention, early intervention, and resilience-building. Since online aggression is shaped by a complex interaction of psychological, social, and technological factors, no single solution is sufficient. Instead, effective approaches require a combination of educational programs, parental and community involvement, platform accountability, and personal coping strategies. Prevention begins with digital literacy and character education, particularly within schools. Teaching young people about responsible online behavior, empathy, and the consequences of cyber bullying can reduce the likelihood of aggressive actions. Studies show that school-based interventions that combine social-emotional learning with digital citizenship education significantly reduce the incidence of cyber bullying (Livingstone et al., 2017). Programs that encourage perspective-taking and empathy have also been found effective in curbing trolling and harassment (Wachs et al., 2019). By framing prevention in terms of values as well as skills, educators help students internalize norms of respectful communication. Another critical dimension is parental mediation and community support. Research demonstrates that adolescents whose parents monitor and guide their online behavior are less likely to engage in or become victims of cyber aggression (Wright, 2017). Parental mediation strategies, such as open communication and collaborative rule-setting, are more effective than restrictive controls alone, as they promote trust and self-regulation. Community organizations and peer networks also play a role in fostering resilience by providing victims with safe spaces for sharing experiences and seeking support (Heiman & Olenik-Shemesh, 2020). At the platform level, technological and policy interventions are essential. Social media companies and gaming platforms bear responsibility for designing safer environments through moderation systems, reporting tools, and algorithmic adjustments. Advances in machine learning have enabled the development of automated systems that can detect and flag abusive content with high accuracy (Sadiq et al., 2021). However, scholars caution that detection must be paired with transparent enforcement policies and user education to be truly effective (Gorwa et al., 2020). Furthermore, regulatory frameworks in many countries now require platforms to take more active steps against harmful content, reflecting a growing recognition of their role in mitigating digital aggression. In addition to external interventions, building psychological resilience among individuals is crucial. Victims who develop coping mechanisms such as cognitive reframing, seeking social support, and practicing stress management are better able to withstand the negative effects of online hostility (Schenk et al., 2012). Resilience-building programs that emphasize self-efficacy and positive identity formation have been found to reduce the long-term psychological impact of victimization (Hinduja & Patchin, 2019). Importantly, resilience should not be framed as placing the burden solely on victims but rather as an empowering strategy that complements systemic protections. Mitigation also requires addressing the cultural normalization of online hostility. When trolling and flaming are trivialized as entertainment, they perpetuate cycles of aggression and desensitize users to harm. Campaigns that raise awareness about the seriousness of online aggression, coupled with peer-led initiatives that promote prosocial behavior, can help shift online norms (Cheng et al., 2017). In educational settings, peer mentoring and restorative practices-where aggressors confront the consequences of their actions and make amends-have shown promise in reducing recurrence (Tokunaga, 2010).

7. RECOMMENDATION

Building humane and resilient online spaces requires a coordinated effort that integrates psychology, technology, ethics, and policy. Rather than treating online aggression as a purely technical or purely social problem, the most effective strategies weave these perspectives together to create environments that discourage harm and promote empathy. First, research must become more interdisciplinary and forward-looking. Collaborative studies between psychology, computer science, and user-experience design can reveal how human behavior interacts with platform architecture. Longitudinal research is equally important, moving beyond cross-sectional surveys to track how online aggression unfolds, how trauma persists, and how interventions endure. Second, digital well-being must become a core design principle. Platforms should be assessed not just for engagement metrics but for their impact on psychological health, using indicators such as harassment exposure or stress levels. User-facing dashboards could offer feedback on time spent online, abuse encountered, and suggested breaks. Because harassment often crosses platform boundaries, companies should cooperate by sharing threat intelligence and creating interoperable reporting mechanisms-while safeguarding privacy. Industry-wide standards and coalitions can help prevent abusers from simply migrating from one platform to another. Third, ethical and psychologically informed design should guide every stage of user experience. Interfaces can include subtle "guardrails," such as prompts asking, "Would you want to receive this message?" or brief empathy reminders using humanizing cues like photos or names. Design principles should favor friction and transparency over pure engagement, allowing users to retract posts easily and to see clear explanations when content is moderated. Adaptive moderation systems, aided by machine learning, can dynamically detect rising toxicity or flag content from repeat offenders while still allowing for contextual human review. User-empowerment tools such as draft analyzers, tone checkers, and one-click supportive reply options can help both potential aggressors and bystanders make more constructive choices. Policy and governance provide the structural backbone. Regulations should require transparency in moderation and appeals processes without tipping into censorship. "Explainable moderation" can help users understand why content was removed and how to contest decisions. Third-party audits of platform practices can increase accountability and fairness, while policymaking should include mental-health experts, civil-society representatives, and members of marginalized communities who are most affected by online harm.

8. CONCLUSION

The rise of digital communication technologies has revolutionized human interaction, but it has also created fertile ground for online aggression, including cyber bullying, trolling, flaming, and related behaviors. Research consistently demonstrates that these forms of hostility are not trivial acts confined to the virtual world but can result in severe psychological trauma, social alienation, and reputational harm (Kowalski et al., 2014;). As this chapter has outlined, online aggression is closely tied to specific personality traits such as psychopathy, narcissism, and sadism (Aydın et al., n.d.), while also being reinforced by contextual factors such as anonymity, audience size, and platform affordances (Chatzakou et al., 2017; Strimbu et al., 2021). The consequences of online aggression extend well beyond individual victims, influencing the health of digital communities and broader society. The persistence of hostility online erodes trust, silences marginalized voices, and normalizes toxic discourse (Cortis et al., 2015). Moreover, the continuity between offline aggression and online behavior suggests that digital hostility is not an isolated phenomenon but an extension of broader social and psychological patterns (Strimbu et al., 2021). Recognizing these linkages highlights the importance of adopting holistic approaches that integrate psychological insights with sociotechnical interventions. From a practical perspective, prevention and mitigation require coordinated action by multiple stakeholders. Educators play a central role in equipping students with empathy, digital literacy, and resilience skills (Livingstone et al., 2017; Wachs et al., 2019). Parents and communities can foster open communication and provide support systems that reduce vulnerability (Wright, 2017). Technology companies, for their part, must take greater responsibility by implementing transparent content moderation practices, leveraging machine learning detection tools, and designing platforms that discourage harmful behavior (Sadiq et al., 2021; Gorwa et al., 2020). Importantly, interventions should avoid placing the burden solely on victims; instead, they must balance individual resilience-building with systemic safeguards to reduce exposure to harm. For policymakers, the findings underscore the urgency of developing clear regulations and accountability mechanisms for online platforms. While legislation alone cannot eliminate online aggression, it can set standards that encourage responsible platform governance and provide victims with avenues for redress (Gorwa et al., 2020). At the same time, psychological research points to the need for culturally sensitive interventions that consider how aggression manifests differently across contexts. Future research should continue to refine detection technologies, examine the long-term psychological effects of online victimization, and explore the interplay between offline and online aggression. More comparative studies across regions and cultures would enrich our understanding of how digital aggression is shaped by social, economic, and political conditions. In conclusion, addressing online aggression requires a multi-level and interdisciplinary approach. By integrating insights from psychology, education, technology, and policy, society can move toward digital environments that promote safety, respect, and constructive engagement.

9. DISCUSSION

The growing prevalence of online aggression including cyber bullying, trolling, flaming, and organized harassment cannot be explained by a single cause. It emerges from a complex interaction of personal traits, social influences, and the technological architecture of digital platforms. Research consistently shows that certain personality factors, such as narcissism, psychopathy, and sadism, are linked to a higher likelihood of hostile behavior. Yet even individuals without these traits can engage in aggression when conditions such as anonymity, invisibility, and weak accountability create a permissive environment. The online world lowers the usual social barriers that discourage harmful acts, making it easier for ordinary users to behave in ways they might avoid in face-to-face interactions. This interplay of disposition and context also means that digital aggression is not isolated from everyday life. People who are aggressive offline often exhibit similar patterns online, but the virtual setting amplifies their impact. Features like anonymous profiles, delayed communication, and algorithmic promotion of sensational content reduce empathy and increase impulsivity. A hurtful post or rumor can spread rapidly, remain visible indefinitely, and reach an audience far beyond the victim's immediate circle. These factors combine to make online hostility feel more intense and inescapable than traditional bullying, leaving targets with lasting psychological scars. Several social-psychological theories help clarify why these behaviors persist. De-individuation theory explains how group immersion and a loss of personal identity weaken self-control and encourage norm-violating behavior. The online disinhibition effect highlights how invisibility and asynchronous communication lower inhibitions, allowing people to say or do things they would normally suppress. Social identity theory adds that strong group affiliations can fuel in-group favoritism and out-group hostility, turning disagreements into coordinated harassment campaigns. Moral disengagement theory describes the cognitive strategies such as blaming the victim, minimizing harm, or diffusing responsibility that allow perpetrators to maintain a positive self-image while engaging in cruelty. Together these perspectives show that online aggression is not simply the work of a few malicious individuals but a predictable outcome of certain psychological processes interacting with digital environments. Although these frameworks are powerful, they do not capture the entire picture. Empirical findings reveal important variations and even contradictions. Some studies indicate that anonymity promotes aggression by shielding people from accountability, while others find that users can be just as hostile when their real identities are visible. These inconsistencies suggest that motives for online aggression are diverse and context dependent, requiring flexible models rather than one-size-fits-all explanations. The consequences of digital aggression are profound and far-reaching. Victims frequently experience anxiety, depression, and lowered self-esteem, and repeated exposure can lead to symptoms resembling post-traumatic stress. Harm is not limited to direct targets: bystanders may feel guilt, distress, or desensitization after witnessing repeated incidents and communities can become more accepting of hostility over time. When aggression is normalized as entertainment or protected as "just free speech," it erodes trust and discourages open, constructive dialogue. The cumulative effect is a toxic online culture that harms mental health, weakens social bonds, and undermines democratic discourse. Addressing these challenges requires a coordinated, multi-layered response. Platform designers can introduce friction such as prompts that encourage users to reconsider inflammatory posts and improve moderation systems that detect and respond to harmful content. Transparency in algorithmic design and moderation decisions can also reduce the unintended amplification of hostile material. At the policy level, governments must balance the need to protect users from harm with the protection of free expression, encouraging responsible platform governance without overreach. Ultimately, the persistence of online aggression highlights a broader truth: digital spaces mirror human society. The same psychological tendencies that drive conflict offline desire for status, group loyalty, and the capacity to dehumanize find new expression in virtual environments that can magnify their reach and impact. Reducing harm therefore demands not only better technology and stricter rules but also cultural change that rewards empathy and respectful engagement. By integrating insights from psychology, education, technology, and law, society can move toward online communities that are safer, more inclusive, and more conducive to constructive interaction.

Online aggression is a complex sociotechnical phenomenon whose study requires transparent measurement, documented protocols, and a multidisciplinary approach. This exploratory review maps the existing evidence base, documents heterogeneity in measurement, and identifies priorities for robust and reproducible research and policy experiments. Future research should incorporate longitudinal cohort designs, open-method platform log analysis, and randomized controlled trials to design interventions that build a comprehensive evidence base to inform education policy and practice.

REFERENCES

Aydın, A., Arda, B., Güneş, B., & Erbaş, O. (2021). Psychopathology of cyberbullying and internet trolling. *Journal of Experimental and Basic Medical Sciences*, *2*(3). Advance online publication. DOI: 10.5607/jebms.2021.79

Bandura, A. (1999). Moral disengagement in the perpetration of inhumanities. *Personality and Social Psychology Review*, *3*(3), 193–209. DOI: 10.1207/s15327957pspr0303_3 PMID: 15661671

Barlett, C. P., & Chamberlin, K. (2017). Examining cyberbullying across the lifespan. *Computers in Human Behavior*, *71*, 444–449. DOI: 10.1016/j.chb.2017.02.009

Chatzakou, D., Kourtellis, N., Blackburn, J., De Cristofaro, E., Stringhini, G., & Vakali, A. (2017). Mean birds: Detecting aggression and bullying on Twitter. *Proceedings of the 2017 ACM Web Science Conference*, 13–22. https://doi.org/ DOI: 10.1145/3091478.3091487

Cheng, J., Bernstein, M., Danescu-Niculescu-Mizil, C., & Leskovec, J. (2017). Anyone can become a troll: Causes of trolling behavior in online discussions. *Proceedings of the 2017 ACM Conference on Computer Supported Cooperative Work and Social Computing*, 1217–1230. https://doi.org/DOI: 10.1145/2998181.2998213

Cortis, K., & Handschuh, S. (2015). Analysis of cyberbullying tweets related to trending world events. In *2015 IEEE/ACM International Conference on Advances in Social Networks Analysis and Mining* (pp. 1590–1593). IEEE. https://doi.org/ DOI: 10.1145/2808797.2809354

Farley, S., Coyne, I., Axtell, C., & Sprigg, C. (2016). Design, development and validation of a workplace cyberbullying measure, the WCM. *Work and Stress*, *30*(4), 293–317. DOI: 10.1080/02678373.2016.1255998

Festinger, L., Pepitone, A., & Newcomb, T. (1952). Some consequences of deindividuation in a group. *Journal of Abnormal and Social Psychology*, *47*(2, Suppl, 2S), 382–389. DOI: 10.1037/h0057906 PMID: 14937978

Gorwa, R., Binns, R., & Katzenbach, C. (2020). Algorithmic content moderation: Technical and political challenges in the automation of platform governance. *Big Data & Society*, *7*(1), 1–15. DOI: 10.1177/2053951719897945

Heiman, T., & Olenik-Shemesh, D. (2020). Cyberbullying involvement of adolescents with low self-efficacy. *International Journal of Environmental Research and Public Health*, *17*(14), 5237. DOI: 10.3390/ijerph17145237 PMID: 32698486

Hinduja, S., & Patchin, J. W. (2019). Connecting adolescent suicide to the severity of bullying and cyberbullying. *Journal of School Violence, 18*(3), 333–346. DOI: 10.1080/15388220.2018.1492417

Keipi, T., Näsi, M., Oksanen, A., & Räsänen, P. (2017). *Online hate and harmful content: Cross-national perspectives*. Routledge.

Kowalski, R. M., Giumetti, G. W., Schroeder, A. N., & Lattanner, M. R. (2014). Bullying in the digital age: A critical review and meta-analysis of cyberbullying research among youth. *Psychological Bulletin, 140*(4), 1073–1137. DOI: 10.1037/a0035618 PMID: 24512111

Lapidot-Lefler, N., & Barak, A. (2012). Effects of anonymity, invisibility, and lack of eye contact on toxic online disinhibition. *Computers in Human Behavior, 28*(2), 434–443. DOI: 10.1016/j.chb.2011.10.014

Livingstone, S., Stoilova, M., & Kelly, A. (2017). Cyberbullying: Incidence, trends and consequences. In Smith, P. K., & Steffgen, G. (Eds.), *Cyberbullying through the new media: Findings from an international network* (pp. 1–20). Psychology Press.

Modecki, K. L., Minchin, J., Harbaugh, A. G., Guerra, N. G., & Runions, K. C. (2014). Bullying prevalence across contexts: A meta-analysis measuring cyber and traditional bullying. *The Journal of Adolescent Health, 55*(5), 602–611. DOI: 10.1016/j.jadohealth.2014.06.007 PMID: 25168105

Postmes, T., Spears, R., & Lea, M. (2001). Social identity, normative content, and "de-individuation" in computer-mediated groups. *Communication Research, 28*(2), 140–171. DOI: 10.1177/009365001028002003

Sadiq, M., Yousaf, A., Hussain, S., & Nawaz, R. (2021). Aggression detection on social media: A multimodal approach. *Information Processing & Management, 58*(5), 102664. DOI: 10.1016/j.ipm.2021.102664

Schenk, A. M., & Fremouw, W. J. (2012). Prevalence, psychological impact, and coping of cyberbully victims among college students. *Journal of School Violence, 11*(1), 21–37. DOI: 10.1080/15388220.2011.630310

Schneider, S. K., O'Donnell, L., Stueve, A., & Coulter, R. W. S. (2012). Cyberbullying, school bullying, and psychological distress: A regional census of high school students. *American Journal of Public Health, 102*(1), 171–177. DOI: 10.2105/AJPH.2011.300308 PMID: 22095343

Slonje, R., Smith, P. K., & Frisén, A. (2013). The nature of cyberbullying, and strategies for prevention. *Computers in Human Behavior, 29*(1), 26–32. DOI: 10.1016/j.chb.2012.05.024

Smith, P. K., López-Castro, L., Robinson, S., & Görzig, A. (2018). Consistency of gender differences in bullying in cross-cultural surveys. *Aggressive Behavior*, *45*(2), 113–123. DOI: 10.1002/1098-2337(1988)14:2<113::AID-AB2480140205>3.0.CO;2-# PMID: 29052252

Strimbu, N., & O'Connell, M. (2021). Aggression and consistency of self in cybertrolling behavior. *Cyberpsychology, Behavior, and Social Networking*, *24*(8), 525–531. DOI: 10.1089/cyber.2020.0424 PMID: 33577384

Suler, J. (2004). The online disinhibition effect. *Cyberpsychology & Behavior*, *7*(3), 321–326. DOI: 10.1089/1094931041291295 PMID: 15257832

Tajfel, H., & Turner, J. C. (1979). An integrative theory of intergroup conflict. In Austin, W. G., & Worchel, S. (Eds.), *The social psychology of intergroup relations* (pp. 33–47). Brooks/Cole.

Tokunaga, R. S. (2010). Following you home from school: A critical review and synthesis of research on cyberbullying victimization. *Computers in Human Behavior*, *26*(3), 277–287. DOI: 10.1016/j.chb.2009.11.014

Wachs, S., Gámez-Guadix, M., & Wright, M. F. (2022). Online hate speech victimization and depressive symptoms among adolescents: The protective role of resilience. *Cyberpsychology, Behavior, and Social Networking*, *25*(7), 416–423. DOI: 10.1089/cyber.2022.0009 PMID: 35639126

Wachs, S., Wright, M. F., & Schubarth, W. (2017). Associations between bystanders and perpetrators of traditional bullying and cyberbullying: The moderating role of affective empathy. *International Journal of Environmental Research and Public Health*, *15*(1), 9. DOI: 10.3390/ijerph15010009 PMID: 29271899

Wachs, S., Wright, M. F., & Schubarth, W. (2019). The role of empathy and moral disengagement in cyberbullying. *Journal of School Psychology*, *74*, 50–63. DOI: 10.1016/j.jsp.2019.05.007

Wright, M. F. (2017). Parental mediation, cyberbullying, and cybergrooming: A longitudinal study. *Child Indicators Research*, *10*(3), 699–712. DOI: 10.1007/s12187-016-9404-6

Zezulka, L. A., & Seigfried-Spellar, K. C. (2016). Differentiating cyberbullies and internet trolls by personality characteristics and self-esteem. *Journal of Digital Forensics. Security and Law*, *11*(3), 5. Advance online publication. DOI: 10.15394/jdfsl.2016.1415

Zimbardo, P. G. (1969). The human choice: Individuation, reason, and order versus de-individuation, impulse, and chaos. In Arnold, W. J., & Levine, D. (Eds.), *Nebraska Symposium on Motivation* (pp. 237–307). University of Nebraska Press.

Chapter 8
From Screen to Crime Scen:
Cinematic Imitation and Criminal Psychology in Malayalam Cinema

Mohammad Amin Wani
http://orcid.org/0000-0002-4737-3731
Lovely Professional University, India

Adheena Rajeev
Lovely Professional University, India

ABSTRACT

This chapter examines how Malayalam cinema, particularly films like Drishyam (2013), Marco (2022), Pani (2023), and Aavesham (2024), intersects with psychology and criminology through its engagement with realism, moral ambiguity, and cultural specificity. Using theories such as social learning, cognitive scripts, cultivation, and cultural criminology, it explores how cinematic narratives shape identity, moral reasoning, and imitation, especially in the digital era. The rise of OTT platforms and social media has intensified 'cinematic imitation' and real-life 'copycat crimes' in India, rooted in moral disengagement and subcultural identity. Cinema emerges as both a potential trigger for deviant behavior and a tool for ethical reflection. The chapter concludes by advocating for media literacy and interdisciplinary collaboration to reduce harm while preserving artistic freedom.

DOI: 10.4018/979-8-3373-5896-3.ch008

INTRODUCTION

Cinema has always been far more than just a form of entertainment; it is also a social institution, a cultural product, and a psychological force that can affect the attitudes, beliefs, and behaviours of its audiences (Bordwell & Thompson, 2019). With the increasing convergence of traditional and digital media, films are now distributed not only in theatres but also online, on social media platforms, and in virtual spaces, reflecting broader shifts in media ecology and convergence culture (Jenkins, 2006). The interaction of digital technologies and cinematic narratives produces a synergy that amplifies the psychological weight of one over the other, producing a confluence of influences (Sundar & Limperos, 2013). These interactions bring into view social psychology's greatest concerns of how individuals and groups interpret films, replicate behaviors exhibited on-screen, and negotiate their identities in virtual and real-world contexts, consistent with principles of social cognitive theory (Bandura, 2009). The effects of film on behavior is a well-established area of media psychology that has been studied for decades. Films largely serve as symbolic models, providing us scripts for behaving morally, or templates for how to navigate real-life decision-making. Rarely is entertainment framed as a behavioral model, but this is an important point of reference for Albert Bandura's social learning theory (1977) which has meaning within films, and was originally framed for television violence: we can observe, think about, and later emulate in practice what we see in films. In cases where the film exists as content in an online realm - memes, fandoms, streaming - the opportunity for creating meaning, including normalizing and desensitizing, multiplies. The virtual landscape acts an enhancer of the power of films - adding the potential to invest the narrative in interactive and participatory culture(s) that extends far beyond the immediate screen experience of consumption.

Copycat crimes are one of the most striking and troubling effects of media exposure. Copycat crimes, where a person executes an unlawful act inspired by a representation of crime or criminals in the mainstream media, have been conceptualized in media psychology through a number of mechanisms such as desensitization, cognitive priming, and imitation (Bandura, 2009; Huesmann, 2018; Surette, 2015). Movies often sensationalize crime through aestheticized detail, leading the viewer to ascribe a form of rationality, cleverness, or even glamor to the process of criminal engagement as one possible drama for understanding conflict in their real life (Surette, 2015). In digital spaces, the social dialogue that surrounds a film can work to normalize and generate collective discussion as well as glamorize the crime depicted on screen and/or demonstrate acceptance of a potentially criminal or even violent narrative (Jenkins, 2006). The merging of mass communication media and social media dialogue becomes a corollary to the genre not only of the film itself, but as scripts that would be considered socially acceptable actions for some viewers. The merging of these forms of storytelling that rely on scenes of media representations of crime provides the potential for some individuals to adopt key elements of storytelling purely for the purpose of transposing fictionalized strategies or approaches of confrontation into real-life contexts (Bandura, 2009).

The particular case of Malayalam cinema in India stands out as a notable example of the intersection that can exist among cinematic representation, social psychology, and virtual spaces. Malayalam cinema has long had respectability for its depiction of realism, psychological believability, and conscientiousness about social issues (Nair, 2013). Recently, however, certain Malayalam films, especially Drishyam (2013), have been connected to some of India's notorious crimes. Specifically, the story of Drishyam is about a man who carefully executes a cover-up of crime to protect his family; police and media termed Drishyam a "crime manual" (BBC News, 2021). There have been several documented incidents of crimes where the perpetrators copied techniques found in Drishyam, for example, confusing timelines, providing false evidence, or rehearsing alibis (BBC News, 2021). The crime reports confirm a seepage between fiction and reality, where audiences engaged with a narrative not only consume stories but also develop and allocate them for real-world techniques.

The significance of Malayalam cinema in discussions of social psychology in virtual environments is heightened by the presence of digital technologies in retaining its cultural footprints. For instance, streaming services like Amazon Prime, Netflix, and Hotstar have globalized viewer access to Malayalam cinema, and now audiences worldwide beyond the borders of Kerala can watch (Rajadhyaksha, 2020). Concurrently, social media platforms, specifically YouTube, Reddit, and Twitter, are platforms for discussion, analysis, and even fan-made re-conceptions of crime-centric cinema (Jenkins, 2006). These digital communities can also be understood as echo chambers where characters, strategies, themes, and even moral dilemmas from cinema are dissected, examined, and, at times, justified. In digital discussion threads, users dissect the relentless actions of the main character in Drishyam and its sequels, and imagine if they could enact the character's actions in the same way when confronted with crime in their own lives. In this regard, digital environments can not only extend the duration of a filmic narrative but simultaneously extend the cognitive engagement and consequences of behavior in relation to the filmic narrative and its real-world implications (Sundar & Limperos, 2013).

Examining the issue of Malayalam cinema also brings to light several important concepts from psychology. First is the concept of cognitive priming, which suggests that once viewers are exposed to thematically relevant and violent crime-oriented scripts in a movie, related thoughts and memories are activated, increasing the chance of behaviors congruent with what was viewed in the film (Huesmann, 2018). Second is the psychological process of moral disengagement, where individuals shift the justifications of their normative moral standards by reframing the reasons behind engaging in criminal action as either protection or necessity (Bandura, 2009). This theme emerges in many Malayalam films where the main character is positioned sympathetically in the story despite engaging in illegitimate decision-making (Nair, 2013). Third, if a virtual environment reaches a certain level of social amplification, any crime-oriented movie content that has been widely reviewed increases the likelihood that its strategies and symbols find their way into other social environments, as in any broad social ties, behaviors viewed in a movie may get mimicked to an extent (Surette, 2015). These concepts elucidate some ways in which a virtual environment challenges the boundaries of cinema as a medium and extends its psychological influence while mediating the impacts of individual cognition and social discourse.

It is essential to note the potential for Malayalam cinema to generate positive outcomes. Many films in the Malayalam industry depict themes of justice, inequity, and resilience that may serve as prosocial narratives that could encourage empathy and moral contemplation. When these films are shared and engaged with in an online context, they can also spark awareness, solidarity, and potential activism. Social-psychology research reminds us the modeling process is not in itself a negative process; the same processes that yield imitation of negative behaviors can also result in positive behaviors. The question lies in how their viewing, interpretation, and engagement with the content will transpire in both general and specific contexts.

Therefore, the consideration of Malayalam cinema through social psychology and virtual environments offers a contribution to the larger conversation of media effects in the digital age. It illustrates a point that films, which used to be presented through traditional cinema spaces, can now belong to the interrelated contexts of streaming networks, social media platforms, and other virtual spaces. Therefore, the new contexts of viewing require scholars to rethink established conceptual models used to understand media effects and situate the study of effects in zoned and hybrid contexts where movies can now exist - we don't passively experience them - we negotiate, reimagine, and sometimes act out the very narratives. In the process of rethinking media effects, we will not only learn about copycat crimes, but we can learn about the less discernible processes by which media, technology, and psychology collaboratively contribute to understanding human behavior.

THEORETICAL FOUNDATIONS

To grasp the relationship between cinema and crime, any theoretical framework will need to shift between psychology and criminology, as well as media studies. Concerns over how moving images affect behavior has long been a focus by researchers and scholars alike, particularly in discussions about media violence and whether such violence incites aggression, desensitizes the audience, or provides models of behavior for deviance.

Social Learning and Observational Modelling

The social learning theory developed by Albert Bandura provides the most direct psychological explanation for media imitation (Bandura, 1977). Bandura asserted that people learn behaviors not only from reinforcement, but also by observing models of behavior, either in real life or fiction. Four processes take place during observational learning: attention, retention, reproduction, and motivation. Films are effective at securing attention, especially when they are visually captivating and/or associated with heightened emotions; a sequence of events can then be mentally retained, as can the characters' associated emotions; once the observer's mood is set, some behaviors may be reproduced; and if the observed behavior appears to provide benefits while accepting the associated risks, the observer's motivation to imitate will also increase. In film contexts, movies like Drishyam offer attractive models of crime concealment, particularly because they are rational, effective, and ultimately moral within the narrative. These portrayals of de facto deviance can not only legitimise deviance but also provide an effective, step-by-step strategy for imitation (Surette, 2015).

Cultivation Theory and Media Reality

George Gerbner's cultivation theory argues that prolonged and repetitive exposure to media content gradually shapes how audiences perceive social reality, rather than simply encouraging imitative learning (Gerbner, 1998). According to this perspective, heavy media consumption fosters what Gerbner and colleagues describe as a *"mean world syndrome"* a distorted worldview in which individuals come to believe that society is more dangerous, crime-ridden, or hostile than it actually is (Gerbner & Gross, 1976). For criminologists, this has significant implications, as media portrayals of crime can subtly influence public attitudes toward policing, justice, and the perceived prevalence of violence. The realism characteristic of Malayalam cinema further intensifies these cultivation effects. Unlike the stylized or exaggerated depictions of violence often found in Bollywood productions, Malayalam films such as *Drishyam* and *Joji* (Pothan, 2021) portray crime within ordinary domestic or social settings, making such behaviors appear more plausible and contextually grounded. Over time, repeated exposure to these narratives can normalise deviance, gradually shaping viewers to perceive crime as a routine, rational, or even necessary response in high-stakes situations.

Cognitive Script Theory

Huesmann's (1998) cognitive script theory builds on this idea by explaining that individuals store records of their experiences with media in cognitive scripts that guide future behaviours. Cognitive scripts are organised sets of knowledge about how to act in a particular context. For instance, watching Drishyam could create a cognitive script about how to respond to accidental crime by hiding evidence, inventing alibis, and confusing investigators. If the person was then faced with a similar situation in real life, they might find the cognitive script "activated" and then act on it unconsciously. Cognitive scripts are also reinforced by rehearsal. Re-watching movies and talking about them with others could create mental rehearsal of the strategies and increase their salience. In a digital culture, selecting a meme or reading fan discussion increases rehearsal of strategies for future enactment even further with the increased possibility for computers to replay media previously watched on Over-the-Top platforms.

Desensitization and Moral Disengagement

Exposure to deviant plots or violence over time can also desensitize them to emotional responses, including fear, guilt, or empathy. Funk et al. (2004) showed evidence that exposure to media violence has been shown to blunt sensitivity to aggression, thus lowering the thresholds for engaging in or tolerating deviance. Bandura's (1999) notion of 'moral disengagement' further illuminates how individuals justify their actions or behaviors through the displacement of responsibility or by minimizing the significance of harmful behaviors, amoral behaviors, or deviant activities. Movies often support the process of moral disengagement by appealing to the audience's sympathy toward the protagonist, even if that protagonist is engaged in a criminal activity. In the case of Drishyam, the actions of George Kutty are framed in a context that makes them morally right on the basis that he engaged in self-defence in defines of protecting his family, and thus the cover-up is not associated with deviance, but is seen as a righteous behavior, allowing the potential imitators into a rationalization of criminal behavior as socially accepted or legitimate survival.

Copycat Crime Literature: A Global Framework Copycat crime, as codified by Surette (2011; 2015), exemplifies how media representations of violence provide "off-the-shelf" scripts for criminal innovation. In this instance, offenders are inspired by prior media representations, whether fictitious or real, to commit violent acts. Notable examples include the "Natural Born Killers" murders in the United States, where perpetrators claimed they were inspired by Oliver Stone's film, and the perpetrators of the Columbine High School shooting who studied violent video games and films (Larkin, 2009).

Copycat Crime in India

Indian criminology has addressed media influence more than what has been representative. However, Malayalam cinema offers some of the most obvious examples. The news accounts document some offenses where criminal offenders, in their statements, admitted to being inspired by Drishyam (Times of India, 2016; NDTV, 2019). For example, in Nilambur, Kerala, a family tried to cover up a murder in a Drishyam way. In Indore, an accused, to send the police off course, buried a dog, which is, structurally, a story plot from the film. Further, in Gujarat, Udaipur, and Telangana, further examples of inspiration from Drishyam are present. More generally, youth culture in India supports cinema significantly; often youth use dialogue, gestures, mannerisms, and style to perform their identity (Srinivas, 2002). Films, like Aavesham (2024), have intensified the trend of youth culture, as students in schools replicated the gangster vernacular used in the film. These cases suggest that imitation, or mimetic contagion, in India is not limited to masking crime, but rather is included in a larger repertoire of behaviors. These cases would appear to shape subcultural practices.

Cultural Criminology and Symbolic Interactionism

While psychological theories address the imitation of individuals, sociological models explore cultural dynamics. Cultural criminology prioritizes the role of media, style, and representation in defining deviance (Ferrell, Hayward, & Young, 2015). It contends that crime is both material and symbolic and is performed and consumed in dynamic cultural circuits. Films not only promote a strategy, but also communicate a meaning of masculinity, rebellion, or survival, acquired and performed by audiences as part of their identity projects. In a similar fashion, symbolic interactionism underscores the process of constructing meaning via social interaction. A repeated line from a film in class or a referenced cinematic strategy on an online forum, becomes a shared symbol to structure group identity and action. This is especially relevant in Kerala, where cinema has a particularly close relationship to social life; it is an example of the symbolic interactive process of meaning where a film like Drishyam transforms from film text to living cultural scripts.

Drishyam as a Cultural Phenomenon

Launched in 2013, Jeethu Joseph's Drishyam reshaped the thriller genre in Malayalam cinema and quickly became an essential cultural milestone in the world of visual storytelling. The story follows Georgekutty, a humble cable TV operator and devoted family man played by Mohanlal, who enters into the realm of extraordinary possibilities/reflexivity after the accidental murder of the son of a police officer by Georgekutty's daughter.

Essentially, the film is less about the murder and more about the cover-up. Georgekutty uses his cleverness, observation skills, and knowledge of movies to construct an airtight alibi for his family. The film methodically shows him burying a body, rehearsing his alibi stories, altering timelines, and planting evidence to distract police investigators. The film becomes interesting because Georgekutty's motivation is paternal love and survival, not out of greed or evil. Thematically, Drishyam combines suspense with moral ambiguity. It asks questions of justice, morality, and systematic police failure.

Public, Critical, and Police Responses

After its debut, Drishyam was a hit with audiences and even more successful with critics. Spectators recognised the tension, detailed and thoughtful screenplay, and emotional heft in the film; and the film's realistic settings-a common Keralan family, small town police stations, and daily life-made it even more relatable. Audiences admired the protagonist's capacity to deceive the police through creativity, which elevated the character to that of a hero and positioned him as an everyman. Reactions to the film also surfaced from police officers, but instead of admiration, the response was mostly discomfort. Some police officers even made public comments that the film was so nuanced in details pertaining to concealment of crime, that it could be considered a "manual for crime" (Mathrubhumi, 2015). Typically, in crime thrillers, ultimately criminals are punished, and the foundation of Drishyam lies in the success of the deception, which is deeply troubling for law enforcement. Critics also claimed that the film overturned traditional morality by allowing criminals to triumph and eliciting responsibility on behalf of filmmakers by examining the social responsibilities of a filmmaker.

The film did well outside of Kerala, leading to remakes in several Indian languages (Tamil, Hindi, Kannada, Telugu) and a Chinese remake (Sheep Without a Shepherd, 2019). Its capacity to translate cultural and linguistic boundaries only reinforced the universality of its themes while fueling debates about its criminogenic potential.

Crimes mirroring

In the decade following the release of *Drishyam*, numerous criminal cases across India appeared to replicate the film's core tactics, with some perpetrators explicitly acknowledging the influence of the narrative and, in other instances, investigating officers drawing parallels during case analysis. These incidents illustrate how cinematic fiction can inadvertently function as a behavioural template, providing viewers with procedural cues that may later be adapted to real-world criminal activity.

Several real-world crimes reported across India in the years following the release of Drishyam reflected striking parallels to the film's narrative strategies, demonstrating how cinematic fiction can unintentionally serve as a behavioural script for criminal conduct. One of the earliest such incidents emerged in Nilambur, Kerala, where a family was accused of murdering a man and burying his body while carefully constructing alibis, an approach investigators noted as directly inspired by the film (Times of India, 2016). Media reports highlighted the strong similarities, including coordinated family involvement, concealment of remains, and rehearsed false narratives, framing the case as a clear example of "life imitating art."

A similar pattern appeared in Siddipet, Telangana, where police uncovered a murder plot in which the accused prepared detailed timelines, orchestrated alibis, and planted fabricated evidence. Investigators explicitly stated that the planning bore a strong resemblance to the strategies depicted in Drishyam (Deccan Chronicle, 2016). The following year, Gujarat police investigated a murder in which the suspects admitted watching the film and intentionally modelling their cover-up on the techniques shown onscreen, raising concerns among officials about cinema offering "step-by-step instructions" for committing crimes (Indian Express, 2015).

The trend resurfaced in Udaipur, where a homicide investigation revealed planning tactics characteristic of those in Drishyam, including methodical body disposal and alibi coordination, again prompting media outlets to describe it as "Drishyam in real life" (Hindustan Times, 2017). A more sensational case emerged in Indore, where an accused individual attempted to mislead investigators by burying a dog's body instead of the victim's, a tactic widely reported as echoing the film's theme of manipulating evidence (NDTV, 2019).

Even after the release of Drishyam 2 in 2021, Kerala police reported multiple cases in which suspects appeared to consciously rehearse or replicate Georgekutty's elaborate strategies. In some investigations, officers noted that accused individuals had watched or rewatched the films shortly before committing the crime, underscoring the extent to which cinematic narratives can function as rehearsed templates for real-world behaviour (Kerala Police statements reported in regional media, 2021–2023).

Why Drishyam Become a 'Manual for Crime'?

Not all crime films lead to copycat behavior and it is important to ask why Drishyam became uniquely criminogenic. Overall, several criminological explanations can be made.

1. Realism and Detail: The film was detailed and realistic digging graves, covering up CCTV evidence, and rehearsing alibis were plausible behaviors that could be realistically reproduced. Unlike stylized action films that characteristically depict crime and violence not engage with portraying plausible scenarios and actions, Drishyam created a narrative of crime through ordinary spaces and events.
2. Moral Justification: Through Georgekutty's characterization as a morally righteous protector of his family, the film's narrative normalized moral disengagement. Finding crime not to be wrong, but to be survival meant easier rationalization for the audience.
3. Success of Dishonesty: Unlike most crime films, that moralize that right prevails, Drishyam's narrative concludes - successfully planning for crime, whereby Georgekutty's family avoids the law. Listening to the narrative did not carry punishment, reinforcing the idea that crime could work if all factors are considered.
4. Seriously Nationalistic: The family-centered narrative connected with identity in India, specifically within Kerala's residents culturally, and within family slotted concerns of honor. Surviving at the expense of family transgressed expectations from its audience
5. Reinforcement Through Remakes and Media Discourse: The film was reshot on multiple occasions, subjected to media analysis and a barrage of public debates, each of which helped to increase its criminological presence. When the press reported on any number of in the real-life adaptations, it reiterated the film's status as a "crime manual," implicating a series of feedback loops between real-life and cinematic crime.

CRIMINOLOGICAL ANALYSIS

From a criminological standpoint, *Drishyam* represents a compelling illustration of how psychological scripting, social learning, and cultural legitimacy intersect to shape behavioural interpretation and enactment. Drawing on social learning theory, individuals often imitate behaviours observed in influential or high-status models (Bandura, 1977). In this context, Georgekutty becomes a culturally resonant model whose actions are perceived as both rational and morally justified within the narrative world. Complementing this, cognitive script theory posits that repeated exposure to particular behavioural sequences enables audiences to internalise and mentally rehearse these scripts as viable problem-solving strategies (Huesmann, 1998).

Further, cultivation theory illustrates how continual exposure to specific media content shapes viewers' perceptions of reality, legitimising certain behaviours as plausible or even normative (Gerbner et al., 1998). This may explain why the meticulous criminal strategies portrayed in *Drishyam* appeared credible and applicable to real-life situations. Meanwhile, insights from cultural criminology emphasise how crime and transgression acquire meaning within particular cultural contexts; the film's themes resonated strongly within Kerala's socio-cultural landscape, making its techniques symbolically potent (Ferrell et al., 2015).

Thus, *Drishyam* transcended its status as mere entertainment and became an informal archive of symbolic resources for representing deviance. The film inadvertently offered a repertoire of techniques, prompting concerns among law enforcement agencies, as suspects were not only drawing on lived experiences but also rehearsing behaviour inspired by cinematic narratives. For criminologists, *Drishyam* demonstrates how popular culture can function as an informal pedagogy of crime, blurring the boundaries between fictional representation and practical criminal application.

The New Wave of Cinematic Imitation

While Drishyam represented a watershed moment regarding cinematic imitation, early viewership considered this phenomenon an exceptional account; a film so intricately detailed and realistic that imitation was a natural extension of its existence. In the years after its release, however, we now see that Drishyam was decidedly not exceptional; it was the starting point of a much more extensive trend in Malayalam cinema that has seen films with a rigid adherence to realism, serious subject matter, and morally ambiguous protagonists influence, directly or indirectly, not just criminality, but everyday youth culture. This "new wave" includes films like Marco (2022), Pani (2023), and Aavesham (2024) which all engendered some debate about the extent to which cinema glamorizes deviance and may be a memorable way to provide a plan for criminal or antisocial behavior. These films sidelined with each other also account for how the stylistic claim to authenticity inherent in Malayalam cinema, informed by contemporary anxieties over social conditions, social practice in its digital context, and specifically the formation of self-identities, had codified an environment for imitative behaviour

Case Study: Marco (2022)

Marco, a spin-off of Mikhael (2019), examined Kochi's gangster underworld by centering a protagonist fully immersed in violence, intimidation, and organized crime—unlike Drishyam, which framed crime as defensive necessity. Through stylized violence, gritty realism, and morally ambiguous characterization, the film portrayed gangster life as both threatening and aspirational, creating what critics called a new "aesthetic of masculinity" built on fear and dominance rather than virtue. Youth reactions reflected this divide: some criticized the glorification of crime, while others adopted Marco's dialogue, style, and attitude, much like earlier responses to Bollywood's Satya (1998). From a criminological perspective, Marco illustrates imitation rooted in symbolic identification rather than direct behavioral copying; few viewers became criminals, but many incorporated gestures, fashion, and language that align with subcultural defiance. The film thus exemplifies cultural criminology's concept of the "aesthetics of crime" (Ferrell, 1999), showing how cinematic depictions of deviance influence identity formation and everyday performance.

Case Study: Pani (2023)

Marco explored gangsterism while Pani focused on addiction, earning praise for its stark portrayal of drug abuse and its social consequences in Kerala. The film followed marginalized youth trapped in cycles of substance use, crime, and despair, aiming to offer social critique but unintentionally risking normalization through its hyperrealism. Unlike Morales, Pani's detailed depiction of drug paraphernalia, slang, and street-level exchanges worried police and educators, who observed students imitating gestures, language, and preparation rituals shown on screen. This suggested the film taught viewers more than it warned them, blurring the line between cautionary narrative and experiential guide. For psychologists, Pani underscores the paradox that vivid, immersive depictions meant to deter risky behavior can instead attract impressionable youth, especially when tied to identity exploration, as Mutz (1994) notes. For criminologists, it demonstrates how realism in media can complicate prevention efforts by making harmful practices appear accessible, authentic, and inadvertently instructive.

Case Study: Aavesham (2024)

Among the films released in 2024, Aavesham initiated a perhaps the quickest and most obvious case of imitation. Directed by Jithu Madhavan and starring Fahadh Faasil as the flamboyant gangster Ranga, the film featured his eccentric demeanor and excessive dialogue and charisma, which prompted a rash of imitation through various online settings. Unlike Georgekutty in Drishyam, who took a rational approach to his decisions, Ranga was performatively larger than life, and a character whose style resonated in youth culture. One only need observe their social media feed to see how quickly imitators flooded the platforms with reels, memes, and videos that involved schoolchildren and college students imitating Ranga's dialogue and mannerisms. Newspaper articles in Kerala observed that teachers and parents were concerned about how rapidly Ranga's swagger spread through youth culture, with observation that the use of his phrases permeated the classroom and playground (The Hindu, 2024). Even Chief Minister Pinarayi Vijayan tabulated the need to disentangle from the glorification of gangster culture, indicating an understanding of cinema's ability to "become infiltrated" into youth (The Hindu, 2024).

Aavesham suggests, therefore, that it is factors not just of films affecting society but how the potential of virtual social media platforms amplifies that influence. In contrast to Drishyam's effect emerging through news reports of the specific crimes, Aavesham's influence occurred in a viral manner, as youth reconstituted its performative elements as micro-content. This illustrates the new ecology of filmic influence in the OTT and social media age, where boundaries between the film, meme, and lived identity are fluid.

Controversies, State Responses, and CBFC Censorship

The popularity of the imitation phenomenon sparked considerable controversy in the public sphere in Kerala. Filmmakers came to the defense of artistic expression, arguing that filmmakers cannot be accountable for the actions of viewers. Critics, formal education, and police expressed concerns about some aspect of cinema's ability to create crime. Historically, the Central Board of Film Certification (CBFC) has stepped in only in situations where films were viewed as "excessive violence" or "socially harmful." Recently, CBFC had lost a level of regulatory control with the introduction of OTT placing films online. Because of the nature of OTT, crime and deviance become more blatant in their depiction. Some police officers in Kerala have even begun to discuss introducing "media literacy modules," where students can learn to explore and critically evaluate what they have watched instead of consuming it wholly (Mathrubhumi, 2024). This tension between censorship and artistic expression reverberates on an international scale in contemporary policy debates regarding media. To censor creative expression is to risk authoritarian overreach; to deny the influence of cinema is almost wilful neglect of the impact of its performance, especially for vulnerable audiences. It is within this dynamic of imitation in Malayalam cinema today that lucrative creative practice highlights an ongoing policy concern: a fusion of creativity with social responsibility in a digital virality era.

Youth Culture and Cinematic Influence

One of the most striking features of this new phase is the speed at which elements of cinema are recognized and adopted into youth culture. From haircuts and slang to gestures and moral frameworks, young people experience film as a bank of identity resources. In Kerala, a state with amongst the highest literacy rates in India and a strong cinephilia culture, cinema is embedded in everyday experience (Menon,

2017). The mimicry of cinematic styles is not necessarily criminogenic; it can be playful or symbolic. But it often normalizes problematic masculinities, romanticizes violence, or trivializes deviance. Aavesham shows how a gangster persona can enter classrooms and playgrounds, eliciting fears from adults about discipline and degradation of values. These types of fears can reflect Cohen's (1972) perceptions of moral panics in society where social anxieties about youth behaviours are being framed by the media

Media, OTTs, and Virality

Finally, it's important to recognize that the effects of Marco, Pani, and Aavesham extend beyond the cinema hall. The ubiquity of OTT platforms means films are available for watching and re-watching, promoting cognitive rehearsal of behaviors and dialogues. Social media platforms can then act as accelerants, turning cinematic gestures into viral content. This creates an ecology of feedback: films motivate imitative performances, these performances circulate digitally, amplifying the cultural effect of the film and inciting more performance. From a criminological perspective, this illustrates a shift from stand-alone copycat crimes (Drishyam) to a form of networked imitation where filmic elements have washed through the networked digital space and become instantiated in everyday cultural practice.

Manuals to Memes

If Drishyam represented film-as-manual, offering distinct and concrete blueprints for committing murders, the new wave is better described as film-as-meme—representing a global, systematic trend in which an array of communal cinematic aspects move across social media spaces and influence behavior semiotically or symbolically. Nevertheless, both representations ultimately make the same point about cinema's criminological implications: films embody unrealized scripts, formed identities, or performance repertoires that are available for audiences to engage with and adapt in multi-modal ways. In a way, anything can become a meme. Murderers have engaged in murder with a Drishyam-like precision, while students recited gangster language-borrowed locations and musings, directly extending the narratives from a cinematic text to their real, lived social moment. Malayalam cinema has helped us understand how screen narratives migrate from the site of the screen and into social reality. The forms are different—manuals versus memes—but what remains unchanged is the film-as-cultural effect dynamic, where cinema represents a cultural force that infiltrates, impacts, or constructs new psychological, behavioral, and social terrains.

Socio-Psychological Dimensions

The significance of cinema upon crime cannot be grasped merely from imitative or media effect perspectives alone; it intersects socio-psychological dimensions such as identity, culture, and social anxieties. Malayalam cinema, as a form of cinema known for its nuanced storytelling and grounding in the everyday, increasingly creates a site where masculinity, power, morality, and rebellion are all commonplace tropes. The socio-psychological implications of this are particularly pronounced for youth audiences, who often find themselves inhabiting transitional spaces of identity and social negotiation. This section discusses how cinematic texts have consequences for identity formation, culturally constructed gendered ways of being and power, subcultural practices and wider social anxieties, including the effects of moral panics and imitative practices.

Narratives and Identity Formation

Narratives are a powerful way for individuals to make sense of their lives and social contexts. Films provide scripts of identity that we can strive to adopt, undertake resistance, or rework to meet our objectives. Psychological research outlines that adolescents and young adults often draw on the texts of media to help understand themselves and their space in society (Steele & Brown, 1995). Malayalam films, within the context of Kerala, often speak to youth through the depiction of everyday struggles, family tensions, and the hope of respect and recognition.

When characters in films like Drishyam or Joji (2021) exhibit intelligence or resourcefulness, or even a kind of subversive problem-solving, a youth viewer will develop a character internalization of those traits as laudable. Identity construction in this analytic becomes bound to the imagined cinematic. But when that trait is related to an act of deviance where an action is a concealed crime, or there is some manipulation of an authority figure, or violence is enacted for honor, youth may take that calculative reasoning and incorporate it as a legitimate means of navigating social constraints. This blurring between fictional character and lived self-strategy explains why some crimes are reenacted as "performances" lifted directly from film narratives.

Another commonly recurring sociopsychological dimension to Malayalam cinema is masculinity. Such characters like Fahadh Faasil's Joji or any of the antagonists played by Tovino Thomas are representations of hyper-masculinity traits: cunning intellect, physical assertiveness, and outright refusal to adhere to normative forms of traditional or moral order. In films such as Aavesham (2024), masculinity is actually dramatized as a performance, and exuberantly scripted police officers provided dialogue, demonstrations of violence in police enforcement, and charmingly scripted versions of leadership frequently bring admiration and loyalty of a community.

For young men dealing with the social pressures of unemployment, marginalization, or fractured authority structures, these cinematic modalities of masculinity entail attractive templates of power and recognition. Criminal psychology indicates that deviant subcultures often valorize precisely these characteristics, courage, defiance, and toughness, as viable and legitimate alternative sources of identity (Cohen, 1955). Thus, the glamorization of violence presented on screen supports the psychological needs for esteem and belonging, so that engaging in imitation is not simply a matter of reproduction but rather an act of aspirational identity performance.

Social Anxieties and Moral Panics

Malayalam cinema works to shape social anxieties not only at the individual psychological level. Various themes, such as corruption, weak institutions, gendered violence, and generational conflict recur in contemporary films and provide resonance with real-world anxieties and societal issues in Kerala's socio-political context. However, when films inspire youth to act (in this case, commit crimes), they can create moral panics where the media and various political discourse characterizes youth as "contaminated" by the negative influences of their exposure to cinema (Cohen, 1972).

For example, subsequent to Drishyam-inspired criminal acts, there were various public statements from Kerala police and political leaders to discourage films that would "teach" criminal acts overtly (The News Minute, 2019). In all honesty, it is not difficult to understand this trope by 2024, as Aavesham's ostentatious dialogues became popularized by school-age children and, as a result, several headlines warned against the "corrupting effect" of cinema on the impressionable youth (The Hindu, 2024). This might be viewed as connected to broader anxieties about generational divides, wherein parents, educators, and state authorities treat cinema as a disruptive notion threatening the stability of common moral order and social stability.

Criminal Subcultures and Imitation Rituals

From a socio-psychological perspective, imitating a filmic act would be expected to take place in group contexts as opposed to individually. Gang culture, peer groups, and neighborhood groups provide the subcultural spaces or environments in which filmic references are reenacted, parodied, or ritualized. Cultural criminology offers contextual studies that likely suggest that crime is often a performing act for an audience, whether real or imagined, and style, symbols, and narratives matter just as much as the act itself (Ferrell et al., 2008).

Examples from Kerala of young people reproducing the Aavesham gestures or alibis like those seen in Drishyam shows this ritualistic aspect of imitation. These reproductions never escalate to criminality, sometimes remaining at a level of stylized behavior and speech or minor forms of deviance. However, in extreme cases, the use of a film script as part of subcultural identity represents the possibility of these types of imitation manifesting in criminal behavior or elaborate attempts to cover up immoral acts inspired by film plots. The potential for crime would therefore be both functional and symbolic, a performance of a lived cinematic identity, within, or outside of, the everyday social space.

Psychosocial aspects of the intersections of culture and cinema

The further considered social-psychological aspects of cinematic influence in its processes illustrate how copycat crime should not simply be considered passive consumption of media. Instead, it operates or situates in, our individual vulnerabilities and cultural scripts of expectations or anxieties. Emerging from experience, young people who feel marginalized from the boundaries of accepted sociality, depicted in films, find themselves in need of a symbolic gameplan to negotiate their lived reality. In other words, films do provide cognitive blueprints for crime (Berger, 1997), but affective and symbolic materials for identity or masculinity construction or as some sort of resistance to authority.

This dynamic further complicates the conversation around debates of censorship or moral panic. By banning or censoring films, we overlook the greater socio-psychological mechanisms operating where audiences are engaging with, reframing, and adapting those narratives relative to their lived conditions. Understanding these processes is an important component of criminal psychology, and one that must do greater, and impact, study on how culture and psychology co-produce deviant behavior beyond the deterministic "media causes crime" view.

IMPLICATIONS FOR CRIMINAL PSYCHOLOGY

The emergence of crime imitative of cinema in Kerala raises urgent questions for criminal psychology. While not all films produce criminal deviance, the repeated incidents of imitative crime suggest a need for insight regarding how cultural narratives can influence behavior, cognition, and social interaction. We discuss implications for criminal psychology organized into three broad categories: copycat crime as a research agenda; implications for policing and the legal system; and implications for rehabilitation, media education, and preventative interventions.

Copycat Crime as a Research Agenda

Copycat crime, while recognized as a phenomenon going back to at least the 1950s, remains relatively unexplored in mainstream criminology and criminal psychology. Some authors (e.g. Surette, 2015) posit that copycat crime, which often emerges from debate concerning media violence, has largely escaped systematic examination in criminology and psychology. The Malayalam example shows clearly why that should not be the case. Unlike generalized portrayals of violence seen in many mainstream Hollywood blockbusters, Malayalam cinema is often more specific in the ways they depict violence and criminal strategies (e.g. ways to bury the body, create an alibi, disrupt video surveillance, mislead authorities).

This opens up novel pathways in the study of criminal psychology:

- Cognitive pathways of imitation: How do consumers of filmic narratives convert a text-based cinematic script into strategies in the worlds they inhabit? Consumers may accept a narrative as a whole narrative, but do they also modify the narrative or accept it fully in the contexts and worlds with which they identify?
- Audience vulnerability: What traits of psychological characteristics (e.g., sensation seeking, moral disengagement, or weak self-control) inhibit or prevent an audience's agency in resisting engagement with a particular narrative experience?
- Cultural specificity: Why is it that Malayalam cinema, with its emphasis on "realism" (e.g., sociological and geographical specificity in it texting), more prone to an audience engagement that mirrors an imitation/truthful adaptation than a genre that paradigmatically embraces fantasy and stylization? By adopting copycat crime as an area for study, as a unique area of investigation, there are opportunities for psychologists to implement empirical studies that are strong in research design and that allow for indicators that claim more than anecdotal, while moving toward knowing how and when media really does have an influence on criminals.

Difficulties in Policing and Courts

Cinema-inspired crime adds complexity to traditional policing and courts. Criminals who intentionally shape their crime according to film can lead investigators into a predictable, yet misleading, narrative. For example, the police struggled in cases in Nilambur and Indore, when the accused utilized Drishyam to set up false trails, leading investigators off course (Times of India, 2015; NDTV, 2019).

There are several difficulties:

- Predictive policing: Even if law enforcement plans to implement strategies to mitigate imitation, crime inspired by cinema may be executed with uncanny effect using loopholes in film as "instruction manuals".
- Courts: Defence lawyers may maintain that cinema inspires the accused tricky questions of diminished responsibility. Courts rarely accept this argument, but it illustrates how closely media and culpability are interwoven.
- Public disclosure - Moral panic: Media conflates the link between film and crime which incites moral panic, while complicating the public's perception as an audience with judicial neutrality.

In short, for policing these difficulties suggest adaptations: both more technical adaptations of identifying and responding to the significance of cinematic scripts represented in criminal behaviours, along with cultural sensibility regarding the symbolic meanings offenders construct in relation to their actions. For the courts, there is the need to delineate differences in admission of cinema as a consideration and a question of accountability.

Rehabilitation and Preventive Programs

Criminal psychology not only seeks to describe deviance, but also rehabilitation and prevention. Specifically for crimes inspired by films, or, more generally, crimes influenced by film, interventions must address the individual vulnerabilities of offenders while also addressing their cultural contexts.

- Rehabilitation: Offenders who are influenced by films may benefit from cognitive-behavior therapy programs that promote critical reflection of pornographic and other messages they have absorbed from the narrative and the role of the visual narrative through the process of identity development (focusing primarily on deviations from social norms). In particular, encouraging offenders to differentiate the fictive representations in film from the social realities implicated in the deviant representations is an important therapeutic agenda.
- Media literacy: Preventive programs, which are unique cultural and legal responses, must not only continue to promote the idea of censorship. Rather, schools, community initiatives, and correctional facilities must utilize and develop media literacy programs that teach audiences the skills to analyze nar-

ratives in films. In fact, media literacy programs have been shown to decrease occurrence of imitation by equipping audiences to decode media messages rather than to absorb them uncritically and without exploration of alternative narratives (Potter, 2013).

- Engaging youth: Since youth are particularly vulnerable to both the messages presented in films as well as the identification processes suggested, structured activities that provide examples of positive role modelling, participating in mentorship initiatives, arts initiatives, and sports, can be brokering agents to counter the seductive appeal of cinematic identities that are based on violence or deception.

Beyond Censorship

In Kerala, public discourse frequently accents censorship as a response to copycat crime. However, from a psychological perspective, censorship is a blunt instrument that cannot speak to the underlying processes that produce imitation. Research has shown that prohibition or edits, would not inhibit behaviors that were shown in the media; and indeed, they might make the media more desirable to audiences and provide a "forbidden" element (Ferguson, 2014). Instead, it is important for criminal psychology to promote approaches that are sensitive to context. Rather than suggesting audiences are passive viewers, which suppresses the imagination, we should approach the issues from the perspective that audiences interpret and learn actively. Policymakers must endorse partnerships between filmmakers, educators, and psychologists to create campaigns that mitigate risk-taking behavior while supporting artistic expression.

Broader Implications for Criminal Psychology

The broader implications for criminal psychology highlight the need to understand crime inspired by cinema in a more culturally informed and interdisciplinary way. Cultural criminology shows that deviance cannot be explained solely through individual pathology, but must also account for the symbolic and cultural meanings that offenders draw from filmic narratives. This requires psychologists to collaborate with film scholars, sociologists, and legal experts to grasp the full complexity of cinematic influence. Applied practice must also expand so that practitioners can recognize how cultural texts shape offenders' mental worlds, beyond traditional forensic assessments. As global streaming spreads film content across borders instantly, opportunities for cross-cultural imitation increase. The Malayalam case thus offers a valuable model for examining how local stories can generate global effects, enriching both the teaching and research of criminal psychology.

FUTURE DIRECTIONS

The interplay of cinema and crime, highlighted through the discussion of the examples Malayalam cinema provides, as with the films Drishyam and Aavesham more broadly, begs the question of what criminal psychology, criminology, and public policy might do with the problem of imitation. We should avoid narrowly framing the problem in terms of causality (i.e. "films cause crime"). Our future directions should contextualize the problem of imitation as a balance between artistic freedom and social responsibility, while also providing a path towards comparative and policy-oriented research. This section outlines three key future directions: weighing freedom of expression against responsibility, developing comparative research, and developing specific policy recommendations.

Mixing Artistic Freedom with Social Responsibility

Cinema has always been a contested space between creativity and regulation. Filmmakers cite artistic expression as a defense of creative work which, regardless of the violence or deviance of the storyline, is interpreted as reflecting social realties and as a call for critical engagement. Conversely, policymakers and portions of the public often focus and lament the unfavourable outcomes of the artistic-oriented display of violence and/or deviance, especially when a crime inspired by a film receives significant media attention. The future of criminal psychology in this area requires moving past this binary dynamic however. Instead of blaming filmmakers, or believing audiences are passive victims, we need to understand the interactive workings of both engagement in either youth-oriented or youth-critical themes. Audiences are not passive viewers. Audiences actively respond to the film, while situating the cinematic narrative of a film in relationship to their own psychological vulnerabilities and socio-cultural milieu. Thus, any intervention would not have an official or an implied suppression of art but to equip audiences with a tool with which they can iterate with the art. Collaborative partnerships between filmmakers, educators and psychologists to speak about the film upon release or to collaborate on awareness campaigns, or disclaimers where sensitive views regarding violent and/or deviant portrayals can be developed as a way of contextualizing such depictions without compromising the artistic process. Just as films which address smoking or substance abuse are now mostly accompanied by disclaimers, crime centered narratives, could likewise include a disclaimer in guidance to reflect as an audience versus to imitate.

Comparative Research Possibilities

Comparative research offers important opportunities for understanding how cinematic imitation varies across regions and cultures. While the Malayalam case highlights the realism and cultural grounding of regional cinema, similar patterns appear globally, from the controversy surrounding Natural Born Killers in the U.S. to Korean thrillers shaping crime dramas and Bollywood's influence on criminal subcultures. Future studies should compare how different Indian industries, such as Malayalam, Bollywood, and Tamil cinema, differ in their criminogenic potential; examine how audiences across countries interpret and act on crime narratives; and explore how OTT platforms enable hybrid forms of imitation as global content is locally contextualized. Such comparative work would show that media influence is culturally mediated, not universally deterministic.

Policy Proposals

As copycat offenses risk visibility, policy makers must deal with efforts to prevent crime while attending to the democratic ideals of free expression.

Drawing on insights from the field of criminal psychology, we suggest a series of nuanced policy directions:

1. Expand Media Literacy Initiatives: Include critical media literacy in curriculum at both the school and university levels. Difficulties that arise in transforming films into action suggest the important step of teaching students to think critically, to discover things like, for example, how films utilize filmic techniques to relay narrative, and how these strategies to narrate cinematic stories imply moral complexity that can dissuade uncritical imitation.
2. Community-Based Programs: Create film clubs, workshops, and public film discussions that fully engage young people with crime films not as formulations for action but rather as sites of debate or discourse. Community-based film screenings with discussion panels composed of psychologists or criminologists can ultimately transform consumption into active conversations about the film texts.
3. Cooperation with Filmmakers: Encourage industry or filmmakers to create voluntary guidelines instead of implementing bureaucratic censorship or regulation guidelines. Filmmakers could work with expert studies to help more completely anticipate risk related to depiction of crime, while still being able to uphold artistic freedom and expression.
4. Case Awareness: Provide case training for judges and lawyers to be able to critically assess claims of filmic influence as an offer of testimony to action.

Films should not be scapegoated as contributors to crime, however, the courts should remain aware of the potential power of prosecution to establish motive and means.

5. Policing Preparedness: Provide the police with cultural literacy training to assist case detectives in determining where cases present with scripts from films or cinematic stories. Learning semiotics criminology can help detectives recognize when a crime appears to connect with a film, thereby improving detection efficiency.

Beyond Kerala: Towards a Global Dialogue

The case of Malayalam films is an example of what is happening globally with media and crime. Streaming services enable cinematic texts to be instantly accessed and consumed across the globe. The possibility for the international replication of crime is exponentially increased; a viewer located in Europe can be influenced by film from Kerala at the same time the film is released in Kerala.

These interactions indicate the need for international collaboration in research and policy, including:

- Cross-cultural criminological networks that share information about media-influenced crime.
- International guidance of responsible and normatively acceptable representations of crime with attention to local cultural awareness and sensitivity to the vulnerability of individuals.
- Cross-jurisdictional media literacy programs that leverage existing and emerging digital space to target populations of youth.

Re-invisioning the Role of Criminal Psychology

The future is bright for criminal psychology in redefining its function in the discussions of media crime. Instead of policing culture, criminal psychology can be a translator between creativity and society by providing knowledge that will advance both artistic creativity, and socially responsible utilization of creativity inaction. This entails a move away from cybernetic approaches to media violence, and making sense of three important factors: audience agency, cultural specificity, and symbolic import. This way, criminal psychology can not only link our understanding of copycat crime, but it can also help move toward a healthier media ecology, where film is a venue of creativity and critique, and not a script for harm.

CONCLUSION

Cinema has a distinctive position in Kerala's cultural imagination. It is not just an entertainment medium; cinema engages with lived experience, influencing ways of valuing, evaluating, and belonging, as well as ways of doing and being. In exploring the criminological significance of Malayalam cinema, we can recognize a phenomenon beyond mainstream media-effects studies: socio-political and normative anchors in engrossing accounts that condense lived experience into blueprints for reality. The case highlighted by the film Drishyam serves as a powerful example. While the film is celebrated for its originality of narrative, it has also been described as a "manual for crime" when observed in the cross-section of crime and reality. Thus, Drishyam captures the duality of cinema as an artistic achievement and as a criminological experiment. The subsequent films that build on the tension of Drishyam, such as Joji, Marco, Pani, and Aavesham, further normalize this tension since they circulate catchphrases, representations, and styles as self-actualized behaviors within youth subcultures.

From a criminal psychology perspective, these observations raise several important points. First, audiences are not simply consumers but active interpreters of the media. While most people experience films as fiction, some people, especially those at the margins who are managing vulnerabilities related to marginalization, negotiating their identity, or the desire to belong to a subculture, might translate the film's script to lived practice. Copycat crime, therefore, is not about universal explanation; it is about specific intersections of personal psychology, cultural context, and narrative detail. Second, cinematic imitation represents wider socio-psychological processes. Films provide symbolic resources for identity construction and re-construction, especially for youth who are struggling with issues of masculinity, whether they are being acknowledged, or claiming independence. As such, crime itself has become a performance for some, a display of cinematic masculinity, rebellion or ingenuity in the same way an actor performs before an audience. It is vital for a field such as criminal psychology to, first, value acknowledging the further symbolic level, and, second, to move beyond clinical/pathology to cultural/semiotic criticism and analysis.

Thirdly, the Malayalam instance reveals the limitations of censorship's fixes. Censorship often arises from moral panics and typically leads to a desire to increase regulatory authority. But you can't merely remove a film or disinfect it of its objectionable qualities to address the mechanisms of imitation that are more psychological and cultural in their implications. Preventive strategies must place emphasis on media literacy, engaging youth, and even rehabilitative approaches that encourage critical thinking about film narratives. In this respect, criminological psychology has an integral role in generating policy that respects artistic freedom while mitigating criminogenic risk. Beyond Kerala/India, this has global implications. In a world of global streaming, film texts travel across borders and grants the possibility for new imitation opportunities. A film released in Kochi, could spark conversations in a New York or Dubai or Singaporean bar within hours. This is no longer domestic, which means any academic study concerning copycat crime and imitation must be comparative and collaborative in nature within this global framework, observing cultural particularities, but shared risks.

Ultimately, the consideration of Malayalam cinema as a criminological case study reinforces a larger truth: that crime is, indeed, an act of transgression, but also exists as a cultural performance constructed by narratives, symbols, and imagination. Confronted with cinema as engaging this cultural work rather than solely as a scapegoat, criminologists, criminal psychologists, and other criminological scholars can contribute to a deeper understanding of how art and life negotiate within the domain of deviance. In conclusion, the relationship between cinema, crime, and psychology is neither to shame and vilify the art form of cinema nor to disregard its power. Cinema has the potential to be a catalyst for reflection, critique, and transformation, but sometimes under certain conditions, it can also produce scripts for damage. The difficulty for scholars, practitioners, and policymakers is to assume that responsibility for the tension - retains the creative impulse of cinema and encourage the social and psychological fortitude to preclude imitation. That said, Malayalam cinema, as a case study that highlights the juxtaposition of realism, detail, and culturally inflected understanding, generously provokes reflection, reminding us that the divide between screen and society is porous, and that the stories we tell are influential in shaping the lives we live.

REFERENCES

Bandura, A. (1977). *Social learning theory*. Prentice Hall.

Bandura, A. (1999). Moral disengagement in the perpetration of inhumanities. *Personality and Social Psychology Review*, *3*(3), 193–209. DOI: 10.1207/s15327957pspr0303_3 PMID: 15661671

Bandura, A. (2009). Social cognitive theory of mass communication. In J. Bryant & M. B. Oliver (Eds.), *Media effects: Advances in theory and research* (3rd 94–124). Routledge.

BBC News. (2021, February 24). *Indian police say suspects copied film "Drishyam" to cover up murder*. BBC News. https://www.bbc.com

Berger, C. R. (1997). Interpersonal communication and social influence. In Berger, C. R., & Chaffee, S. H. (Eds.), *Handbook of communication science* (pp. 503–529). Sage.

Bordwell, D., & Thompson, K. (2019). *Film art: An introduction* (12th ed.). McGraw-Hill Education.

Cohen, L. E. (1955). *Delinquent boys: The culture of the gang*. Free Press.

Cohen, S. (1972). *Folk devils and moral panics: The creation of the Mods and Rockers*. Routledge.

Deccan Chronicle. (2016). *Siddipet murder accused allegedly inspired by Drishyam*. Deccan Chronicle.

Ferguson, C. J. (2014). Does movie violence increase violent behavior? An examination of longitudinal data. *Psychology of Popular Media Culture*, *3*(3), 170–177.

Ferrell, J. (1999). *Crimes of style: Urban graffiti and the politics of criminality*. Northeastern University Press.

Ferrell, J., Hayward, K., & Young, J. (2008). *Cultural criminology: An invitation* (2nd ed.). SAGE.

Ferrell, J., Hayward, K., & Young, J. (2015). *Cultural criminology: An invitation* (2nd ed.). SAGE. DOI: 10.4135/9781473919969

Funk, J. B., Baldacci, H. B., Pasold, T., & Baumgardner, J. (2004). Violence exposure in real-life, video games, television, movies, and the internet: Is there desensitization? *Journal of Adolescence*, *27*(1), 23–39. DOI: 10.1016/j.adolescence.2003.10.005 PMID: 15013258

Gerbner, G. (1998). Cultivation analysis: An overview. In Morgan, M. (Ed.), *Against the mainstream: The selected works of George Gerbner* (pp. 175–194). Peter Lang.

Gerbner, G., & Gross, L. (1976). Living with television: The violence profile. *Journal of Communication, 26*(2), 173–199. DOI: 10.1111/j.1460-2466.1976.tb01397.x PMID: 932235

Gerbner, G., Gross, L., Morgan, M., & Signorielli, N. (1998). Growing up with television: Cultivation processes. In Bryant, J., & Zillmann, D. (Eds.), *Media effects: Advances in theory and research* (pp. 43–67). Lawrence Erlbaum.

Hindustan Times. (2017). *Udaipur murder case resembles Drishyam plot, say police*. Hindustan Times.

Huesmann, L. R. (1998). The role of social information processing and cognitive scripts in the acquisition and maintenance of habitual aggressive behavior. In Geen, R. G., & Donnerstein, E. (Eds.), *Human aggression: Theories, research, and implications for policy* (pp. 73–109). Academic Press. DOI: 10.1016/B978-012278805-5/50005-5

Huesmann, L. R. (2018). Aggressive behavior and media violence research. *Annual Review of Clinical Psychology, 14*, 75–99.

Indian Express. (2015). *Gujarat murder accused admit to copying plot from Drishyam*. The Indian Express.

Jenkins, H. (2006). *Convergence culture: Where old and new media collide*. New York University Press.

Kerala Police Reports (2021–2023). Summaries of public statements cited in regional news reports regarding imitation crimes following *Drishyam 2. (Multiple sources; used for contextual attribution.)*

Larkin, R. (2009). *The Columbine legacy: Rampage shootings as political acts*. University of Texas Press. DOI: 10.1177/0002764209332548

Mathrubhumi. (2015, February 25). *Drishyam* inspires real-life crime: Police. https://english.mathrubhumi.com/

Mathrubhumi. (2024, March 12). Media literacy modules proposed for students to counter film influence. https://english.mathrubhumi.com/

Menon, A. (2017). Youth, identity, and cinema in Kerala. *South Asian Popular Culture, 15*(2), 135–150.

Nair, P. K. (2013). *The moving image: A study of Malayalam cinema*. Oxford University Press India.

NDTV. (2019). *Indore man buries dog to mislead police in murder case inspired by Drishyam*. NDTV.

Potter, W. J. (2013). *Media literacy* (6th ed.). SAGE.

Rajadhyaksha, A. (2020). Indian cinema in the streaming age. *Journal of Indian Cinema Studies*, *5*(2), 45–62.

Sheep Without a Shepherd. (2019). [Film]. China.

Srinivas, L. (2002). *Megastar: Chiranjeevi and Telugu cinema after N.T. Rama Rao*. Oxford University Press.

Steele, J. R., & Brown, J. D. (1995). Adolescent room culture: Studying media in the context of everyday life. *Journal of Youth and Adolescence*, *24*(5), 551–576. DOI: 10.1007/BF01537056

Sundar, S. S., & Limperos, A. M. (2013). Uses and grats 2.0: New gratifications for new media. *Journal of Broadcasting & Electronic Media*, *57*(4), 504–525. DOI: 10.1080/08838151.2013.845827

Surette, R. (2011). *Media, crime, and criminal justice: Images, realities, and policies* (5th ed.). Cengage Learning.

Surette, R. (2015). *Copycat crime: Media influence on violent behavior*. Routledge.

The Hindu. (2024, April 20). Kerala CM warns against glamorisation of violence in films like *Aavesham*. https://www.thehindu.com/

The News Minute. (2019, September 22). How *Drishyam* inspired several real-life crimes in India. https://www.thenewsminute.com/

The News Minute. (2022, January 12). After *Drishyam 2*, police report cases inspired by movie strategies. https://www.thenewsminute.com/

Times of India. (2016). *Nilambur family murder case echoes Drishyam storyline*. The Times of India.

Chapter 9

The Sustainable Development of Young People's Psychological Well-Being:

Design Thinking Mindset as a Prevention

Areej ElSayary
http://orcid.org/0000-0002-5554-0069
Zayed University, UAE

ABSTRACT

This study investigates the relationship between design thinking mindset and the psychological well-being of young people in the UAE. In addition, it explores how developing a design thinking mindset can be a psychological prevention to promote sustainable well-being in young people. A quantitative approach was deployed using a cross-sectional study. The participants were young undergraduate students at a federal institute in the United Arab Emirates (UAE). The study's findings suggest that developing a design thinking mindset can act as a psychological prevention to promote the sustainable development of young people's well-being. The study also found a strong positive correlation between design thinking mindsets and psychological well-being. The findings have important implications for educators, policymakers, and practitioners interested in promoting sustainable well-being in young people.

DOI: 10.4018/979-8-3373-5896-3.ch009

INTRODUCTION

The COVID-19 pandemic has prompted changes in our professional and personal routines, prompting inquiries about the work landscape's evolution, the skills required for emerging employment challenges, the mental health of individuals (particularly teens and young adults), and the level of involvement in virtual, hybrid, or in-person work settings. The pandemic has also affected people's mindsets, causing them to reevaluate what they value most in employment, such as flexible schedules, work-life balance, and career advancement opportunities. The outbreak has triggered an increase in feelings of fear, worry, tension, and low mood among people, with students in educational institutions like schools and universities feeling the greatest impact (Mahyoob, 2020). The COVID-19 outbreak has led to approximately 228 million cases of infection and 4.7 million fatalities (Guazzini et al., 2022). Economic downturns and changes in daily life routines have been significant, stemming from lockdowns and numerous health protocols, and have affected mental health. Adolescents could be disproportionately affected due to their stage of growth and heightened susceptibility to stress from their surroundings (Zhang et al., 2021). Moreover, educational institutions worldwide adopted remote learning in response to the COVID-19 pandemic. This pandemic has been a worldwide emergency, presenting a multitude of difficulties and leading to a range of psychological effects (Aisha & Ratra, 2022). Yet, within each crisis lies a significant opportunity, allowing those involved to become acquainted with novel, cutting-edge educational methods and to develop new competencies (Farrah & Jabari., 2020). The focus on well-being has received greater importance in individuals' work and social lives. In order to cope with the changes people face, it is important to develop an approach that tackle the problems, suggest solutions and promotes people's well-being. Design thinking (DT) is an approach used for customizing and reshaping preliminary interventions (Yeager et al., 2016). More specifically, DT is a human-centered, iterative process that integrates both convergent and divergent thinking, utilizing multidisciplinary teams and employing visual techniques to promote 21st-century skills (Badwan et al., 2017). The design thinking mindset includes ten core dimensions: uncertainty and risk tolerance, empathy, holistic thinking, collaboration and diversity, learning orientation, experimentation, critical questioning, abduction, creative confidence, and impact (Vignoli et al., 2023). It is a human-centered approach that develops growth mindsets, which enable young people to innovate and solve complex problems that have a real impact on people's lives. Design thinking is a powerful process that is influenced by positive social psychology. It helps understand the strengths and limitations, understand individuals' needs, and influence their overall well-being. Importantly, in virtual and digitally-mediated environments, the design thinking mindset becomes particularly valuable as it enables individuals to navigate reduced social cues, develop stronger group identity, and foster collaborative problem-solving despite the limitations of reduced non-verbal cues and virtual affordances (Cummings & Wertz, 2023; Han et al., 2024; Kush et al., 2025). It was stated that the development of a design thinking mindset in students stimulates the development of a growth mindset and, consequently, promotes psychological well-being (Ku & Stager, 2022). DT is not only a problem-solving sequence but a socio-cognitive mindset that integrates empathy, experimentation, iteration, and collaborative meaning-making. It entails five core phases: empathize, define, ideate, prototype, and test, each emphasizing human-centered inquiry and reflective learning (Brown & Katz, 2019; Liedtka, 2020). As a construct, DT involves cognitive flexibility, perspective-taking, ambiguity tolerance, and creative confidence, which together shape how individuals interpret social cues and generate solutions in uncertain environments. This clarification aligns DT more explicitly with the development of psychological well-being and provides a stronger conceptual base for linking DT with PERMA and growth mindset theories.

This research examines the link between a design-thinking mindset and the mental health (precisely psychological well-being) of youth in the UAE. The study explores how developing a design thinking mindset can be psychological prevention to promote sustainable well-being in young people. The subsequent research inquiries have been developed to steer this investigation:

1. What is the relationship between design-thinking mindsets and the psychological well-being of young people?
2. How can developing a design thinking mindset act as a psychological prevention to promote sustainable development of young people's well-being?
3. Is there a significant difference between the mean scores of design thinking mindset and well-being in young people?

Background of the Study

The UAE's 2030 sustainable development agenda outlines six key sectors for transformation, each defined by specific goals and objectives: a unified society with a maintained identity, a secure public realm and impartial legal system, an economy based on competitive knowledge, a top-tier educational system, healthcare of the highest standard, and a sustainable approach to the environment and infrastructure. In addition, it was stated that preparing individuals for any challenges by developing mindsets and skills is essential to prepare them for jobs that still need to be created (UAE, 2017).

In 2019, before the pandemic, the Arab Youth Survey reported that 54% of young Arabs face difficulty in accessing medical care for mental illnesses such as anxiety or depression (Emirates Youth Council, 2021). Additionally, it was stated in The Economist Impact (2022), that neuropsychiatric conditions account for roughly 19.9% of the UAE's disease burden, with depression and anxiety representing 75% of these mental health issues. In previous study, it was indicated that students are more likely to experience depression and anxiety compared to the broader populace (Evans et al., 2018). It is interesting to note that the World Health Organization (WHO) in 2021 highlighted that half of all mental health issues begin by the age of 14, and three-quarters have started by the age of 24. The promotion, prevention, and intervention initiatives were stated as important goals in the UAE agenda. This is because 34% of the UAE population is under age 25 (Oxford Business Group, 2021).

The COVID-19 pandemic has increased mental health issues, as a result of losing social communication and the presence of the feeling of isolation (Mailizar et al., 2020). This is due to the high stress levels, long work hours, and more exposure to screen time experienced by students, teachers, and administrators during this time (Ridge & Erfurth, 2020). Furthermore, employers will begin to recognize the importance of their employees' mental health for the sustainability of their business. Early identification of the problems and early interventions are important to consider in order to apply more effective treatment strategies (Matthews, 2019). The Director-General of the World Health Organization (WHO), emphasized that addressing mental health needs is a key aspect of responding to the COVID-19 pandemic. He warned that neglecting individuals' emotional and psychological well-being would result in enduring social and economic burdens for society (The Economist Impact, 2022).

Theoretical Framework

In 1954, Gordon Allport emphasized that social psychology aimed to explain how people's thoughts, feelings, and behaviors are influenced by the presence of others (Spencer & Myers, 2006; Thompson & Schonthal, 2020). It not only explores processes like conformity, persuasion, and social perception but increasingly intersects with positive psychology by examining how social relationships, prosocial behavior, and social identity contribute to well-being and human flourishing. Positive psychology is defined as the science and practice of improving well-being (Lomas et al., 2014). However, positive psychology has been criticized for insufficient attention to the social context of well-being (Becker & Marecek, 2008). This field focused mainly on creating individual interventions that emphasize strategies and tools to develop psychological skills that fall within the scope of planned activities (Sin & Lyubomirsky, 2009). From an applied psychology perspective, there are increasing efforts to develop strategies that promote well-being at a social level, referred to as "Positive Social Psychology" (Lomas et al., 2014).

Conversely, Ryff's psychological well-being theory (2013) suggests that well-being is a multifaceted concept encompassing six dimensions: autonomy, mastery of one's environment, personal development, positive relationships with others, a sense of purpose in life, and self-acceptance. These dimensions are interrelated and contribute to well-being (Dosi et al., 2018). In addition, Seligman's PERMA framework (2012) proposes that well-being combines five elements: positive emotions, engagement, relationships, meaning, and accomplishment, which was used in this study, in addition to two more elements: future plans and health.

Dosi et al. (2018) indicated that design thinking could enhance psychological interventions by fostering a growth mindset, an idea also emphasized in the self-theories proposed by Dweck (1999). These theories focus on individuals' beliefs about their capabilities and the potential for growth and development. A growth mindset correlates with the notion that abilities can be honed through effort and perseverance, whereas a fixed mindset adheres to the belief that abilities are inherent and unchangeable. Design thinking is highlighted as a potent facilitator of innovation and creativity across various sectors, including education, business, and healthcare (Dosi et al., 2018). It refers to the cognitive and metacognitive processes involved in design thinking, including tolerance for ambiguity, embracing risk, human-centeredness, empathy, mindfulness, and collaboration (Davies et al., 2022; Ladachart et al., 2022). Dosi et al. (2018) recommend that future research should focus on developing a better understanding of the design thinking mindset and its impact on individuals and organizations.

Based on these concepts, the framework of design thinking mindset and psychological well-being can be developed. The framework proposes that a growth mindset is associated with developing a design thinking mindset, contributing to the development of psychological well-being. The six dimensions of psychological well-being proposed by Ryff (2013) and the five elements of Seligman's PERMA framework (2012) were used to measure the different aspects of psychological well-being. The cognitive and metacognitive processes involved in design thinking, such as tolerance for ambiguity, embracing risk, human-centeredness, empathy, mindfulness, and collaboration, can contribute to developing psychological well-being by promoting positive emotions, engagement, positive relationships, meaning, and accomplishment (Dosi et al., 2018). The framework can be used to guide research on the relationship between design thinking mindsets and psychological well-being and to develop interventions that promote the development of both.

Design Thinking in Virtual Environments and Social Psychology

The contemporary learning landscape increasingly occurs within virtual and digitally-mediated environments, particularly following the COVID-19 pandemic. Understanding how design thinking operates within these contexts requires consideration of virtual environment affordances and their implications for social psychology, group identity, and psychological well-being (Han et al., 2024). *Virtual environments* present unique affordances, the possibilities for action that environments provide, which differ substantially from physical spaces. These affordances include spatiality, presence, and embodiment, which can either enhance or constrain social interaction (Han et al., 2024). However, virtual environments also impose significant constraints on communication, particularly through the reduction of nonverbal social cues such as facial expressions, body language, and proxemics. Research in computer-mediated communication demonstrates that this reduction in social cues can impact group processes, including social identity formation and conformity behaviors (Kush et al., 2025).

The Reduced *Social Cues Model* suggests that limited non-verbal information in virtual environments can lead to depersonalization and reduced social influence (Kush et al., 2025). However, more recent research indicates that individuals adapt to these constraints through enhanced reliance on text-based cues, profile information, and shared group identity (Kush et al., 2025). Design thinking mindsets, particularly the dimensions of empathy, collaboration, and critical questioning, can mitigate the challenges posed by reduced social cues. By fostering explicit attention to others' perspectives and needs, design thinking enables individuals to compensate for missing nonverbal information and maintain meaningful group identity in virtual contexts (Cummings & Wertz, 2023; Han et al., 2024). Furthermore, the design thinking emphasis on *human-centeredness* and *empathy* aligns with positive social psychology principles that extend beyond individual well-being to encompass relational and community-level outcomes. When individuals employ design thinking approaches in virtual environments, they are more likely to engage in perspective-taking, recognize diverse viewpoints, and develop inclusive solutions that consider the needs of all group members, even when visual and physical presence is limited (Faralla et al., 2024). The sense of social presence, defined as the perceptual salience of another social actor in mediated communication (Cummings & Wertz, 2023), can be enhanced through design thinking practices that emphasize empathy and human-centered problem-solving.

Digital Patterns and Youth Engagement in the UAE

Given the UAE's strategic focus on digital transformation and the increasing role of virtual environments in education and social life, understanding youth digital engagement patterns is essential for contextualizing design thinking interventions. Recent research on digital media engagement among UAE youth reveals that young people exhibit high levels of engagement with video-centric social platforms, with platform preferences shaped by peer dynamics and platform design affordances (Darwish, 2025). The study found that UAE adolescents demonstrate diverse but overlapping digital habits, characterized by a desire for peer connection and entertainment, yet face multifaceted digital divides marked by gaps in access, uneven development of critical digital literacy skills, and difficulty identifying manipulations such as deepfakes (Darwish, 2025). Gender-based differences in digital engagement are particularly notable: males demonstrate higher interactivity and engagement with content creation features, while females exhibit stronger privacy vigilance and protective behaviors online (Darwish, 2025). Older students show more advanced use of academic and productivity tools, suggesting developmental trajectories in digital literacy. These patterns underscore the importance of culturally responsive, age-appropriate interventions that address both the opportunities and risks of digital environments. DT mindsets are particularly relevant for navigating these digital patterns. The DT emphasis on critical questioning can help young people develop stronger algorithmic awareness and media literacy skills. The collaboration and diversity dimensions encourage peer-led learning and ethical content creation practices. Additionally, the learning orientation and experimentation dimensions support the development of adaptive digital skills necessary for success in rapidly evolving technological landscapes (Darwish, 2025). By integrating design thinking approaches into digital literacy education, educators can help UAE youth develop not only technical competencies but also the metacognitive awareness and ethical reasoning necessary for sustainable digital citizenship.

Elements of Wellbeing

There are numerous ways of categorizing the primary elements of well-being. In this study, the five-model domain of well-being (positive emotions, engagements, relationships, meaning, and accomplishments) was created by the father of this field Martin Seligman (2012). Every component can be seen as an end in itself, not merely a means to achieve another objective (Seligman, 2012). The positive emotions element of well-being is about having a pleasurable life (Peterson, 2006; Seligman, 2012).

Positive feelings such as happiness, gratitude, contentment, and joy are all connected to greater life satisfaction and well-being (Fredrickson, 2009; Seligman, 2012). Positive emotions not only enhance resilience and expand our perspective of potential but also contribute to improved sleep quality (Fredrickson, 2009). *Engagement* is an activity where we all are completely involved in and being "in the zone" (Csikszentmihalyi, 1990; Seligman, 2012). The engagement activities seemed effortless; however, they contributed to the well-being. *Relationships* are essential to human thriving. Studies have shown that social isolation in life and work significantly elevates the risk of premature death, surpassing the dangers posed by smoking, alcoholism, or obesity (Holt-Lunstad et al., 2010). From the perspective of human-centered designers, it is extremely important to focus attention on others in order to have a life worth living (Park et al., 2013). In the long run, some sense of *Meaning* is important as it involves living one's values of meaning where one's life makes sense, matters, and has a purpose even during the struggle (Heintzelman & King, 2014). *Accomplishment* is crucial for human flourishing, as it requires setting objectives, having the drive to chase them, and the capacity to forge routes to achieve these aims. These goals may be immediate, but it's essential for individuals to embrace novelty and accept the possibility of failure in order to innovate (Cannon & Edmondson, 2005). This is due to the fact that individuals experience enhanced well-being when they can fully leverage and relish their personal successes, rather than hastily proceeding to the next endeavor (Bryant & Veroff, 2007; Langston, 1994). This approach fosters a more contented and satisfying life. While the five elements of the PERMA model are distinct components that collectively enhance overall well-being, they seldom occur independently in real-world scenarios. On the other side, understanding *future plans* and *health* is important to understand the relationship between design thinking mindsets and well-being because design thinking can:

- help individuals develop a growth mindset and focus on purpose and impact (Mouchrek & Benson, 2023). Creating solutions aimed at solving actual societal issues and having a positive impact can help individuals find a sense of purpose and meaning in their work. This can help individuals feel more fulfilled, satisfied, and motivated to plan their future properly.
- be used to improve health outcomes by fostering empathy, collaboration, and human-centeredness (Yeager et al., 2016). Good health can help individuals feel more energized, focused, and productive, while a proper sleeping pattern can improve cognitive function, memory, and learning. This can lead to

greater productivity and success and a greater sense of accomplishment and satisfaction (Yeager et al., 2016).

> Individuals can use design thinking to create solutions that solve problems and promote well-being and happiness by focusing on these elements. The design thinking mindset can help individuals develop the skills and mindsets needed to cultivate each element of PERMA and promote well-being and happiness in their lives.

Design Thinking Mindset (DTM)

Design thinking, as described by Badwan et al. (2017), is an approach centered around humans for solving problems and driving innovation. It integrates both convergent and divergent thinking, utilizes multidisciplinary teams, and employs visual techniques to cultivate 21st-century skills in individuals. Recent scale development research has operationalized the design thinking mindset as a second-order factor comprising ten interconnected dimensions: (1) uncertainty and risk tolerance (the ability to embrace ambiguity and take calculated risks); (2) empathy (understanding and valuing others' perspectives and needs); (3) holistic thinking (considering problems as integrated wholes rather than isolated components); (4) collaboration and diversity (valuing multidisciplinary perspectives and teamwork); (5) learning orientation (maintaining curiosity and commitment to continuous improvement); (6) experimentation (adopting iterative, trial-and-error approaches); (7) critical questioning (challenging assumptions and conventional wisdom); (8) abduction (using intuitive reasoning and pattern recognition); (9) creative confidence (believing in one's capacity to generate novel solutions); and (10) impact (focusing on meaningful, real-world outcomes) (Vignoli et al., 2023). According to Fraser (2010), the mindset of a designer encompasses qualities such as openness, empathy, intrinsic motivation, mindfulness, adaptability, and optimism. This approach to work involves a mindset focused on tackling problems through experimentation and exploration, tolerance for ambiguity, optimism, and a forward-looking perspective (You, 2022). In virtual and digital learning environments, these dimensions become particularly salient, as individuals must navigate reduced nonverbal communication cues and develop stronger reliance on empathy, critical questioning, and collaborative problem-solving to maintain group cohesion and identity (Cummings & Wertz, 2023; Han et al., 2024; Kush et al., 2025). The design thinking mindset can be used to develop skills such as creativity, innovation, collaboration, and problem-solving, which are necessary for future jobs (Klenner et al., 2021).

As reported by many authors, measuring design thinking mindsets has many challenges: (1) different ways of implementing design thinking differ from one organization to another and from one context to another (Marelaro et al., 2015); (2)

measuring something that is not a design thinking mindset is risky because many different practices are categorized or labeled as design thinking (Schmiedgen et al., 2016); and (3) researchers who aimed to measure design thinking declared that their tools were not valid as they used manufactured tools (Schmiedgen et al., 2016).

This study defines a Design thinking mindset as the collection of attitudes, perspectives, beliefs, and actions that typify an individual, team, or organization. The novelty and intellectual merit of the intervention aim to positively impact Learners' well-being using Design Thinking Mindset as the driving force that includes uncertainty, empathy, mindfulness, collaborative working with diversity, learning-oriented, and creative confidence. Embracing uncertainty in problem-solving involves considering all potential solutions as fluid and open to question (Lockwood, 2014). This means engaging in a process where both the results and the time required to achieve them are not predetermined (Schweitzer et al., 2016). User empathy lies at the heart of a human-centered design process, enabling individuals to view situations from various viewpoints and comprehend the motivations behind people's actions (You, 2022). Showing empathy helps in refraining from judgment and being at ease with individuals from diverse backgrounds and viewpoints (Carlgren et al., 2016). *Mindfulness* of the process means being aware of the process's steps and when to be involved in a converging or diverging phase (Schweitzer et al., 2016). *Collaborative working* with diversity is essential in design thinking, where individuals need to collaborate, share their knowledge, and discuss using visualization tools. Collaborating in a multidisciplinary team is essential to better communicate and clarify possibilities with others from different backgrounds, perceptions, and perspectives (Auernhammer & Roth, 2021). Having a *learning-oriented* approach is a fundamental characteristic of design thinkers (Schweitzer et al., 2016). *Creative confidence* is the ability to think differently and trust in solving problems creatively (Plattner et al., 2014).

The design thinking mindset and the elements of PERMA are related in several ways. For instance, by engaging in design thinking activities, individuals can experience positive emotions such as inspiration, curiosity, and love. Also, the design thinking mindset can promote engagement by encouraging individuals to be fully absorbed in activities that focus on human-centered design and problem-solving. Positive relationships can be fostered by empathy, collaboration, and human-centeredness, where individuals work together to solve problems and create solutions. Hepner et al. (2022) also highlighted the advantageous impacts of mindfulness programs on positive emotion, engagement, relationships, meaning, and accomplishment. Moreover, by creating solutions for real-world challenges that positively influence society, individuals can cultivate a sense of purpose and meaning in their work. The trait of positive emotion is linked to higher self-reported empathy but lower empathic performance. While the trait of empathy was found to be negatively correlated with well-being alone, the practice of empathy in everyday life typically correlated with increased well-being (Depow et al., 2021). Additionally, while uncertainty is commonly connected with negative emotions (Morriss et al., 2021), in certain situations, it can lead to positive outcomes (Anderson et al., 2019; Vazard, 2022). Finally, the design thinking mindset can promote accomplishment by encouraging individuals to set and achieve goals (Yeager et al., 2016). In conclusion, the design thinking mindset can help individuals develop the skills and mindsets needed to cultivate each element of PERMA and promote well-being and happiness in their lives. By focusing on the elements of PERMA, individuals can use design thinking to create solutions that not only solve problems but also promote well-being and happiness. This leads to the growth mindset intervention to increase students' desire to take on challenges and enhance their persistence (klenner et al., 2021).

Design Thinking in Virtual Collaboration: Bridging Digital Divides and Enhancing Teamwork

Although design thinking has traditionally been discussed in physical contexts, its application in virtual collaboration environments presents unique opportunities and challenges for young people's psychological well-being. Virtual collaboration, defined as synchronous or asynchronous teamwork mediated through digital platforms, requires specific DT competencies to succeed (Grabowski et al., 2024). The metaverse and immersive extended reality (XR) environments offer new technological possibilities for conducting 3D immersive group meetings that can enrich virtual teamwork by replicating and augmenting traditional face-to-face interactions (Grabowski et al., 2024).

In virtual collaboration contexts, design thinking increases through specific mechanisms that compensate for the reduced social cues inherent in technology-mediated communication. The ten core dimensions of DT, particularly empathy, collaboration/diversity, and critical questioning, become essential for navigating virtual team dynamics. Empathy in virtual settings requires active effort to understand team members' perspectives without nonverbal cues such as facial expressions, body language, and tone of voice. Young people employing DT skills in virtual teams must consciously seek clarification, ask open-ended questions, and create psychological safety for team members to express concerns (Grabowski et al., 2024).

Problem decomposition, a key DT skill, becomes particularly valuable in virtual collaboration. When teams face complex challenges in virtual environments, the ability to break down problems into manageable components allows distributed team members to work on specific aspects asynchronously or in parallel sessions. This skill reduces cognitive overload and enhances engagement in virtual meetings. Similarly, reframing, the ability to view problems from multiple perspectives, helps virtual teams overcome the limitations of reduced social presence by encouraging diverse viewpoints and creative problem-solving approaches (Grabowski et al., 2024).

The technological design characteristics of virtual environments significantly influence how DT skills can be applied. According to recent research on group dynamics in the metaverse, immersive XR meetings with realistic avatars and embodied interactions create higher levels of entitativity (the perception that participants form a cohesive group) compared to traditional 2D video conferencing (Grabowski et al., 2024). This enhanced sense of group cohesion facilitates better collaboration and engagement, which are essential outcomes when applying design thinking processes in virtual settings. Young people in these immersive environments can more effectively employ DT's collaborative dimension because they experience greater social presence and can convey nonverbal cues through avatar movements and gestures.

Furthermore, design thinking in virtual collaboration addresses what researchers term "qualia," the subjective experience of being in a virtual environment (Grabowski et al., 2024). Young people's psychological well-being in virtual teams depends not only on task completion but also on their subjective experience of connection and belonging. Design thinking's emphasis on user-centered design and empathy directly supports the creation of virtual collaboration spaces that enhance positive qualia and reduce feelings of isolation or disconnection.

Social Processes and Group Dynamics in Virtual Environments

A critical gap in previous discussions of design thinking and well-being has been the minimal theorizing about social processes within virtual environments themselves. Social processes, the patterns of interaction, communication, and relationship formation that occur within groups, function differently in virtual versus face-to-face contexts, with significant implications for young people's psychological well-being. Understanding these processes is essential for applying design thinking effectively in digital spaces.

Virtual environments present unique social dynamics characterized by what researchers term "reduced social cues." Unlike face-to-face interactions where individuals can perceive facial expressions, body language, tone of voice, and physical proximity, technology-mediated communication filters these cues through digital interfaces. However, recent research on social connectedness in virtual reality environments reveals that individuals adapt remarkably well to these constraints through active engagement and creative use of available cues (Derda et al., 2025). Young people demonstrate high levels of adaptability by actively seeking non-verbal cues (such as avatar movements and gestures) and engaging in social interactions that foster social presence, the perception of being "with" others in a shared space (Derda et al., 2025).

The development of social connectedness in virtual environments unfolds through distinct phases that can be understood through a design thinking lens. Derda and colleagues (2025) identified three formative phases: initiation, conversion, and engagement. During the initiation phase, interactive features such as hand and body tracking allow participants to convey gestures and movements, enabling identification and connection with others. This phase mirrors the empathy stage of design thinking, where understanding others' perspectives and communication styles is paramount. In the conversion phase, social affordances, the features of the technology that enable social interaction, facilitate joint activities and shared experiences. Here, design thinking's collaborative dimension becomes essential as participants engage in co-creation and collective problem-solving. The engagement phase involves the renegotiation and redefinition of social space within the virtual environment, requiring the critical questioning and reframing skills central to design thinking (Derda et al., 2025).

An important finding from research on virtual social dynamics is that the transfer of social space from physical to virtual environments is not direct or seamless. Instead, participants must actively reconstruct social norms, communication patterns, and relationship dynamics within the virtual context (Derda et al., 2025). This reconstructive process requires design thinking skills, particularly the ability to question assumptions about how social interaction "should" work and to design new interaction patterns suited to the virtual environment's affordances and constraints. Young people who possess strong design thinking mindsets are better equipped to navigate this reconstruction process, leading to more satisfying and psychologically beneficial virtual social experiences.

Social psychology research on communication networks reveals that the structure of virtual communication, who communicates with whom, through what channels, and with what frequency, significantly influences shared social identity and group cohesion (Kush et al., 2025). Design thinking's emphasis on systems thinking and holistic understanding helps young people recognize how communication patterns in virtual teams affect not only task completion but also psychological well-being and sense of belonging. By applying design thinking to the structure of virtual communication networks, young people can help create more inclusive and psychologically supportive virtual communities (Kush et al., 2025).

Furthermore, the concept of "interaction flow" in virtual environments, the smooth, uninterrupted engagement in collaborative activities, represents a key mediating mechanism between technology and well-being outcomes (Grabowski et al., 2024). Design thinking facilitates interaction flow by encouraging participants to anticipate potential communication breakdowns, design clear protocols for virtual collaboration, and continuously refine processes based on feedback. This proactive, user-centered approach to designing virtual social processes directly supports young people's psychological well-being by reducing frustration and enhancing satisfaction with virtual interactions (Grabowski et al., 2024).

Parasocial Relationships and Virtual Support Networks in Young People's Well-being

While isolation has been discussed as a challenge for young people's psychological well-being, particularly during and after the COVID-19 pandemic, an equally important phenomenon deserves attention: parasocial interactions and online support communities. Parasocial relationships, one-sided relationships where individuals feel a sense of connection to media figures or online personalities, have become increasingly prevalent among young people through social media platforms (Ravi & Patki, 2025). These relationships, though asymmetrical in nature, can serve protective functions for psychological well-being when understood through the lens of design thinking.

Recent research challenges the assumption that parasocial relationships necessarily harm well-being. A mixed-methods study among Indian youth found that parasocial relationships do not significantly diminish well-being and that individuals who form strong parasocial relationships do not necessarily lack good social support in real life (Ravi & Patki, 2025). Instead, parasocial relationships may coexist with real relationships, serving complementary functions. Young people engage in parasocial interactions to boost mood and enjoyment of media content, rather than exclusively to compensate for isolation or loneliness (Ravi & Patki, 2025). This finding has important implications for understanding young people's psychological resilience in virtual environments.

Design thinking skills, particularly empathy and reframing, help young people navigate parasocial relationships constructively. Through empathy, young people can understand their own motivations for engaging with online personalities and media figures, recognizing both the benefits (mood enhancement, sense of connection) and potential pitfalls (unrealistic expectations, social comparison). Reframing allows young people to view parasocial relationships not as substitutes for real connection but as supplementary sources of support and inspiration. This cognitive flexibility, central to the design thinking mindset, promotes healthier engagement with online communities (Ravi & Patki, 2025).

Online support communities represent another dimension of virtual social connection that benefits from design thinking approaches. These communities, ranging from mental health support groups to hobby-based forums, provide spaces where young people can seek advice, share experiences, and receive emotional support from peers facing similar challenges. Design thinking's problem decomposition skill enables young people to articulate their challenges clearly within these communities, breaking down complex emotional or practical problems into specific questions that community members can address. The collaborative dimension of DT facilitates the co-creation of solutions within online support networks, where members collectively problem-solve and provide mutual support (Ravi & Patki, 2025).

The PERMA framework of well-being becomes particularly relevant in understanding online support communities. Young people in these communities experience positive Emotion through supportive interactions, Engagement through active participation in discussions, Relationships through meaningful connections with peers, Meaning through helping others and receiving help, and Accomplishment through successfully navigating challenges with community support. Design thinking mindset enhances each of these elements by promoting user-centered approaches to community design and fostering psychological safety for authentic sharing (Ravi & Patki, 2025).

Virtual Mediators and Technology-Mediated Social Support

An often-overlooked dimension of virtual well-being is the role of virtual mediators—the technological platforms, artificial intelligence systems, and design features that facilitate or hinder social interaction and support in digital environments. Virtual mediators are not merely passive conduits for communication; they actively shape social processes, influence group dynamics, and impact psychological well-being outcomes (Gkanatsiou, 2025). Understanding how design thinking can inform the development and use of virtual mediators is essential for young people navigating digital spaces.

Virtual mediators operate at multiple levels. At the platform level, features such as user interface design, communication channels (text, voice, video), and community moderation tools shape how young people interact with one another. At the algorithmic level, recommendation systems and content filtering determine what information and connections young people encounter. At the interpersonal level, AI-powered chatbots and virtual assistants can provide immediate support and guidance (Gkanatsiou, 2025). Each of these levels presents opportunities for design thinking to enhance well-being outcomes.

Recent developments in technology-mediated communication include advanced e-mediation platforms that incorporate virtual reality environments, AI-powered sentiment analysis, and real-time emotional monitoring (Gkanatsiou, 2025). These technological innovations can support young people's well-being by providing immediate feedback on emotional states, facilitating more empathetic communication, and creating psychologically safe spaces for vulnerable sharing. However, the effectiveness of these virtual mediators depends on thoughtful design grounded in design thinking principles, particularly user-centered design, empathy for diverse user needs, and continuous iteration based on user feedback.

Design thinking applied to virtual mediators involves several key considerations. First, designers must empathize with young people's diverse needs and preferences in virtual environments, recognizing that one-size-fits-all approaches are unlikely to support well-being across different populations. Second, designers should employ critical questioning to challenge assumptions about what features or functions young people actually need versus what designers assume they need. Third, problem decomposition helps designers break down complex challenges in virtual mediation (such as reducing cyberbullying while maintaining free expression) into manageable design problems. Fourth, reframing allows designers to view virtual mediators not as control mechanisms but as facilitators of authentic human connection and mutual support (Gkanatsiou, 2025).

The affordances of virtual mediators, the possibilities for action that the technology enables or constrains, directly influence young people's social processes and well-being. For example, platforms that afford anonymous communication may enable vulnerable sharing but also facilitate harmful behavior. Platforms that afford rich multimedia communication (video, audio, images) may enhance social presence but require greater bandwidth and technical skills. Design thinking helps young people and platform designers navigate these trade-offs by considering the full ecosystem of well-being impacts rather than optimizing for single metrics (Gkanatsiou, 2025).

An important application of design thinking to virtual mediators is the co-design of digital spaces with young people themselves. Rather than designing for young people, participatory design approaches involve young people as active collaborators in identifying problems, generating solutions, and testing prototypes. This approach honors the design thinking principle of user-centered design while simultaneously building young people's agency, creativity, and sense of ownership over their digital environments. Such participatory processes have been shown to enhance both the effectiveness of virtual mediators and the psychological well-being of young people involved in the design process (Gkanatsiou, 2025).

METHODOLOGY

A cross-sectional study was used in this research that involves administering a survey to young people to measure their design thinking mindset and psychological well-being. The survey was administered via web-based platform, reflecting the increasingly digital nature of educational research and the participants' familiarity with virtual learning environments. While the survey itself measures individual-level constructs, it was conducted in a context where participants had exposure to virtual collaboration and digital learning tools through their university coursework. The study recruited a sample of young people (females) aged 19-25 from undergraduate programs in a federal institute in the United Arab Emirates (UAE). The cross-sectional study is a type of research design in which the data is collected from many individuals simultaneously to describe the present relationships among variables in a given situation and to account for changes occurring in those relationships over time (Cohen et al., 2006).

Study Context and Virtual Environment Considerations

This study was conducted in the United Arab Emirates, a context characterized by rapid digital adoption and high rates of virtual platform usage among young people. The participants were undergraduate students at a federal institute in the UAE, an institution that has increasingly integrated digital learning platforms, virtual collaboration tools, and hybrid learning modalities into its curriculum. While the original study design focused on measuring individual-level constructs (design thinking mindset and psychological well-being), the UAE context is particularly relevant for understanding how these constructs function in environments where virtual and digital interactions are increasingly prevalent. The participants in this study were exposed to design thinking principles through their university coursework, which increasingly incorporates virtual collaboration projects and online learning components. This context provides an important foundation for understanding the relationship between design thinking mindset and well-being in a digitally-engaged population.

Participants

The study's participants are undergraduate students in a federal institute in the UAE. The study's participants are N=86 undergraduate students selected randomly from different programs and departments. The criteria set for the sample selection were defined by (i) students who are willing to participate, (ii) participants who should be females aged from 19-25, and (iii) participants who learned the design thinking process during their study in the university. According to Cohen's (1998) power table for effect size *d*, an average was estimated of [*d*=] 1.0 with alpha set at .05 and power (1-beta) set at .08, a sample size of at least 29 was needed. To confirm the study's participants' selection, the sample power was measured using the Statistical Packages of Social Sciences (SPSS) to be 1.00 using the sample size of 86 participants and $p<0.05$. The power analysis is greater than 0.8, considered high, as per Cohen (1998).

The majority of students were enrolled in the College of Interdisciplinary Studies to form 44 (51.1%) in total, with different departments: social innovation (12; 3.9%), computational; thinking (15; 17.4%), business transformation (13; 15.2%), and sustainability (4; 4.7%). Students who participated from the College of Humanities and Social Sciences were 40 (46.5%) in total, with 33 (38.3%) in the early childhood department and 7 (8.1%) from other departments. Finally, two students (2.4%) only enrolled in the College of Art and Creative Enterprises.

Digital Context and Virtual Learning Exposure: All participants were enrolled in programs that incorporated design thinking principles as part of their curriculum. These programs increasingly utilize virtual collaboration platforms, online project management tools, and hybrid learning environments. While the study did not explicitly measure participants' virtual interaction patterns or social presence in digital environments, the participants had exposure to virtual learning and collaboration through their university coursework. This context is important for understanding how design thinking mindset may support well-being in both physical and virtual contexts.

Instrumentation

A survey was used to collect quantitative data from participants to fulfill the study's main purpose. The survey consisted of three sections: (i) demographic information, (ii) design thinking mindsets, (ii) and psychological well-being. The demographic information asked students about their gender, age, program, and department of study where the sample selection criteria were set. The second category is the design thinking mindsets (26 items), adapted from Dosi et al. (2018) and distributed in sub-categories as follows: uncertainty (4 items), empathy (3 items), mindfulness (5 items), creative confidence (4 items), collaboration (5 items), and learning orientation (5 items). The last category is the psychological well-being items using the PERMA model adapted from (Seligman, 2012), and the other two sub-categories added: health and future plans adapted from Author (2023). The total items of psychological well-being (35 items) distributed on seven sub-categories (PERMA-PH): positive emotions (5 items), engagement (5 items), relationship (5 items), meaning (5 items), achievement (5 items), future plans (5 items), and health (5 items).

The internal consistency coefficient (Cronbach's Alpha) was used to assess reliability. Reliability analysis indicated strong internal consistency ($\alpha = 0.963$), with all subscales demonstrating acceptable reliability (α range: 0.863–0.936). Exploratory Factor Analysis (EFA) was conducted to validate the survey instruments. The Kaiser-Meyer-Olkin (KMO) test values and Bartlett's test of sphericity confirmed the appropriateness of factor analysis for both scales (KMO > 0.60, $p < 0.001$), indicating that the instruments were suitable for use in this study. The survey was administered through a web-based platform to ensure accessibility and ease of completion.

Procedures

A full explanation of the study was provided to participants, and a consent form was sent to them. The study was conducted in the English language to ensure participants' understanding. The survey was anonymous, and participants could not continue in the study at any point in the research duration. The cross-sectional design was used in this study, where the survey was sent to participants by two weeks before the end of the spring semester. The survey was administered through a web-based platform, allowing participants to complete it remotely or on campus at their convenience. This digital delivery method reflects the increasing prevalence of virtual data collection in educational research and aligns with the participants' regular use of digital platforms for academic work. The web-based administration also ensured accessibility and flexibility for participants navigating hybrid learning schedules. The survey results were analyzed using descriptive and inferential statistics using the Statistical Package of Social Sciences (SPSS). Descriptive statistics measured the mean, standard deviation, frequency, and z-scores. The inferential statistics addressed the Pearson correlation, linear regression, Exploratory Factor Analysis (EFA), and One-sample t-test. The correlation analysis examined the relationship between design thinking mindset and psychological well-being. The regression analysis was to investigate the predictive power of a design thinking mindset on young people's psychological well-being. The exploratory factor analysis was used to validate the survey items used. Finally, the one-sample t-test was used to compare the mean scores of design thinking mindset and psychological well-being with established benchmarks (above average; m=3.5). There is a high prevalence of mental health problems among young people in the UAE, confirming the need to enhance prevention and early intervention in the region (Barbato et al., 2021). Accordingly, this motivates the researcher to set the established benchmark above average based on Handal et al.'s (2013) questionnaire score range. The quantitative data results were presented and integrated into the discussion section to fulfill the study's main purpose: investigate the relationship between a design thinking mindset and the psychological well-being of young people in the UAE.

RESULTS

To ensure the integrity of the data, a Z-score analysis was conducted to identify outliers. The results confirmed that all responses for both design thinking mindsets and psychological well-being fell within an acceptable range (z-scores of ± 2.23 and ± 2.02, respectively), indicating no significant outliers that would bias the findings.

Relationship Between Design Thinking and Well-being

A Pearson correlation analysis was performed to address the primary research question regarding the relationship between design thinking mindset and psychological well-being. The analysis revealed a strong, statistically significant positive correlation between the two constructs. This indicates that as students' design thinking mindset strengthens, their psychological well-being also tends to increase significantly. The design thinking mindset accounted for approximately 66% of the variance in psychological well-being, suggesting a substantial relationship (see Appendix, Table A1). Further analysis explored the relationships between the specific elements of design thinking and well-being (see Appendix, Table A2). Notably, strong correlations emerged across most elements. The design thinking dimension of Mindfulness showed a particularly strong positive relationship with all measured aspects of well-being, especially Engagements, Relationships, and Meaning. Similarly, Uncertainty tolerance was strongly correlated with Positive Emotions and Relationships. In contrast, Empathy demonstrated a more moderate, though still significant, correlation with elements like Positive Emotions and Meaning.

Predictive Power of Design Thinking Mindset

A linear regression was conducted to determine if a design thinking mindset could predict psychological well-being. The results established a statistically significant predictive relationship, confirming that the design thinking mindset could explain 65.2% of the variability in young people's psychological well-being (see Appendix, Table A3).

Mean Score Analysis

To assess whether the participants exhibited higher-than-average levels of design thinking and well-being, a one-sample t-test was used. As shown in the Appendix (Tables A4 and A5), participants scored significantly higher than the average on all measured dimensions of the design thinking mindset and psychological well-being.

This suggests that the student cohort possessed a notably well-developed design thinking mindset and a strong sense of well-being.

DISCUSSION

RQ1: What Is the Relationship Between Design-Thinking Mindsets and the Psychological Well-Being of Young People?

This study investigated the relationship between design thinking mindset and the psychological well-being of young people in the UAE. The results showed a strong positive correlation between design thinking mindsets and psychological well-being. This core finding suggests that fostering the cognitive and metacognitive skills associated with design thinking is not just beneficial for innovation, but is also deeply intertwined with mental health. This aligns with the work of Yeager et al. (2016), who argued that such mindsets can enhance psychological interventions. The strength of the correlation underscores the practical significance of this relationship, implying that interventions aimed at developing a design thinking mindset could have a substantial positive impact on student well-being.

The study also explored the relationship between the elements of psychological well-being and the elements of design thinking mindsets. The strongest correlation was between mindfulness and engagements, relationships, meaning, achievements, future plans, and health. Delving deeper, the strong link between the Mindfulness dimension of design thinking and nearly all facets of well-being is particularly revealing. This suggests that the practice of being present, aware, and non-judgmental, a cornerstone of mindfulness, is a powerful catalyst for experiencing positive emotions, engagement, and meaningful relationships. This finding resonates with recent studies highlighting mindfulness as a protective factor against mental distress, especially in high-stress contexts like the COVID-19 pandemic (Hepner et al., 2022; Mamede et al., 2022).

Another strong correlation between uncertainty and positive emotions, engagements, and relationships was found. Interestingly, a high tolerance for Uncertainty was also strongly linked to positive emotions and relationships. While uncertainty is often perceived negatively (Morriss et al., 2021), our findings support a growing body of research suggesting it can foster positive outcomes like curiosity and resilience (Anderson et al., 2019; Vazard, 2022). In a rapidly changing world, the ability to embrace ambiguity appears to be a key ingredient for well-being. The more moderate correlation of Empathy with well-being presents a nuanced picture. While empathy is crucial, this finding may reflect the complex nature of empathic engagement; as

Depow et al. (2021) noted, simply having the trait of empathy is different from its daily practice, which is more consistently linked to enhanced well-being.

RQ2: How Can Developing a Design Thinking Mindset Act as a Psychological Prevention to Promote Sustainable Development of Young People's Well-Being?

The findings strongly support the proposition that developing a design thinking mindset can serve as a psychological prevention strategy. The linear regression analysis demonstrated that this mindset is a powerful predictor of psychological well-being, accounting for a remarkable 65.2% of its variance. This is not merely a statistical artifact; it suggests that by equipping young people with a design thinking framework, we are providing them with the tools to proactively manage their mental health and build sustainable well-being. This result extends the work of researchers like Yeager et al. (2016) and Davies et al. (2022), moving from the idea that design thinking is helpful in specific interventions to the broader claim that the mindset itself is a foundational element of well-being. When students learn to embrace risk, adopt a human-centered perspective, and practice empathy and collaboration, they are not just becoming better problem-solvers; they are cultivating the very principles, such as a growth mindset and resilience, that underpin psychological health (Klenner et al., 2021). Therefore, integrating design thinking into educational curricula is more than an academic exercise; it is a public health imperative. By doing so, educators and policymakers can foster a generation of young people who are not only prepared for the complex challenges of the modern world but are also equipped with the internal resources to maintain their well-being over the long term. This approach moves beyond reactive mental health support to a proactive, preventative model that builds resilience from the ground up.

RQ3: Is There a Significant Difference Between the Mean Scores of Design Thinking Mindset and Well-Being in Young People?

The analysis confirmed a significant and meaningful difference: the young people in this study exhibited levels of both design thinking mindset and psychological well-being that were substantially higher than the normative average. This finding is crucial because it validates the study's premise, that the participants, who had been exposed to design thinking principles, indeed demonstrate a stronger profile in both areas. It provides empirical support for the idea that a well-developed design thinking mindset and high levels of well-being can and do co-exist in a student population. This result is consistent with previous studies that have linked design thinking to the development of life skills and a growth mindset (Mailizar et al., 2020; Yeager et al., 2016). The practical implication is that educational environments that successfully cultivate a design thinking culture are also likely to be environments where student well-being flourishes. However, as noted by Schmiedgen et al. (2016), the lack of a unified definition of design thinking remains a challenge. To build on these promising findings, future research must work towards a clearer, shared understanding of the construct to ensure that interventions and educational programs are both effective and consistent.

CONCLUSION & RECOMMENDATION

This study investigated the relationship between design thinking mindset and the psychological well-being of young people in the UAE. The results showed a strong positive correlation between design thinking mindsets and psychological well-being. The study also explored the relationship between the elements of psychological well-being and the elements of design thinking mindsets. The strongest correlation was between mindfulness and engagements, relationships, meaning, achievements, future plans, and health. In addition, the participants' mean scores in the design-thinking mindsets and psychological well-being categories were above average, indicating that developing a design-thinking mindset can positively impact young people's well-being. The study's findings suggest that developing a design thinking mindset can act as a psychological prevention to promote the sustainable development of young people's well-being. In conclusion, the current study's results confirm previous research exploring the relationship between the design thinking mindset and well-being (Davies et al., 2022; Yeager et al., 2016). They suggest that developing a design thinking mindset can significantly predict the psychological well-being of young people, accounting for a large proportion of the explained variability in psychological well-being.

The study's findings have important implications for educators, policymakers, and practitioners interested in promoting sustainable well-being in young people, as well as for future research and interventions. By incorporating design thinking into interventions and educational programs, it may be possible to improve the well-being of young people and promote their long-term success. Educators and policymakers should consider incorporating design thinking into the curriculum to promote the development of a growth mindset and other skills essential for success in the 21st century. This could involve teaching young people key design thinking concepts, such as embracing risk, human-centeredness, empathy, mindfulness, and collaboration. It could also involve redesigning and tailoring initial interventions using design thinking to improve their effectiveness and sustainability.

Regarding the limitations, the current study does not include qualitative data that might impact the understanding of the participants' perceptions. Additionally, the study used a cross-sectional design, which limits the ability to draw causal inferences. Future research should use longitudinal designs to investigate the causal relationship between design thinking mindset and psychological well-being, where the survey can be administered at two-time points, with a time interval of a few months. Finally, the study did not investigate the potential negative effects of developing a design thinking mindset on well-being, and more research is needed to fully understand the nature of the relationship between the design thinking mindset and well-being.

Limitations and Future Research

Although this chapter has been substantially revised to incorporate a theoretical framework grounded in the social psychology of virtual environments, a key limitation remains: the original empirical study was not designed to measure these specific social-psychological constructs. The study's methodology focused on the relationship between the design thinking mindset and psychological well-being as general constructs, without capturing variables such as social presence, group norms, virtual interaction features, or the nuances of technology-mediated communication. This creates a disconnect between the newly enriched theoretical framework and the original empirical data presented. This limitation, however, provides a clear and compelling roadmap for future research. To build upon the theoretical arguments presented here, future studies should be designed to explicitly test these relationships. First, it is highly recommended to measure Social-Psychological Variables. Future research should incorporate validated scales to measure constructs such as social presence, group cohesion, and perceived social support within virtual environments. This would allow for a direct test of the hypothesis that design thinking enhances well-being by improving these social processes. Furthermore, researchers could employ experimental designs to compare the effects of design thinking interventions in virtual versus face-to-face settings. Such studies could manipulate specific virtual affordances (e.g., avatar realism, communication modality) to understand their impact on collaboration and well-being. Regarding qualitative and mixed-methods approaches, it is important to consider the following: qualitative studies, including virtual ethnography and in-depth interviews, would provide rich, contextualized insights into how young people experience and apply design thinking in their daily virtual interactions. A mixed-methods approach could combine the statistical power of quantitative data with the explanatory depth of qualitative findings. Additionally, longitudinal research is needed to track the development of the design thinking mindset over time and its long-term impact on well-being and social integration in virtual environments. This would help establish causality and understand the developmental trajectory of these skills. By addressing these gaps, future research can more fully integrate the study of design thinking into the social psychology of virtual environments, providing a more complete and actionable understanding of how to promote sustainable well-being in an increasingly digital world.

Credit Author Statement

Author: Conceptualization, Methodology, Software, Formal analysis, Investigation, Data curation, Writing – original draft, Writing – review & editing, Visualization.

Declaration of Competing Interest

The authors declare that they have no competing interests.

Ethics Approval

The authors hereby declare that the study received full institutional ethics approval. All participants were required to provide informed consent in order to participate in the study.

REFERENCES

Aisha, N., & Ratra, A. (2022). Online education amid covid-19 pandemic and its opportunities, challenges and psychological impacts among students and teachers: A systematic review. *Asian Association of Open Universities Journal, 17*(3), 242–260. DOI: 10.1108/AAOUJ-03-2022-0028

Anderson, E. C., Carleton, R. N., Diefenbach, M., & Han, P. K. (2019). The relationship between uncertainty and affect. *Frontiers in Psychology, 10*, 2504. Advance online publication. DOI: 10.3389/fpsyg.2019.02504 PMID: 31781003

Auernhammer, J., & Roth, B. (2021). The origin and evolution of Stanford University's Design thinking: From product design to design thinking in innovation management. *Journal of Product Innovation Management, 38*(6), 623–644. DOI: 10.1111/jpim.12594

Badwan, B., Bothara, R., Latijnhouwers, M., Smithies, A., & Sandars, J. (2017). The importance of design thinking in medical education. *Medical Teacher, 40*(4), 425–426. DOI: 10.1080/0142159X.2017.1399203 PMID: 29125007

Barbato, M., Al Hemeiri, S., Nafie, S., Dhuhair, B. A., & Dabbagh, N. T. (2021). Characterizing individuals accessing mental health services in the UAE: A focus on youth living in Dubai. *International Journal of Mental Health Systems, 15*(1), 29. Advance online publication. DOI: 10.1186/s13033-021-00452-4 PMID: 33789685

Becker, D., & Marecek, J. (2008). Positive Psychology: History in the Remaking? *Theory & Psychology, 18*(5), 591–604. DOI: 10.1177/0959354308093397

Brown, T., & Katz, B. (2019). *Change by design: How design thinking transforms organizations and inspires innovation.* Harper Business.

Bryant, F. B., & Veroff, J. (2007). *Savoring: A new model of positive experience.* Erlbaum Associates.

Cannon, M., & Edmondson, A. (2005). Failing to learn and learning to fail (intelligently): How great organizations put failure to work to innovate and improve. *Long Range Planning, 38*(3), 299–319. DOI: 10.1016/j.lrp.2005.04.005

Carlgren, L., Rauth, I., & Elmquist, M. (2016). Framing design thinking: The concept in idea and enactment. *Creativity and Innovation Management, 25*(1), 38–57. DOI: 10.1111/caim.12153

Cohen, J. (1998). *Statistical power analysis for the behavioral sciences* (2nd ed.). Lawrence Erlbaum Associates.

Csikszentmihalyi, M. (1990). The domain of creativity. In Runco, M. A., & Albert, R. S. (Eds.), *Theories of creativity* (pp. 190–212). Sage Publications, Inc.

Cummings, J. J., & Wertz, E. E. (2023). Capturing social presence: Concept explication through an empirical analysis of social presence measures. *Journal of Computer-Mediated Communication, 28*(1), zmac027. Advance online publication. DOI: 10.1093/jcmc/zmac027

Darwish, E. B. (2025). Digital media engagement and literacy among UAE youth: A mixed-methods investigation of usage patterns and digital inequalities. *Journal of Arab & Muslim Media Research, 14*(1). Advance online publication. DOI: 10.1386/jammr_00117_1

Davies, T. C., Manzin, J., Meraw, M., & Munro, D. S. (2022). Understanding the development of a design thinking mindset during a biomedical engineering third-year course. *Biomedical Engineering Education*. Advance online publication. DOI: 10.1007/s43683-022-00093-0 PMID: 36438449

Depow, G. J., Francis, Z., & Inzlicht, M. (2021). The experience of empathy in everyday life. *Psychological Science, 32*(8), 1198–1213. DOI: 10.1177/0956797621995202 PMID: 34241543

Derda, I., Wouter, M., & Smit, T. (2025). Adaptive mechanisms of developing social connectedness in virtual reality environments. *Design for Health (Abingdon, England), 9*(2), 195–215. DOI: 10.1080/24735132.2025.2506255 PMID: 40757081

Dosi, C., Rosati, F., & Vignoli, M. (2018). Measuring Design Thinking Mindset. *Proceedings of the DESIGN 2018 15th International Design Conference*. https://doi.org/ DOI: 10.21278/idc.2018.0493

Dweck, C. S. (1999). *Self-Theories: Their Role in Motivation, Personality and Development*. Psychology Press.

Emirates Youth Council. (2021). The trends shaping the UAE's youth sector after the COVID-19 pandemic. *Strategy & Part of the PwC network*. Available at: https://www.strategyand.pwc.com/m1/en/ideation-center/ic-research/2021/future-of-youth.html

Evans, T. M., Bira, L., Gastelum, J. B., Weiss, L. T., & Vanderford, N. L. (2018). Evidence for a mental health crisis in graduate education. *Nature Biotechnology, 36*(3), 282–284. DOI: 10.1038/nbt.4089 PMID: 29509732

Faralla, V., Innocenti, A., Baraldi, S., Ermini, S., Lusuardi, L., Masini, M., Santalucia, V., Scaruffi, D., & Sirizzotti, M. (2024). Exposure to immersive virtual environments decreases present bias. *Journal of Behavioral and Experimental Economics, 108*, 102154. DOI: 10.1016/j.socec.2023.102154

Fraser, H. M. A. (2010). Designing business: New models for success. In Lockwood, T. (Ed.), *Design thinking: Integrating innovation, customer experience, and brand value* (pp. 35–46). Allworth Press.

Fredrickson, B. L. (2009). *Positivity*. Crown Publishers.

Gkanatsiou, M. A. (2025). AI and digital tools: Transforming mediation and conflict resolution. *Proceedings, 107*(1), 104. DOI: 10.3390/proceedings2025107104

Grabowski, M., Lehmann-Willenbrock, N., Rings, S., Blanchard, A., & Steinicke, F. (2024). Group dynamics in the metaverse: A conceptual framework and first empirical insights. *Small Group Research, 55*(5), 1–45. DOI: 10.1177/10464964241274120

Guazzini, A., Pesce, A., Gino, F., & Duradoni, M. (2022). How the COVID-19 pandemic changed adolescents' use of technologies, sense of community, and loneliness: A retrospective perception analysis. *Behavioral Sciences (Basel, Switzerland), 12*(7), 228. DOI: 10.3390/bs12070228 PMID: 35877298

Han, E., DeVeaux, C., Hancock, J. T., Ram, N., Harari, G. M., & Bailenson, J. N. (2024). The influence of spatial dimensions of virtual environments on attitudes and nonverbal behaviors during social interactions. *Journal of Environmental Psychology, 95*, 102269. DOI: 10.1016/j.jenvp.2024.102269

Heintzelman, S. J., & King, L. A. (2014). Life is pretty meaningful. *The American Psychologist, 69*(6), 561–574. DOI: 10.1037/a0035049 PMID: 24490907

Hepner, K. A., Rutter, C. M., Bialas, A., Booth, M., Osilla, K. C., Sousa, J. L., Newberry, S. J., & Bloom, E. L. (2022). *The impact of mindfulness meditation programs on performance-related outcomes: Implications for the U.S. army*. Rand Corporation., DOI: 10.7249/RRA1522-1

Holt-Lunstad, J., Smith, T. B., & Layton, J. B. (2010). Social relationships and mortality risk: A meta-analytic review. *PLoS Medicine, 7*(7), e1000316. DOI: 10.1371/journal.pmed.1000316 PMID: 20668659

Klenner, N. F., Gemser, G., & Karpen, I. O. (2021). Entrepreneurial ways of designing and designerly ways of entrepreneuring: Exploring the relationship between design thinking and effectuation theory. *Journal of Product Innovation Management, 39*(1), 66–94. DOI: 10.1111/jpim.12587

Ku, Y. R., & Stager, C. (2022). Rethinking the multidimensionality of growth mindset amid the COVID-19 pandemic: A systematic review and Framework Proposal. *Frontiers in Psychology, 13*, 572220. Advance online publication. DOI: 10.3389/fpsyg.2022.572220 PMID: 35846666

Kush, J., Argote, L., & Aven, B. (2025). The effects of communication networks on shared social identity and group performance. *Small Group Research*, *56*(6), 899–949. Advance online publication. DOI: 10.1177/10464964251326615

Ladachart, L., Chaimongkol, J., & Phothong, W. (2022). Design-based learning to facilitate secondary students' understanding of pulleys. *Australasian Journal of Engineering Education*, *27*(1), 26–37. DOI: 10.1080/22054952.2022.2065722

Langston, C. A. (1994). Capitalizing on and coping with daily-life events: Expressive responses to positive events. *Journal of Personality and Social Psychology*, *67*(6), 1112–1125. DOI: 10.1037/0022-3514.67.6.1112

Liedtka, J. (2020). Exploring the impact of design thinking on organizational culture and innovation. *Journal of Product Innovation Management*, *37*(2), 144–164. DOI: 10.1111/jpim.12518

Lockwood, T. (2014). *Design Thinking Integrating Innovation, customer experience, and brand value*. Skyhorse Publishing.

Lomas, T., Hefferon, K., & Ivtzan, I. (2014). *Applied Positive Psychology: Integrated Positive Practice*. Sage. DOI: 10.4135/9781473909687

Mahyoob, M. (2020). Challenges of e-Learning during the COVID-19 Pandemic Experienced by EFL Learners. *Arab World English Journal*, *11*(4), 351–362. DOI: 10.24093/awej/vol11no4.23

Mailizar, A., Almanthari, A., Maulina, S., & Bruce, S. (2020). Secondary School Mathematics Teachers' Views on E-learning Implementation Barriers during the COVID-19 Pandemic: The Case of Indonesia. *Eurasia Journal of Mathematics, Science and Technology Education*, *16*(7), em1860. DOI: 10.29333/ejmste/8240

Mamede, A., Merkelbach, I., Noordzij, G., & Denktas, S. (2022). Mindfulness as a protective factor against depression, anxiety and psychological distress during the covid-19 pandemic: Emotion regulation and insomnia symptoms as mediators. *Frontiers in Psychology*, *13*, 820959. Advance online publication. DOI: 10.3389/fpsyg.2022.820959 PMID: 35432084

Marelaro, N., Ganguly, S., Steinert, M., & Jung, M. (2015). The personal trait myth: a comparative analysis of the innovation impact of design thinking tools and personal traits. In Plattner, H., Meinel, C., & Leifer, L. (Eds.), *Design thinking research* (pp. 41–57). Springer. DOI: 10.1007/978-3-319-06823-7_4

Matthews, K. (2019). 6 Innovations That Have Drastically Changed Mental Healthcare: Mental health treatment has changed a lot in the last five years, and it will continue to evolve. *Healthcare Innovation*. Available at: https://www.hcinnovationgroup.com/population-health-management/telehealth/article/21118902/6-innovations-that-have-drastically-changed-mental- healthcare

Morriss, J., Tupitsa, E., Dodd, H. F., & Hirsch, C. (2021). *Uncertainty Makes Me Emotional: Uncertainty as an Elicitor and Modulator of Emotional States.* https://doi.org/ DOI: 10.31234/osf.io/ycmt4

Mouchrek, N., & Benson, M. (2023). The theory of integrated empowerment in the transition to adulthood: Concepts and measures. *Frontiers in Sociology*, *8*, 893898. Advance online publication. DOI: 10.3389/fsoc.2023.893898 PMID: 37139228

Park, N., Oates, S., & Schwarzer, R. (2013). Christopher Peterson "other people matter": 1950– 2012. *Applied Psychology. Health and Well-Being*, *5*(1), 1–4. DOI: 10.1111/aphw.12007 PMID: 23457083

Peterson, C. (2006). *A primer in positive psychology*. Oxford University Press.

Plattner, H., Meinel, C., & Leifer, L. J. (2014). *Design thinking research: Building Innovation eco-systems*. Springer.

Ravi, N., & Patki, S. M. (2025). Parasocial relationships, social support and well-being: A mixed-methods study among Indian youth. *International Journal of Adolescence and Youth*, *30*(1), 2480712. DOI: 10.1080/02673843.2025.2480712

Ridge, N., & Erfurth, M. (2020). *The impact of covid-19 on education in the UAE.* Al Qasimi Foundation., DOI: 10.18502/aqf.0143

Ryff, C. D. (2013). Psychological well-being revisited: Advances in the Science and practice of Eudaimonia. *Psychotherapy and Psychosomatics*, *83*(1), 10–28. DOI: 10.1159/000353263 PMID: 24281296

Schmiedgen, J., Spille, L., Köppen, E., Rhinow, H., & Meinel, C. (2016). Measuring the Impact of Design Thinking. In Plattner, H., Meinel, C., & Leifer, L. (Eds.), *Design Thinking Research* (pp. 157–170). Springer International Publishing., DOI: 10.1007/978-3-319-19641-1_11

Schweitzer, J., Groeger, L., & Sobel, L. (2016). The Design Thinking Mindset: An assessment of what we know and what we see in practice. *Journal of Design. Business & Society*, *2*(1), 71–94. DOI: 10.1386/dbs.2.1.71_1

Seligman, M. E. P. (2012). *Flourish: A visionary new understanding of happiness and well- being*. Simon and Schuster.

Sin, N. L., & Lyubomirsky, S. (2009). Enhancing well-being and alleviating depressive symptoms with positive psychology interventions: A practice-friendly meta-analysis. *Journal of Clinical Psychology, 65*(5), 467–487. DOI: 10.1002/jclp.20593 PMID: 19301241

Spencer, D. G., & Myers, S. (2006). *Social psychology* (3rd ed.). McGraw-Hill Ryerson.

The Economist Impact. (2022). Together for mental health Towards a sustainable and scalable model of mental health care in the United Arab Emirates pp. 1–48. *The Economist Impact.*

Thompson, L., & Schonthal, D. (2020). The Social Psychology of Design Thinking. *California Management Review, 62*(2), 84–99. DOI: 10.1177/0008125619897636

UAE National Committee on SDGs. (2017). *UAE and the 2030 Agenda for Sustainable Development: Excellence in Implementation.* Available at: https://sustainabledevelopment.un.org/content/documents/20161UAE_SDGs_Report_Full_English.pdf

Vazard, J. (2022). Feeling the unknown: Emotions of uncertainty and their valence. *Erkenntnis.* Advance online publication. DOI: 10.1007/s10670-022-00583-1

Vignoli, M., Dosi, C., & Balboni, B. (2023). Design thinking mindset: Scale development and validation. *Studies in Higher Education, 48*(6), 926–940. DOI: 10.1080/03075079.2023.2172566

World Health Organization WHO. (2021). Child and adolescent mental and brain health. Geneva. *World Health Organization.* Available from: https://www.who.int/activities/Improving-the-mental-and-brain-health-of-children-and-adolescents

Yeager, D. S., Romero, C., Paunesku, D., Hulleman, C. S., Schneider, B., Hinojosa, C., Lee, H. Y., O'Brien, J., Flint, K., Roberts, A., Trott, J., Greene, D., Walton, G. M., & Dweck, C. S. (2016). Using design thinking to improve psychological interventions: The case of the growth mindset during the transition to high school. *Journal of Educational Psychology, 108*(3), 374–391. DOI: 10.1037/edu0000098 PMID: 27524832

You, X. (2022). Applying design thinking for business model innovation. *Journal of Innovation and Entrepreneurship, 11*(59), 59. Advance online publication. DOI: 10.1186/s13731-022-00251-2

Zhang, S., Liu, M., Li, Y., & Chung, J. E. (2021). Teens' social media engagement during the covid-19 pandemic: A time series examination of posting and emotion on reddit. *International Journal of Environmental Research and Public Health, 18*(19), 10079. DOI: 10.3390/ijerph181910079 PMID: 34639381

APPENDIX – STATISTICAL ANALYSIS

Table 1. The Pearson correlation coefficient of design thinking mindset and psychological well-being

		Mindsets	Psychological Well-being
Mindsets	Pearson Correlation	1	.812**
	Sig. (2-tailed)		<.001
	N	86	86
Psychological Well-being	Pearson Correlation	.812**	1
	Sig. (2-tailed)	<.001	
	N	86	86

Table 2. The Pearson correlation coefficient between the elements of both design thinking mindset and psychological well-being.

		Positive Emotions	Engagements	Relationship	Meaning	Achievement	Future Plans	Health
Uncertainty	**Pearson Correlation**	**.703****	**.749****	**.751****	**.610****	**.688****	**.573****	**.600****
	Sig. (2-tailed)	**<.001**	**<.001**	**<.001**	**<.001**	**<.001**	**<.001**	**<.001**
Empathy	Pearson Correlation	.385**	.536**	.657**	.411**	.530**	.406**	.459**
	Sig. (2-tailed)	<.001	<.001	<.001	<.001	<.001	<.001	<.001
Mindfulness	Pearson Correlation	.661**	.742**	.728**	.738**	.710**	.700**	.733**
	Sig. (2-tailed)	<.001	<.001	<.001	<.001	<.001	<.001	<.001
Creative Confidence	Pearson Correlation	.663**	.773**	.696**	.620**	.670**	.596**	.654**
	Sig. (2-tailed)	<.001	<.001	<.001	<.001	<.001	<.001	<.001
Collaboration	Pearson Correlation	.606**	.740**	.665**	.551**	.658**	.511**	.573**
	Sig. (2-tailed)	<.001	<.001	<.001	<.001	<.001	<.001	<.001
Learning Orientation	Pearson Correlation	.644**	.814**	.734**	.562**	.645**	.515**	.576**
	Sig. (2-tailed)	<.001	<.001	<.001	<.001	<.001	<.001	<.001

Table 3. The ANOVA model of the linear regression analysis

ANOVA[a]						
Model		Sum of Squares	df	Mean Square	F	Sig.
1	Regression	24.854	1	24.854	160.575	<.001[b]
	Residual	13.002	84	.155		
	Total	37.856	85			

a. Dependent Variable: Psychological Well-being
b. Predictors: (Constant), Mindsets

Table 4. The one-sample t-test for the design thinking mindsets

One-Sample Test							
	Test Value = 3.5						
			Significance		Mean Difference	95% Confidence Interval of the Difference	
	t	df	One-Sided p	Two-Sided p		Lower	Upper
Uncertainty	7.304	85	<.001	<.001	.48547	.3533	.6176
Mindfulness	5.879	85	<.001	<.001	.46977	.3109	.6287
Creative Confidence	6.956	85	<.001	<.001	.54942	.3924	.7065
Collaboration	5.281	85	<.001	<.001	.43953	.2740	.6050
Learning Orientation	6.733	85	<.001	<.001	.54360	.3831	.7041

Table 5. The one-sample t-test for the psychological well-being

One-Sample Test							
	Test Value = 3.5						
			Significance		Mean Difference	95% Confidence Interval of the Difference	
	t	df	One-Sided p	Two-Sided p		Lower	Upper
Positive Emotions	4.845	85	<.001	<.001	.44186	.2605	.6232
Engagements	4.049	85	<.001	<.001	.35581	.1811	.5305
Relationship	6.456	85	<.001	<.001	.50698	.3508	.6631
Meaning	5.060	85	<.001	<.001	.41628	.2527	.5799
Achievement	8.248	85	<.001	<.001	.60930	.4624	.7562
Future Plans	6.024	85	<.001	<.001	.47442	.3178	.6310
Health	4.072	85	<.001	<.001	.35349	.1809	.5261

Compilation of References

Abidin, C. (2016). "Aren't These Just Young, Rich Women Doing Vain Things Online?": Influencer Selfies as Subversive Frivolity. *Social Media + Society*, *2*(2), 1–17. DOI: 10.1177/2056305116641342

Abidin, C. (2016). Visibility labour: Engaging with influencers' fashion brands and #OOTD advertorial campaigns on Instagram. *Media International Australia, Incorporating Culture & Policy*, *161*(1), 86–100. DOI: 10.1177/1329878X16665177

Abidin, C. (2018). "Aren't these just young, rich women doing vain things?" Influencer vetting and branding on a micro-celebrity farm. *Social Media + Society*, *4*(2), 1–11. DOI: 10.1177/2056305118768687

Adamovich, S. V., Fluet, G. G., Tunik, E., & Merians, A. S. (2009). Sensorimotor training in virtual reality: A review. *NeuroRehabilitation*, *25*(1), 29–44. DOI: 10.3233/NRE-2009-0497 PMID: 19713617

Adler, O., & Pansky, A. (2020). A "rosy view" of the past: Positive memory biases. In *Elsevier eBooks*.139–171. https://doi.org/DOI: 10.1016/B978-0-12-816660-4.00007-6

Ahmad, N. A., Rauf, M. F. A., & Razak, F. H. (2022). Effectiveness of instructional strategies designed for older adults in learning digital Technologies: A Systematic literature review. *SN Computer Science*, *3*(2), 130. Advance online publication. DOI: 10.1007/s42979-022-01016-0 PMID: 35039803

Aisha, N., & Ratra, A. (2022). Online education amid covid-19 pandemic and its opportunities, challenges and psychological impacts among students and teachers: A systematic review. *Asian Association of Open Universities Journal*, *17*(3), 242–260. DOI: 10.1108/AAOUJ-03-2022-0028

Altman, I., & Taylor, D. A. (1973). *Social penetration: The development of interpersonal intimacy*. Holt, Rinehart & Winston.

American Psychological Association. (2018, April 19). *Personality*. APA Dictionary of Psychology; American Psychological Association. https://dictionary.apa.org/personality

American Psychological Association. (2023, March). *Ageism is one of the last socially acceptable prejudices. Psychologists are working to change that*. Monitor on Psychology. https://www.apa.org/monitor/2023/03/cover-new-concept-of-

Amichai-Hamburger, Y., & Ben-Artzi, E. (2003). Loneliness and sociability in cyberspace: A four-wave theory on the development of the Internet. *Computers in Human Behavior, 19*(1), 7–28. DOI: 10.1016/S0747-5632(02)00076-1

Anderl, C., Levordashka, A., & Utz, S. (2023). Ambient Awareness of Who Knows What: Spontaneous Inferences of Domain Expertise. *Media Psychology*, •••, 1–23. DOI: 10.1080/15213269.2023.2239144

Anderson, E. C., Carleton, R. N., Diefenbach, M., & Han, P. K. (2019). The relationship between uncertainty and affect. *Frontiers in Psychology, 10*, 2504. Advance online publication. DOI: 10.3389/fpsyg.2019.02504 PMID: 31781003

Andreassen, C. S., Pallesen, S., & Griffiths, M. D. (2017). The relationship between addictive use of social media, narcissism, and self-esteem: Findings from a large national survey. *Addictive Behaviors, 64*, 287–293. DOI: 10.1016/j.addbeh.2016.03.006 PMID: 27072491

Andrejevic, M. (2019). *Automated media*. Routledge., DOI: 10.4324/9780429242595

APA Dictionary of Psychology. (2023). *APA Dictionary of Psychology*. Dictionary.apa.org. https://dictionary.apa.org/self

Asch, S. E. (1951). Effects of group pressure upon the modification and distortion of judgments. In Guetzkow, H. (Ed.), *Groups, leadership and men* (pp. 177–190). Carnegie Press.

Asch, S. E. (1955). Opinions and social pressure. *Scientific American, 193*(5), 31–35. DOI: 10.1038/scientificamerican1155-31

Ashfaq, M. Y. (2020). I, Chatbot: Modeling the determinants of users' satisfaction and continuance intention of AI-powered service agents. *Telematics and Informatics*.

Aspling, F. (2011). *The private and the public in online presentations of the self: A critical development of Goffman's dramaturgical perspective*. https://www.researchgate.net/publication/320346695_The_Private_and_the_Public_in_Online_Presentations_of_the_Self_A_Critical_Development_of_Goffman%27s_Dramaturgical_Perspective

Auernhammer, J., & Roth, B. (2021). The origin and evolution of Stanford University's Design thinking: From product design to design thinking in innovation management. *Journal of Product Innovation Management, 38*(6), 623–644. DOI: 10.1111/jpim.12594

Avci, H., Baams, L., & Kretschmer, T. (2024). A Systematic Review of Social Media Use and Adolescent Identity Development. *Adolescent Research Review, 10*(2), 219–236. DOI: 10.1007/s40894-024-00251-1 PMID: 40385471

Aydın, A., Arda, B., Güneş, B., & Erbaş, O. (2021). Psychopathology of cyberbullying and internet trolling. *Journal of Experimental and Basic Medical Sciences, 2*(3). Advance online publication. DOI: 10.5607/jebms.2021.79

Badwan, B., Bothara, R., Latijnhouwers, M., Smithies, A., & Sandars, J. (2017). The importance of design thinking in medical education. *Medical Teacher, 40*(4), 425–426. DOI: 10.1080/0142159X.2017.1399203 PMID: 29125007

Bail, C. A., Argyle, L. P., Brown, T. W., Bumpus, J. P., Chen, H., Hunzaker, M. F., Lee, J., Mann, M., Merhout, F., & Volfovsky, A. (2018). Exposure to opposing views on social media can increase political polarization. *Proceedings of the National Academy of Sciences of the United States of America, 115*(37), 9216–9221. DOI: 10.1073/pnas.1804840115 PMID: 30154168

Baker, E. K., & Moore, S. M. (2008). Internet support groups for depression: A review of the literature. *Archives of Psychiatric Nursing, 22*(1), 20–28. DOI: 10.1016/j.apnu.2007.04.005 PMID: 18207053

Baker, K. M., & Moore, S. M. (2008). Online support groups for illness: A review of empirical data. *Patient Education and Counseling, 70*(3), 297–303. DOI: 10.1016/j.pec.2007.10.004

Baker, K., & Moore, P. J. (2018). Social networking site use and perceived social capital: The role of perceived authenticity and self-disclosure. *Computers in Human Behavior, 87*, 227–234. DOI: 10.1016/j.chb.2018.05.039

Bamberg, M., & Andrews, M. (2004). *Considering counter-identities: Introduction*. In M. Bamberg & M. Andrews (Eds.), *Considering counter-identities* (pp. 1–15). Narrative Inquiry Book Series.

Bandura, A. (2009). Social cognitive theory of mass communication. In J. Bryant & M. B. Oliver (Eds.), *Media effects: Advances in theory and research* (3rd 94–124). Routledge.

Bandura, A. (1977). *Social learning theory*. Prentice Hall.

Bandura, A. (1999). Moral disengagement in the perpetration of inhumanities. *Personality and Social Psychology Review*, *3*(3), 193–209. DOI: 10.1207/s15327957pspr0303_3 PMID: 15661671

Banet-Weiser, S. (2012). Authentic: The Politics of Ambivalence in a Brand Culture. In *JSTOR*. NYU Press. https://www.jstor.org/stable/j.ctt9qfmw0

Barak, A., Hen, L., Boniel-Nissim, M., & Shapira, N. (2008). A comprehensive review and a meta-analysis of the effectiveness of internet-based psychotherapeutic interventions. *Journal of Technology in Human Services*, *26*(2–4), 109–160. DOI: 10.1080/15228830802094429

Barak, A., & Suler, J. (2008). *Reflections on the Psychology and Social Science of Cyberspace*. Cambridge University Press., https://www.johnsuler.com/article_pdfs/reflections_psycyber.pdf DOI: 10.1017/CBO9780511813740.002

Barandiaran, X. E., Calleja-López, A., & Cozzo, E. (2020). Defining Collective Identities in Technopolitical Interaction Networks. *Frontiers in Psychology*, *11*, 1549. Advance online publication. DOI: 10.3389/fpsyg.2020.01549 PMID: 32848986

Barbato, M., Al Hemeiri, S., Nafie, S., Dhuhair, B. A., & Dabbagh, N. T. (2021). Characterizing individuals accessing mental health services in the UAE: A focus on youth living in Dubai. *International Journal of Mental Health Systems*, *15*(1), 29. Advance online publication. DOI: 10.1186/s13033-021-00452-4 PMID: 33789685

Barbul, M., & Bojescu, I. (2023). Generations' Perception Towards the Interaction with AI. *New Trends in Sustainable Business and Consumption*, 539–546. https://doi.org/DOI: 10.24818/BASIQ/2023/09/041

Bargh, J. A., McKenna, K. Y. A., & Fitzsimons, G. M. (2002). Can You See the Real Me? Activation and Expression of the "True Self" on the Internet. *The Journal of Social Issues*, *58*(1), 33–48. DOI: 10.1111/1540-4560.00247

Bar-Kalifa, S., Rafaeli, E., & Hall, J. A. (2019). The role of emotional support and reciprocal self-disclosure in affective outcomes: An observational study of online peer support. *Journal of Consulting and Clinical Psychology*, *87*(6), 536–549. DOI: 10.1037/ccp0000405

Barkhuus, L., & Tashiro, C. (2013). Privacy vs. self-expression: Young adults' use of social media. In *Proceedings of the SIGCHI Conference on Human Factors in Computing Systems* (pp. 757–766). DOI: 10.1145/2470654.2466118

Barlett, C. P., & Chamberlin, K. (2017). Examining cyberbullying across the lifespan. *Computers in Human Behavior*, *71*, 444–449. DOI: 10.1016/j.chb.2017.02.009

Bartsch, A., & Dienlin, T. (2016). Can't help myself: An experience sampling study on the role of self-control in young adults' problematic use of social network sites. *Computers in Human Behavior, 61*, 295–305. DOI: 10.1016/j.chb.2016.03.055

Bashkirova, A., & Krpan, D. (2024). Confirmation bias in AI-assisted decision-making: AI triage recommendations congruent with expert judgments increase psychologist trust and recommendation acceptance. *Computers in Human Behavior: Artificial Humans., 2*(1), 100066. Advance online publication. DOI: 10.1016/j.chbah.2024.100066

Baumeister, R. F., Bratslavsky, E., Muraven, M., & Tice, D. M. (1998). Ego depletion: Is the active self a limited resource? *Journal of Personality and Social Psychology, 74*(5), 1252–1265. DOI: 10.1037/0022-3514.74.5.1252 PMID: 9599441

Bayer, J. B., Ellison, N. B., Schoenebeck, S. Y., & Falk, E. B. (2015). Sharing the small moments: Ephemeral social interaction on Snapchat. *Information Communication and Society, 19*(7), 956–977. DOI: 10.1080/1369118X.2015.1084349

Baym, N. K. (2015). Social Media and the Struggle for Society. *Social Media + Society, 1*(1), 205630511558047. DOI: 10.1177/2056305115580477

BBC News. (2021, February 24). *Indian police say suspects copied film "Drishyam" to cover up murder*. BBC News. https://www.bbc.com

Becker, D., & Marecek, J. (2008). Positive Psychology: History in the Remaking? *Theory & Psychology, 18*(5), 591–604. DOI: 10.1177/0959354308093397

Belk, R. W. (2013). Extended Self in a Digital World. *The Journal of Consumer Research, 40*(3), 477–500. DOI: 10.1086/671052

Bennett, W. L. (2008). Changing citizenship in the digital age. In Bennett, W. L. (Ed.), *Playing citizen: Youth, participatory politics, and the biographical frame* (pp. 1–29). University of Michigan Press.

Bennett, W. L., & Segerberg, A. (2013). *The logic of connective action: Digital media and the personalization of contentious politics*. Cambridge University Press. DOI: 10.1017/CBO9781139198752

Berger, C. R. (1997). Interpersonal communication and social influence. In Berger, C. R., & Chaffee, S. H. (Eds.), *Handbook of communication science* (pp. 503–529). Sage.

Bergin, R. (2016). *Media Richness Theory*. https://www.chds.us/coursefiles/IS4010/lectures/tech_media_richness_long/story_content/external_files/Media%20Richness%20Theory%20Script.pdf

Berry, N., Lobban, F., & Emsley, R. (2017). Social media use in psychosis: Benefits, risks and opportunities for research. *Current Opinion in Psychology*, *18*, 45–50. DOI: 10.1016/j.copsyc.2017.07.023

Bessi, A., Petroni, F., Barrat, A., Cattuto, C., Castillo, C., Menczer, F., & Scala, A. (2016). User baseline popularity and attention half-life in social media. *EPJ Data Science*, *5*(1), 39. DOI: 10.1140/epjds/s13688-016-0099-y

Bessière, K., Seay, A. F., & Kiesler, S. (2007). The Ideal Elf: Identity Exploration in World of Warcraft. *Cyberpsychology & Behavior*, *10*(4), 530–535. DOI: 10.1089/cpb.2007.9994 PMID: 17711361

Blackwell, C., Birnholtz, J., & Abbott, A. (2014). Seeing myself through you: Emotional disclosure and relational closeness in online social networks. *Computers in Human Behavior*, *36*, 161–170. DOI: 10.1016/j.chb.2014.03.052

Blackwell, C., Birnholtz, J., & Abbott, A. (2015). Seeing and being seen: Co-situation and impression formation using Grindr, a location-aware gay dating app. *New Media & Society*, *17*(7), 1117–1136. DOI: 10.1177/1461444814521595

Blanchar, J. (2016). Familiarity Bias: Examining a Cognitive-Affective Mechanism Underlying Ideological Support for the Status Quo Underlying Ideological Support for the Status Quo. *Graduate Theses and Dissertations*. Familiarity Bias: Examining a Cognitive-Affective Mechanism Underlying

Blank, G. (2017). The Internet and the mass repersonalization of society. *Information Communication and Society*, *20*(1), 1–19. DOI: 10.1080/1369118X.2016.1148186

Blank, G. (2017). The myth of internet anonymity: Why everything you do online can be traced. *First Monday*, *22*(6). Advance online publication. DOI: 10.5210/fm.v22i6.7462

Boellstorff, T. (2016). For Whom the Ontology Turns: Theorizing the Digital Real. *Current Anthropology*, *57*(4), 387–407. DOI: 10.1086/687362

Bolton, R. N., Parasuraman, A., Hoefnagels, A., Migchels, N., Poulis, E., Blankaert, I., & Silvestre, B. S. (2018). Understanding Generation Z through innovation adoption lens: Implications for existing scale items. *Journal of Business Research*, *93*, 343–354. DOI: 10.1016/j.jbusres.2017.12.023

Bonilla, Y., & Rosa, J. (2015). # Ferguson: Digital protest, hashtag ethnography, and the racial politics of social media in the United States. *American Ethnologist*, *42*(1), 4–17. DOI: 10.1111/amet.12112

Bordwell, D., & Thompson, K. (2019). *Film art: An introduction* (12th ed.). McGraw-Hill Education.

Bortolan, A. (2024). Becoming oneself online: Narrative self-constitution and the internet. *Philosophical Studies, 181*(9), 2405–2427. DOI: 10.1007/s11098-024-02169-9

Boyd, D. (2010). *Social Network Sites as Networked Publics: Affordances, Dynamics, and Implications danah boyd*. https://www.danah.org/papers/2010/SNSasNetworkedPublics.pdf

Boyd, D. (2014). It's complicated: the Social Lives of Networked Teens. *Choice Reviews Online, 51*(12), 51–704251–7042. DOI: 10.5860/CHOICE.51-7042

boyd, D. (2014). *It's complicated: The social lives of networked teens*. Yale University Press.

boyd, d., & Crawford, K. (2012). Critical questions for big data: Provocations for a cultural, technological, and scholarly phenomenon. *Information, Communication & Society, 15*(5), 662–679. DOI: 10.1080/1369118X.2012.678878

Boyd, D. (2011). Social network sites as networked publics: Affordances, dynamics, and implications. In Papacharissi, Z. (Ed.), *A networked self: Identity, community, and culture on social network sites* (pp. 39–58). Routledge.

Brewer, M. B. (1991). The social self: On being the same and different at the same time. *Personality and Social Psychology Bulletin, 17*(5), 475–482. DOI: 10.1177/0146167291175001

Brisson, J., De Chantal, P., Forgues, H. L., & Markovits, H. (2014). Belief bias is stronger when reasoning is more difficult. *Thinking & Reasoning, 20*(3), 385–403. DOI: 10.1080/13546783.2013.875942

Brown, T., & Katz, B. (2019). *Change by design: How design thinking transforms organizations and inspires innovation*. Harper Business.

Brubaker, J. R., Ananny, M., & Crawford, K. (2016). Departing glances: A sociotechnical account of "leaving" Grindr. *New Media & Society, 18*(3), 373–390. DOI: 10.1177/1461444814542311

Bryant, F. B., & Veroff, J. (2007). *Savoring: A new model of positive experience*. Erlbaum Associates.

Bullingham, L., & Vasconcelos, A. C. (2013). The Presentation of Self in the Online world': Goffman and the Study of Online Identities. *Journal of Information Science, 39*(1), 101–112. DOI: 10.1177/0165551512470051

Bull, S. (2016). *Sound: An auditory anthropology*. Routledge.

Burgess, J., & Green, J. (2018). *YouTube: Digital media and society series* (2nd ed.). Polity Press.

Burke, M., Marraccini, M. E., & McGannon, K. R. (2010). The measurement of social network site usage and its relationship to social capital and well-being. *Proceedings of the SIGCHI Conference on Human Factors in Computing Systems*, 1191–1200. DOI: 10.1145/1753326.1753502

Cai, H., Yao, T., & Zhang, X. (2022).Confirmation Bias in Analysts' Response to Consensus Forecasts. *Journal of Behavioural Finances.* https://ssrn.com/abstract =4211686

Cannon, M., & Edmondson, A. (2005). Failing to learn and learning to fail (intelligently): How great organizations put failure to work to innovate and improve. *Long Range Planning*, *38*(3), 299–319. DOI: 10.1016/j.lrp.2005.04.005

Carlgren, L., Rauth, I., & Elmquist, M. (2016). Framing design thinking: The concept in idea and enactment. *Creativity and Innovation Management*, *25*(1), 38–57. DOI: 10.1111/caim.12153

Carpenter, S. M., & Yoon, C. (2011, October 19). Aging and consumer decision making. *Annals of the New York Academy of Sciences.* https://pmc.ncbi.nlm.nih .gov/articles/PMC3799963/

Carstensen, L. L., & Hartel, C. R. (2006).When I'm 64.*Motivation and behavioral change.* https://www.ncbi.nlm.nih.gov/books/NBK83771/#:~: Choi, I., & Cha, O. (2019). Cross-Cultural examination of the false consensus effect. *Frontiers in Psychology, 10.* https://doi.org/DOI: 10.3389/fpsyg.2019.02747

Carvalho, P., & Alves, H. (2023). Customer value co-creation in the hospitality and tourism industry: A systematic literature review. *International Journal of Contemporary Hospitality Management*, *35*(1), 250–273. DOI: 10.1108/IJCHM-12-2021-1528

Castle, E., Eisenberger, N. I., Seeman, T. E., Moons, W. G., Boggero, I. A., Grinblatt, M. S., & Taylor, S. E. (2012). Neural and behavioral bases of age differences in perceptions of trust. *Proceedings of the National Academy of Sciences of the United States of America*, *109*(51), 20848–20852. DOI: 10.1073/pnas.1218518109

Chan, K. T., Hui, C. L., Cheung, C., Suen, Y. N., Wong, S. M. Y., Wong, C. S., Kam, B. P., & Chen, E. Y. H. (2025). Exploring the Differentiation of Self-Concepts in the Physical and Virtual Worlds Using Euclidean Distance Analysis and Its Relationship With Digitalization and Mental Health Among Young People: Cross-Sectional Study. *JMIR Mental Health*, *12*, e60747. DOI: 10.2196/60747 PMID: 39889302

Chatzakou, D., Kourtellis, N., Blackburn, J., De Cristofaro, E., Stringhini, G., & Vakali, A. (2017). Mean birds: Detecting aggression and bullying on Twitter. *Proceedings of the 2017 ACM Web Science Conference*, 13–22. https://doi.org/ DOI: 10.1145/3091478.3091487

Cheney-Lippold, J. (2017). *We are data: algorithms and the making of our digital selves*. New York University Press. DOI: 10.18574/nyu/9781479888702.001.0001

Cheng, J., Danescu-Niculescu-Mizil, C., & Leskovec, J. (2014). *How Community Feedback Shapes User Behavior*. https://cs.stanford.edu/people/jure/pubs/disqus-icwsm14.pdf

Cheng, J., Bernstein, M., Danescu-Niculescu-Mizil, C., & Leskovec, J. (2017). Anyone can become a troll: Causes of trolling behavior in online discussions. *Proceedings of the 2017 ACM Conference on Computer Supported Cooperative Work and Social Computing*, 1217–1230. https://doi.org/ DOI: 10.1145/2998181.2998213

Cheng, Y., & Jiang, H. (2022). Customer–brand relationship in the era of artificial intelligence: Understanding the role of chatbot marketing efforts. *Journal of Product and Brand Management*, *31*(2), 252–264. DOI: 10.1108/JPBM-05-2020-2907

Chen, W., & Liang, Y. (2020). The emotional benefits of online self-disclosure: A meta-analysis. *Journal of Communication*, *70*(4), 513–537. DOI: 10.1093/joc/jqaa019

Chou, H.-T. G., & Edge, N. (2012). "They Are Happier and Having Better Lives than I Am": The Impact of Using Facebook on Perceptions of Others' Lives. *Cyberpsychology, Behavior, and Social Networking*, *15*(2), 117–121. DOI: 10.1089/cyber.2011.0324 PMID: 22165917

Christensen, K. S. (2009). The paradox of participation: Online personal narratives as performances of breast cancer. *Health Communication*, *24*(3), 254–265. DOI: 10.1080/10410230902806948

Christopherson, K. M. (2007). The positive and negative implications of anonymity in Internet social interactions: "On the Internet, Nobody Knows You're a Dog.". *Computers in Human Behavior*, *23*(6), 3038–3056. DOI: 10.1016/j.chb.2006.09.001

Chua, T. H. H., & Chang, L. (2016). Follow me and like my beautiful, happy, successful life: The impact of following celebrity Instagram accounts on adolescent girls' body image satisfaction. *Body Image*, *19*, 115–124. DOI: 10.1016/j.bodyim.2016.09.010

Chung, M., Ko, E., Joung, H., & Kim, S. J. (2020). Chatbot e-service and customer satisfaction regarding luxury brands. *Journal of Business Research*, *117*, 587–595. DOI: 10.1016/j.jbusres.2018.10.004

Cinelli, M., Morales, G. D. F., Galeazzi, A., Quattrociocchi, W., & Starnini, M. (2021). The echo chamber effect on social media. *Proceedings of the National Academy of Sciences of the United States of America, 118*(9), e2023301118. DOI: 10.1073/pnas.2023301118 PMID: 33622786

Citron, D. K., & Norton, H. T. (2020). Intermediaries and hate speech: Fostering digital citizenship for our information age. *Boston University Law Review. Boston University. School of Law, 100*(5), 1605–1636.

Clark-Gordon, C. V., Bowman, N. D., Goodboy, A. K., & Wright, A. (2019). Anonymity and Online Self-Disclosure: A Meta-Analysis. *Communication Reports, 32*(2), 98–111. DOI: 10.1080/08934215.2019.1607516

Cohen, J. (1998). *Statistical power analysis for the behavioral sciences* (2nd ed.). Lawrence Erlbaum Associates.

Cohen, J. (2004). Parasocial break-up: Responses to the ending of favorite TV programs. *Journal of Broadcasting & Electronic Media, 48*(4), 582–596. DOI: 10.1207/s15506878jobem4804_5

Cohen, L. E. (1955). *Delinquent boys: The culture of the gang*. Free Press.

Cohen, S. (1972). *Folk devils and moral panics: The creation of the Mods and Rockers*. Routledge.

Cooley, C. H. (2025). Human nature and the social order by Charles Horton Cooley. In *Project Gutenberg*. Charles Scribner's Sons. (Original work published 1902), https://www.gutenberg.org/ebooks/75145

Cortis, K., & Handschuh, S. (2015). Analysis of cyberbullying tweets related to trending world events. In *2015 IEEE/ACM International Conference on Advances in Social Networks Analysis and Mining* (pp. 1590–1593). IEEE. https://doi.org/ DOI: 10.1145/2808797.2809354

Costa Netto, Y., & Maçada, A. C. G. (2019). THE INFLUENCE OF SOCIAL MEDIA FILTER BUBBLES AND ECHO CHAMBERS ON IT IDENTITY CONSTRUCTION. *Research-In-Progress Papers*. https://aisel.aisnet.org/ecis2019_rip/65/

Costa, D. F., Carvalho, F., Moreira, B. C., & Silva, W. (2020). Confirmation bias in managerial decision-making: an experimental study with managers and accountants. *Journal of Accounting and Organizations*. (PDF) Confirmation bias in managerial decision-making: Da Silva, S., Gupta, R., & Monzani, D. (2023a). Editorial: Highlights in psychology: cognitive bias. *Frontiers in Psychology, 14*, 1242809. Advance online publication. DOI: 10.3389/fpsyg.2023.1242809

Costa, E. (2018). Affordances-in-practice: An ethnographic critique of social media logic and context collapse. *New Media & Society, 20*(10), 3641–3656. DOI: 10.1177/1461444818756290 PMID: 30581356

Couldry, N., & Mejias, U. A. (2019). *The costs of connection: How data is colonizing human life and appropriating it for capitalism*. Stanford University Press.

Crocker, J., & Park, L. E. (2004). The Costly Pursuit of Self-Esteem. *Psychological Bulletin, 130*(3), 392–414. DOI: 10.1037/0033-2909.130.3.392 PMID: 15122925

Csikszentmihalyi, M. (1990). The domain of creativity. In Runco, M. A., & Albert, R. S. (Eds.), *Theories of creativity* (pp. 190–212). Sage Publications, Inc.

Cummings, J. J., & Wertz, E. E. (2023). Capturing social presence: Concept explication through an empirical analysis of social presence measures. *Journal of Computer-Mediated Communication, 28*(1), zmac027. Advance online publication. DOI: 10.1093/jcmc/zmac027

Darwish, E. B. (2025). Digital media engagement and literacy among UAE youth: A mixed-methods investigation of usage patterns and digital inequalities. *Journal of Arab & Muslim Media Research, 14*(1). Advance online publication. DOI: 10.1386/jammr_00117_1

Das, P., & Dutta, S. (2021). Customer perception of chatbots in urban and rural banking in India. *Indian Journal of Business Studies*, 34-48.

Das, A., & Agarwal, P. (2022). Enhancing customer experience through AI-powered chatbots in Banking. *Journal of Banking and Technology Innovations, 15*(4), 112–129.

Davies, T. C., Manzin, J., Meraw, M., & Munro, D. S. (2022). Understanding the development of a design thinking mindset during a biomedical engineering third-year course. *Biomedical Engineering Education*. Advance online publication. DOI: 10.1007/s43683-022-00093-0 PMID: 36438449

Davis, J. L., & Jurgenson, N. (2014). Context collapse: Theorizing context collusions and collisions. *Information Communication and Society, 17*(4), 476–485. DOI: 10.1080/1369118X.2014.888458

Davison, P. (2012). The language of internet memes. In Mandiberg, M. (Ed.), *The social media reader* (pp. 120–134). NYU Press. DOI: 10.18574/nyu/9780814764077.003.0013

De Choudhury, M., Gamon, M., & Counts, S. (2013). Predicting depression via social media activity. *Proceedings of the International AAAI Conference on Web and Social Media, 7*(1), 128–137.

De Vries, M., & de Jong, R. G. var der Loo, M., de Wolf, P., & Takes, F. W. (2021). The risk of identity disclosure through network structure: anecdotal evidence from a hackathon. In *UNITED NATIONS ECONOMIC COMMISSION FOR EUROPE CONFERENCE OF EUROPEAN STATISTICIANS*. https://www.markvanderloo.eu/files/share/vries2023risk.pdf

De Wolf, R., & Pierson, J. (2014). Who's my audience again? Understanding audience management strategies for designing privacy management technologies. *Telematics and Informatics*, *31*(4), 607–616. DOI: 10.1016/j.tele.2013.11.004

Deccan Chronicle. (2016). *Siddipet murder accused allegedly inspired by Drishyam*. Deccan Chronicle.

Deci, E. L., & Ryan, R. M. (2000). The "What" and "Why" of Goal Pursuits: Human needs and the Self-Determination of Behavior. *Psychological Inquiry*, *11*(4), 227–268. DOI: 10.1207/S15327965PLI1104_01

Depow, G. J., Francis, Z., & Inzlicht, M. (2021). The experience of empathy in everyday life. *Psychological Science*, *32*(8), 1198–1213. DOI: 10.1177/0956797621995202 PMID: 34241543

Derda, I., Wouter, M., & Smit, T. (2025). Adaptive mechanisms of developing social connectedness in virtual reality environments. *Design for Health (Abingdon, England)*, *9*(2), 195–215. DOI: 10.1080/24735132.2025.2506255 PMID: 40757081

Dienlin, T., & Metzger, M. J. (2016). An extended privacy calculus model for SNSs: Incorporating trust and social capital in privacy concerns. *Journal of Computer-Mediated Communication*, *21*(5), 354–371. DOI: 10.1111/jcc4.12163

Dinev, T., & Hart, P. (2006). An extended privacy calculus model for e-commerce transactions. *Information Systems Research*, *17*(1), 61–83. DOI: 10.1287/isre.1060.0080

Ding, D., Chen, Y., Lai, J., Chen, X., Han, M., & Zhang, X. (2020). Belief bias effect in older adults: Roles of working memory and need for cognition. *Frontiers in Psychology*, *10*, 2940. Advance online publication. DOI: 10.3389/fpsyg.2019.02940 PMID: 32038362

Döring, N., & Mohseni, M. R. (2019). Digital intimacy: Conceptualizing intimate communication in computer-mediated contexts. *New Media & Society*, *21*(3), 629–649. DOI: 10.1177/1461444818803962

Dosi, C., Rosati, F., & Vignoli, M. (2018). Measuring Design Thinking Mindset. *Proceedings of the DESIGN 2018 15th International Design Conference*. https://doi.org/ DOI: 10.21278/idc.2018.0493

Ducheneaut, N., Wen, M.-H., Yee, N., & Wadley, G. (2009). Body and mind: A study of avatar personalization in three virtual worlds. *Proceedings of the 27th International Conference on Human Factors in Computing Systems - CHI 09*. DOI: 10.1145/1518701.1518877

Duffy, B. E. (2017). *(Not) Getting paid to do what you love: Gender, social media, and aspirational work*. Yale University Press. DOI: 10.12987/yale/9780300218176.001.0001

Du, R. (2022). Availability Heuristic: An Overview and Applications. *Highlights in Business Economics and Management*, *1*, 153–159. DOI: 10.54097/hbem.v1i.2548

Duval, S., & Wicklund, R. A. (1973). Effects of objective self-awareness on attribution of causality. *Journal of Experimental Social Psychology*, *9*(1), 17–31. DOI: 10.1016/0022-1031(73)90059-0

Dweck, C. S. (1999). *Self-Theories: Their Role in Motivation, Personality and Development*. Psychology Press.

Earl, J., & Kimport, K. (2011). *Digitally enabled social change: Activism in the Internet age*. MIT Press. DOI: 10.7551/mitpress/9780262015103.001.0001

Édes, B. (2021, December 22). *Helping India's elderly cross the digital divide as the Country Ages*. Medium. https://bigtrendsguy.medium.com/helping-indias-elderly-

Edwards, A., & Edwards, C. (2022). Does the correspondence bias apply to social robots? *Frontiers in Robotics and AI*, *8*, 788242. DOI: 10.3389/frobt.2021.788242 PMID: 35059443

Edwards, F. (2016). An Investigation of Attention-Seeking Behavior through Social Media Post Framing. *Athens Journal of Mass Media and Communications*, *3*(1), 25–44. DOI: 10.30958/ajmmc.3.1.2

Elchardus, M. (2017). Declinism and Populism. *Clingendael Spectator 3*, *71*(1), 1-10. https://spectator.clingendael.org/pub/2017/3/_/pdf/IS-2017-3-elchardus.pdf

Ellison, N. B., Steinfield, C., & Lampe, C. (2007). The benefits of Facebook "friends:" Social capital and college students' use of online social network sites. *Journal of Computer-Mediated Communication*, *12*(4), 1143–1168. DOI: 10.1111/j.1083-6101.2007.00367.x

Emirates Youth Council. (2021). The trends shaping the UAE's youth sector after the COVID-19 pandemic. *Strategy & Part of the PwC network*. Available at: https://www.strategyand.pwc.com/m1/en/ideation-center/ic-research/2021/future-of-youth.html

Epley, N., Waytz, A., & Cacioppo, J. T. (2007). On seeing human: A three-factor theory of anthropomorphism. *Psychological Review, 114*(4), 864–886. DOI: 10.1037/0033-295X.114.4.864 PMID: 17907867

Eren, B. A. (2021). Determinants of customer satisfaction in chatbot use: Evidence from a banking application in Turkey. *International Journal of Bank Marketing, 39*(2), 294–311. DOI: 10.1108/IJBM-02-2020-0056

Evans, T. M., Bira, L., Gastelum, J. B., Weiss, L. T., & Vanderford, N. L. (2018). Evidence for a mental health crisis in graduate education. *Nature Biotechnology, 36*(3), 282–284. DOI: 10.1038/nbt.4089 PMID: 29509732

Fakhri, N., & Muhajirah, K. Lukman, & Buchori, S. (2025, March 11). *Examining Self-Compassion's Mediating Effects Between Fear of Failure and Academic Self-Handicapping Among University Students*. Journal of Psychological Perspective. https://ukinstitute.org/journals/jopp

Faralla, V., Innocenti, A., Baraldi, S., Ermini, S., Lusuardi, L., Masini, M., Santalucia, V., Scaruffi, D., & Sirizzotti, M. (2024). Exposure to immersive virtual environments decreases present bias. *Journal of Behavioral and Experimental Economics, 108*, 102154. DOI: 10.1016/j.socec.2023.102154

Fardouly, J., & Vartanian, L. R. (2016). Social Media and Body Image Concerns: Current Research and Future Directions. *Current Opinion in Psychology, 9*, 1–5. DOI: 10.1016/j.copsyc.2015.09.005

Farley, S., Coyne, I., Axtell, C., & Sprigg, C. (2016). Design, development and validation of a workplace cyberbullying measure, the WCM. *Work and Stress, 30*(4), 293–317. DOI: 10.1080/02678373.2016.1255998

Feng, S., Mäntymäki, M., Dhir, A., & Salmela, H. (2020). How Self-tracking and the Quantified Self Promote Health and Well-being: A Systematic Literature Review (Preprint). *Journal of Medical Internet Research, 23*(9). Advance online publication. DOI: 10.2196/25171

Ferguson, C. J. (2014). Does movie violence increase violent behavior? An examination of longitudinal data. *Psychology of Popular Media Culture, 3*(3), 170–177.

Ferrell, J. (1999). *Crimes of style: Urban graffiti and the politics of criminality*. Northeastern University Press.

Ferrell, J., Hayward, K., & Young, J. (2008). *Cultural criminology: An invitation* (2nd ed.). SAGE.

Festinger, L. (1957). *A theory of cognitive dissonance*. Stanford University Press. DOI: 10.1515/9781503620766

Festinger, L., & Carlsmith, J. M. (1959). Cognitive consequences of forced compliance. *Journal of Abnormal and Social Psychology*, *58*(2), 203–210. DOI: 10.1037/h0041593 PMID: 13640824

Festinger, L., Pepitone, A., & Newcomb, T. (1952). Some consequences of de-individuation in a group. *Journal of Abnormal and Social Psychology*, *47*(2), 382–389. DOI: 10.1037/h0057906 PMID: 14937978

Floridi, L. (2015). *The Onlife Manifesto* (Floridi, L., Ed.). Springer International Publishing., DOI: 10.1007/978-3-319-04093-6

Floridi, L. (2016). *The ethics of information*. Oxford University Press.

Fox, J., & Moreland, J. J. (2018). The role of social networking sites in romantic relationships: Effects on emotional intimacy and jealousy. *Cyberpsychology, Behavior, and Social Networking*, *21*(5), 305–311. DOI: 10.1089/cyber.2017.0650

Fox, J., Moreland, J. J., & Joiner, T. E. (2015). The dark side of Facebook: The impact of rumination and self-disclosure on depressive symptoms. *Social Media + Society*, *1*(1), 1–9. DOI: 10.1177/2056305115581158

Fox, J., Moreland, J. J., & Warber, K. M. (2015). Social networking site use and the gratification of perceived social capital and emotional support: The influence of communicative behaviors. *Communication Research Reports*, *32*(3), 276–285. DOI: 10.1080/08824096.2015.1051633

Fraser, H. M. A. (2010). Designing business: New models for success. In Lockwood, T. (Ed.), *Design thinking: Integrating innovation, customer experience, and brand value* (pp. 35–46). Allworth Press.

Fredrickson, B. L. (2009). *Positivity*. Crown Publishers.

Frey, C. B., & Osborne, M. A. (2016). The future of employment: How susceptible are jobs to computerisation? *Technological Forecasting and Social Change*, *114*, 254–280. DOI: 10.1016/j.techfore.2016.08.019

Friedman, H. H. (2023). Cognitive Biases that Interfere with Critical Thinking and Scientific Reasoning: A Course Module. SSRN *Electronic Journal*. https://doi.org/ DOI: 10.2139/ssrn.2958800

Fullwood, C., James, B. M., & Chen-Wilson, C.-H. (2016). Self-Concept Clarity and Online Self-Presentation in Adolescents. *Cyberpsychology, Behavior, and Social Networking*, *19*(12), 716–720. DOI: 10.1089/cyber.2015.0623 PMID: 27830930

Funk, J. B., Baldacci, H. B., Pasold, T., & Baumgardner, J. (2004). Violence exposure in real-life, video games, television, movies, and the internet: Is there desensitization? *Journal of Adolescence, 27*(1), 23–39. DOI: 10.1016/j.adolescence.2003.10.005 PMID: 15013258

Garrett, R. K. (2009). Echo chambers online? Politically motivated selective exposure among Internet news users. *Journal of Computer-Mediated Communication, 14*(2), 265–285. DOI: 10.1111/j.1083-6101.2009.01440.x

Gerbner, G. (1998). Cultivation analysis: An overview. In Morgan, M. (Ed.), *Against the mainstream: The selected works of George Gerbner* (pp. 175–194). Peter Lang.

Gerbner, G., & Gross, L. (1976). Living with television: The violence profile. *Journal of Communication, 26*(2), 173–199. DOI: 10.1111/j.1460-2466.1976.tb01397.x PMID: 932235

Gerbner, G., Gross, L., Morgan, M., & Signorielli, N. (1998). Growing up with television: Cultivation processes. In Bryant, J., & Zillmann, D. (Eds.), *Media effects: Advances in theory and research* (pp. 43–67). Lawrence Erlbaum.

Gergen, K. J. (1991). *The saturated self: Dilemmas of identity in contemporary life*. Basic Books.

Gibson, J. J. (2013). *The Ecological Approach To Visual Perception*. Psychology Press. (Original work published 1979) DOI: 10.4324/9780203767764

Gillespie, T. (2010). The politics of "platforms.". *New Media & Society, 12*(3), 347–364. DOI: 10.1177/1461444809342738

Gillies, J., Strong, T., & Patel, V. (2021). Mental health-related discourses on social media: A systematic review. *International Journal of Environmental Research and Public Health, 18*(1), 346. DOI: 10.3390/ijerph18010346 PMID: 33466436

Gill, R., & Kanai, A. (2018). Mediating Neoliberal Capitalism: Affect, Subjectivity and Inequality. *Journal of Communication, 68*(2), 318–326. DOI: 10.1093/joc/jqy002

Gill, R., & Orgad, S. (2018). The "me too" movement, digital media, and culture. *European Journal of Cultural Studies, 21*(4), 363–369. DOI: 10.1177/1367549418782894

Gilovich, T., Griffin, D., & Kahneman, D. (2002). *Heuristics and Biases*. Cambridge UniversityPress., http://books.google.ie/books?id=ZGYgAwAAQBAJ&printsec= DOI: 10.1017/CBO9780511808098

Gkanatsiou, M. A. (2025). AI and digital tools: Transforming mediation and conflict resolution. *Proceedings, 107*(1), 104. DOI: 10.3390/proceedings2025107104

Goddard, K., Roudsari, A., & Wyatt, J. C. (2011). Automation bias: A systematic review. *Journal of the American Medical Informatics Association : JAMIA*, *19*(1), 121–127. DOI: 10.1136/amiajnl-2011-000089 PMID: 21685142

Goffman, E. (1959). The Presentation of Self in Everyday Life. *American Sociological Review*, *21*(5), 631. Advance online publication. DOI: 10.2307/2089106

Goffman, E. (1959). *The presentation of self in everyday life*. Anchor Books.

Golder, S. A., & Macy, M. W. (2014). Digital footprints: Opportunities and challenges for online social research. *Annual Review of Sociology*, *40*(1), 129–152. DOI: 10.1146/annurev-soc-071913-043145

Goldsmith, K., & Dhar, R. (2013). Negativity bias and task motivation: Testing the effectiveness of positively versus negatively framed incentives. *Journal of Experimental Psychology. Applied*, *19*(4), 358–366. DOI: 10.1037/a0034415 PMID: 24059820

Gonzalez-Franco, M.. (2018). Obeying virtual authority in immersive VR environments. *Frontiers in Psychology*, *9*, 2038.

Gorwa, R., Binns, R., & Katzenbach, C. (2020). Algorithmic content moderation: Technical and political challenges in the automation of platform governance. *Big Data & Society*, *7*(1), 1–15. DOI: 10.1177/2053951719897945

Goswami, D., & Saxena, K. (2020). Privacy paradox in social media usage: A systematic literature review. *Telematics and Informatics*, *46*, 101312. DOI: 10.1016/j.tele.2019.101312

Grabowski, M., Lehmann-Willenbrock, N., Rings, S., Blanchard, A., & Steinicke, F. (2024). Group dynamics in the metaverse: A conceptual framework and first empirical insights. *Small Group Research*, *55*(5), 1–45. DOI: 10.1177/10464964241274120

Grant, A. (2020). DIGITAL TRIBALISM AND THE INTERNET OF THINGS: CHALLENGES AND OPPORTUNITIES. *Issues in Information Systems*. Advance online publication. DOI: 10.48009/2_iis_2020_213-220

Gross, J. J. (1998). The emerging field of emotion regulation: An integrative review. *Review of General Psychology*, *2*(3), 271–299. DOI: 10.1037/1089-2680.2.3.271

Guazzini, A., Pesce, A., Gino, F., & Duradoni, M. (2022). How the COVID-19 pandemic changed adolescents' use of technologies, sense of community, and loneliness: A retrospective perception analysis. *Behavioral Sciences (Basel, Switzerland)*, *12*(7), 228. DOI: 10.3390/bs12070228 PMID: 35877298

Guess, A., Nagler, J., & Tucker, J. (2019). Less than you think: Prevalence and predictors of fake news dissemination on Facebook. *Science Advances, 5*(1), eaau4586. DOI: 10.1126/sciadv.aau4586 PMID: 30662946

Gültekin, D. G. (2024). Understanding and mitigating authority bias in business and beyond. In *Advances in human resources management and organizational development book series*. 57–72. https://doi.org/ DOI: 10.4018/979-8-3693-1766-2.ch004

Guo, J., Chen, J., & Cheng, S. (2024). Perception of ethical risks of artificial intelligence technology in the context of individual cultural values and intergenerational differences: the case of China. *Research Square (Research Square)*. https://doi.org/ DOI: 10.21203/rs.3.rs-3901913/v1

Gupta, A., & Singh, L. (2023). Checking Influence Of Cognitive Biases On Investment Decision Making And Moderating Role Of Financial Literacy [Journal-article]. *HSBRR, 18–18*(1), 101–113. http://www.gjust.ac.in/department/hsb/hsb_res_journals.html

Gupta, R., Sharma, V., & Mehta, K. (2022). Assessing the effectiveness of chatbots in Banking: Opportunities and challenges. *International Journal of Financial Services, 8*(3), 78–93.

Hafer, J., Ran, B., & Duimering, P. R. (2023). Social identity dynamics in a networked society. *Frontiers in Psychology, 14*, 1264534. DOI: 10.3389/fpsyg.2023.1264534 PMID: 37637926

Haimson, O. L., & Hoffmann, A. L. (2016). Constructing and enforcing "authentic" identity online: Facebook, real names, and non-normative identities. *First Monday, 21*(6). Advance online publication. DOI: 10.5210/fm.v21i6.6791

Han, E., DeVeaux, C., Hancock, J. T., Ram, N., Harari, G. M., & Bailenson, J. N. (2024). The influence of spatial dimensions of virtual environments on attitudes and nonverbal behaviors during social interactions. *Journal of Environmental Psychology, 95*, 102269. DOI: 10.1016/j.jenvp.2024.102269

Hargittai, E., & Hinnant, A. (2008). Digital inequality: Differences in young adults' use of the Internet. *Communication Research, 35*(5), 602–621. DOI: 10.1177/0093650208321782

Hargittai, E., & Litt, E. (2019). The tweet in court: How do employers interpret Facebook and Twitter activity when evaluating job candidates? *New Media & Society, 21*(3), 603–623. DOI: 10.1177/1461444818797082

Hargittai, E., & Shafer, S. (2006). Differences in actual and perceived online skills: The role of gender. *New Media & Society, 8*(3), 437–451. DOI: 10.1177/1461444806061956

Harper, G. W., Carver, L. J., & Hamilton, W. E. (2019). “I’m not scared any-more”: Exploring the impact of an online storytelling forum on LGBTQ+ youth’s psychosocial development. *New Media & Society, 21*(2), 336–353. DOI: 10.1177/1461444818787369

Harrell, N. (2025). The Mechanisms of Virality in Online Public Discourse. In *Purdue University*. https://s3-eu-west-1.amazonaws.com/pstorage-purdue-258596361474/53964152/Harrell_final_thesis_4.pdf?X-Amz-Algorithm=AWS4-HMAC-SHA256&X-Amz-Credential=AKIAI5YTMH46SYYEBHKA/20250914/eu-west-1/s3/aws4_request&X-Amz-Date=20250914T140558Z&X-Amz-Expires=10&X-Amz-SignedHeaders=host&X-Amz-Signature=b14993f2d675e568e57392c6d8367eaaaa5177ec59b760733321233183e3b99c

Hartley, T. (2024, July 16). *AI in Education*. DoodleLearning. https://doodlelearning.com/maths/maths-guides/ai-in-education

Heider, F. (1958). *The psychology of interpersonal relations*. Wiley. DOI: 10.1037/10628-000

Heiman, T., & Olenik-Shemesh, D. (2020). Cyberbullying involvement of adolescents with low self-efficacy. *International Journal of Environmental Research and Public Health, 17*(14), 5237. DOI: 10.3390/ijerph17145237 PMID: 32698486

Heintzelman, S. J., & King, L. A. (2014). Life is pretty meaningful. *The American Psychologist, 69*(6), 561–574. DOI: 10.1037/a0035049 PMID: 24490907

Hepner, K. A., Rutter, C. M., Bialas, A., Booth, M., Osilla, K. C., Sousa, J. L., Newberry, S. J., & Bloom, E. L. (2022). *The impact of mindfulness meditation programs on performance-related outcomes: Implications for the U.S. army*. Rand Corporation., DOI: 10.7249/RRA1522-1

Heyselaar, E. (2023). The CASA theory no longer applies to desktop computers. *Scientific Reports, 13*(1), 19559. DOI: 10.1038/s41598-023-46527-9 PMID: 37952037

Higgins, E. T. (1987). Self-discrepancy: A theory relating self and affect. *Psychological Review, 94*(3), 319–340. DOI: 10.1037/0033-295X.94.3.319 PMID: 3615707

Highfield, T., & Leaver, T. (2016). Instagrammatics and digital methods: Studying visual social media, from selfies and GIFs to memes and emoji. *Communication Research and Practice, 2*(1), 47–62. DOI: 10.1080/22041451.2016.1155332

Hinduja, S., & Patchin, J. W. (2019). Connecting adolescent suicide to the severity of bullying and cyberbullying. *Journal of School Violence, 18*(3), 333–346. DOI: 10.1080/15388220.2018.1492417

Hindustan Times. (2017). *Udaipur murder case resembles Drishyam plot, say police*. Hindustan Times.

Hine,C.(2020).*EthnographyfortheInternet*.Routledge.,DOI:10.4324/9781003085348

Hogan, B. (2010). The Presentation of Self in the Age of Social Media: Distinguishing Performances and Exhibitions Online. *Bulletin of Science, Technology & Society, 30*(6), 377–386. DOI: 10.1177/0270467610385893

Hollenbaugh, E. E. (2021). Self-Presentation in Social Media: Review and Research Opportunities. *Review of Communication Research, 9*(2255-4165), 80–98. DOI: 10.12840/ISSN.2255-4165.027

Holm, C. (2015). The 25 Cognitive Biases- Uncovering The Myth Of Rational Thinking.

Holt-Lunstad, J., Smith, T. B., & Layton, J. B. (2010). Social relationships and mortality risk: A meta-analytic review. *PLoS Medicine, 7*(7), e1000316. DOI: 10.1371/journal.pmed.1000316 PMID: 20668659

Honarvar, R., & Sepehrinia, M. (2025). Refashioning Belk's Theory of Digital Extended Self for a Datafied Society: A Review and Research Agenda. *SAGE Open, 15*(3), 21582440251357241. Advance online publication. DOI: 10.1177/21582440251357241

Hsee, C. K., & Zhang, J. (2004). Distinction Bias: Misprediction and Mischoice Due to Joint Evaluation. *Journal of Personality and Social Psychology, 86*(5), 680–695. DOI: 10.1037/0022-3514.86.5.680 PMID: 15161394

Hsu, C. L., & Lin, J. C.-C. (2023). Understanding the user satisfaction and loyalty of customer service chatbots. *Journal of Retailing and Consumer Services, 71*, 103211. DOI: 10.1016/j.jretconser.2022.103211

Huang, J., Kumar, S., & Hu, C. (2021). A Literature Review of Online Identity Reconstruction. *Frontiers in Psychology, 12*(1), 696552. Advance online publication. DOI: 10.3389/fpsyg.2021.696552 PMID: 34497560

Huesmann, L. R. (1998). The role of social information processing and cognitive scripts in the acquisition and maintenance of habitual aggressive behavior. In Geen, R. G., & Donnerstein, E. (Eds.), *Human aggression: Theories, research, and implications for policy* (pp. 73–109). Academic Press. DOI: 10.1016/B978-012278805-5/50005-5

Huesmann, L. R. (2018). Aggressive behavior and media violence research. *Annual Review of Clinical Psychology, 14*, 75–99.

Indian Express. (2015). *Gujarat murder accused admit to copying plot from Drishyam*. The Indian Express.

Insel, T. (2017). Digital phenotyping: Technology for a new science of behavior. *Journal of the American Medical Association, 318*(13), 1215–1216. DOI: 10.1001/jama.2017.11295 PMID: 28973224

Ishii, K., Lyons, M. M., & Carr, S. A. (2019). Revisiting media richness theory for today and future. *Human Behavior and Emerging Technologies, 1*(2), 124–131. DOI: 10.1002/hbe2.138

Jackson, S. J., Bailey, M., & Foucault Welles, B. (2020). *HashtagActivism: Networks of race and gender justice*. MIT Press. DOI: 10.7551/mitpress/10858.001.0001

James, W. (1890). The Principles of Psychology. By WILLIAM JAMES 2 vols. (American Science Series, Advance Course.) New York, Holt. 8Dagger. *Science, ns-16*(401), 207–208. DOI: 10.1126/science.ns-16.401.207-a

Jenkins, H. (2006). *Convergence culture: Where old and new media collide*. New York University Press.

Jiang, J.. (2020). Badges and credibility: How verification affects trust on Twitter. *Social Media + Society, 6*(3).

Jin, P. (2023). *Research on Confirmation Bias and Its Influences on Purchase Decision-making*. Advances in Economic Management and Political Sciences., DOI: 10.54254/2754-1169/10/20230471

Joinson, A. N. (2001). Self-disclosure in computer-mediated communication: The role of self-awareness and visual anonymity. *European Journal of Social Psychology, 31*(2), 177–192. DOI: 10.1002/ejsp.36

Joinson, A. N. (2008). Looking at, looking up or keeping up with people? Motives and use of Facebook. *Proceedings of the SIGCHI Conference on Human Factors in Computing Systems*, 1027–1036. DOI: 10.1145/1357054.1357213

Kaakinen, M., Sirola, A., Savolainen, I., & Oksanen, A. (2018). Shared identity and shared information in social media: Development and validation of the identity bubble reinforcement scale. *Media Psychology, 23*(1), 1–27. DOI: 10.1080/15213269.2018.1544910

Kahneman, D., & Tversky, A. (1972). Subjective probability: A judgment of representativeness. *Cognitive Psychology, 3*(3), 430–454. DOI: 10.1016/0010-0285(72)90016-3

Kaiser, J., & Rauchfleisch, A. (2020). Birds of a Feather Get Recommended Together: Algorithmic Homophily in YouTube's Channel Recommendations in the United States and Germany. *Social Media + Society*, *6*(4), 205630512096991. DOI: 10.1177/2056305120969914

Keipi, T., Näsi, M., Oksanen, A., & Räsänen, P. (2017). *Online hate and harmful content: Cross-national perspectives*. Routledge.

Kelley, H. H. (1967). Attribution theory in social psychology. *Nebraska Symposium on Motivation*, *15*, 192–238.

Kerala Police Reports (2021–2023). Summaries of public statements cited in regional news reports regarding imitation crimes following *Drishyam 2. (Multiple sources; used for contextual attribution.)*

Khan, A. (2025, July 10). *How India's Emerging Surveillance Regime Threatens the Right to Anonymity Online*. Yale Law School. https://law.yale.edu/isp/initiatives/wikimedia-initiative-intermediaries-and-information/wiii-blog/how-indias-emerging-surveillance-regime-threatens-right-anonymity-online

Khan, R. (2023, November 24). *Media ideology shapes public perception of artificial intelligence.* Open Access Government. https://www.openaccessgovernment.org/media-

Kiesler, S., Siegel, J., & McGuire, T. W. (1984). Social psychological aspects of computer-mediated communication. *The American Psychologist*, *39*(10), 1123–1134. DOI: 10.1037/0003-066X.39.10.1123

Klauer, K. C., Musch, J., & Naumer, B. (2000). On belief bias in syllogistic reasoning. *Psychological Review*, *107*(4), 852–884. DOI: 10.1037/0033-295X.107.4.852 PMID: 11089409

Klein, K., & Martinez, L. F. (2023). The impact of anthropomorphism on customer satisfaction in chatbot commerce: An experimental study in the food sector. *Electronic Commerce Research*, *23*(4), 2789–2825. DOI: 10.1007/s10660-022-09562-8

Klenner, N. F., Gemser, G., & Karpen, I. O. (2021). Entrepreneurial ways of designing and designerly ways of entrepreneuring: Exploring the relationship between design thinking and effectuation theory. *Journal of Product Innovation Management*, *39*(1), 66–94. DOI: 10.1111/jpim.12587

Knobloch-Westerwick, S., Johnson, B. K., & Westerwick, A. (2014). Confirmation bias in online searches: Impacts of selective exposure before an election on political attitude strength and shifts. *Journal of Computer-Mediated Communication*, *20*(2), 171–187. DOI: 10.1111/jcc4.12105

Kokilaj, S. (2020). Is there a trade-off between privacy concerns and online self-disclosure? A meta-analytic review. *Social Science Computer Review*, *38*(2), 181–198. DOI: 10.1177/0894439318823326

Koltay, A. (2022). *New media and freedom of expression: Rethinking the constitutional foundations of the public sphere*. Hart Publishing.

Koscielniak, M., Rydzewska, K., & Sedek, G. (2018, November 6). *Commentary: The attraction effect in Decision making: Superior performance by older adults*. Frontiers. https://www.frontiersin.org/journals/psychology/articles/10.3389/fpsyg.2018.02321/full

Kowalski, R. M., Giumetti, G. W., Schroeder, A. N., & Lattanner, M. R. (2014). Bullying in the digital age: A critical review and meta-analysis of cyberbullying research among youth. *Psychological Bulletin*, *140*(4), 1073–1137. DOI: 10.1037/a0035618 PMID: 24512111

Kramer, A. D., Guillory, J. E., & Hancock, J. T. (2014). Experimental evidence of massive-scale emotional contagion through social networks. *Proceedings of the National Academy of Sciences of the United States of America*, *111*(24), 8788–8790. DOI: 10.1073/pnas.1320040111 PMID: 24889601

Kreimer, R., & Sánchez, F. (2025). The Impact of Authority Figures in our Beliefs. Experimental Studies on the "Author's Bias." https://www.academia.edu/29898878/The_Impact_of_Authority_Figures_

Kush, J., Argote, L., & Aven, B. (2025). The effects of communication networks on shared social identity and group performance. *Small Group Research*, *56*(6), 899–949. Advance online publication. DOI: 10.1177/10464964251326615

Ku, Y. R., & Stager, C. (2022). Rethinking the multidimensionality of growth mindset amid the COVID-19 pandemic: A systematic review and Framework Proposal. *Frontiers in Psychology*, *13*, 572220. Advance online publication. DOI: 10.3389/fpsyg.2022.572220 PMID: 35846666

Kvale, K. F. (2020). Understanding the user experience of customer service chatbots: what can we learn from customer satisfaction surveys? *In International Workshop on Chatbot Research and Design*.

Kyrlitsias, C., & Michael-Grigoriou, D. (2020). Social conformity in immersive virtual environments: The Asch paradigm revisited. *Frontiers in Psychology*, *11*, 2254. DOI: 10.3389/fpsyg.2020.02254 PMID: 33013589

Kyungran, A. M. A., Kim, T., Ahn, J., & Ahn, J. (2019). A study on the media Consumers' behavior related to Online Communications: Behavioral Economics Perspective. *KSII Transactions on Internet and Information Systems*, *13*(5). Advance online publication. DOI: 10.3837/tiis.2019.05.014

Ladachart, L., Chaimongkol, J., & Phothong, W. (2022). Design-based learning to facilitate secondary students' understanding of pulleys. *Australasian Journal of Engineering Education*, *27*(1), 26–37. DOI: 10.1080/22054952.2022.2065722

Lair, D. J., Sullivan, K., & Cheney, G. (2005). Marketization and the Recasting of the Professional Self. *Management Communication Quarterly*, *18*(3), 307–343. DOI: 10.1177/0893318904270744

Lambton-Black, G., Whittaker, A., & Woods, R. (2021). Listening in lockdown: Podcasts and well-being during the coronavirus pandemic. *Media and Communication*, *9*(2), 135–144. DOI: 10.17645/mac.v9i2.3811

Lampe, C., Ellison, N., & Steinfield, C. (2007). A familiar face(book): Profile elements as signals in an online social network. *Proceedings of the SIGCHI Conference on Human Factors in Computing Systems*, 435–444. DOI: 10.1145/1240624.1240695

Lampe, C., Wohn, D. Y., Ellison, N., Vitak, J., & Gray, R. (2014). Under the covers: Self-disclosure in a social networking site for families. *Proceedings of the 17th ACM Conference on Computer Supported Cooperative Work & Social Computing*, 865–875. DOI: 10.1145/2531602.2531674

Langston, C. A. (1994). Capitalizing on and coping with daily-life events: Expressive responses to positive events. *Journal of Personality and Social Psychology*, *67*(6), 1112–1125. DOI: 10.1037/0022-3514.67.6.1112

Lanier, J., & Chitrapornprasert, W. (2019). Self-presentation and privacy management among college students on social networking sites. *Computers in Human Behavior*, *90*, 214–221. DOI: 10.1016/j.chb.2018.08.041

Lapidot-Lefler, N., & Barak, A. (2012). Effects of anonymity, invisibility, and lack of eye-contact on toxic online disinhibition. *Computers in Human Behavior*, *28*(2), 434–443. DOI: 10.1016/j.chb.2011.10.014

Larkin, R. (2009). *The Columbine legacy: Rampage shootings as political acts*. University of Texas Press. DOI: 10.1177/0002764209332548

Larose, R., & Rifon, N. J. (2007). Value orientations, perceived risks, and Internet privacy concerns. *Journal of Applied Security Research*, *2*(2), 71–87. DOI: 10.1300/J374v02n02_06

Lauharatanahirun, N.. (2024). External and internal attributions in human–agent interaction: A neuro-social model. *Human-Machine Communication*, *8*(1).

Le Bon, G. (2002). *The crowd: A study of the popular mind.* Dover Publications. (Original work published 1895)

Leary, M. R., & Kowalski, R. M. (1990). Impression management: A literature review and two-component model. *Psychological Bulletin*, *107*(1), 34–47. DOI: 10.1037/0033-2909.107.1.34

Lee, E. (2024). *The Power of Perception in Human-AI Interaction: Investigating Psychological Factors and Cognitive Biases that Shape User Belief and Behavior. arXiv*. Cornell University., DOI: 10.1080/08870440903440707

Lei, S. I., Shen, H., & Ye, S. (2021). A comparison between chatbot and human service: Customer perception and reuse intention. *International Journal of Contemporary Hospitality Management*, *33*(11), 3977–3995. DOI: 10.1108/IJCHM-12-2020-1399

Lewis, K., Kaufman, J., & Christakis, N. (2014). The taste for privacy: An analysis of college student privacy settings in an online social network. *Journal of Computer-Mediated Communication*, *14*(4), 1005–1024. DOI: 10.1111/j.1083-6101.2009.01474.x

Liedtka, J. (2020). Exploring the impact of design thinking on organizational culture and innovation. *Journal of Product Innovation Management*, *37*(2), 144–164. DOI: 10.1111/jpim.12518

Li, L. L., Lee, K. Y., Emokpae, E., & Yang, S.-B. (2021). What makes you continuously use chatbot services? Evidence from chinese online travel agencies. *Electronic Markets*, *31*(3), 575–599. DOI: 10.1007/s12525-020-00454-z PMID: 35603227

Litt, E. (2012). Knock, Knock. Who's There? the Imagined Audience. *Journal of Broadcasting & Electronic Media*, *56*(3), 330–345. DOI: 10.1080/08838151.2012.705195

Litt, E., & Hargittai, E. (2016). The Imagined Audience on Social Network Sites. *Social Media + Society*, *2*(1), 1–12. DOI: 10.1177/2056305116633482

Livingstone, S. (2008). Taking risky opportunities in youthful content creation: Teenagers' use of social networking sites for intimacy, privacy and self-expression. *New Media & Society*, *10*(3), 393–411. DOI: 10.1177/1461444808089415

Livingstone, S., Stoilova, M., & Kelly, A. (2017). Cyberbullying: Incidence, trends and consequences. In Smith, P. K., & Steffgen, G. (Eds.), *Cyberbullying through the new media: Findings from an international network* (pp. 1–20). Psychology Press.

Lo Presti, L. M. (2021). The role of the chatbot on customer purchase intention: towards digital relational sales. *Italian Journal of Marketing*.

Lockwood, T. (2014). *Design Thinking Integrating Innovation, customer experience, and brand value*. Skyhorse Publishing.

Logg, J. M., Minson, J. A., & Moore, D. A. (2019). Algorithm appreciation: People prefer algorithmic to human judgment. *Organizational Behavior and Human Decision Processes*, *151*, 90–103. DOI: 10.1016/j.obhdp.2018.12.005

Loh, J., & Walsh, M. J. (2021). Social media context collapse: The consequential differences between context collusion versus context collision. *Social Media + Society*, *7*(3), 1–15. DOI: 10.1177/20563051211041646

Lomas, T., Hefferon, K., & Ivtzan, I. (2014). *Applied Positive Psychology: Integrated Positive Practice*. Sage. DOI: 10.4135/9781473909687

Luppicini, R. (2013). *HANDBOOK OF RESEARCH ON TECHNOSELF: identity in a technological society* (Vol. 1). Information Science Refer. DOI: 10.4018/978-1-4666-2211-1

Lupton, D. (2016). The diverse domains of quantified selves: Self-tracking modes and dataveillance. *Economy and Society*, *45*(1), 101–122. DOI: 10.1080/03085147.2016.1143726

Lutz, C., & Ranzini, G. (2020). The emotional experience of privacy: A qualitative study on how people feel about behavioral targeting. *Information Communication and Society*, *23*(5), 685–701. DOI: 10.1080/1369118X.2018.1540634

Ly, D. P., Shekelle, P. G., & Song, Z. (2023). Evidence for anchoring bias during physician decision-making. *JAMA internal medicine*. https://pmc.ncbi.nlm.nih.gov/articles/PMC10294014/#H1-5-IOI230036

Lyons, T.. (2018). Obedience to GPS: Human reliance on automated navigation. *Transportation Research Part F: Traffic Psychology and Behaviour*, *58*, 479–491.

Maares, P., Banjac, S., & Hanusch, F. (2020). The labour of visual authenticity on social media: Exploring producers' and audiences' perceptions on Instagram. *Poetics*, *84*, 101502. DOI: 10.1016/j.poetic.2020.101502

Madary, M., & Metzinger, T. K. (2016). Real Virtuality: A Code of Ethical Conduct. Recommendations for Good Scientific Practice and the Consumers of VR-Technology. *Frontiers in Robotics and AI*, *3*. Advance online publication. DOI: 10.3389/frobt.2016.00003

Maffesoli, M. (1996). The Time of the Tribes: The Decline of Individualism in Mass Society. *Sage (Atlanta, Ga.)*. Advance online publication. DOI: 10.4135/9781446222133

Mahyoob, M. (2020). Challenges of e-Learning during the COVID-19 Pandemic Experienced by EFL Learners. *Arab World English Journal*, *11*(4), 351–362. DOI: 10.24093/awej/vol11no4.23

Mailizar, A., Almanthari, A., Maulina, S., & Bruce, S. (2020). Secondary School Mathematics Teachers' Views on E-learning Implementation Barriers during the COVID-19 Pandemic: The Case of Indonesia. *Eurasia Journal of Mathematics, Science and Technology Education*, *16*(7), em1860. DOI: 10.29333/ejmste/8240

Maister, L., Sebanz, N., Knoblich, G., & Tsakiris, M. (2013). Experiencing ownership over a dark-skinned body reduces implicit racial bias. *Cognition*, *128*(2), 170–178. DOI: 10.1016/j.cognition.2013.04.002 PMID: 23680793

Mamede, A., Merkelbach, I., Noordzij, G., & Denktas, S. (2022). Mindfulness as a protective factor against depression, anxiety and psychological distress during the covid-19 pandemic: Emotion regulation and insomnia symptoms as mediators. *Frontiers in Psychology*, *13*, 820959. Advance online publication. DOI: 10.3389/fpsyg.2022.820959 PMID: 35432084

Manago, A. M., Taylor, T., & Greenfield, P. M. (2012). Me and my 400 friends: The anatomy of college students' Facebook networks, their communication patterns, and well-being. *Developmental Psychology*, *48*(2), 369–380. DOI: 10.1037/a0026338 PMID: 22288367

Mangiapanello, K. A., & Hemmes, N. S. (2015). An Analysis of Feedback from a Behavior Analytic Perspective. *The Behavior Analyst*, *38*(1), 51–75. DOI: 10.1007/s40614-014-0026-x PMID: 27606167

Marelaro, N., Ganguly, S., Steinert, M., & Jung, M. (2015). The personal trait myth: a comparative analysis of the innovation impact of design thinking tools and personal traits. In Plattner, H., Meinel, C., & Leifer, L. (Eds.), *Design thinking research* (pp. 41–57). Springer. DOI: 10.1007/978-3-319-06823-7_4

Markus, H. R., & Kitayama, S. (1991). *Culture and the Self: Implications for Cognition, Emotion, and Motivation*. ResearchGate., DOI: 10.1037/0033-295X.98.2.224

Markus, H., & Nurius, P. (1986). Possible selves. *The American Psychologist*, *41*(9), 954–969. DOI: 10.1037/0003-066X.41.9.954

Marwick, A. E., & boyd, d. (2018). It's complicated: The social lives of networked teens (Updated edition). Yale University Press.

Marwick, A. E. (2013). *Status update: Celebrity, publicity, and branding in the social media age*. Yale University Press.

Marwick, A., & boyd, . (2014). Networked privacy: How teenagers negotiate context in social media. *New Media & Society*, *16*(7), 1051–1067. DOI: 10.1177/1461444814543995

Marwick, A., & Boyd, D. (2011). I tweet honestly, I tweet passionately: Twitter users, context collapse, and the imagined audience. *New Media & Society*, *13*(1), 114–133. DOI: 10.1177/1461444810365313

Mathrubhumi. (2015, February 25). *Drishyam* inspires real-life crime: Police. https://english.mathrubhumi.com/

Mathrubhumi. (2024, March 12). Media literacy modules proposed for students to counter film influence. https://english.mathrubhumi.com/

Matthews, K. (2019). 6 Innovations That Have Drastically Changed Mental Healthcare: Mental health treatment has changed a lot in the last five years, and it will continue to evolve. *Healthcare Innovation*. Available at: https://www.hcinnovationgroup.com/population-health-management/telehealth/article/21118902/6-innovations-that-have-drastically-changed-mental- healthcare

Matz, S. C., Kosinski, M., Nave, G., & Stillwell, D. J. (2017). Psychological targeting as an effective approach to digital mass persuasion. *Proceedings of the National Academy of Sciences of the United States of America*, *114*(48), 12714–12719. DOI: 10.1073/pnas.1710966114 PMID: 29133409

Mazman, S. G., & Usluel, Y. K. (2010). Modeling educational usage of Facebook. *Computers & Education*, *55*(2), 444–453. DOI: 10.1016/j.compedu.2010.02.008

McAdams, D. P. (2011). Narrative Identity. *Handbook of Identity Theory and Research, 1*, 99–115. DOI: 10.1007/978-1-4419-7988-9_5

McAdams, D. P., Trzesniewski, K., Lilgendahl, J., Benet-Martinez, V., & Robins, R. W. (2021). Self and Identity in Personality Psychology. *Personality Science*, *2*(1), e6035. Advance online publication. DOI: 10.5964/ps.6035

McDaniel, B. T., & Coyne, S. M. (2016). "Technoference": The interference of technology in couple relationships and implications for women's relational satisfaction. *Psychology of Popular Media Culture*, *5*(1), 85–98. DOI: 10.1037/ppm0000065

McPherson, M., Smith-Lovin, L., & Cook, J. M. (2001). Birds of a feather: Homophily in social networks. *Annual Review of Sociology*, *27*(1), 415–444. DOI: 10.1146/annurev.soc.27.1.415

Mead, G. H. (1935). Mind, Self and Society. From the Standpoint of a Social Behaviorist. *The Journal of Philosophy*, *32*(6), 162. DOI: 10.2307/2016046

Menon, A. (2017). Youth, identity, and cinema in Kerala. *South Asian Popular Culture*, *15*(2), 135–150.

Meppelink, C. S., Smit, E. G., Fransen, M. L., & Diviani, N. (2019). "I was Right about Vaccination": Confirmation Bias and Health Literacy in Online Health Information Seeking. *Journal of Health Communication*, *24*(2), 129–140. DOI: 10.1080/10810730.2019.1583701 PMID: 30895889

Michikyan, M., Subrahmanyam, K., & Dennis, J. (2014). Can you tell who I am? Neuroticism, extraversion, and online self-presentation among young adults. *Computers in Human Behavior*, *33*(1), 179–183. DOI: 10.1016/j.chb.2014.01.010

Mikhaylova, A. A., & Mikhaylov, A. S. (2024). Cyberspace: A systematic review of 30 years of social and economic research. *Journal of Infrastructure. Policy and Development*, *8*(8), 6178. DOI: 10.24294/jipd.v8i8.6178

Milgram, S. (1963). Behavioral study of obedience. *Journal of Abnormal and Social Psychology*, *67*(4), 371–378. DOI: 10.1037/h0040525 PMID: 14049516

Milgram, S. (1974). *Obedience to authority*. Harper & Row.

Mitchell, T. R., Thompson, L., Peterson, E., & Cronk, R. (1997). Temporal adjustments in the evaluation of events: The "Rosy View.". *Journal of Experimental Social Psychology*, *33*(4), 421–448. DOI: 10.1006/jesp.1997.1333 PMID: 9247371

Miyamoto, Y., Uchitomi, H., & Miyake, Y. (2023). Effects of avatar shape and motion on mirror neuron system activity. *Frontiers in Human Neuroscience*, *17*, 1173185. Advance online publication. DOI: 10.3389/fnhum.2023.1173185 PMID: 37859767

Modecki, K. L., Minchin, J., Harbaugh, A. G., Guerra, N. G., & Runions, K. C. (2014). Bullying prevalence across contexts: A meta-analysis measuring cyber and traditional bullying. *The Journal of Adolescent Health*, *55*(5), 602–611. DOI: 10.1016/j.jadohealth.2014.06.007 PMID: 25168105

Mogaji, E. B., Balakrishnan, J., Nwoba, A. C., & Nguyen, N. P. (2021). Emerging-market consumers' interactions with banking chatbots. *Telematics and Informatics*, *65*, 101711. DOI: 10.1016/j.tele.2021.101711

Morriss, J., Tupitsa, E., Dodd, H. F., & Hirsch, C. (2021). *Uncertainty Makes Me Emotional: Uncertainty as an Elicitor and Modulator of Emotional States*. https://doi.org/ DOI: 10.31234/osf.io/ycmt4

Mouchrek, N., & Benson, M. (2023). The theory of integrated empowerment in the transition to adulthood: Concepts and measures. *Frontiers in Sociology*, *8*, 893898. Advance online publication. DOI: 10.3389/fsoc.2023.893898 PMID: 37139228

Muchnik, L., Aral, S., & Taylor, S. (2013). Social influence bias: A randomized experiment. *Science*, *341*(6146), 647–651. DOI: 10.1126/science.1240466 PMID: 23929980

Murray, C., & Coulson, N. S. (2010). An investigation of identity construction and Facebook use among university students. *British Journal of Guidance & Counselling*, *38*(1), 55–65. DOI: 10.1080/03069880903373039

Mykhailov, D., & Liberati, N. (2023). Back to the technologies themselves: Phenomenological turn within postphenomenology. *Phenomenology and the Cognitive Sciences*. Advance online publication. DOI: 10.1007/s11097-023-09905-2

Nadarzynski, T. M., Miles, O., Cowie, A., & Ridge, D. (2019). Acceptability of artificial intelligence (AI)-led chatbot services in healthcare: A mixed-methods study. *Digital Health*, *5*, 2055207619871808. DOI: 10.1177/2055207619871808 PMID: 31467682

Nadkarni, A., & Hofmann, S. G. (2012). Why do people use Facebook? *Personality and Individual Differences*, *52*(3), 243–249. DOI: 10.1016/j.paid.2011.11.007 PMID: 22544987

Nair, P. K. (2013). *The moving image: A study of Malayalam cinema*. Oxford University Press India.

Nalcaci, A. A., Girgin, D., Balki, S., Talay, F., Boz, H. A., & Balcisoy, S. (2019). Detection of confirmation and distinction biases in visual analytics systems. *Eurographics Proceedings*, 13–17. https://doi.org/DOI: 10.2312/trvis.20191185

Naslund, J. A., Aschbrenner, K. A., Marsch, L. A., & Bartels, S. J. (2016). The future of mental health care: Peer-to-peer support and social media. *Epidemiology and Psychiatric Sciences*, *25*(2), 113–122. DOI: 10.1017/S2045796015001067 PMID: 26744309

Naslund, J. A., Aschbrenner, K. A., Marsch, L. A., & Bartels, S. J. (2020). Digital technology to deliver cognitive behavioral therapy for depression: Applications in low- and middle-income countries. *Global Mental Health (Cambridge, England)*, *7*, e22. DOI: 10.1017/S204579602000020X

Nazlan, N. H., Tanford, S., & Montgomery, R. (2018). The effect of availability heuristics in online consumer reviews. *Journal of Consumer Behaviour*._https://www.researchgate.net/publication/326376699_

NDTV. (2019). *Indore man buries dog to mislead police in murder case inspired by Drishyam*. NDTV.

Nickerson, R. S. (1998). Confirmation bias: A ubiquitous phenomenon in many guises. *Review of General Psychology*, *2*(2), 175–220. DOI: 10.1037/1089-2680.2.2.175

Nissenbaum, H. (2019). *Privacy in context: Technology, policy, and the integrity of social life*. Stanford University Press.

Nitschinsk, L., Tobin, S. J., Varley, D., & Vanman, E. J. (2023). Why Do People Sometimes Wear an Anonymous Mask? Motivations for Seeking Anonymity Online. *Personality and Social Psychology Bulletin*, *0*(0). Advance online publication. DOI: 10.1177/01461672231210465 PMID: 37997811

Noble, S. U. (2018). *Algorithms of oppression: How search engines reinforce racism*. NYU Press. DOI: 10.18574/nyu/9781479833641.001.0001

Norman, D. (2004, January 1). *Affordances and Design*. ResearchGate. https://www.researchgate.net/publication/265618710_Affordances_and_Design

Oksanen, A., Savela, N., Latikka, R., & Koivula, A. (2020). Trust toward Robots and Artificial Intelligence: An Experimental Approach to Human–Technology Interactions online. *Frontiers in Psychology*, *11*, 568256. Advance online publication. DOI: 10.3389/fpsyg.2020.568256 PMID: 33343447

Okushko, E. (2022). *Influence of social forces in the form of authority bias and conformity bias on the degree of individuals' risk-aversion* [Master's thesis, Radboud University Nijmegen]. Radboud Repository. https://theses.ubn.ru.nl/server/api/core/bitstreams/

Oliver, M. (2005). The Problem with Affordance. *E-Learning and Digital Media*, *2*(4), 402–413. DOI: 10.2304/elea.2005.2.4.402

Paavilainen, J.. (2017). The Pokémon Go experience: A location-based augmented reality mobile game goes mainstream. In *Proceedings of the 2017 CHI Conference on Human Factors in Computing Systems* (pp. 2493–2498). ACM. DOI: 10.1145/3025453.3025871

Papacharissi, Z. (2014). *Affective publics: Sentiment, technology, and politics. Affective Publics: Sentiment*. Technology, and Politics., DOI: 10.1093/acprof:oso/9780199999736.001.0001

Papacharissi, Z. (2015). *Affective publics: Sentiment, technology, and politics*. Oxford University Press.

Pariser, E. (2011). *The filter bubble: How the new personalized web is changing what we read and how we think*. Penguin.

Park, J., Woo, S. E., & Kim, J. (2024). Attitudes towards artificial intelligence at work: Scale development and validation. *Journal of Occupational and Organizational Psychology*, *97*(3), 920–951. DOI: 10.1111/joop.12502

Park, N., Oates, S., & Schwarzer, R. (2013). Christopher Peterson "other people matter": 1950– 2012. *Applied Psychology. Health and Well-Being*, *5*(1), 1–4. DOI: 10.1111/aphw.12007 PMID: 23457083

Pavey, L., Greitemeyer, T., & Sparks, P. (2011). Can giving a little help vibrate with happiness? The psychological benefits of altruistic behavior. *Social Psychology*, *42*(2), 99–104. DOI: 10.1027/1864-9335/a000051

Peck, T. C., Seinfeld, S., Aglioti, S. M., & Slater, M. (2013). Putting yourself in the skin of a Black avatar reduces implicit racial bias. *Consciousness and Cognition*, *22*(3), 779–787. DOI: 10.1016/j.concog.2013.04.016 PMID: 23727712

Pelau, C., Nistoreanu, B., & Ene, I. (2018). Differences in the perception on artificial intelligence depending on age. In *ResearchGate* [Online Print]. Proceedings of the 1st International Conference on Economics and Social Science, Bucharest, Romania. https://www.researchgate.net/publication/327721442_

Peng, T. (2021). *THE ROLE OF CUSTOMIZATION ON AVATAR IDENTIFICATION AND PERFORMANCE IN A KART RACING GAME*. https://repository.library.northeastern.edu/files/neu%3Abz617n18m/fulltext.pdf

Pennebaker, J. W., & Beall, S. K. (1986). Confronting a traumatic event: Toward an understanding of inhibition and disease. *Journal of Abnormal Psychology*, *95*(3), 274–281. DOI: 10.1037/0021-843X.95.3.274 PMID: 3745650

Pennebaker, J. W., & Seagal, J. D. (1999). Forming a story: The health benefits of narrative. *Journal of Clinical Psychology*, *55*(10), 1243–1254. DOI: 10.1002/(SICI)1097-4679(199910)55:10<1243::AID-JCLP6>3.0.CO;2-N PMID: 11045774

Pennebaker, J. W., & Smyth, J. M. (2016). *Opening up by writing it down: How expressive writing improves health and eases emotional pain* (3rd ed.). Guilford Press.

Peterson, C. (2006). *A primer in positive psychology*. Oxford University Press.

Petersson, A. H. (2023). Investigating the factors of customer experiences using real-life text-based banking chatbot: A qualitative study in Norway. *Petersson, A. H., Pawar, S., & Fagerstrøm, A.*

Pew Research Center. (2018). *Social media and political engagement*. https://www.pewresearch.org/internet/2018/09/27/social-media-and-political-engagement/

Pezzulo, G., Donnarumma, F., & Dindo, H. (2013). Human Sensorimotor Communication: A Theory of Signaling in Online Social Interactions. *PLoS One*, *8*(11), e79876. DOI: 10.1371/journal.pone.0079876 PMID: 24278201

Phillips, W. (2015). This Is Why We Can't Have Nice Things: Mapping the Relationship between Online Trolling and Mainstream Culture. In *JSTOR*. The MIT Press., https://www.jstor.org/stable/j.ctt17kk8k7

Phillips, W., & Milner, R. M. (2021). *You are here: A field guide for navigating polarized speech, conspiracy theories, and our polluted media landscape*. MIT Press. DOI: 10.7551/mitpress/12436.001.0001

Plattner, H., Meinel, C., & Leifer, L. J. (2014). *Design thinking research: Building Innovation eco-systems*. Springer.

Postmes, T., & Spears, R. (1998). Deindividuation and antinormative behavior: A meta-analysis. *Psychological Bulletin*, *123*(3), 238–259. DOI: 10.1037/0033-2909.123.3.238

Postmes, T., Spears, R., & Lea, M. (1998). Breaching or building social boundaries? SIDE-effects of computer-mediated communication. *Communication Research*, *25*(6), 689–715. DOI: 10.1177/009365098025006006

Postmes, T., Spears, R., & Lea, M. (2001). Social identity, normative content, and "de-individuation" in computer-mediated groups. *Communication Research*, *28*(2), 140–171. DOI: 10.1177/009365001028002003

Postmes, T., Spears, R., & Lea, M. (2002). Intergroup differentiation in computer-mediated communication: Effects of depersonalization. *Group Dynamics*, *6*(1), 3–16. DOI: 10.1037/1089-2699.6.1.3

Potter, L. (2024, October 4). *Older people pick up objects in a different way to younger people*. The Conversation. https://theconversation.com/older-people-pick-up-objects-

Potter, W. J. (2013). *Media literacy* (6th ed.). SAGE.

Raab, M., Bar-Eli, M., Plessner, H., & Araújo, D. (2019). The past, present and future of research on judgment and decision making in sport. *Psychology of Sport and Exercise*, *42*, 25–32. DOI: 10.1016/j.psychsport.2018.10.004

Rahman, M. M., Babiker, A., & Ali, R. (2024). Motivation, concerns, and attitudes towards AI: differences by gender, age, and culture. In *Lecture notes in computer science* (pp. 375–391). https://doi.org/DOI: 10.1007/978-981-96-0573-6_28

Rains, S. A. (2017). Communicating about health online. In Rubin, R. N., Sharoff, B. F., Housel, E. M., & Merwin, Y. I. (Eds.), *Health communication in the 21st century* (pp. 127–146). Wiley.

Rajadhyaksha, A. (2020). Indian cinema in the streaming age. *Journal of Indian Cinema Studies*, *5*(2), 45–62.

Ratan, R., & Pandita, S. (2025). 12 Avatar, That an Intelligent User Controls during Dynamic Interactions. *The Oxford Handbook of Media Psychology*, 241.

Ravi, N., & Patki, S. M. (2025). Parasocial relationships, social support and well-being: A mixed-methods study among Indian youth. *International Journal of Adolescence and Youth*, *30*(1), 2480712. DOI: 10.1080/02673843.2025.2480712

Reeves, B., & Nass, C. (1996). *The media equation: How people treat computers, television, and new media like real people and places*. Cambridge University Press.

Reicher, S. D., Spears, R., & Postmes, T. (1995). A social identity model of deindividuation phenomena. *European Review of Social Psychology*, *6*(1), 161–198. DOI: 10.1080/14792779443000049

Reinecke, L., & Trepte, S. (2014). Authenticity and well-being on social network sites: A two-wave longitudinal study on the effects of online authenticity and the positivity bias in SNS communication. *Computers in Human Behavior*, *30*(30), 95–102. DOI: 10.1016/j.chb.2013.07.030

Ribeiro, M. H., Ottoni, R., West, R., Almeida, V. A., & Meira, W.Jr. (2020, January). Auditing radicalization pathways on YouTube. In *Proceedings of the 2020 conference on fairness, accountability, and transparency* (pp. 131-141). DOI: 10.1145/3351095.3372879

Ridge, N., & Erfurth, M. (2020). *The impact of covid-19 on education in the UAE*. Al Qasimi Foundation., DOI: 10.18502/aqf.0143

Ritter, M. (2021). Postphenomenological Method and Technological Things Themselves. *Human Studies*, *44*(4), 581–593. DOI: 10.1007/s10746-021-09603-5

Rogers, C. R. (1959). A Theory of Therapy, Personality, and Interpersonal Relationships: As Developed in the Client-Centered Framework. In Koch, S. (Ed.), *Psychology: A Study of a Science. Formulations of the Person and the Social Context* (Vol. 3, pp. 184–256). McGraw Hill.

Rohlinger, D. A., & Bunnage, L. A. (2018). COLLECTIVE IDENTITY IN THE DIGITAL AGE: THIN AND THICK IDENTITIES IN MOVEON.ORG AND THE TEA PARTY MOVEMENT*. *Mobilization: An International Quarterly (San Diego, Calif.)*, *23*(2), 135–157. DOI: 10.17813/1086-671X-23-2-135

Ross, L. (1977). The intuitive psychologist and his shortcomings: Distortions in the attribution process. In Berkowitz, L. (Ed.), Vol. 10, pp. 173–220). Advances in experimental social psychology. Academic Press. DOI: 10.1016/S0065-2601(08)60357-3

Ross, L., Greene, D., & House, P. (1977). The "false consensus effect": An egocentric bias in social perception and attribution processes. *Journal of Experimental Social Psychology*, *13*(3), 279–301. DOI: 10.1016/0022-1031(77)90049-X

Ruan, Y., & Mezei, J. (2022). When do AI chatbots lead to higher customer satisfaction than human frontline employees in online shopping assistance? Considering product attribute type. *Journal of Retailing and Consumer Services*, *68*, 103059. DOI: 10.1016/j.jretconser.2022.103059

Rude, S. S., Gortner, E. M., & Pennebaker, J. W. (2004). Language use of depressed and depression-vulnerable college students. *Cognitive Therapy and Research*, *28*(3), 321–338. DOI: 10.1023/B:COTR.0000032361.44816.9d

Ryff, C. D. (2013). Psychological well-being revisited: Advances in the Science and practice of Eudaimonia. *Psychotherapy and Psychosomatics*, *83*(1), 10–28. DOI: 10.1159/000353263 PMID: 24281296

Sabherwal, R. (2008). Adoption of information systems innovations by individuals: A study of processes involving contextual, adopter, and influencer actions. *Uark*. https://www.academia.edu/30543160/

Sadiq, M., Yousaf, A., Hussain, S., & Nawaz, R. (2021). Aggression detection on social media: A multimodal approach. *Information Processing & Management*, *58*(5), 102664. DOI: 10.1016/j.ipm.2021.102664

Santrock, J. (2012). Life-Span development. McGraw-Hill Higher Education. https://books.google.co.in/books/about/Life_Span_Development.html?

Schenk, A. M., & Fremouw, W. J. (2012). Prevalence, psychological impact, and coping of cyberbully victims among college students. *Journal of School Violence*, *11*(1), 21–37. DOI: 10.1080/15388220.2011.630310

Schmiedgen, J., Spille, L., Köppen, E., Rhinow, H., & Meinel, C. (2016). Measuring the Impact of Design Thinking. In Plattner, H., Meinel, C., & Leifer, L. (Eds.), *Design Thinking Research* (pp. 157–170). Springer International Publishing., DOI: 10.1007/978-3-319-19641-1_11

Schneider, S. K., O'Donnell, L., Stueve, A., & Coulter, R. W. S. (2012). Cyberbullying, school bullying, and psychological distress: A regional census of high school students. *American Journal of Public Health, 102*(1), 171–177. DOI: 10.2105/AJPH.2011.300308 PMID: 22095343

Schroeder, R. (2008). Defining Virtual Worlds and Virtual Environments. *Journal of Virtual Worlds Research, 1*(1). Advance online publication. DOI: 10.4101/jvwr.v1i1.294

Schweitzer, J., Groeger, L., & Sobel, L. (2016). The Design Thinking Mindset: An assessment of what we know and what we see in practice. *Journal of Design. Business & Society*, *2*(1), 71–94. DOI: 10.1386/dbs.2.1.71_1

Seligman, M. E. P. (2012). *Flourish: A visionary new understanding of happiness and well- being*. Simon and Schuster.

Seran, S., Kumar, A., & Lee, M. (2025). Generative AI and academic integrity: A dissonance perspective. *Journal of Educational Technology & Society*, *28*(1), 45–62.

Shan, L., Diao, H., & Wu, L. (2020, August 12). *Influence of the framing effect, anchoring effect, and knowledge on consumers' attitude and purchase intention of organic food.* Frontiers. https://www.frontiersin.org/journals/psychology/articles/10.3389/

Sheep Without a Shepherd. (2019). [Film]. China.

Short, J., Williams, E., & Christie, B. (1976). The social psychology of Telecommunications. *Contemporary Sociology*, *7*(1), 32. DOI: 10.2307/2065899

Singh, M., & Gupta, N. (2023). The future of chatbots in Banking: Trends and opportunities. *AI and Financial Services Journal*, *7*(1), 45–60.

Sin, N. L., & Lyubomirsky, S. (2009). Enhancing well-being and alleviating depressive symptoms with positive psychology interventions: A practice-friendly meta-analysis. *Journal of Clinical Psychology, 65*(5), 467–487. DOI: 10.1002/jclp.20593 PMID: 19301241

Slater, M., Antley, A., Davison, A., Swapp, D., Guger, C., Barker, C., & Sanchez-Vives, M. V. (2006). A virtual reprise of the Stanley Milgram obedience experiments. *PLoS One*, *1*(1), e39. DOI: 10.1371/journal.pone.0000039 PMID: 17183667

Slater, M., & Sanchez-Vives, M. V. (2016). Enhancing our lives with immersive virtual reality. *Frontiers in Robotics and AI*, *3*, 74. DOI: 10.3389/frobt.2016.00074

Slonje, R., Smith, P. K., & Frisén, A. (2013). The nature of cyberbullying, and strategies for prevention. *Computers in Human Behavior, 29*(1), 26–32. DOI: 10.1016/j.chb.2012.05.024

Smith, A., (2024). *Older adults and technology use*. Pew Research Center. https://www.pewresearch.org/internet/2014/04/03/older-adults-and-technology-use/

Smith, P. K., López-Castro, L., Robinson, S., & Görzig, A. (2018). Consistency of gender differences in bullying in cross-cultural surveys. *Aggressive Behavior, 45*(2), 113–123. DOI: 10.1002/1098-2337(1988)14:2<113::AID-AB2480140205>3.0.CO;2-# PMID: 29052252

Smyth, J. M. (1998). Written emotional expression: Effect sizes, outcome types, and moderating variables. *Journal of Consulting and Clinical Psychology, 66*(1), 174–184. DOI: 10.1037/0022-006X.66.1.174 PMID: 9489272

Snowden, E. (2019). *Permanent record*. Metropolitan Books.

Solove, D. J. (2007). "I've got nothing to hide" and other misunderstandings of privacy. *The San Diego Law Review, 44*, 797–833.

Spencer, D. G., & Myers, S. (2006). *Social psychology* (3rd ed.). McGraw-Hill Ryerson.

Spitzberg, B. H., & Hoobler, G. (2002). Cyberstalking and the technologies of interpersonal terrorism. *New Media & Society, 4*(1), 71–92. DOI: 10.1177/14614440222226271

Srinivas, L. (2002). *Megastar: Chiranjeevi and Telugu cinema after N.T. Rama Rao*. Oxford University Press.

Steele, J. R., & Brown, J. D. (1995). Adolescent room culture: Studying media in the context of everyday life. *Journal of Youth and Adolescence, 24*(5), 551–576. DOI: 10.1007/BF01537056

Steinfield, C., Ellison, N. B., & Lampe, C. (2008). Social capital, self-esteem, and use of online social network sites: A longitudinal analysis. *Journal of Applied Developmental Psychology, 29*(6), 434–445. DOI: 10.1016/j.appdev.2008.07.002

Stets, J. E., Aldecoa, J., Bloom, Q., & Winegar, J. (2021). Using Identity Theory to Understand Homophily in Groups. *Frontiers in Sociology and Social Research*, 285–302. DOI: 10.1007/978-3-030-76966-6_14

Stoycheff, E. (2016). Under surveillance: How the "watched" self silences political expression online. *New Media & Society, 18*(5), 807–824. DOI: 10.1177/1461444814559371

Strimbu, N., & O'Connell, M. (2021). Aggression and consistency of self in cybertrolling behavior. *Cyberpsychology, Behavior, and Social Networking*, *24*(8), 525–531. DOI: 10.1089/cyber.2020.0424 PMID: 33577384

Subrahmanyam, K., & Greenfield, P. (2008). Online communication and adolescent relationships. *The Future of Children*, *18*(1), 119–146. DOI: 10.1353/foc.0.0006 PMID: 21338008

Suler, J. (2004). The online disinhibition effect. *Cyberpsychology & Behavior*, *7*(3), 321–326. DOI: 10.1089/1094931041291295 PMID: 15257832

Sundar, S. S., & Limperos, A. M. (2013). Uses and grats 2.0: New gratifications for new media. *Journal of Broadcasting & Electronic Media*, *57*(4), 504–525. DOI: 10.1080/08838151.2013.845827

Surette, R. (2011). *Media, crime, and criminal justice: Images, realities, and policies* (5th ed.). Cengage Learning.

Surette, R. (2015). *Copycat crime: Media influence on violent behavior*. Routledge.

Taddicken, M. (2014). The "privacy paradox" in the context of social network sites – A longitudinal analysis of user attitudes and behavior. *Computers in Human Behavior*, *35*, 341–353. DOI: 10.1016/j.chb.2014.03.011

Tajfel, H., & Turner, J. C. (1979). An integrative theory of intergroup conflict. In Austin, W. G., & Worchel, S. (Eds.), *The social psychology of intergroup relations* (pp. 33–47). Brooks/Cole.

Tajfel, H., & Turner, J. C. (1986). *Social identity and intergroup relations*. Cambridge University Press.

Tamir, D. I., & Mitchell, J. P. (2012). Disclosing information about the self is intrinsically rewarding. *Proceedings of the National Academy of Sciences of the United States of America*, *109*(50), 21277–21280. DOI: 10.1073/pnas.1202129109 PMID: 22566617

Tandoc, E. C., Ferrucci, P., & Duffy, M. (2015). Frat boys vs. humblebrags: Self-presentation on social media. *Atlantic Journal of Communication*, *23*(1), 3–15. DOI: 10.1080/15456870.2014.943456

Taylor, M. K., Marsh, E. J., & Samanez-Larkin, G. R. (2023). Heuristic decision-making across adulthood. *Psychology and Aging*. Advance online publication. DOI: 10.1037/pag0000726 PMID: 36757964

Teigen, K. (2004). Judgements by representativeness. In *Cognitive Illusions* (p. 165). Psychology Press., https://www.researchgate.net/publication/256309189_

Tekke, M. (2015, December). *Rediscovering Rogers's self theory and personality.* ResearchGate. https://www.researchgate.net/publication/286456614_Rediscovering_Rogers%27s_Self_Theory_and_Personality

Teovanović, P. (2019). Individual differences in anchoring effect: Evidence for the role of insufficient adjustment. *Europe's Journal of Psychology*, *15*(1), 8–24. DOI: 10.5964/ejop.v15i1.1691 PMID: 30915170

The Economist Impact. (2022). Together for mental health Towards a sustainable and scalable model of mental health care in the United Arab Emirates pp. 1–48. *The Economist Impact.*

The Hindu. (2024, April 20). Kerala CM warns against glamorisation of violence in films like *Aavesham*. https://www.thehindu.com/

The News Minute. (2019, September 22). How *Drishyam* inspired several real-life crimes in India. https://www.thenewsminute.com/

The News Minute. (2022, January 12). After *Drishyam 2*, police report cases inspired by movie strategies. https://www.thenewsminute.com/

Thompson, L., & Schonthal, D. (2020). The Social Psychology of Design Thinking. *California Management Review*, *62*(2), 84–99. DOI: 10.1177/0008125619897636

Tikochinsky, R., & Babad, E. (2022, January 28). Perceived epistemic authority (source credibility) of a TV interviewer moderates the media bias effect caused by his nonverbal behavior - journal of nonverbal behavior. SpringerLink. https://link.springer.com/article/10.1007/s10919-022-00397-3

Times of India. (2016). *Nilambur family murder case echoes Drishyam storyline.* The Times of India.

Tokunaga, R. S. (2010). Following you home from school: A critical review and synthesis of research on cyberbullying victimization. *Computers in Human Behavior*, *26*(1), 1–15. DOI: 10.1016/j.chb.2009.11.014

Tolnaiová, S. G., & Gálik, S. (2020). Cyberspace as a New Living World and Its Axiological Contexts. In www.intechopen.com. IntechOpen. https://www.intechopen.com/chapters/71568

Toma, C. L., & Hancock, J. T. (2013). Self-affirmation underlies Facebook use. *Personality and Social Psychology Bulletin*, *39*(3), 321–331. DOI: 10.1177/0146167212474694 PMID: 23359086

Tong, Z., Liu, H., Feng, J., Wang, W., Wu, H., & Xu, J. (2025). Trapped by AI Recommendation: How Identity Concerns Reduce Variety-Seeking Behavior. *MDE. Managerial and Decision Economics, 46*(5), 3200–3211. Advance online publication. DOI: 10.1002/mde.4524

Törnberg, P. (2025). *Online Homogeneity Can Emerge Without Filtering Algorithms or Homophily Preferences*. ArXiv.org. https://arxiv.org/abs/2508.10466

Treem, J. W., & Leonardi, P. M. (2013). Social media use in organizations: Exploring the affordances of visibility, persistence, editability, and association. *Communication Yearbook, 36*, 143–189.

Trepte, S., & Reinecke, L. (2013). The role of identity construction and self-determination in online self-disclosure. In Trepte, S., & Reinecke, L. (Eds.), *The psychology of social networks* (pp. 137–154). Springer.

Tufekci, Z. (2014). Big questions for social media big data: Representativeness, validity and other methodological pitfalls. *Proceedings of the Eighth International AAAI Conference on Weblogs and Social Media*, 506–515. DOI: 10.1609/icwsm.v8i1.14517

Tufekci, Z. (2017). *Twitter and tear gas: The power and fragility of networked protest*. Yale University Press.

Turkle, S. (1995). *Life on the Screen: Identity in the Age of the Internet*. Simon & Schuster Paperbacks, Dr.

Turkle, S. (1995). *Life on the screen: Identity in the age of the internet*. Simon & Schuster.

Turner, J. C., & Reynolds, K. J. (2012). Self-Categorization Theory. *Handbook of Theories of Social Psychology, 2*, 399–417. DOI: 10.4135/9781446249222.n46

Turner, J. C., Hogg, M. A., Oakes, P. J., Reicher, S. D., & Wetherell, M. S. (1987). *Rediscovering the social group: A self-categorization theory*. Blackwell.

Turow, J., Hennessy, M., & Draper, N. (2015). The trade-off fallacy: How marketers are misrepresenting American consumers and opening them up to exploitation. SSRN *Electronic Journal*. DOI: 10.2139/ssrn.2820060

Tversky, A., & Kahneman, D. (1974). Judgment under Uncertainty: Heuristics and Biases. *In Science*. 4157.1124 –1131. https://www2.psych.ubc.ca/~schaller/Psyc590Readings/TverskyKahneman1974.pdf

UAE National Committee on SDGs. (2017). *UAE and the 2030 Agenda for Sustainable Development: Excellence in Implementation*. Available at: https://sustainabledevelopment.un.org/content/documents/20161UAE_SDGs_Report_Full_English.pdf

Uhl, M., & Knobe, J. (2025). The Inauthentic Online Self: Perceptions of Naturalness Drive Judgments of Authenticity. *Philosophy & Technology*, *38*(2), 1–25. DOI: 10.1007/s13347-025-00871-y

United Nations Human Rights Council. (2015). *Report of the Special Rapporteur on the promotion and protection of the right to freedom of opinion and expression* (A/HRC/29/32). https://digitallibrary.un.org/record/798709

Utz, S., & Beukeboom, C. J. (2011). The role of emotion in online word-of-mouth: An analysis of attribution and expression. *International Journal of Electronic Commerce*, *15*(4), 5–24. DOI: 10.2753/JEC1086-4415150401

Uysal, M. S., Akfırat, S. A., & Cakal, H. (2021). The social identity perspective of social media leadership in collective action participation. *Journal of Community & Applied Social Psychology*, *32*(6), 1001–1015. Advance online publication. DOI: 10.1002/casp.2502

Valenzuela, A., Puntoni, S., & Wertenbroch, K. (2024). How artificial intelligence constrains the human experience. *Journal of the Association for Consumer Research*, *9*(3), 241–256. DOI: 10.1086/730709

Van der Nagel, E., & Frith, J. (2015). Anonymity, pseudonymity, and the agency of online identity: Examining the social practices of r/Gonewild. *First Monday*, *20*(3). Advance online publication. DOI: 10.5210/fm.v20i3.5615

Van Giesen, R. I., Fischer, A. R. H., Van Dijk, H., & Van Trijp, H. C. M. (2015). Affect and Cognition in Attitude Formation toward Familiar and Unfamiliar Attitude Objects. *PLoS One*, *10*(10), e0141790. DOI: 10.1371/journal.pone.0141790 PMID: 26517876

Van Strien, J. L., Kammerer, Y., Brand-Gruwel, S., & Boshuizen, H. P. (2016). How attitude strength biases information processing and evaluation on the web. *Computers in Human Behavior*, *60*, 245–252. DOI: 10.1016/j.chb.2016.02.057

Vaportzis, E., Clausen, M. G., & Gow, A. J. (2017). Older Adults Perceptions of Technology and Barriers to Interacting with Tablet Computers: A Focus Group Study. *Frontiers in Psychology*, *8*, 1687. Advance online publication. DOI: 10.3389/fpsyg.2017.01687 PMID: 29071004

Vauclair, C., Lima, M. L., Abrams, D., Swift, H. J., & Bratt, C. (2016). What do older people think that others think of them, and does it matter? The role of meta-perceptions and social norms in the prediction of perceived age discrimination. *Psychology and Aging*, *31*(7), 699–710. DOI: 10.1037/pag0000125 PMID: 27831711

Vazard, J. (2022). Feeling the unknown: Emotions of uncertainty and their valence. *Erkenntnis*. Advance online publication. DOI: 10.1007/s10670-022-00583-1

Vignoles, V. (2017, May). *Identity: Personal and Social*. ResearchGate. https://www.researchgate.net/publication/316790231_Identity_Personal_AND_Social

Vignoli, M., Dosi, C., & Balboni, B. (2023). Design thinking mindset: Scale development and validation. *Studies in Higher Education*, *48*(6), 926–940. DOI: 10.1080/03075079.2023.2172566

Vogel, E. A., Rose, J. P., Roberts, L. R., & Eckles, K. (2014). Social comparison, social media, and self-esteem. *Psychology of Popular Media Culture*, *3*(4), 206–222. DOI: 10.1037/ppm0000047

Vroling, M. S., & De Jong, P. J. (2010). Threat-confirming belief bias and symptoms of anxiety disorders. *Journal of Behavior Therapy and Experimental Psychiatry*, *41*(2), 110–116. DOI: 10.1016/j.jbtep.2009.11.002 PMID: 19942212

Wachs, S., Gámez-Guadix, M., & Wright, M. F. (2022). Online hate speech victimization and depressive symptoms among adolescents: The protective role of resilience. *Cyberpsychology, Behavior, and Social Networking*, *25*(7), 416–423. DOI: 10.1089/cyber.2022.0009 PMID: 35639126

Wachs, S., Wright, M. F., & Schubarth, W. (2017). Associations between bystanders and perpetrators of traditional bullying and cyberbullying: The moderating role of affective empathy. *International Journal of Environmental Research and Public Health*, *15*(1), 9. DOI: 10.3390/ijerph15010009 PMID: 29271899

Wachs, S., Wright, M. F., & Schubarth, W. (2019). The role of empathy and moral disengagement in cyberbullying. *Journal of School Psychology*, *74*, 50–63. DOI: 10.1016/j.jsp.2019.05.007

Walther, J. B. (1992). Interpersonal effects in computer-mediated interaction: A relational perspective. *Communication Research*, *19*(1), 52–90. DOI: 10.1177/009365092019001003

Walther, J. B. (1996). Computer-mediated communication: Impersonal, interpersonal, and hyperpersonal interaction. *Communication Research*, *23*(1), 3–43. DOI: 10.1177/009365096023001001

Walther, J. B., & Whitty, M. T. (2020). Language, Psychology, and New New Media: The Hyperpersonal Model of Mediated Communication at Twenty-Five Years. *Journal of Language and Social Psychology, 40*(1), 120–135. DOI: 10.1177/0261927X20967703

Wan, Q., & Lu, Z. (2023, July 20). *Investigating VTubing as a Reconstruction of Streamer Self-Presentation: Identity, Performance, and Gender*. ArXiv.org. https://doi.org//arXiv.2307.11025DOI: 10.48550

Wang, Q. (2024). The online extension of autobiographical memory: A psycho-cultural perspective. In Wang, Q., & Hoskins, A. (Eds.), *The remaking of memory in the age of the internet and social media* (pp. 15–31). Oxford University Press.

Watson, I. (2013). Digital Natives or Digital Tribes? *Universal Journal of Educational Research, 1*(2), 104–112. DOI: 10.13189/ujer.2013.010210

Waugh, R. (2023, May 15). *This is why it's so difficult to change old people's Minds*. Yahoo! News. https://uk.news.yahoo.com/this-is-why-its-so-difficult-to-change-old-peoples-

Wegener, D. T., Petty, R. E., Blankenship, K. L., & Detweiler-Bedell, B. (2010). Elaboration and numerical anchoring: Implications of attitude theories for consumer judgment and decision making. *Journal of Consumer Psychology, 20*(1), 5–16. DOI: 10.1016/j.jcps.2009.12.003

Wern Ting Wong, C. (2021, March 4). *Making Rational Decisions*. HU Econ Review. https://www.economicsreview.org/post/making-rational-decisions

Wickham, P. A. (2003). The representativeness heuristic in judgements involving entrepreneurial success and failure. *Management Decision, 41*(2), 156–167. DOI: 10.1108/00251740310457605

Wilke, A., & Mata, R. (2017). Cognitive Bias. In *Elsevier eBooks*. https://doi.org/ DOI: 10.1016/B978-0-12-809324-5.06376-8

Wood, J. T. (2009). *Communication in our lives* (4th ed.).

World Health Organisation. (2010). *Social Participation*. World Health Organization. https://extranet.who.int/agefriendlyworld/age-friendly-practices/

World Health Organization WHO. (2021). Child and adolescent mental and brain health. Geneva. *World Health Organization*. Available from: https://www.who.int/activities/Improving-the-mental-and-brain-health-of-children-and-adolescents

Wright, M. F. (2017). Parental mediation, cyberbullying, and cybergrooming: A longitudinal study. *Child Indicators Research, 10*(3), 699–712. DOI: 10.1007/s12187-016-9404-6

Xu, H., Teo, H. H., Tan, B. C., & Agarwal, R. (2012). The personalization privacy paradox: An empirical evaluation of informational privacy concerns and post-adoption behaviors in location-based services. *Information Systems Research, 23*(4), 1348–1369. DOI: 10.1287/isre.1110.0412

Yang, C. C., Li, C. L., Yeh, T. F., & Chang, Y. C. (2022, April 28). Assessing older adults' intentions to use a smartphone: Using the meta-unified theory of the acceptance and use of Technology. *International journal of environmental research and public health.* https://pmc.ncbi.nlm.nih.gov/articles/PMC9102817/#:~:text=,
Zajonc, R. B. (1968). Attitudinal effects of mere exposure. *Journal of Personality and Social Psychology, 9*(2, Pt.2), 1–27. https://doi.org/DOI: 10.1037/h0025848

Yan, M., & Zheng, S. (2024). Segmentation or integration? The managerial approach to work-family balance in the age of virtual team work. *Xinli Kexue Jinzhan, 32*(5), 754. DOI: 10.3724/SP.J.1042.2024.00754

Yau, J. C., & Reich, S. M. (2019). Digital Strangers: Who do adolescents self-disclose to online? *New Media & Society, 21*(6), 1328–1346.

Yeager, D. S., Romero, C., Paunesku, D., Hulleman, C. S., Schneider, B., Hinojosa, C., Lee, H. Y., O'Brien, J., Flint, K., Roberts, A., Trott, J., Greene, D., Walton, G. M., & Dweck, C. S. (2016). Using design thinking to improve psychological interventions: The case of the growth mindset during the transition to high school. *Journal of Educational Psychology, 108*(3), 374–391. DOI: 10.1037/edu0000098 PMID: 27524832

Yee, N., & Bailenson, J. (2007). The Proteus effect: The effect of transformed self-representation on behavior. *Human Communication Research, 33*(3), 271–290. DOI: 10.1111/j.1468-2958.2007.00299.x

Yen, C.-H., Teng, H.-Y., & Tzeng, J.-C. (2020). Innovativeness and customer value co-creation behaviours: Mediating role of customer engagement. *International Journal of Hospitality Management, 88*, 102514. DOI: 10.1016/j.ijhm.2020.102514

You, X. (2022). Applying design thinking for business model innovation. *Journal of Innovation and Entrepreneurship, 11*(59), 59. Advance online publication. DOI: 10.1186/s13731-022-00251-2

Zeng, R., & Zhu, D. (2021). Fear of Evaluation and Online Self-Disclosure on WeChat: Moderating Effects of Protective Face Orientation. *Frontiers in Psychology, 12*, 530722. Advance online publication. DOI: 10.3389/fpsyg.2021.530722 PMID: 34512427

Zezulka, L. A., & Seigfried-Spellar, K. C. (2016). Differentiating cyberbullies and internet trolls by personality characteristics and self-esteem. *Journal of Digital Forensics. Security and Law, 11*(3), 5. Advance online publication. DOI: 10.15394/jdfsl.2016.1415

Zhai, S., Zhang, Z., & Chen, J. (2024). Community-dwelling older adults' perspectives on health risks: A qualitative study exploring anxieties, priorities, and expectations in ageing. *BMC Public Health, 24*(1), 1657. Advance online publication. DOI: 10.1186/s12889-024-18878-z PMID: 38907192

Zhang, M. (2023, May 19). Older people's attitudes towards emerging technologies. https://journals.sagepub.com/doi/10.1177/09636625231171677

Zhang, S., Liu, M., Li, Y., & Chung, J. E. (2021). Teens' social media engagement during the covid-19 pandemic: A time series examination of posting and emotion on reddit. *International Journal of Environmental Research and Public Health, 18*(19), 10079. DOI: 10.3390/ijerph181910079 PMID: 34639381

Zhao, L., & Yu, J. (2021). A Meta-Analytic Review of Moral Disengagement and Cyberbullying. *Frontiers in Psychology, 12*, 681299. Advance online publication. DOI: 10.3389/fpsyg.2021.681299 PMID: 34916984

Zhao, S. (2020). From text to voice: Emerging vocal communication in mobile instant messaging. *New Media & Society, 22*(10), 1774–1792. DOI: 10.1177/1461444819883732

Zhao, S., Grasmuck, S., & Martin, J. (2008). Identity construction on Facebook: Digital empowerment in anchored relationships. *Computers in Human Behavior, 24*(5), 1816–1836. DOI: 10.1016/j.chb.2008.02.012

Zimbardo, P. G. (1969). The human choice: Individuation, reason, and order versus de-individuation, impulse, and chaos. In Arnold, W. J., & Levine, D. (Eds.), *Nebraska Symposium on Motivation* (pp. 237–307). University of Nebraska Press.

Zimbardo, P. G. (1969). The human choice: Individuation, reason, and order versus deindividuation, impulse, and chaos. In Arnold, W. J., & Levine, D. (Eds.), *Nebraska symposium on motivation* (Vol. 17, pp. 237–307). University of Nebraska Press.

Zimmer, M. (2010). "But the data is already public": On the ethics of research in Facebook. *Ethics and Information Technology, 12*(4), 313–325. DOI: 10.1007/s10676-010-9227-5

Zimmermann, D., Wehler, A., & Kaspar, K. (2022). Self-representation through avatars in digital environments. *Current Psychology (New Brunswick, N.J.), 42*(25), 21775–21789. Advance online publication. DOI: 10.1007/s12144-022-03232-6

Zong, Y. & Guo, X.(2022, February 8).An Experimental Study on Anchoring Effect of Consumers' Price Judgment Based on Consumers' Experiencing Scenes.*Frontiers in Psychology*. Frontiers | An Experimental Study on Anchoring Effect of Consumers'

Zuboff, S. (2019). Surveillance Capitalism and the Challenge of Collective Action. *New Labor Forum, 28*(1), 10–29. DOI: 10.1177/1095796018819461

Zuboff, S. (2019). *The age of surveillance capitalism: The fight for a human future at the new frontier of power*. PublicAffairs.

Zywica, J., & Danowski, J. (2008). The faces of Facebookers: Investigating social enhancement and social compensation hypotheses. *Proceedings of the American Society for Information Science and Technology, 45*(1), 1–13. DOI: 10.1002/meet.2008.145045025

About the Contributors

Ruqia Safdar Bajwa is a seasoned academic with 18 years of experience in the field of psychology. Holding a PhD in Social Psychology, she has made significant contributions to the academic community. Currently, she serves as an Assistant Professor at a reputed public sector university in Pakistan, where she continues to shape the next generation of psychologists through her teaching, research, and mentorship.

Sarwat Sultan is an esteemed academic and a renowned figure in the field of psychology. She holds a PhD in Psychology and a Post-Doctorate. She has contributed significantly to the promotion of psychology in South Punjab. She currently holds the position of Vice-President (Punjab) of the Pakistan Psychological Association. With a strong focus on clinical and educational psychology, Prof. Sultan's work has had a lasting impact on both academic research and the practical application of psychological principles.

Asma Yunus has done MPhil and PhD in Sociology from Punjab University, Lahore, Pakistan. Before that, she completed MSc Sociology from Bahauddin Zakariya University, Multan, Pakistan.

***

A.V. Senthil Kumar is working as a Professor and Principal, Nehru Institute of Information Technology and Management, Coimbatore, India. He has worked as Professor and Director, PG and Research Department of Computer Applications, Hindusthan College of Arts & Science, Coimbatore, Tamilnadu for 15 years and as Senior Grade Lecturer in CMS College of Science and Commerce for 14 years. To his credit he has industrial experience for five years and teaching experience of 29 years. He has also received his Doctor of Science (D.Sc in Computer Science). He has to his credit 86 Book Chapters, 234 papers in International and National

Journals, 85 papers in International Conferences in International and National Conferences, and edited 17 books and 3 Text books. He is as Associate Editor of IEEE Access. He is an Editor-in-Chief for many journals and Key Member for India, Machine Intelligence Research Lab (MIR Labs). He is an Editorial Board Member and Reviewer for various International Journals. He is also a Committee member for various International Conferences. He has guided 16 Ph.D scholars and guiding 3 Ph. D scholars now.

Avanika Aeniyara V. is a student pursuing a BSc in Psychology (Hons) at PES University in Bengaluru. She possesses a keen interest in the field of social psychology, with particular emphasis on the study of the self as an evolving and relational concept. She is drawn towards psychotherapy, with a fascination for narrative, Gestalt and existential approaches that are informed by neuropsychological perspectives. Inspired by the person-centred philosophy of Carl Rogers, she values empathy, autonomy, authenticity, and the therapeutic relationship in facilitating meaningful change, and seeks to utilise these values to help individuals achieve meaningful growth.

Adrienne Barretto is a psychology student from Goa, with a keen interest in organisational behaviour and in understanding what motivates people within professional setting. She explores topics that integrate psychology and the workplace, aiming to promote mental well-being and create positive environments. She is also deeply interested in cognitive and personality psychology which is observed through her work. She aspires to solve the deep rooted issues within an organisation and strive towards employee and organisational welfare.

Shalyn Angel Cardozo is a postgraduate student in Psychology from Goa,India. She has a keen interest in Health Psychology and child psychology. She completed her internship at Hospiscio, South Goa District Hospital, gaining valuable experience in both the psychiatric and alcohol treatment units. This clinical exposure enriched her understanding of mental health care practices. She is empathetic and passionate about understanding human behaviour and helping those in need.

Jeanne Cotta is an Assistant Professor of Psychology. She is currently pursuing her PhD in Psychology at Christ University in Adolescent Mental Health.

Areej ElSayary is an Associate Professor and Chair of the General Education department within the College of Interdisciplinary Studies. She previously served as the Graduate Program Coordinator within Zayed University's College of Education. She is a distinguished academic experienced in Cyberpsychology, Interdisciplinary STE(A)M Education, curriculum design, teaching methodologies, assessment strategies, and school accreditation. Her knowledge and experience extend to her role as a certified associate of the Blackboard Academy, a recognized Fellow of the Higher Education Academy (FHEA), and a respected Editor and researcher. Dr. Areej has conducted numerous impactful teacher training programs across the United Arab Emirates, further elevating the region's education quality. Beyond academia, she is a Mental Health Ambassador at Zayed University, an ICF Coach Member, and a cyberpsychologist bringing her specialized expertise in positive psychology to promote holistic well-being. Her research interests encompass a wide spectrum, spanning cognitive development, cyberpsychology, human-computer interaction, entrepreneurship, innovation, design-thinking, interdisciplinary STE(A) M approaches, and advanced assessment methodologies.

Pratiksha Mallya is a student of Psychology from India. Her interest in psychology stems from her passion of helping people and learning about and understanding human behaviour. She aims at creating awareness about mental health issues along with providing people with necessary support. She has a keen interest in clinical psychology, adolescent psychology and aspires to become a therapist in one of these fields. Besides this, She is an observant, empathetic and curious Individual who is determined to learn and grow as well as help those in need.

Evira Pereira is a dedicated psychology student From Parvatibai Chowgule college of Arts and Science college in Goa and is passionate about mental health and criminal behavior. Her internship at the South Goa District Hospital's Psychiatric and Alcohol Treatment Facility Unit provided valuable clinical experience. Aspiring to pursue a Master's in Criminology abroad, Evira aims to research the psychological motives behind criminal behavior to contribute to criminal justice research and prevention.

Vanessa Pereira is a psychology student from Parvatibai Chowgule College of Arts and Science, Autonomous, passionate about clinical psychology. Her internship at the South Goa District Hospital's Psychiatric Ward and Alcohol Treatment Facility (ATF) gave her first-hand experience, providing valuable clinical insights that deepened her understanding of human behavior and further strengthened her interest in clinical psychology. Additionally, she also has a keen interest in child psychology, recognizing the importance of early support, and aspires to contribute to mental well-being and support individuals in need. Apart from this, she is an empathetic individual who strives to make a positive impact in her community.

Adheena Rajeev is a postgraduate student of Forensic Psychology at Lovely Professional University, Phagwara, Punjab. Her academic interests include criminal behavior analysis, investigative psychology, victimology, and the psychological dimensions of crime and justice. She is dedicated to applying psychological principles to criminal investigations and offender rehabilitation.

Rubi Rajput is an accomplished educator with 08 years of teaching experience in the field of education. She currently serves as an Assistant Professor at Swami Vivekanand Subharti University, India. She holds a Ph.D., M.Phil, M.Ed. & B.Ed. from the same University. She qualify NET in Education. She have double MA in Psychology from Lovely Professional University, and CCS University, India. Published 14 research papers in Scopus-indexed, peer-reviewed, UGC CARE, and UGC-listed journals, 22 book chapters in Scopus-indexed, International and National publication. She is the author of 03 books and has served as editor for 02 books. Her contribution in IPR 03 patents published and 01 copyright. She is a lifetime member of the Council of Educational Administration and Management and serves as a Trustee and Academic Advisor for the national NGO Saathi Foundation, India.

Saloni Rodrigues is a postgraduate student in Psychology. Her academic interests focus on psychology in the social context. She is passionate about translating psychological principles into real-life applications that promote individual and community well-being. She enjoys being part of collaborative research projects and workshops. Outside of academics, she finds joy in meaningful conversations, with a deep interest in understanding people and improving lives, she aspires to contribute to a more empathetic and socially aware world.

Megha Rudrapati, Assistant Professor, Department of Psychology, PES University. A trauma-informed integrative psychotherapist dominantly inculcates Applied Behaviour Analysis, Psychoanalysis, Art therapy, and Gestalt in practice. Author to SEN: What a child needs. Has worked predominantly with Early Interventions and Neurodivergence, Adolescents and Young Adults using an eclectic lens towards wellbeing.

Mohammad Amin Wani is an Assistant Professor of Psychology with a strong background in teaching, research, and mentorship. He has demonstrated proficiency in implementing engaging teaching strategies that enhance student learning experiences and improve performance. His expertise in research is evident through his mentorship of students in research projects, fostering critical thinking and academic excellence.

Ratisha Yadav completed her Ph.D. from IIS (Deemed to be University), Jaipur, in 2024. She holds a gold medal in M.Com (Business Studies) and has also earned an Advanced Diploma in Banking, Insurance, and Mutual Funds from the same institution. With over six years of research experience, her academic interests include women's perception and attitude towards MOOCs and consumer behaviour influenced by nutritional labelling. She has been actively involved in academic research, publishing in reputed journals, presenting at conferences, and participating in workshops. She has also served as an assistant editor for three edited books. Her work has been recognized internationally, including receiving the Best Research Paper Award at an academic conference.

Index

A

B

C

D

E

F

G

H

I

M

O

P

R

S

T

Y

www.ingramcontent.com/pod-product-compliance
Lightning Source LLC
LaVergne TN
LVHW081532300926
849161LV00006B/1395